The Prose of Royall Tyler

Silhouette of Royall Tyler dating about 1800 when he was in his early 40's. At this time he was at the peak of his fame as a novelist, essayist and versifier, and about to enter the climax of his public career as Chief Justice of the Vermont Supreme Court. *In the Royall Tyler Collection of the Vermont Historical Society, gift of Helen Tyler Brown.* Superimposed is Tyler's signature, taken from a letter written in 1800.

The Prose of Royall Tyler

COLLECTED AND EDITED BY

MARIUS B. PÉLADEAU

Published jointly by

The Vermont Historical Society
Montpelier, Vermont

The Charles E. Tuttle Company
Rutland, Vermont

REPRESENTATIVES
Continental Europe: BOXERBOOKS, INC., Zurich
British Isles: PRENTICE-HALL INTERNATIONAL, INC., London
Australasia: PAUL FLESCH & CO., PTY. LTD., Melbourne
Canada: M. G. HURTIG LTD., Edmonton

Published by the Charles E. Tuttle Company, Inc.
of Rutland, Vermont & Tokyo, Japan
with editorial offices at
2–6, Suido 1-chome, Bunkyo-ku, Tokyo, Japan

Copyright in Japan, 1972, by
The Charles E. Tuttle Company, Inc.
All rights reserved
First edition, 1972

Library of Congress Catalog Card No. 70-152113
International Standard Book No. 0-8048-0970-4

PRINTED IN JAPAN

List of Illustrations

Contents

From that endless variety of objects, held up to pursuit in civilized society, this essential advantage flows, that to genius of every species, opportunity is given, to exert itself in its proper sphere. . . . None can attain eminence in all, but each in some of the vocations of life. . . . Even this solitary soldier, who belongs to none of the *regiments* of life, finds a *peculiar* employment: Now choosing as a centinel, to ascend the watchtower and *survey,* and now, as a cavalier, to throw a gauntlet, and break a lance with the champions of vice and folly.

ROYALL TYLER
"The Saunterer"
1794

Yes, there was now a germ of an American literature; distinct; on its own root; growing; vigorous; not to be poohpoohed, or trampled under foot; or easily done to death any more. . . .

Assuredly the time will arrive when the Americans as a people will take pride in a literature of their own and realize that a National Literature is a National Power.

JAMES KIRKE PAULDING
The Dutchman's Fireside
1831

Preface

THIS collection of Royall Tyler's prose is intended to be a companion volume to the compilation of his efforts in verse. Although his poems give us an insight into the man and serve as a reflection of his age, Tyler's prose unfolds even more clearly the man's personality and talents and allows us to examine more thoroughly his motivations, emotions and thoughts.

The essays present us with a matchless picture of Federalist and Republican politics and illustrate how an educated man became deeply involved in the events which permeated the everyday life of United States citizens during the turbulent years between 1790 and 1825. The autobiographical "Bay Boy," on the other hand, gives us a first-hand account of what it was like to be a young boy growing up in Boston during the exciting years immediately preceding the outbreak of the American Revolution.

Several sources have been tapped in assembling this collection of Tyler's prose. Most important are his manuscripts. Although a number of most important holograph works which once existed have been lost or misplaced in recent years, those that survive bulk considerably in this volume.

This edition also collects for the first time the Tyler prose which was published during his lifetime and which can still be attributed to him. Because most of Tyler's prose was printed under pseudonyms in newspapers and other periodical publications, which had a high mortality rate due to their ephemeral nature, it is not easily obtainable.

As stated in the edition of Tyler's verse, this inaccessibility of his works has prevented a serious study of the man's role as one of the early Republic's foremost novelists, essayists and versifiers. It is the hope that this volume will help rectify the problems by presenting for the first time as complete as possible a corpus of Tyler's prose works, both published and in manuscript.

Outside of the short eulogy on George Washington, this volume does not include that prose which appeared as separate imprints. *The Contrast, The Algerine Captive* and the *Reports of Cases* have all been reprinted. *The Yankey in London,* the only title which has never been reissued, is catalogued in several prominent libraries across the country.

In the compilation of this work, Mr. Thomas B. Ragle, president of Marlboro College, Vermont, has been most helpful. To the Honorable and Mrs. William Royall Tyler of Washington, D.C., I am most grateful, not only for making available the miniature of Tyler used on the dust jacket, but for their many years of support and interest.

Most of the manuscripts at the Vermont Historical Society are in the "Royall Tyler Collection, gift of Helen Tyler Brown." Mrs. Dorothy S.

Melville and Allan D. Sutherland, M.D., the heirs of Miss Brown, were most generous in granting their permission to examine and publish the papers. Mr. Howard C. Rice, Jr., assistant librarian for rare books and special collections at Princeton University, and Doctor T. D. Seymour Bassett, curator of the Wilbur Collection at the University of Vermont, have been extremely liberal in their assistance and encouragement. I would also like to thank Mrs. Thomas J. Walsh and Miss June Haley for their continued efforts over several years duration.

Tyler's prose would not have been collected without the encouragement of the late Charles V. S. Borst of the Charles E. Tuttle Company, Inc., and the interest and assistance of Charles T. Morrissey, Director of the Vermont Historical Society. The dedication of Roland A. Mulhauser in seeing this book into print has been invaluable.

This study would have been impossible wthout the patience and for-bearance of the staffs of the several libraries and historical and literary societies visited during the course of the research. I especially want to thank the directors, librarians and staffs of the Boston Athenaeum, the Boston Public Library Manuscript Division, the American Antiquarian Society, the Vermont Historical Society, the University of Vermont Guy W. Bailey Library's Wilbur Collection, the Brattleboro, Vermont, Brooks Library, and the Library of Congress Microfilm, Law and Rare Books Divisions.

Finally, to the John P. Clement Memorial Fund should go the credit for making possible the publication of this volume. John P. Clement of Rut-land, Vermont, was a Life Member of the Vermont Historical Society and it President from 1959 to 1965. On December 5, 1968, he died of injuries received in an automobile accident in Rutland. Upon his death his friends felt that a memorial would best carry on the aims to which he had devoted his distinguished talents. Since he was a noted bibliophile and student of Vermont's history it was further decided that a book published in his memory, especially a book pertaining to Vermont, would be a most suitable memorial. Contributions from 36 individuals and two Rutland business firms provided almost half of the funds necessary for the Vermont Historical Society to co-publish this volume with the Charles E. Tuttle Company. The remaining funds were drawn from the Society's Research Fund. Thus I am grateful to the contributors to the John P. Clement Memorial Fund, and to the Vermont Historical Society, for their indis-pensable support. And I am honored that John P. Clement's memory can be perpetuated by publication of *The Prose Of Royall Tyler*.

MARIUS B. PÉLADEAU

Washington, D.C.

Introduction

ROYALL TYLER'S prose serves as an excellent indicator of the man's personality. Initially, it illustrates his quick wit, wide reading habits, mastery of language and facile ability to turn a good phrase. But the prose tells us much more than just this. It allows us to look more deeply into Tyler's character and how it reflected his era.[1]

Most of Tyler's works are short in nature—the letters, essays and his other prose are usually no more than a couple of pages in length. Even his longer efforts, such as *The Algerine Captive, Yankey in London* and the unfinished "Bay Boy" are episodic in character so that the chapters did not have to be written in sequence. So loose is the picaresque structure of *The Algerine Captive* and "The Bay Boy" that Tyler could (and did) employ chapters or parts of chapters from the former in the latter.

Both works deal with the life of a fictional character, autobiographical in nature, called Dr. Updike Underhill. Outside of the bare requisites laid down by the chronological development of Updike's life, Tyler had no restrictions of plot which confined him in his development of the story line. The *Yankey in London,* on the other hand, is a series of widely disjointed epistles on many subjects which also did not demand composition in any particular sequence.

Thus, even Tyler's longer pieces contain very little sustained writing, but are rather snatches set down when time and inclination permitted, to be gathered together at a convenient later date. In fact, from his correspondence we can determine that Tyler composed his novels and longer essays at the demands of the publishers, sending off sections or even individual pages as the printer needed them to complete a chapter or gathering of pages.

All this shows Tyler's extreme impatience and restlessness. He did not possess the desire to concentrate on his literary endeavors for sustained periods. If a verse or essay did not come easily, it was quickly laid aside and forgotten. As a rapid and incessant writer, Tyler was not one to labor long over rhymes or phrases. These were hinderances with which he had no patience.

The problem was that words, wit and wisdom came too easily for Tyler. When writing involved hard work it ceased to interest him. He had always been able to rise—in the courtroom, at the banquet, or in public—and turn the correct and pretty phrase, the well-chosen word. It was an innate talent,

---

[1] For further comments on Tyler's relationship to his age see G. Thomas Tanselle, *Royall Tyler* (Cambridge, 1967), pp. 208–9 (hereafter cited as *Royall Tyler*); and Marius B. Péladeau, *The Verse of Royall Tyler* (Charlottesville, 1968), pp. xxxiv-xxxix.

but one to which he gave little thought or saw little need to develop further. In the end, it was this basic facility to compose readily, plus his wide reading, which allowed Tyler to make a pleasurable avocation out of writing essays or sermons for his friends or the several New England newspapers and periodicals without seriously disturbing his law career.

A good number of Tyler's manuscripts survive and they tell us much of how his talents were transferred to the written or printed page. He was not one to laboriously revise or rewrite his prose. It is obvious that his thoughts came tumbling out and were put down on the paper as they came, and that the initial results were so good (or good enough) that Tyler never gave serious thought to revising or rewriting his manuscripts.[2]

Since the majority of Tyler's prose was originally printed in newspapers and other ephemeral periodicals, it was probably not reworked after being set in type. Nor are there clues which would lead us to believe Tyler bothered to make revisions in the galley proofs of his longer works, such as *The Algerine Captive* and *Yankey in London*.

One of the interesting facets of Tyler's talent was his ability to write intelligently on many subjects. It is not sufficient to pass this off by simply saying it was the result of his college education—in a day when this was not available to all—and his reading everything on which he could lay his hands. Undoubtedly both contributed their share, but it was more than that. Tyler had a retentive and discerning mind, able to range widely and digest minutely and cogently. He was able to assimilate much and synthesize the intake so that when it came time to write the product was a blending of many sources, but still uniquely Tyler.

No matter how lofty his source, Tyler never took for granted anyone else's judgements. With a harmonious blending of vision and reflection, Tyler had the courage to trust his own mind, his own deductions. He never

[2] Joseph T. Buckingham, who rose to become a noted Boston publisher, first met Tyler when the young Buckingham served as a printer's devil for the *Farmer's Weekly Museum* in Walpole, N.H. He always entertained a high regard for both Tyler and Joseph Dennie and spoke well of them in his memoirs.

Many years after Tyler's death Buckingham had this to say of Tyler's skills: "He wrote rapidly, and could vary his style 'from grave to gay, from lively to severe,' as easily as he could draw on his glove. Most of the articles . . . 'from the Shop of Messrs. Colon & Spondee,' were written by him; the poetical pieces, I believe are all of his composition. These he generally threw off with a dash of the pen, seldom taking pains to revise them. They are noted for inaccuracy of rhymes,—a defect, which he thought hardly worthy of his attention; but they are remarkable for sprightliness of thought and expression, and an easy flow of language." See Joseph T. Buckingham, *Specimens of Newspaper Literature: With Personal Memoirs, Anecdotes, and Reminiscences* (Boston, 1850), II, 203.

let someone else's conclusions rest unchallenged, or an assumption unexplored—no matter how many people believed in them.

Tyler was a product of his age's education. The topics to which he devoted the most attention throughout his life were religion, morals, politics and the new American Republic. By the time Tyler had reached maturity he had formed definite opinions on all of these. As he grew, however, we can trace the development of his intellect and his change of outlook on these and other subjects.

In religion, he started as a rather orthodox Episcopalian, albeit one profoundly touched by the all-pervading Calvinistic heritage of the New England colonies. The deep satire of "The Bay Boy" and other works reflects his preoccupation with this subject in his later years. This point will be touched upon in more detail in the discussion of "The Bay Boy."[3]

In politics we see a definite maturing of opinion. As an impressionable youth, with an upbringing in the prosperous merchant class of Boston, he naturally became a staunch Federalist. As he grew older, living and working among the individualistic rural Yankee of northern New England, he gradually became disenchanted and finally revolted by the aristocratic caste that came to dominate the Federalist Party.

Tyler's greatest talent was the ability to make what was real a matter of general awareness in a manner understandable to the proverbial "man-in-the-street." As literature it would be unfair to judge Tyler's efforts by present standards or again by contemporary works in England, for he had a practical end to accomplish with an audience whose limitations he knew and endeavored to meet. His greatest ambition was to be a useful rather than an accomplished writer.

He was one of our first satirists, the predecessor of a line which has sometimes amused and sometimes perplexed foreign readers. In satire, as in everything else, Tyler's main effort was to make his meaning clear and he took no risks for the sake of delicacy, as his audience would not have had him. Tyler was always understood. The new nation had not yet completely attained to the graces of literaure, but the strength and vigor which ought to precede these were abundant.

In a way, Tyler contributed little new to the developing American tradition, although he was an intimate part of that tradition and it was reflected deeply in his life and writing. What he did contribute in a small way, was a new outlook, an incisive and self-searching look into the American spirit and particularly its developing religious and political philosophies. Tyler spared no one, not even himself, in revealing all he felt needed to be revealed

[3] See below, pp. 21–40.

if the American people were to be channeled into what he hoped would be a purely "American thought."

In his day Tyler exerted no mean influence on his contemporaries. He raised by several notches the intellectual tone of the thousands who read faithfully his essays and newspaper columns. In short, Tyler can be said to have put literary tone into many people's front parlor.

There was no abrupt change in literary habits following the independence of the colonies from British rule. A people could not adjust themselves to a new condition of liberty in a day or year after their life of a century and three-quarters as subject provinces. Neither could they get out of the ruts of thought and expression in which they had been brought up.

Tyler spanned a transitional age. His early work was done in an era of literary barrenness, itself the natural sequence of disturbed conditions in the country which the War of 1812 helped to settle. But before that all American authors had to do imitative work before they began to quarry the wealth of material close at hand. Tyler went through this apprenticeship as did everyone else.

Moreover, in the years immediately following the end of the war there were causes which continued to impart to literature the complexion it had during the revolutionary conflict. Opposition and disputation was the order of the day. The Declaration of Independence was passed with difficulty; the war was prolonged by dissent and disagreement and the plan of union was to be several years in getting itself adjusted to provincial notions.

This process made a continuation of political literature inevitable. Many of those who had in the years of fighting the British kept up a wordy war protracted it even after the Constitution was adopted, believing that the fruits of the sacrifice made would be lost with the rejection of their own theories of government. Hence followed a new installment of political literature whose importance in tiding the nation over dangerous shoals cannot be overestimated. It was in these eventful times that Tyler and Joseph Dennie made the public politically aware in their famous "Colon and Spondee" essays and poems.

On the other hand, during the second half of his life Tyler was writing in an age of developing exuberant nationalism. The years after the War of 1812 were ones of emergent patriotism that rose to a high pitch in the following decades. The spread-eagle posture in writing and oratory was assumed by nearly everyone; Tyler was no exception.

Doctor Oliver Wendell Holmes called Ralph Waldo Emerson's "Phi Beta Kappa Oration" of 1837 the American intellectual "Declaration of Independence." This, however, ignores the fact that many others had spoken out for a truly national literature to be created by "native writers" dealing with "native themes." If nothing else, Tyler's materials were as native as they could be, and the direction in which he was pointing was obvious to all who read him.

Tyler is an easy man to categorize—he is a man of his day, of his period. And yet he is not a mere type. Sometimes he looked beyond his age and although he rarely outstripped it, he often had a sensitive vision of the future few of his contemporaries possessed.

Although several chapters of "The Bay Boy" and other of his prose efforts deal with the religious turmoil of mid-18th century New England in a light and satirical fashion, Tyler was deeply disturbed by the question of religion and personal and social morality.

The Puritans were characterized by their continual attempt to maintain the delicate balance between ideal and behavior, to straddle the fence between the strong desire for moral withdrawal from the world and the equally powerful pull of capitulation to the world. This was the plight of the Puritans, whose concern for consistency in thought and purpose was also a potential victim to the demands of practical action.

These opposites, held in fruitful tension in the early years of our history, had gone their own way by the end of the 18th century. The delicate balance had been upset. Americans talked one way and acted another. The result was moral confusion. How much of this Tyler could perceive concretely we do not know, but that the ferment affected him is clear. Although he probably could not realize it completely, the task of Tyler and others like him was to help shape and create a new moral style and a new consciousness for a people unwilling to confront the discrepancies of their daily lives.

Tyler was the epitome of a reflective people in a time when the shadow of gloom had not entirely passed. Knowing of this deep strain in the American people—and himself—Tyler sought to lead them out of it by the best means at his disposal. Despite his sarcasm, he was a sympathetic observer of what was good and worthwhile in people. He was one quick to draw lessons from and point out the good and bad in life. He found guidance in the foibles of people and their day-by-day existence. It was a sober inheritance from the country's 17th century ancestry.

Tyler had his limitations, as does every writer who contributes to a nation's literature without attempting too much in it. He did not aspire to a great novel, being content with an enjoyable picaresque tale. He did not pretend to be a great essayist, although he turned out some of his age's most readable prose in this form. He did not aspire to be a deathless satirist, although biting and witty he could be.

Beyond the narrow compass of his talents he did not venture, but within these limitations he gave boundlessly to all men of what he had.

There are men who are never at rest with themelves or with the world in which they live. They are pioneers who cannot adjust themselves to any social entity but must always blaze trails across uncharted lands and search beyond the horizon for adventure and stimulus. These have their counterpart in literature, the innovative, imaginative ones who pioneer in new forms or themes. To them history rightfully affords a well-lighted and prominently placed niche.

On the other hand, there are those men of vision, who although not timid or afraid, feel that the cause of advancing a civilization or a culture can best be accomplished through the utilization of existing means of expression and channels of progress. There are men such as this in the field of literary endeavor. Tyler was one of them. He was not a pioneer in the sense of blazing new paths: he preferred to labor diligently within the context of his age and of the people with whom he lived.

Even though a man of foresight, he felt that the great future of America and American letters could be brought about initially by building upon a solid present. Although most often working with a serious intent, he believed that his avocation of literature was one which should give himself and his audience enjoyment. It is one of the reasons why he so delighted in exercising his considerable talents as a satirist. Tyler did not take himself or his productions seriously and neither did his contemporaries; it would be a mistake for twentieth century readers to do so.

It would be preferable, therefore, to look upon him as a wide-ranging commentator of American life, rather than a shaper of it. Tyler loses nothing in comparison with other "universal men" of his era; he was as widely read and as knowledgeable as any of his contemporaries and an examination of the contents of this volume will show that there was no subject which escaped his searching examination.

Tyler's only drawback was that he lived in frontier Vermont rather than in the population and cultural centers of the eastern seaboard where, as he called it, the "tinsel glory" of fame would have "bespangled" him more obviously. But being a modest, unassuming man not especially interested in the glories of this world the lack of worldly fame never bothered him and it should also not color how the present day judges his sincere efforts to preserve in writing a picture of his age.

A Bibliographic Note

BECAUSE of the extensive use in this volume of manuscripts and published material from relatively inaccessible sources, some editorial problems had to be resolved before proceeding with the editing of the text.

The decision was made that the prime purpose of this edition would be to gather together all of Tyler's attributable prose and present it in a readable fashion without the burden of unnecessarily weighty scholarly apparatus. Some authors, because of ther rank as literary figures, deserve and require critical renderings of their manuscripts. Tyler does not fit into this category.

Although Tyler's writing is a fine reflection of his age, his education and his talents, it was not felt that his standing in literary history depended on the exact charting of every manuscript variant or the placement of every apostrophe.

In presenting the manuscripts, therefore, readability has been the prime determining factor. An exact, scholarly rendering of the various manuscript fragments, in their various stages of completion, with all the vagaries of unfinished texts, would have resulted in great unevenness. Some of Tyler's manuscripts are mere rough drafts while others are in the final stages of polish ready for the typesetter. Still other manuscripts are in Mrs. Tyler's hand, written from her husband's dictation during the final years of his life.[1]

Tyler's paragraphing and punctuation were most erratic. He rarely employed apostrophes and commas and periods were practically unknown

---

[1] The manuscripts posed one common problem. Because of careless storage and the fragility of certain old papers, some of Tyler's manuscripts are in poor condition. This has made the deciphering of certain words and phrases most difficult.

Until about 1820 Tyler's penmanship was quite legible, but in the final six years of his life the cancer of the face, which affected his eyes and finally caused his near blindness, resulted in a serious deterioration of his handwriting. In the final years the cancerous growth became so bad that Tyler either dictated to his wife or wrote on large slates and had her transcribe his writing onto paper. Mrs. Tyler's handwriting is most legible.

In order to clarify the presentation of the manuscript texts, the following textual devices have been employed:

[. . .], [. . . .]	One or two words missing or illegible and not conjecturable.
[roman]	Conjectural reading for missing or illegible words or phrases. A question mark is inserted before the closing bracket if the reading is doubtful.
[*italic*]	Editorial insertion in the text. Missing articles and prepositions, however, are silently added.

to him. Hyphens and dashes (of varying lengths) served as common sub-
stitutes for commas, periods, semi-colons and even as indicators of the start
of a new paragraph. Both the author and his wife had a most irregular concept of possessives and capitalization—as was common with their age—and
they also indulged themselves in some very personal interpretations of the
rules of spelling. All-in-all, however, Tyler in manuscript is most readable
despite these faults. His grammer was generally excellent and although his
sentences are usually long and involved they are structurally sound.

Since verse and prose rolled so effortlessly from his mind and he was so
impatient to get his thoughts on paper, Tyler probably felt inconsistencies
in spelling or punctuation were minor details which could be cleaned up
later by the publisher or typesetter. In a letter to Isaac Riley about the
publication of Tyler's *Law Reports,* the author showed how much he left
these affairs to the taste of the publisher. Tyler said:

I leave all matters of decoration to you; having omitted even to score the Capitals;
convinced that elegance in typography depends on fashion; and believing, from what
I have seen from your press, that you are at the tip of the American mode.[2]

Joseph T. Buckingham, who published Tyler's verse and prose in both
the *Polyanthos* and *New-England Galaxy,* also pointed out the inadequacies
of Tyler's texts in the following exerpt from a letter of May 20, 1806. The
editor asked Tyler, "Does my punctuation please you? If it do not, you will
please to point all favourite passages."[3]

Even his close friends politely chided Tyler about these faults. His literary
partner, Joseph Dennie, told him: "Be not too impatient; hurry in writing
and overweening zeal with the fair, are both dangerous. Horace, and the
rest of those dull fellows, advise slowness in composition; but I know thy
pride, and the naughtiness of thy heart." A short time later Dennie again
said: "I exhort you to industry. A little Latin will do you no harm; and . . .
the elements of penmanship and punctuation are indispensable."[4]

These passages show that since Tyler himself placed so little importance
on capitalization, paragraphing and punctuation, it was not something

[2] The letter is quoted in Thomas Pickman Tyler, "Memoirs of Honorable Royall
Tyler, late Chief Justice of Vermont," p. 255. This manuscript memoir is in the Royall
Tyler Collection, gift of Helen Tyler Brown, at the Vermont Historical Society.
Hereafter cited as "TPT Memoir." It was started by Tyler's son in 1873.
[3] The communication is in the Royall Tyler Collection. Hereafter to be cited as "RT
Collection." For further comment on the rapidity of Tyler's composition see above,
p. 12.
[4] The letters are quoted in Laura G. Pedder, ed., *The Letters of Joseph Dennie, 1768–
1812* (Orono, Me., 1936), pp. 156, 165.

which should weigh heavily now in presenting a readable canon of the author's prose. For that reason, these aspects of grammer have been normalized and spelling silently emended except where odd usages or contemporary spellings preserve the flavor of Tyler's style.

As mentioned above, it is not felt that Tyler's reputation requires a variorum edition. Therefore, none of the material canceled by Tyler in his manuscripts has been included here. In most instances the cancels were not decipherable and could not be transcribed. Secondly, a great part of those that were legible consisted of mere routine corrections of spelling, verb tenses and minor points of grammar.

At all times the guiding principle has been to present the prose without burdening it with unnecessary editorial intrusions.

The works that were published during Tyler's lifetime in contemporary newspapers, journals and magazines presented less of a problem. They are reprinted here as they originally appeared with the quaint use of italics and other typographical devices for emphasis. None of these seriously obstruct a smooth reading of the texts. By retaining them, on the other hand, it is felt we are preserving the spirit of the printers of the era to whom Tyler gave so much leeway in presenting his prose "at the tip of the mode."

Typesetters and even some publishers were often unlettered or, at the least, individualistic in their interpretations of the rules of punctuation and spelling. This has resulted in several variant readings of Tyler's published essays and other prose works. With some of his more popular "Colon and Spondee" columns, which were picked up and reprinted in as many as half a dozen newspapers, it is not unusual to find that many different versions. For this edition, however, the text used is that employed in the first appearance of any particular work.

"The Bay Boy," because it bulks the largest in Tyler's prose canon and because it holds the greatest importance of all his surviving unpublished works, is presented first. The other works are given, as much as possible, in chronological order, starting with the Sermon and Prayer he delivered on Christmas Day in 1793 and ending with the few surviving fragments of "Utile Dulci" which Tyler completed at the end of his life.

Manuscript title page of Tyler's last major effort, "The Bay Boy." Although uncompleted, the surviving portions have been gathered together for the first time in this volume. It was to have been a sequel to Tyler's earlier novel, *The Algerine Captive*, published in 1797. *In the Royall Tyler Collection of the Vermont Historical Society, gift of Helen Tyler Brown.*

"The Bay Boy"

"THE BAY BOY," Tyler's unfinished autobiographical novel was the natural outgrowth of *The Algerine Captive*, his first published book-length narrative.[1] In order to trace the genesis of "The Bay Boy" it is necessary to outline the history of *The Algerine Captive*.

Under the pseudonymn of Dr. Updike Underhill, Tyler used *The Algerine Captive* as a convenient vehicle to put before the public his views on domestic politics, religion, the medical profession, education, the slavery question, foreign policy and American life in general. In a total of 69 chapters Tyler traced Updike's life from birth through his teens and his six years imprisonment in Algiers after his capture by some Barbary pirates.

The book is episodic in nature, moving from one event to another with few digressions from the main story line. The picaresque structure of the book is one of its weak points. Like all other novels of incident there is no unfolding of situations, no interweaving of events to form a plot, no clearly defined objective outside of a chronological one and, therefore, little suspense.

Despite these faults, Tyler partly succeeded in refuting the contention of most foreign observers of his age that the American nation was too raw and too barren to bring forth a culture and a literature based on native traditions and materials. *The Algerine Captive*—and "The Bay Boy" which was to follow—are purely American. The narrator, which is in reality Tyler speaking through the medium of his hero, Updike, is a complete Yankee and the setting of the book, outside of Updike's stay in Algeria, was the eastern seaboard of the United States from the District of Maine to Virginia. Heightening the import of the choice of locale and characters was Tyler's impassioned plea for a native literature in the preface and throughout the work. He definitely said that the stated purpose of *The Algerine Captive* was "to display a portrait of New England, hitherto unattempted."

The first mention of the book is in May, 1795, when young Edward

---

[1] The work was first printed by David Carlisle at Walpole, N.H., in 1797. It was reprinted by G. and J. Robinson in London in 1802. Because most of this edition was lost due to a fire in the publishers' warehouse, it was reissued by the Robinsons in 13 installments in their journal, *The Lady's Magazine,* in 1804. The third and final edition was printed by Peter B. Gleason and Co. in Hartford, Conn., in 1816.

A facsimile of the first London edition, with an introduction by Jack B. Moore, was published by Scholars' Facsimiles and Reprints in 1967. For a full bibliographical description of the various editions see Tanselle, "Some Uncollected Authors XLII. Royall Tyler, 1757–1826," *The Book Collector,* XV, No. 3 (Autumn, 1966), 311–4.

Palmer, Tyler's brother-in-law, wrote to his mother: "Mr. Tyler sett me a writing his Algerine Captive." In October the manuscript was still in the formative stage because Tyler said in a letter to Dennie: "I have begun a work for the Walpole press—but as the Angel said to the Evangelist— 'Come and see.' "[2]

By the middle of 1796 the manuscript was apparently completed because Dennie asked Tyler, "What is your present employment at Guilford? . . . meditating new Updikes under old oaks?"[3] The emphasis on the word "new" hints that *The Algerine Captive* was probably finished.

The manuscript went to the printer, David Carlisle of Walpole, New Hampshire, shortly thereafter and rolled off his presses sometimes between the 7th and 12th of August, 1797. *The Farmer's Weekly Museum,* published by Carlisle, carried an advertisement on August 7th that the book was about to be published.[4] The *Columbian Centinel* in Boston stated on August 12th that the novel had just been "lately published."[5] The notice further explained that "this work is with sufficient reason, attributed to *ROYALL TYLER,* Esq. of celebrated and comic powers. It is said to combine the humourous and historical, and, as a lively portrait of *New-England* manners, to surpass everything in the same line that has been written in America."[6]

The first edition of approximately one thousand copies sold fairly well at $1.50 each. Advertisements for the work were carried in a good number of New England and New York newspapers. In general, the notices made no attempt to hide the identity of the author. Although Tyler's name was not carried on the title page the advertisements discreetly or openly stated *The Algerine Captive* was by him.[7]

Reports from friends in both Boston and New York spoke of the book's

[2] Ms. letter from Edward Palmer to Mrs. Joseph P. Palmer, dated from Brattleboro, Vt., May 30, 1795. In the "RT Collection." The Ms. letter from Tyler to Dennie, dated Oct. 7, 1795, is at the New Hampshire Historical Society, Concord.

[3] *The Letters of Joseph Dennie,* p. 152.

[4] *The Farmer's Weekly Museum,* V, No. 227 (Aug. 7, 1797), 1.

[5] *Columbian Centinel,* XXVII, No. 410 (Aug. 12, 1797), 3. Two days later *The Farmer's Weekly Museum* also noted the book was available and printed an exerpt on the back page. See Vol. V, No. 228 (Aug. 14, 1797), 4.

[6] *Columbian Centinel,* XXVII, No. 410 (Aug. 12, 1797), 3. Tyler dedicated the book to David Humphrey, at the time U.S. Ambassador to Portugal. A poet, he had been one of the Hartford Wits and had served under Washington in the Revolution.

[7] For examples of these advertisements see those of the Boston publisher and bookseller, Joseph Nancrede, in the *Columbian Centinel,* XXVIII, No. 7 (Sept. 27, 1797), 3 and No. 9 (Oct. 4, 1797), 4. Despite the frequent linking of Tyler's name to the book many were deceived about the identity of Dr. Underhill. Mrs. Tyler tells in her memoirs that her husband used to read exerpts of Dr. Underhill's adventures to their

favorable reception. Speaking of this during a visit to Boston in August, Dennie could not help commenting on the city's meagre taste for literary productions:

Your novel has been examined by the few and approved. It is, however, extremely difficult for the Bostonians to supply themselves with a book that slumbers in a stall at Walpole, supposed, by the latest and most accurate advertisements, to be situated 400 miles north of their meridian. . . . People are pretty well convinced that you are capable of writing well on any subject; and, for your encouragement, I can assure you that a taste for letters begins gradually to obtain here.[8]

From New York came the encouraging news from William Coleman, Aaron Burr's law partner, that he had received requests for up to 30 copies of *The Algerine Captive,* although he was encountering difficulties obtaining them from New York booksellers. Coleman also said that "when I have heard you mentioned here, with much tribute of applause, for your literary talents, as I have often; and when I see your publication of the 'Algerine' announced with great eclat, as it has repeatedly been in different papers . . . I feel proud that I was once so intimately acquainted with the man and the Author."[9]

There is no doubt that the public acclaim which followed the publication of *The Algerine Captive* led Tyler to give serious thought to coming out with a sequel to Updike's episodes. Within the book itself the author definitely stated he was contemplating a second edition if the demand was sufficient. Updike said, during a visit to Boston:

The remarks I made upon this hospitable, busy, national, town-born people; my observations upon their manners, habits, local virtues, customs, and prejudices; the elocution of their principal clergymen; with anecdotes of public characters—I deal not in private foibles; and a comparative view of their manners at the beginning and near the close of the eighteenth century, are pronounced by the partiality of some friends to

old maid without disclosing his authorship of the book. The woman never realized Tyler was the author and could not understand why Dr. Underhill never came to visit the family in Guilford. See Mary Palmer Tyler, "Memoirs," p. 170. (The original manuscript is in the possession of The Honorable William Royall Tyler, Washington, D. C. and a microfilm copy is in the Manuscript Division, Library of Congress, Washington, D.C. Hereafter cited as "MPT Memoirs.")

Buckingham, in *Specimens of Newspaper Literature,* p. 209, said the first edition "sold rapidly."

[8] Letter from Dennie to Tyler, dated from Boston, Aug. 30, 1797. In "TPT Memoir," p. 116, and *Letters of Joseph Dennie,* p. 165.

[9] Letter from Coleman to Tyler, dated from New York, Sept. 24, 1797. In "TPT Memoir," p. 117. Another anecdote of the Coleman-Tyler friendship is recounted below, pp. 284–85.

be original, and, to those who know the town, highly interesting. If this homespun history of private life [*The Algerine Captive*] shall be approved, these remarks will be published by themselves in a future edition of this work.[10]

The timeliness of the book was praised by several reviewers, and there is no doubt Tyler would have liked to capitalize on the topical value of the work if time had permitted. A notice in *The Farmer's Weekly Museum* said that

the subject of this work is well chosen, the publication well timed, and the execution does great credit to the talents and erudition of the writer. In delineating the national character, and in describing the local peculiarities, in manners, customs, and language, of the people of New England, there is no preceding work, either in Europe or America, which can claim the smallest pretence to rivalship.[11]

Unfortunately, Tyler's growing law career and his service on the Vermont Supreme Court Bench sidetracked his efforts to continue Updike's adventures. Although Tyler found sufficient time in the following decades to write countless verses, essays and other short pieces for the periodical press, he was unable to undertake another full-length novel until near the end of his life.

During the following years, however, there were a number of cries for a new edition of *The Algerine Captive*. Dennie took the lead by writing the following in his magazine, *The Port Folio*.

The editor of "The Farmer's Museum" remarks, that "among the great variety of literary works, which are occasionally published, we find the fate of them to vary, not always in proportion to their merits. A fortunate title to some, will ensure the fate of a third or fourth edition, where the intrinsic value of the work is trivial. . . . Some again are only neglected for a while, till their deserts call them from an unjust oblivion. Amongst the latter, may be classed the Algerine Captive, written by R. Tyler, Esq., a work of much humour and merit, and for which we are happy to see a late and increasing demand." From our partiality for Mr. Tyler, and our conviction of the ingenuity of his mind, we are delighted with the above information. A second edition of his work, enlarged to two volumes octavo . . . is greatly wanted, and would afford the author an opportunity to extend his chapters, which are now too brief, and fill a fine outline, with very captivating colours.[12]

In June, 1803, Dennie noted that *The Algerine Captive* had been reprinted by the Robinsons in London and bemoaned the fact that the English were

[10] *The Algerine Captive*, I, Chap. 16.
[11] *Farmer's Weekly Museum*, VI, No. 264 (April 24, 1798), 4.
[12] *The Port Folio*, II, No. 1 (Jan. 1, 1802), 8.

wont "to treat American Literature wth delicacy and respect" while it was neglected in its own country.[13] Dennie pursued this matter at greater length in a following issue of *The Port Folio*.

"The Algerine Captive," a well written novel, the production of an American, and a favourite friend of the Editor of the Port Folio, is commended in all the literary journals of Great Britain. It must be truly grateful, it must be a soothing *triumph*, to the ingenious author to learn that his book is perused in the country of his *ancestors*. In his native country, his motley fellow *citizens* were too much occupied in the shallow devices of an infamous democracy, and in perusing, with the eagerness of Shylock, "the *bond, the bond*."[14]

By the first decade of the new century the inaccessibility of *The Algerine Captive* caused many of Tyler's friends to call more loudly for a reprinting in the United States. The *Monthly Anthology and Boston Review*, in 1810, said that the book, "an admirable picture of the manners of the interior of New England," was "very undeservedly hastening to oblivion" and urged that it be reissued.[15]

Despite these pleas nothing was done to produce a new American edition until 1816 when *The Algerine Captive* was reissued by Peter Gleason in Hartford. It was a poor reprinting of the London edition and did not include any changes by the author. The new printing, however, sold well apparently and led Tyler to think again of the book's complete revision. The cancer, which was affecting his eyesight, also caused disfigurement of his face and curtailed seriously his law practice. The result was that Tyler once again turned to writing as a means of earning money and occupying his time.

Extreme praise for what Tyler was attempting to accomplish in *The Algerine Captive* came from a most unexpected source in 1822. In the May issue of *The Literary and Scientific Repository, and Critical Review*, its editor, James Fenimore Cooper, lauded both the author and the book in a review of Catherine Maria Sedgwick's *A New-England Tale*. Speaking specifically of books which "illustrate American society and manners" Cooper said:

[13] *Ibid.*, III, No. 23 (June 4, 1803), 181.

[14] *Ibid.*, IV, No. 17 (April 28, 1804), 134. A few months later, however, Dennie became unhappy with the British, accusing them of mutilating the text of *The Algerine Captive* so as to eliminate all traces of its American origin. See *The Port Folio*, IV, No. 35 (Sept. 1, 1804), 277. This charge is refuted by Tanselle, "Early American Fiction in England: The Case of *The Algerine Captive*," *Papers of the Bibliographical Society of America*, LIX, No. 4 (Oct.–Dec., 1965), 367–84.

[15] *Monthly Anthology and Boston Review*, IX (Nov. 1810), 334. The author of the review has been identified as Nathaniel A. Haven. See the *Journal of the Society Which Conducts the Monthly Anthology & Boston Review* (Boston, 1910), p. 242.

We have seen but two attempts of this sort which merit any praise, a story called Salem Witchcraft, and Mr. Tyler's forgotten, and we fear, lost narrative of the Algerine Captive, both of which relate to times long past. Any future collector of our national tales, would do well to snatch these from oblivion, and to give them that place among the memorials of other days, which is due to the early and authentic historians of a country. We say the historians—we do not mean to rank the writers of these tales, among the recorders of statutes, and battles, and party chronicles; but among those true historians which . . . give us just notions of what manner of men the ancient Greeks were, in their domestic affections, and retired deportment; and with whom Fielding classes himself, nearly in these words: "Those dignified authors who produce what is called true histories, are indeed writers of fictions, which I am a true historian, a describer of society as it exists, and of men as they are."[16]

After December, 1822, when his eyesight caused him to lose his position as Register of Probate for Windham County, Tyler was practically completely confined to his home. Seeking to keep occupied, he thought more seriously of rewriting *The Algerine Captive,* probably upon the lines suggested originally by Dennie in 1802. The basic story line—the life and adventures of Dr. Updike Underhill—was to remain. Old chapters would be retained or expanded when possible, new chapters would fill out the story, and new episodes, new secondary characters and new situations would be intertwined around the original chronological development of Updike's career.

Although none of the surviving manuscript fragments are dated, it is possible to determine when Tyler started the revision. Those few pieces in his own hand were probably done before his eyesight became very bad around 1821–23. These efforts, however, were only desultory. It was not until the latter part of 1824 that composition started in earnest. The greater part of the surviving manuscript, in Mrs. Tyler's handwriting, shows that the majority of "The Bay Boy" was accomplished in these last three years of Tyler's life.

Existing correspondence between members of the family and Mrs. Tyler's diary allow the dating of the new manuscript after November, 1824. Initially Tyler contemplated merely a revision of the old *Algerine Captive,* not a completely new novel. It was only later, in 1825, when the rewriting had become so extensive that its author decided to turn the work into a new book, to be entitled "The Bay Boy."

In August, 1824, Tyler received strong encouragement from an extremely

---

[16] The review is in the *Repository,* IV (May, 1822), 336–70. Reprinted in James Fenimore Cooper, *Early Critical Essays, 1820–1822,* ed. James F. Beard, Jr. (Gainesville, Fla., 1955), pp. 97–8.

favorable retrospective review of *The Algerine Captive* in *The Minerva,* a literary magazine in New York. The article said:

It is . . . a wholesome and agreeable pursuit to leave our contemporaries at times, and . . . to bring forth from the dust of the past, the buried treasures of literature.
    In thus recurring backwards, we lately met the work of an American author, Royall Tyler, Esq. some time . . . a Judge of the Court of Common Pleas in some part of Vermont; and certainly lament that a book which affords such strong indications of genius, and is written in such a graceful style, should have been suffered to die on the sale of a first edition. . . . Its republication at this day would add new lustre to the rising reputation of our country, and would richly repay the expenses of the publisher.[17]

But Tyler, extremely discouraged by his poor health, despaired of ever completing both the new edition of *The Algerine Captive* and "Utile Dulci," an anthology of his remnant poems, essays, plays and other miscellaneous works on which he was also working.[18] His wife, writing to their children, urged them to encourage their father to keep writing. On October 4, therefore, Edward, then a student at Yale, wrote to his father:

You must know that I rec'd the notice in the Minerva with much satisfaction. If you can sell another edition of the Alg. Cap. our circumstances render it a duty. . . . The Alg. Cap., as the Reviewer observes contains much fine writing; it is probably, however, capable of improvement, particularly in those respects where the public taste has changed—by omitting, for instance, the long epitomes at the head of the chapters—they sometimes satisfy a lazy reader rather than sharpen his appetite.[19]

Despite the heartening review in *The Minerva* and the support of his family, it was difficult for Tyler to apply himself to the task at hand. For more than a decade he had been taking various remedies for the spreading cancer. He was forced to draw the blinds and remain in a darkened room the majority of the time. Among other medications he tried laudanum and it is obvious from his wife's diary entries that it resulted in many periods when his concentration lagged and his enthusiasm for work disappeared.

Still Mrs. Tyler urged him to write. Large slate writing boards and chalk were purchased so that Tyler could write in big characters to save his eyesight. On November 13, 1824, Mrs. Tyler could proudly write in her diary that "this day My Husband wrote the first slate full of the New Edition of the

[17] *The Minerva,* I (N.S.), No. 21 (Aug. 28, 1824), 331–3.
[18] For a discussion of the composition of "Utile Dulci" see below, pp. 439–41.
[19] Ms. letter from Edward Tyler to Royall Tyler, dated from New Haven, Conn., Oct. 4, 1825. Ms. No. 824544 in the "RT Collection."

Algerine C—."[20] On the following day she added: "I have this evening copied the first page of the manuscript of the Algerine Captive."[21]

From mid-November until mid-December Mrs. Tyler's diary tells of Tyler's feverish attempts to complete "The Bay Boy."[22] Nearly every day Mrs. Tyler mentions her husband's sitting down to compose more of the book. She is obviously confident of its future progress. On November 19 the diary notes the completion of 30 pages and Mrs. Tyler was so pleased she ran to Mrs. Fessenden's home to spread the good news.[23]

By November 24 Tyler was up to 70 pages and by December 10 it was with pride that Mrs. Tyler noted the completion of 100 manuscript pages.[24] By early 1825, however, Tyler's health again weakened and Mrs. Tyler's letter of January 19 to her daughter, Amelia Sophia, in Salem, Massachusetts, was one of mingled optimism as to progress made and discouragement over the possibilities of continuing. The letter shows that although the family was still calling the manuscript "the Captive," the book outlined is definitely "The Bay Boy" as it now exists in manuscript fragments. The letter is quoted at length since it also speaks of the attempts Tyler was making to market the manuscript.

Your Aunt Pickman asks how your Father is managing his Captive. He has gone back to his early years, and given a particular account of his parents and education as a physician in Boston, and made him a student contemporary with General Warren, who was slain at Bunker Hill—which carries the story back to the time when Sir Francis Bernard was Governor in Massachusetts; of course affording many interesting anecdotes of the times, sentiments and feelings of the people of that day of excitement, related in your Father's fascinating manner. But I regret to say, it is now laid by for the present. Your Father's health is weak and he got tired of the Captive. . . . Your Father says in answer to your queries as to when he means to publish—and how or where the Captive will be published—that he has no doubt he shall be able to finish the Captive, that he intends throwing out a great deal of the old work, that we have got about two hundred and forty pages like the old text, which we have ascertained the usual way by counting the words, and that he expects to write nearly as much more, so as to make the work larger than the original. You saw Mr. Houston's first letter and the answer to it, he wrote again and said there was now such a rage especially in England for American literature, that his intention was when the first volume was finished to send it to his

[20] The manuscript diary was kept by Mrs. Tyler, with intermittent gaps, between Dec. 2, 1821–June 9, 1843. It provides an excellent picture of the Tylers' family life. Since the pagination is irregular citations will be by date of entry. Hereafter cited as "Mrs. Tyler's Ms. Diary."

[21] *Ibid.*, Nov. 14, 1824.

[22] *Ibid.* The seventeen entries covering this period are dated between Nov. 17–Dec. 10, 1824.

[23] *Ibid.*, Nov. 19, 1824.

[24] *Ibid.*, Nov. 24 and Dec. 10, 1824.

correspondents in London, and have an Edition printed there at the same time it was printing in New York, and to secure the copy right in both countrys and he had no doubt of a rapid sale. As for terms, he says there were three ways of proceeding: one was for the author to print at his own expense; another, to let some responsible book-seller print at certain shares of profit and the author run all risk of loss; the other, for the author to sell the copy right for fourteen years for such sum as he could get. This last is the only way *we could do,* as you know the destruction of the poor is their poverty. But it is more probable even this way it will command a few hundred dollars, which will be a blessing in our situation.[25]

Mrs. Tyler concluded by saying that although "there is a great deal of writing to do" she hoped that the manuscript would be finished soon so that their son John could take it with him to New York.

By this time *The Algerine Captive* had been so extensively chopped up that Tyler realized he had a new book on his hands. In April comes the first mention that the manuscript was to be called "The Bay Boy," or as the title page said, "the autobiography of a youth of Massachusetts Bay . . . during a period anterior to the Revolution."

Mrs. Tyler's diary on April 25 is doubly significant because it notes the new title of the book and indicates that the manuscript was so well advanced that she could begin copying a final draft "for the press."[26] The last mention of "The Bay Boy" is in May. It comes in a letter from Mrs. Tyler to her son, Edward. It is her most discouraging commentary and indicates that even her perpetually buoyant spirits were adversely affected by her husband's failing health.

Should your Father grow much weaker, I shall not have patience to have you wait till after commencement before you visit us. At present we are busily engaged about the *Bay Boy* . . . it needs all my art and management to induce him to go on, so diffident is he about success, and his bodily sufferings are so great that nothing but the hope I keep alive in his bosom of leaving something behind him that may be of service to his children could possibly give him courage to proceed. . . . Your Father is very feeble indeed. I tremble every day he should be taken suddenly away.[27]

[25] Ms. letter from Mary Palmer Tyler to Amelia Sophia Tyler, dated from Brattleboro, Vt., Jan. 19, 1825. Ms. No. 825119 in the "RT Collection." The reference to Tyler's "education as a physician" is a puzzling one. Previous to this there had never been any indication that he considered medicine as a vocation while in college. Mrs. Tyler, however, is definite in her statement so it appears that before deciding upon a career in law Tyler had given some thought to becoming a physician.

[26] Mrs. Tyler's Ms. Diary, April 25, 1825. The entries for April 28 and 30, 1825, indicate her further progress in the copying but unfortunately a gap occurs in the diary shortly thereafter and Mrs. Tyler did not make any further references to "The Bay Boy", when she resumed writing in the diary.

[27] Ms. letter from Mary Palmer Tyler to Edward Tyler at Goshen, Conn., dated from Brattleboro, Vt., May 15, 1825. In the "RT Collection."

Tyler was to linger on for another 15 months, but from the twelve surviving fragments of the manuscript, it is difficult to know how much of "The Bay Boy" he actually completed before his death in August, 1826.

There is no doubt that many pieces of the manuscript have been lost in the 141 years since Tyler's death. For instance, the first 57 pages of the final draft which Mrs. Tyler said she was copying "for the press" are now missing although it has been posssible to reconstruct most of the missing first four chapters from earlier rough drafts in Tyler's hand. In January, 1825, Mrs. Tyler said that her husband had completed sufficent manuscript to make up 240 printed pages and he expected to at least double this amount.

Marginal notes show Tyler estimated that about four and a half pages of manuscript would equal ten printed pages. Using this as a guide in counting the number of manuscript pages extant, there survives at present sufficient copy to result in approximately 250 pages, nowhere near the more than 590 printed pages the author contemplated.[28] What survives, however (the front matter and fifteen chapters in various stages of finish), is enough to give us an excellent picture of Tyler's skills as a spinner of adventuresome yarns, a fine delineator of character, a sure handler of dialogue and a biting satirist.

Several aspects of "The Bay Boy" deserve special mention. The first is the autobiographical features of the manuscript. Tyler was born in 1757, and even if we did not have Mrs. Tyler's definite statement that her husband had "gone back to his early years" it would be obvious that the work is mostly a clever recounting of Tyler's own childhood in Boston during the turbulent years immediately preceding the Revolution. This is part of the book's great value. It localizes and builds upon much of the material in *The Algerine Captive*.

Of historical importance is Tyler's reflections upon the personalities who lived in Boston during the third quarter of the eighteenth century. The histories of the period and the memoirs of those personally involved go a long way toward substantiating the validity of Tyler's "fictitious" history and show that he was realistically depicting Boston as he knew it in his youth.

The manuscript of "The Bay Boy" is not dated but several internal clues allow us to pinpoint the exact period about which Tyler is writing. There is a reference to a clock in the steeple of the Old South Church. The *Boston Gazette* of April 16, 1770, reports that Gawan Brown had set up "a great clock" in the church steeple.

[28] The marginal notations used by Tyler in counting the rough draft manuscript pages to discover how many printed pages would result have been helpful in arriving at the above figure. These notations have been included as footnotes in the following text of "The Bay Boy."

Updike is also told of the preaching of Dr. George Whitefield, the noted English Methodist evangelist, at the same church. Contemporary accounts inform us that Dr. Whitefield addressed the Old South congregation on August 29 and September 3, 1770. Updike also submits a poem to the *Massachusetts Spy* at a period when Isaiah Thomas was the newspaper's sole owner. This would have been between 1770 and 1775.

Finally, Chapter X revolves around an episode involving Sir Francis Bernard, the Colonial governor of Massachusetts, who was recalled by the British government in 1769. All of these dates, clustered close together, make it possible to place "The Bay Boy" into its proper context with known historical personages and activities.

Considering that "The Bay Boy" is a look at history only about 50 years after the events described, the retrospective glance Tyler provides us of the Massachusetts Bay Colony in the mid-eighteenth century is amazing for its breath and depth of perspection, description and character delineation. Tyler's interest in the American scene as a source for material and as inspiration for literary endeavors remained strong to the end of his life.

Several of the characters in the book are identifiable, such as Tyler's mother and father, Governor Bernard, and others. Some, although they probably loomed large in the life of the period, have faded into the deep shadows of history and are no longer recognizable under the layers of Tyler's satire. In any case, there is no doubt of the artistic merit with which Tyler has portrayed each of these types.

In 1825, when he was contemplating publication of "The Bay Boy," many of the people depicted in the book were still alive and the author probably made definite attempts to disguise the identities of those involved, especially since religion and politics, then as now, were volatile subjects. Some of the characters, on the other hand, are undoubtedly composites of several individuals and attempts to identify them now would be fruitless.

Among those who cannot be identified is the old, eccentric Mrs. Diaway who was Updike's first patient, and the beautiful, brittle Charlotte Love, his first romantic infatuation. Mrs. Diaway is Tyler's most individualized characterization. His presentation of what may be the first neuropathic type in American literature is a veritable tour de force. Mrs. Diaway was obviously someone with whom Tyler was very intimate during his youth and he has handled her personality and its quirks with surety and skill.

During his early years in college and immediately thereafter Tyler had manifested a strong interest in the female sex and it is no coincidence that his hero, Updike, also showed a somewhat amorous propensity. It would be interesting, therefore, if the identity of Charlotte Love was known. There is the outside possibility Tyler is remembering his unfortunate affair with the beautiful Abigail Adams when he tells of Updike's disasterous involvement with the shallow Charlotte. If this is the case, Charles Brightly, Updike's competitor for the charms of Charlotte, may be Col. William Stephens Smith whom Abigail married after her parents broke off the affair with Tyler.[29]

An important personage in "The Bay Boy" is "the celebrated Dr. G—, physician and surgeon" of Marlborough Street, under whom Updike received his introduction as a student of medicine. The sections of the manuscript devoted to a satire of the medical profession are among Tyler's best. Dr. G—, however, is treated with great respect and devotion and it is obvious he was a person for whom Tyler had great regard.

A study of medical histories of the period, together with a close examination of the passages describing Dr. G—, provide definite evidence that Tyler was describing Dr. Silvester Gardiner of Boston. Updike tells us that Dr. G—was a noted surgeon, a druggist of high repute, a Tory and Church of England man, and held in high esteem because of his gentle and kind personality. Dr. Silvester Gardiner was also all of these and other clues provide supporting evidence for this attribution.[30]

As mentioned above, Tyler admitted that Updike's parents were modeled after his own mother and father. Although the family background of both his parents is available in genealogies and the political and civic career of his

[29] This period in Tyler's life has been well covered. See "TPT Memoir," pp. 23–31; "MPT Memoirs," pp. 17, 34–37; Tyler Verse, pp. xvi–xvii; Royall Tyler, pp. 10–19; and Mary Palmer Tyler, Grandmother Tyler's Book, Frederick Tupper and Helen Tyler Brown, eds. (New York, 1925), pp. 76–82. The latter is a condensed and unevenly edited printing of Mrs. Tyler's Ms. "Memoirs." Whenever possible citations are given for the more reliable original manuscript. The printed edition will hereafter be cited as GTB.

The Adams family viewpoint of the affair with Abigail is summarized in L. H. Butterfield, ed., The Earliest Diary of John Adams (Cambridge, 1966), pp. 18–28, and Page Smith, John Adams (Garden City, 1962), I, 531, 572–3; 592–3; II, 658–62, 668, 675.

Although Abigail and her husband never saw "The Bay Boy" they felt that they had been previously satirized by Tyler. Abigail thought that the comparison between Col. Manley, the virtuous American, with the foppish Englishman, Billy Dimple, in The Contrast was meant to point out the differences between Tyler and her husband. (Abigail's letter, privately owned, is quoted in The Earliest Diary of John Adams, p. 29.)

[30] See James Thacher, The American Medical Biography (Boston, 1828), I, 24; and Bertrand W. Chapman, The Nativism of Royall Tyler (University of Vermont Master's Thesis, 1933), p. 75. Chapman, who examined "The Bay Boy" manuscript, was one of the first to evaluate it and attempt to identify the disguised personages. His thesis has been useful in compiling this section. Further details about Dr. Gardiner are presented in "The Bay Boy," Chapter IX, footnotes 2, 3 and 8, pp. 101 & 104.

father has been adequately traced, nothing is known of their individual personalities and their married life.[31]

The depiction of Tyler's parents in the early chapters of "The Bay Boy" is, therefore, the first and only flesh-and-blood record of them. Despite the somewhat unflattering comments on his mother's education (Tyler blames the system, not the person) and his father's method of picking a wife, the picture of them is permeated with love and admiration for two people who clearly imparted much to their son.

Following his permanent departure from Boston in 1791 for Vermont, Tyler was estranged from his mother for the rest of her life. The kind treatment of Updike's mother in "The Bay Boy" is a notable attempt to make amends for what he considered his ungallant treatment of her in her final years.[32]

In contrast to Mr. and Mrs. Underhill, their son Updike—and, therefore, Tyler himself—is never physically described in either *The Algerine Captive* or "The Bay Boy." Updike remains a mere observer and narrator of the events which ebb and flow around him. Tyler's failure to give the reader a mental picture of Updike is due partly to his own innate sense of modesty and partly to the traditional structure of a novel of incident.

On the other hand, the Rev. Ammi Rhuhamah Priest, the minister who plays such an important role in the early chapters of "The Bay Boy," is fully developed. In Tyler's mind he was possibly meant to be a caricature of a specific religious figure who was intimately embroiled in the "Great Awakening" that swept New England in mid-century. Now, however, he is just a stereotype of the many ministers involved in this momentous religious upheaval. Fortunately the loss of Rev. Priest's identity after all these years does not prevent the enjoyment of one of the book's most delightful characters and the brunt of some of Tyler's most incisive satire.

It is possible that the Rev. Priest is a composite character, combining the personalities of some of the religious figures of the period with some of the instructors, tutors and professors whom Tyler had known as a boy at South Latin School or at Harvard College. Certain facets of Rev. Priest, therefore, may be those of the noted Tory and scholar, John Lovell, who was principal at South Latin in 1765 when Tyler entered the school at the age of eight.

[31] The family geneology is charted in *GTB*, Appendix A, pp. 327–34. The civic and political career of Royall Tyler, Sr., is discussed in "TPT Memoir," pp. 3–13. See also *Royall Tyler*, pp. 1–2.

[32] References to Tyler's relationship with his mother, Mary Tyler Whitwell, are found in "MPT Memoirs," pp. 111–2, 127–30, 133, 139–40, 159, 181. Appended (p. 226) is a Ms., letter from Tyler's mother to his wife, dated Aug. 2, 1796. See also *GTB*, pp. 244–5, 170–1, and "TPT Memoir," pp. 146–7.

Although the Reverend Priest has remained unidentified, Chapters III, IV, V and VI, which deal with his influence on young Updike's education and upbringing, and the minister's disastrous involvement in the politics of the town of Shingletrees, are of great import. They show the sociological importance of Tyler's satire of New England religious life in the mid-eighteenth century.

This continent's first settlers were zealous seekers of religious freedom. New Englanders thought themselves in covenant with the Almighty, commissioned to plant true churches in the New World. Nine of Great Britain's 13 colonies created harmony of a sort by establishing state churches of their own, for example, the Congregational in Massachusetts and Connecticut. This led, as in Massachusetts, to the unique link between church and Commonwealth—the establishment of a state Christianity. The government of the state, therefore, came to undertake a divine mission.

The state-church relation of the "Bible Commonwealths" began to give way in the years immediately preceding the Revolution when most of the infant states of the future Republic dropped their legal ties to a particular church. But even earlier the New England religion underwent a tortuous eruption that forever prevented it from falling back into its old ways. If New England ecclesiastical history had any one theme between the first Great Awakening in 1738 and the second at the end of the century, it was complexity and confusion.

Before mid-century Puritanism had undergone an unsettling upheaval. The Great Awakening turned into a religious revival that spread grace and discord in about equal amounts throughout New England. The opponents of the Awakening, called "Old Lights," controlled the consociations in the early 1740's, using them to keep the revivalists "New Lights" out of the pulpits in Connecticut and Massachusetts. Soon the "New Lights" gained sufficient support to control most of the consociations themselves and the discord was compounded.

The religious divisions and debates spawned by the Great Awakening resulted in one of the most critical episodes of American intellectual history. Everyone was swept up in the struggle. The Awakening, and the resultant New Light theology, was of momentous intellectual and cultural significance and led to great richness of American thought and expression for many decades.

The movement also had definite political repercussions. The arguments developed by Jonathan Edwards, Joseph Bellamy, Thomas Foxcroft, Jonathan Meyhew and others shook New England Congregationalism to its foundations and helped shake the colonies out of the British Empire.

At the time, not only had the Great Awakening divided New England Congregationalism into three wings and given rise to some of the new splinter denominations, but it had provided a challenge of lasting significance to the major premises of Calvinist orthodoxy. For revivalism, no matter how justified, rationalized or intellectualized by a professing Calvinist, was simply not compatible with absolute divine sovereignty, election and predestination.

The urban reaction to revivalism, especially in Boston, was sophisticated, theologically liberal and socially conservative. This reflex challenged Calvinism no less than the revivals themselves, and provided a hospitable dwelling place for scientific rationalism and eventually, Unitarianism.

It was in this atmosphere that Tyler's father had been brought up and as a precocious young boy at the proverbial "father's knee," Tyler was able to take in all that he heard and saw. Later, as a young man at Harvard in the 1770's, surrounded by the questioning attitude of both faculty and students, he was further touched by the swelling climate of religious and political change.

Especially significant in "The Bay Boy" are Chapters IV and V. In the former an unfortunate minister had the misfortune to preach on "the obnoxious doctrine of good works." The efforts by the more orthodox members of the cloth to dissuade the minister from his grievous errors undoubtedly is Tyler's sharpest satire on the dissension and bitter feelings caused by the Great Awakening.

In Chapter V Tyler continues his attack by recounting the misfortune of Rev. Priest who was unintentionally pulled into a secular dispute between members of his parish. The people of the community were unable to decide whether a new road to the town should be constructed through the middle of a swamp or around it. The proponents of the direct route were called "Midites," while those who advocated the more circuitous road were termed "Wanderers." The well-meaning Reverend Priest was innocently dragged into the middle of the dispute and lost all. The caricature of the "Old Light" and "New Light" adherents is clear.

There are several other chapters in "The Bay Boy" which are topical in nature and present us with many contemporary events of historical importance from Tyler's viewpoint.

As a well educated and well read man, especially one with growing children, Tyler was very much interested in the educational system of the day and the possibilities of reform. In *The Algerine Captive* (Chapters V, VI and VII), Tyler had sharply criticized the primary education then being received by the majority of youngsters of that day. He repeated this attack in Chapter VII of "The Bay Boy" by recounting Updike's inability to generate sympathy for his teaching methods among the townspeople who had engaged him to run their local school.

College education, particularly at Harvard, also comes in for some unfavorable comments. Although Tyler himself was graduated from Harvard in 1776 with probably as good an education as it was possible to receive at that time, he undoubtedly looked back at his years in Cambridge as somewhat restrictive and maybe even unpleasant. As one with a very individual temperament and intellect, Tyler did not always get along with the college authorities whom he felt were unnecessarily pompous and stuffy.[33]

Religion comes in for more caustic comments in Chapter IX. This time it is the established Church of England, the hotbed of Toryism during the years immediately before the Revolution, which feels the point of Tyler's pen. Tyler recounts an episode in which young Updike attends a Sunday service at old Trinity Church in Boston. All-in-all, however, Tyler treats the church of his youth with some kindness and with a softer hand than he reserved for the warring factions of Congregationalism.

Chapter XII touches upon a subject close to Tyler's heart: the drama. It recounts the trials of a group of schoolboys who tried to produce Addison's *Cato* despite Puritan Boston's ban against theatrical productions. If the episode is at all autobiographical, as it probably is, it gives us a fine insight into the young age at which Tyler took up an interest in the stage and why his first serious excursion into literature was a play, *The Contrast*.[34]

The remaining sections of "The Bay Boy" are set in Boston and its vicinity and give us a keyhole look into everyday existence in the Massachusetts Bay Colony during the middle and end of the eighteenth century. Chapters, IX, XI, XIII and XIV, especially, present magnificent little vignettes of what it was like to be a young lad in those times.

There is a fine picture in Chapter IX of Sir Francis Bernard, the last colonial governor of Massachusetts. The governor's evening encounter with the town warden, with Updike hiding in the background, is handled with masterly skill by Tyler. No better picture could have been provided to illustrate how ineffectual and bumbling British colonial rule had become.

No attempt will be made to delve into every possible object of satire in

---

[33] Tyler's college years are recounted in "TPT Memoir," pp. 13–16; *Tyler Verse*, pp. xiv–xv; and *Royall Tyler*, pp. 4–7.

[34] Although *The Contrast* is Tyler's first known published work, a couple of his childhood and college verses survive. See *Tyler Verse*, pp. 3–5. Especially interesting, because it shows his early interest in the drama, is "A Prologue to be Spoken by Mr. Frankley" (*Ibid.*, pp. 5–7), apparently written while Tyler was a student at Harvard.

"The Bay Boy." Much more could be said about the sections devoted to the religious and political controversies of the period, but Tyler's story-telling ability can be enjoyed without lengthy explication or by wrestling with obscure points of theology or political philosophies.

Except for those sections lifted from *The Algerine Captive*, most of "The Bay Boy" would seem to have been written post-1800. This is ascertained from numerous topical references in the text and, of course, the statements by Mrs. Tyler quoted above.

In Chapter VIII there is a reference to Sir William Congreve and the use of his rockets against the French in 1806 and in Chapter XII there are mentions of the actors George Frederick Cooke, Edmund Kean, John Philip Kemble and Thomas A. Cooper, all of whom reached the pinnacle of their theatrical fame in the early years of the nineteenth century. In Chapter XIV there is an allusion to the Revolution and "a more recent war," indicating Tyler composed this section after the close of the War of 1812 in 1815. Several other clues, which will be cited in the footnotes to each chapter, allow the pinpointing of the majority of the novel's composition in the last decade of the author's life.

In order to outline better the genesis of "The Bay Boy" and to point out the various points of similarity and difference between it and *The Algerine Captive*, the following section will be devoted to a short fragment-by-fragment discussion of the surviving pieces of "The Bay Boy." The numbering of the fragments has been provided by the editor in an attempt to present the segments in an orderly and identifiable manner. This listing of the manuscript fragments should be consulted in coordination with the chart immediately following (page 40). It shows their relationship to sections of *The Algerine Captive*. The initial footnotes to each chapter also give additional bibliographical details.

"THE BAY BOY" FRAGMENTS

Fragment 1: The Title Page
This includes the title, subtitle, dedicatory verse and, on the reverse, a dedication to Mrs. Sarah Holbrook of Brattleboro.[35] (In Tyler's hand.)

---

[35] Tyler also dedicated the other effort of his final years, "Utile Dulci," to Mrs. Holbrook. She was the wife of Capt. John Holbrook, well known and prominent Brattleboro publisher and merchant. The Tylers and Holbrooks were very intimate, especially during Tyler's last years.

Fragment 2: A Preface
To the Mayor and City Officials of Boston in the year 2025, two hundred years after the completion of the manuscript. (In Tyler's hand.)

Fragment 3: A small manuscript notebook[36]
Containing: (a) the last part of Chapter II; (b) a "Preface to the Third Edition"; (c) variant readings of the last two paragraphs of Chapter VIII; (d) a part of Chapter III; (e) a section of Chapter IV; (f) the introductory verse to Chapter V; and (g) a tabulation of the number of pages in various chapters, used in this edition as a "Table of Contents." (The entire notebook is in Tyler's hand.)

Fragment 4: A rough draft of an unnumbered chapter
From its contents it is meant obviously to be Chapter I. (In Tyler's hand.)

Fragment 5: A gathering of pages in rough draft
This includes: (a) the first part of Chapter II, and (b) an insert for Chapter IV. (In Tyler's hand.)

Fragment 6: A gathering of pages in rough draft
Preliminary drafts of Chapters IV and V. (In Tyler's hand.)

Fragment 7: The remainder of the final draft
This is a large gathering of pages, numbered 58 through 148, which is obviously the clean, final draft of the novel as Tyler intended it to be presented to a publisher. Unfortunately, the first 57 pages and those pages after 148 have been lost, which prevents us from knowing how much Tyler had completed before his death. The gathering commences with the final two pages of Chapter IV and continues with Chapters V through XI, and the two unnumbered chapters entitled "First Theatrical Presentation in Boston" [Chapter XII] and "Jealousy" [Chapter XIV]. (All in Mrs. Tyler's hand.)

Fragment 8: An unnumbered chapter
A complete chapter entitled "Thanksgiving and Christmas Days" which is thought to be Chapter XV. (In Tyler's hand.)

---

[36] Miss Helen Tyler Brown noted that this small notebook was "found in C. E. M. H.'s house." This was Miss Carrie E. M. Hatcher of Brattleboro who transcribed and typed many manuscripts for Miss Brown when she was compiling material for her biography of Tyler.

Fragment 9: An unnumbered chapter
A separate chapter considered to be Chapter XIII. (In Tyler's hand.)

Fragment 10: An incomplete rough draft
This includes paragraphs one through four of Chapter VI, to which is appended the introductory poem of Chapter VII, and all of Chapter VIII except the final two paragraphs. (In Tyler's hand.)

Fragment 11: A single sheet
Unattached to Fragment 10, but clearly the last two paragraphs of Chapter VIII. (In Tyler's hand.)

Fragment 12: A gathering of preliminary draft pages
Pages numbered one through 28 contain incomplete versions of Chapter IX and X (initially numbered VII and VIII in this draft). Appended is part of the Preface to the Mayor and officials of Boston. (In Tyler's hand.)

Fragment 13: Preface to the Second Edition
The original manuscript of this preface is now lost. It was, however, copied by Thomas Pickman Tyler, and incorporated in his memoir of his father (pp. 112–3) now at the Vermont Historical Society.

A COMPARISON OF "THE BAY BOY" AND THE ALGERINE CAPTIVE

Sections Unique to "The Bay Boy"	Sections in "The Bay Boy" Similar To Some in *The Algerine Captive*	Remarks
Title Page		
Dedication		
Preface		
Preface to the Second Edition		
Preface to the Third Edition		
Chapters I & II		*AC* I, II, III not in "BB."
	"BB" III composed of *AC* V, paragraphs 1–2.	
Chapter IV		*AC* IV deals with Updike's birth but does not resemble "BB" II.
Chapter V		
	"BB" VI composed of *AC* V, paragraphs 3–4 and *AC* VI with a different headnote poem and notable changes in the transitional paragraphs.	
	"BB" VII composed of *AC* VII and VIII.	
Chapters VIII, IX, & X		
	"BB" XI composed of *AC* IX, X and XI with changes, including a different headnote poem.	
Chapters XII, XIII, XIV & XV		

"THE BAY-BOY"

Or the autobiography of a youth of Massachusetts Bay—chiefly designed to preserve some traces of those evanescent customs, habits, manners, opinions and notions which prevailed among the good people of Boston & its vicinity during a period anterior to the Revolution.

by a native of Boston

"I leave you here a little Book
"For you to look upon
"That you may see your Father's face
"When he is dead and gone."
—John Rodgers—[1]

* * * * *

To Mrs. Sarah Holbrook
Consort
of
John Holbrook, Esqr
Brattleboro, Vermont.

Madam—

I candidly confess that if I had known a better wife or mother, a lady possessing in a higher degree those virtues and accomplishments which constitute that first and most reputable of characters, an American Matron, I should not have presumed to connect your name with the following pages. Sensible, however, that every effort, however feeble, which has for its object the allurement of youth to the practice

---

[1] Rev. John Rogers (1500?–1555), Protestant minister, one of the first martyrs to the Protestant faith following the accession of Queen Mary to the throne. The lines quoted are from his "Advise to His Children," a poem reprinted in the famous *New-England Primer*.

of piety and virtue must ensure your good wishes, I venture without permission to dedicate this little book to your patronage.

*   *   *   *   *

PREFACE

To my very dear friends
And respected fellow citizens, the Mayor, Aldermen
And uncommon Councilmen of the
City of Boston for the year 2025

Enlighten'd Sirs—

In dedicating this my humble work to your especial patronage I am not vain enough to imagine that it will trundle on toward your splendid era upon the high railroad of immortality. No, I rather anticipate that after bustling the brief day assign'd to a new work, figuring in the circulating libraries, soundly criticized and its half binding worn out, it will sink gently with its author into forgetfulness. But yet I cannot but fancy that some profound antiquary of your superexcellent age, while groaping among the rubbish of time, may from some kennel of oblivion fish up my poor book, which by your day will have acquired an extrinsic value like the Roman As, or Denarias of Augustus or Otho; intrinsically of little value but when knawn by the tooth of time is in our day worth its weight in gold.

I do certainly enter with sympathetic glee into the delight and ecstasy with which my learned friend the Antiquary will seize upon this forlorn fragment of past days. How will he cuckle over its dusty pages and gloat upon the awkward stiff style, the obsolete words and redundant spelling, the coarse letter press, the uncouth binding and all the displays of typography which appear so elegant in the present and will furnish so much matter for derision to succeeding eyes. In the words of my rhymes on the chestnut tree, for I do not pretend to write poetry, my dim eyes were never seen "in a phrenzy robing."[1]

---

[1] This phrase must have come from an early version of Tyler's poem, "The Chestnut Tree," since it cannot now be found in any of the extant manuscript texts. For the complete poem see *Tyler Verse*, pp. 194–216.

In the words of my dithyrambic on a horse chestnut tree (I have to cite my own words, for why should a man pilfer the pearls and diamonds of his rich neighbors when he has a plentiful stock of paste and tinsel of his own homespun manufacture, especially when he reflects that the brilliants of Shakespeare and Milton would only by their splendour diminish the lustre of his own meagre text); in the words then of my own rhymes

> Who is that meager, studious wight,
> Who sports the habit of past days,
> And in the reigning modes despite
> His antique coat and vest displays?

> In whose gaunt form from head to feet
> The Antiquarian's air you trace,
> While Hebrew roots, and uncial Greek
> Plot out the features of his face.

> His critic eye is fixed with glee
> On a worm eaten, smoak dried page,
> The time worn paper seems to be
> The relic of some long past age.

> In sooth! it is the manuscript
> Of this poor feeble verse of mine,
> Which in despite of taste and wit
> Has straggled down to future time.

> The bookworm's features scrawl a smile
> While gloating on the musty page;
> As we admire some ruin'd pile,
> Not for its worth, but for its age.

> The sprawling letters, yellow text,
> The formal phrase, the bald stiff style,
> The spelling quaint, the line perplext,
> Provoke his unaccustom'd smile

> Like Kennicott he quotes and cites
> On illustration clear intent;
> And in the margin gravely notes
> A thousand meanings never meant.[2]

I cannot but hope my esteemed friend the Antiquary will at my especial request and out of regard to our long tried friendship be persuaded to *do* or translate my life and adventures into the tasteful vanacular of your elegant age. In which event, enlighten'd sirs, you may as a relaxation from the government of the great literary emporium of the universe be amused with sketches of the manners, customs, habits, opinions and notions of your ancestors when Boston was a mere town of crooked streets, rough pavements and grotesque buildings. When Beacon Hill had not buri'd its venerable head before the sprite of speculation and the genius of architecture. When West Boston was covered with grass and South Boston was a sheep pasture. When the only approaches to the town were by the ferries of Charlestown and Winnesimmet and the narrow neck which connects Boston with Roxbury then its only avenue. When no magnificent mansion house lodged the mayor on the eider down of luxury. When no broad canal or abundant railways brought the produce of the Origon and Rocky Mountains, the St. Lawrence and the Lake of the Woods to your great commercial depot—the Venice of the United States.[3]

And perhaps too extatic thought! Perhaps my lady mayoress may condescend to admit my new edition into the salon of the mansion house, or peruse it by the flame of her gas light closure, or let it repose on the cover of her *steame* piano forte.[4] And perhaps too her lovely daughters may pout their pretty lips with disdain while they learn the millinery notions of their awkward ancestors; or to quote once more from my "Chestnut Tree":

[2] From "The Chestnut Tree," stanzas 155–61.

[3] In predicting transcontinental railways, Tyler was demonstrating a breath of vision and depth of faith not possessed by many in his day. Although George Stephenson's first locomotive drew a train in 1814 and the Stockton & Darlington Railway was opened in 1825, the first locomotive did not reach the United States until 1829, several years after Tyler's death.

[4] The first practical application of gas distilled from coal as an illuminating agent is

Our leghorn straws, and bearskin muffs
And all our dashy modes of dress,
They view as we, the blue starched ruffs
Of Scottish James and old Queen Bess.

Again they look, and laugh again;
Then peer, and smile and giggling, stare;
While all the lovely group exclaim,
"What monstrous frights our grandames were!"[5]

Wishing you, enlighten'd sirs, all that exquisite pleasure which you will doubtless derive from a comparative view of your own notions, with the uncouth notions of your ancestors, and that my lady mayoress and all your interesting wives may be made very merry at the unfashionable, unbecoming dress of their great, great, great, great, great grandmothers, and that your beautiful and accomplished daughters may soon be blest with good husbands with the most enlarged notions

> I subscribe myself your and their
> Fellow Citizen, friend and well wisher.
> The Author.—

* * * * *

PREFACE TO THE SECOND EDITION

IN THE YEAR 1797, when the sufferings of our unfortunate seamen, carried into slavery at Algiers, was the common topic of conversation, and excited the most lively interest throughout the United States, the author (at the suggestion of his lamented friend, the

generally assigned to William Murduck between 1792 and 1802. Tyler probably had read of the first use of gas for lighting purposes in the United States. This was demonstrated by Rembrandt Peale in 1816 at his Baltimore Museum and Gallery of the Fine Arts.

Although there are records of crude steam-operated keyboard instruments in France in the middle of the seventeenth century, the first American calliope is attributed to William Hoyt of Dayton, Ohio, in 1851. The instrument gained wider fame following the 1855 patent to J. C. Stoddard of Worcester, Mass., for a "steam piano."

[5] "The Chestnut Tree," stanzas 44-5.

late Joseph Dennie, Esq., then editor of a popular newspaper printed in Walpole, New Hampshire, and afterwards conductor of the Port Folio in Philadelphia) embodied such information as could then be obtained as to the manners, customs, habits and history of those corsairs in a little work, entitled The Algerine Captive. An impression of 1000 copies was then published by David Carlisle, Printer, at Walpole; and in 1802, a second edition was printed in London for G. & J. Robinson, Paternoster Row, by S. Hamilton, Falcon Court, Fleet Street. This London Edition was treated decorously by the English reviewers; altho' the work was issued at that unpropitious era when, in the words of an English reviewer of great acerbity, "no one ever read an American book."[1] The Algerine Captive was reviewed in a Boston Magazine by some one who had the sagacity to discover that it savored of infidelity.[2] The Author was prepared to meet severe criticism on his style; and various other imperfections; but certainly he never imagined it was objectionable on the score of infidelity, or even scepticism. The part objected to, as far as the Author recollects, was written with a view to do away with the vulgar prejudices against Islamism. He never thought that in adepting the liberality of the good Sale,[3] the translator of the Koran, he was even jeopardising the truths of Christianity; for the Author considered then, and now considers, that, after exhibiting Islamism in its best light, the Mahometan imposture will be obvious to those who compare the language, the dogma, the fables, the monstrous absurdities of the Koran, with the sublime doctrines, morals and language of the Gospel Dispensation.

[1] Tyler would have had to compose this preface (Fragment 13) after 1820 since it was in that year that Sidney Smith, the English critic, made his famous indictment of American literature and the arts in a review of Adam Seybert's Statistical Annals . . . of the United States of America: Founded on Official Documents . . .(Philadelphia, 1818). Smith said, "In the four quarters of the globe, who reads an American book, or goes to an American play, or looks at an American picture or statue?"

[2] The 1810 review of The Algerine Captive in the Monthly Anthology and Boston Review explained that the Christian religion came off second-best in the debate over the relative merits of Islamism and Christianity.

[3] George Sale (1697?–1736). His direct translation of the Koran into English in 1734 was most influential.

PREFACE TO THE THIRD EDITION

WHILE all attempts to pry into futurity which have for ages flattered the credulity of the people at large and even occupied the studies of the philosopher are now justly exploded, while the learned of the present day have ridiculed or frowned judicial astrology, palmistry, the Vergilian lots, with the vulgar witcheries of cards and coffee grounds into contempt, yet they have universally recommended researches into the past as laudable and instructive.

The least crumbling fragments of ancient time have been sought for with avidity and viewed with delight by the learned and unlearned, the latter, however, deriving their enjoyment from mere curiosity, while the former discover in such venerable remains that which may reflect light upon the character of the nation upon whose territory they may have been found. Hence, the gratification of those who have explored the ruins of Pompia and Herculanium, or the mouldering edifices in the deserts of Affricia.

The same laudable desire to be acquainted with the opinions, manners and habits of the generations which have past away is prevalent. I believe no man who has read Hume's History of England has not reperused with delight his citation from Holingshed prefixed to his History, where that author who wrote and pub[lished] his [...] (20 Elis: 1577)[1] gravely laments the introduction of chimneys, the substitution of bolsters for log pillows, of pewter platters for wooden trenchers and the building houses of oak as premotive of luxury which would enervate the nation.

It is true the manners, customs, habits and especially the opinions of our ancestors are frequently preserved in the writings of their age, but

[1] Although Tyler misspelled the names of both Raphael Holinshed (*d.* 1580?) and Sir Henry Ellis (1777–1869), it is possible to decipher this citation. He is referring to Ellis' inclusion of Holinshed's *Chronicles of England, Scotland and Ireland* in a uniform six volume series of chronicles published under Ellis' superintendence in 1807–8. Ellis reprinted Holinshed's 1587 edition with the excisions ordered by the Privy Council replaced.

Tyler's writing is unclear. The date used in the citation may be either 1577 or 1677. The former is the date of Holinshed's first edition.

it is equally true that there is a multitude of minute particulars which are suffered to pass into oblivion which if preserved might serve to develop the character of such age with more precision than those gathered from the writings of the time. When I have perused the scanty details of the customs of former days I have been almost ready to charge the past generation with inexcusable neglect in omitting to tell us more of what is so delightful to know; but it is difficult to imagine that what is familiar and consequently of little interest to us can ever become interesting to others, and every generation, while accusing their predecessors with neglect, are guilty of the same omissions.

The pedestrian of the present day whose shoes are newly accommodated to the right and left foot is heedless that a pair of his shoes, if preserved to a far distant and future day, would be worth more than their weight in gold and be gathered as an invaluable treasure into the museum of the Antiquarian; that if the shoe lasted for the left foot should chance to hop down to posterity what delightful lucubration it might cause. Some Antiquary, after vainly essaying to fit it to the right foot, would gravely declare that the anatomy of their ancestors' pedestals differed from those of their day. Others might conjecture that this shoe was constructed, like those of the Chinese ladies, to cripple the feet or to prevent some [lawyer?] from sauntering away his time in Bond Street or elsewhere.

From this view of the subject I have availed myself of a promise made in the first edition of my adventures,[2] to sketch some of the opinions, manners, habits, customs and amusements of the inhabitants of the town of Boston and its vicinity, designed not so much for the entertainment of the existing generation, who may live too near the scenes described to treat my sketches with due respect, but for the gratification of their descendants who may find in the traits of, to them, a remote age, wonderful delight.

To them, in the words of the motto of my title page, I repeat

[2] The "promise made in the first edition" of *The Algerine Captive* is printed above, pp. 23–24.

I leave you here a little book
For you to look upon
That you may see your father's face
When he is dead and gone.

Thine, Courteous Reader
of every coming generation and sex
in all loving kindness
Updike Underhill.
Shingletrees.—

* * * * *

[A TABLE OF CONTENTS]¹

* * * * *

¹ Although this is not a "Table of Contents" per se, it is the only tabulation of chapters which remains. This list (Fragment 3g) shows some of the new chapters Tyler was planning to include in "The Bay Boy" and how he was counting the manuscript pages to discover how they would bulk once printed. For a discussion of this point see above, pp. 28, 30.

Why Tyler made a mistake in his addition of the last two figures to the subtotal 169 is not known.

CHAPTER I

Quaint fashion too was there,
Whose caprice trims the Indian's wampum
And the crowns of Kings.
                              Author's Manuscript.

MY MOTHER WAS daughter of Mr. Ichabod Anvil, hardware merchant of Boston.[1] In these titled days he would have been styled "Esquire." He certainly had very fair pretensions to this dignified appellation as he had filled the offices of warden, fireward, overseer of the poor and selectman; had been frequently elected moderator in town meetings and repeatedly reposed on the cushioned seats of the Boston bench in the General Court.

He had spared no expense in my mother's education. She was taught every accomplishment then deemed necessary to qualify a young lady to adorn the first circles in society. She cut paper into all sorts and shapes of fly cages, diamond nets to preserve the gilt furniture from this slattern insect, fringes for candlesticks and sconces and pretty devices for watch cases where two enamoured hearts were consumed together on the altar of Hymen or were transfixt by the arrow of Cupid like a pair of chickens, or rather doves, on the same spit. She painted on glass, had worked a famous sampler where all the letters of the alphabet, capitals and small letters, German text and Italian shown resplendent with all sorts of angles and all the colors of the rainbow; besides London smoak, which seems to have been unaccountably overlooked by Sir Isaac Newton in his prismatic analysis[2] and which I here recommend to the investigation of Sir Humphrey Davy;[3] and where the words of King Solomon, "Many daughters have done vir-

---

[1] This chapter, although unnumbered, is complete in itself and was obviously meant by Tyler to come at or near the beginning of the novel. The extant rough draft is in Tyler's hand (Fragment 4).

[2] Optics interested Newton early in his career. He presented an account of his work in this field before the Royal Society in 1672. His paper tells of the composition of white light, i.e., the existence of colors in the spectrum.

[3] Sir Humphrey Davy (1778–1829), English chemist; friend of Coleridge and Southey.

tuously but thou excellest them all," shone conspicuously in German text; the whole concluding with a flaring "Anno Domini," denoting the year of its fabrication by Miss Molly Anvil, aged thirteen, worked in gold and silver thread.

This wonderful performance, so creditable to my mother's early taste for letters, was framed, glazed and hung over the parlor chimney-place and was for several years the pride and delight of my grandfather and grandmother and the admiration of many polite visitors. In the latter days of my mother's celibacy, which, as the reader will soon learn, was rather protracted from some cause or other which I will not attempt to fathom, she very carefully picked out this date which had so mightily delighted her in her early teens. She observed that the fashion of dating samplers, which was always a silly one, was now changed, besides there was an unaccountable mistake in the date, as she persisted in declaring that she was but eight years of age when she quitted school.

With the aid of silk and linen threads, floss silk, cap wire, gum arabic, gamboge and verdigris she made artificial flowers which were said to look as naturally in the winter as in the spring. She made two deep glazed cases of filigree work, filled with paper gilt on the edges and rolled into various shapes—oval, rotund and octagon—at the bottom of which was seen, in virgin's wax, a peep into paradise at that interesting period when the wily serpent was flattering our mother Eve into feasting on the forbidden fruit; where might be seen the lofty Tree of Knowledge with the crooked tempter writhing his lubricious folds around its trunk, and our mother Eve modestly shrouded by her dishevelled tresses extending her fair hand toward the forbidden pippins, while the glazing serpent with his brilliant eyes of glass beads ogles poor Eve and seems to chuckle with the anticipation of his premeditated conquest.[4]

I will venture to observe that this scene seems to have settled a dis-

[4] Early in his career Tyler wrote a most interesting poem, "The Origin of Evil," which gave his version of the fall of Adam and Eve. The poem's erotic imagery unveils a side of Tyler's personality he rarely presented to the public. For the text of the poem see *Tyler Verse*, pp. 11–15.

pute which has long divided the theological world—certain Divines holding that the Mosaical narration is literally correct, while others, with the Jewish historian Josephus, have intimated that the whole account is allegorical: that Eden itself is meant to represent the paradisiacal and innocent state of childhood and that the plucking of the fruit of the Tree of Knowledge of good and evil but a type of our introduction into the scenes of nature life, and its rigid enactments represented by our first parents being cast out to earn their bread by the sweat of their brows. I say my mother's wax work decided this knotty point, for if she hit off a tolerable likeness of the tempter there can be but little doubt that it was the old serpent *in propria persona* who prevailed over the curiosity of our general mother.

My mother was also taught to build sumptuous palaces to occupy the chimney hearth in the summer season, in front of which might be seen the sodded lawn and artfully concealed pewter basons representing duck ponds, in which the cork ducks and geese paddled about and seemed almost to quack and hiss.

My mother was also an adroit sempstress. She could do back stitch, cross stitch, tent stitch, nun's stitch, seed stitch, faggoting, herring bone, tambour stitch, but she knew nothing of botany, chemistry, natural philosophy, astronomy, zoology and the many other abstruse sciences which are apt to bewilder pretty brains in more modern education. As to the Latin tongue, our ancestors thought that one tongue was sufficient for the mistress of a family to scold—no, no—to flatter her domestic into order.

Nor were her literary acquirements deficient. She read her Bible, and had the New England Primer, including the assemblies and shorter catechism, by heart; could repeat "In Adam's fall we sinned all," "Hush, my dear, lie still and slumber," "John Rodgers" and the singular drama at the conclusion.[5] She had likewise read Pamela or Virtue Rewarded, Mrs. Bradstreet's Poems and the fearful end of

---

[5] A child of that day who could not commit large sections of the *New-England Primer* to memory would have been considered seriously delinquent. See above, p. 44.

Francis Spira, and would have read Young's Night Thoughts, only as she said it puzzled her so to make out the rhymes.[6]

But the crown and cap sheaf of all her accomplishments was her performance on the spinet. I wish, reader, you could have seen her as she has been represented to me in all the pride and costume of her maiden glory, seated on her tent stitch joint stool as erect and attractive as a polished shaft from the quiver of Cupid, her hair craped on her lovely head—an operation which required the labor of the barber for only five hours—but no time was lost in the process, as the hair thus fashionably craped would continue five months without the application of the comb. Upon the tip of this toupee a diminutive triangular cap, called a fly cap, cocked like a man's hat, richly edged with point lace, was conspicious; but what the cap lacked in its main structure was made up in its train, as from behind was depended two long pinners which reached half way down her back.

Her hair was turned up behind and secured to the back of her head by a tortoise shell comb resplendent with French paste, excepting one lock, called by the ladies a "favorite" and by the beaux a "love lock," which was suffered to stray over the left shoulder, and wanton down her lovely neck—this with a black patch as big as a pea stuck under her right eye and another at the corner of her mouth gave an air of smartness to the fair one altogether irresistible to the eye of taste.

Her neck was clasped by a brilliant necklace with its dependent solitaire and of the same pattern were her earrings magnified by many a pendant and drop. Her negligee of rich brocade, with deep ruffle cuffs which, as she sat, almost touched the ground, these enclosing ruffles of the finest Brussels lace. Her bust clasped by a stiff pair of stays which terminated in sharp angles at the bottom before and behind and so tightly laced as to excite apprehension that she might break off in the middle, but this was happily prevented by the busk; a silver stayhook set with jewels adorned her lap and served to confine

---

[6] Nathaniel Bacon (1647–1676) was the author of *A Relation of the Fearful Estate of Francis Spira, after he turned apostate from the Protestant Church to Popery.*

Tyler was well acquainted with Edward Young's *The Complaint; or, Night Thoughts.* He quoted from it in the headnote passages preceding "The Origin of Evil."

the strings of her short apron; a pocket hoop and plumpers by their broad expanse served to relieve the slender circuity of the waist. Shoes of white satin ornamented on the instep by a broad fillet of silver lace and heels two inches and a half high were clasped with paste buckles. A pin cushion and scissors suspended by silver hook and chain completed the attractive costume.

When visitors were present—especially of the obnoxious sex—how sweetly would she smile, look arch and throwing back her love knot by way of interlude, after a hundred pressing invitations to play and sing, and a thousand apologies for low spirits and a bad cold, how would she strike the notes, and never did jacks and crowquils breathe such extatic melody while she accompanied the instrument warbling forth the words of that pathetic air—

> Arrah will you marry me, my dear Ally Croaker?
> He talked with her father, and bowed to her mother,
> He romped with her sister and joked with her brother,
> And still the gentle youth bespoke her,
> Arrah will you marry me, my d-e-a-r Ally, Ally, Ally
> Croak—Croak—Croak—Croaker.

There was something so delicate, so dulcet, so sweetly feminine in her voice and words, they seemed to knock so gently at the heart beseeching admission for all the kinder affections that the heart that would refuse them entrance must have been made of gristle cartilage or English bent sole leather.[7] The English may speak in raptures of their Catalani and Billington, I pity them, for they never heard my mother warble Ally Croaker.[8]

[7] At this point in the manuscript there is the marginal notation, "ten pages." This is an example of Tyler counting to see how many printed pages would result from a certain number of manuscript sheets. These notations occur throughout the novel fragments, especially in those in Tyler's hand. The fact that these marginal tabulations rarely occur in the fair copy by Mrs. Tyler reinforces the theory that this was the final recopied draft which was to be sent off to the prospective publisher.

[8] The song "Ally Croaker" was a well-known tune of the day. Mrs. Billington (1770–1818), who starred in popular opera, was much admired by Franz Joseph Haydn and is supposed to have posed for Joshua Reynolds' painting of St. Cecilia. Angelica Catalani (1780–1849), a native of Italy, gained a considerable reputation at La Scala before going to England in 1806.

Facsimiles of the handwriting of eminent personages are now the vogue and it seems to be imagined that the character cannot be completely developed without preserving in their biography an accurate transcript of some scrap of their chirography[9] with all its blots, blurs, interlineations and corrections. I do confess, with all due deference to Lavater, that I cannot subscribe to this fanciful theory,[10] for it appears to me that a great man may write a very mean hand and a very little man make a fine flourish; and it seems as absurd to me, as if in assaying the seamanship of a tar we should inquire in which jaw he chewed his tobacco or whether he tipped his allowance of grog over the right or left thumb. But he who contends with the fashion, whether displayed on bonnets or philosophical axioms, is not very profitably employed. It is better to chime in with the reigning mode and wait patiently till some more rational whim seizes the philosopher or milliner, and so to compleat the exhibition of my mother's maiden accomplishments, I have presented my readers with a facsimile of her handwriting copied from the family cook book, promising, however, by way of glossary, that she uniformly substituted the P for the B, and vice versa—

Resate to macka Boun kake

Tak won Boun of flower
   won dittoe Shugar
   3 quarts dittoe Putter
   9 egges. slice kurrants or reasons or sitturn
   as is jug pest. Pake it in a sloe
   uven

But maugre all my mother's maiden graces she remained single and solitary. She now acknowledged twenty-five while those who recollected the date on the sampler deemed her "thirty and a bit to spare." Indeed she began to shew evident signs of veteran maidenhood, was more and more attentive to her parrot, made daily assignations with the tabby cat and could not abide the noise of children. She

[9] Tyler had originally written "orthography" but crossed it out and substituted "chirography."

[10] Johann Casper Lavater (1741–1801), Swiss writer and founder of physiognomics.

now discovered that the taste of the gentlemen was strangely perverted, that in lieu of being pleased with the company of well educated women they were unaccountably attracted by rosy cheeks and baby faces. She declared she would not accept the hand of any bachelor of her acquaintance. No, that she would not, that's paz!

She now became first peevish and then nervous, her physician recommended change of air, and her father having become acquainted with my grandfather Underhill during the session of the General Court she was invited to spend the summer months at the latter gentleman's seat at Shingletrees, for so I conclude to call the place.

My mother accepted the invitation and took up her abode with my grandfather's family, which consisted at that time of himself and wife, my father, then a hale bachelor of forty, and my Aunt Tabatha. Never did Bath, Balston or Saratoga so renovate the health and spirits of a languishing invalid. My mother was all gaiety and girlishness—everything she saw was novel and exhilarating—she immediately imbibed a passion for rural occupations, following the milk maidens into the barnyard and patted the cows with her fair hand, inhaling their sweet breath as they were milking them. She fed the sheep and the poultry, tripped into the dairy, played with the churn dash, skrewed and unskrewed the cheese-press and declared she believed she was born for a farmer's wife.

These hints were not lost upon my father, not that he imagined she would ever cut the respectable figure she afterwards did as the mistress of a well stocked farm, but because my mother, in a desultory conversation, somehow or other unaccountably dropped a hint that she was possessed of three thousand pounds old tenor, independent of her father, with expectation of an addition on his decease. He therefore humored her in all her rural whimses, strolled with her about the farm, explained the use of all the farming implements from the gingle hook to the log chain and great harrow.

From time immemorial your rural walks have been the haunts where the little loves play hide-and-seek and let fly their tiny shafts at strolling hearts and it so happened here; long before the summer months had expired the business was settled and my father having sought and obtained in form her parents' consent was wedded to my mother, the sack posset drank, the stocking thrown, the wedding cake devoured excepting sundry pieces stuck full of the bridal pins and sent by the bride maids to certain favored young ladies that they might place them under their pillows and dream of those blissful days when their own wedding cake and bridal pins should be in like manner distributed.

On the marriage of my father my grandfather Underhill executed an absolute deed of the farm and took his bond secured by mortgage on the premises to maintain him and my grandmother in sickness and in health for and during their natural lives. The old couple now retired into a suit of apartments projecting from one corner of the house, for our ancestors did not as in modern times erect a great building and have two-thirds of it a receptacle for rats, but they finished what they began, adding building to building by such pavilions as the increase of the family required.[11] Into one of these pavilions the old people retired while the new married pair commenced housekeeping in what was then rather ludicrously called "father's 'tother end."

Perhaps it may be thought that I have portrayed my mother's maiden deportment with a freedom not strictly consistent with filial respect but it should be recollected that her town education was imparted by fashion, and it will be seen that her rural attainments, her conjugal duties and matronly graces were taught by those sage instructors—reason, experience and good sense. Certain it is that her conduct in the marriage state frustrated all the anticipations of her friends and more than gratified her husband's fondest hopes.

When the wedding visits were all received and returned, and the novelty of her new situation and relations in life had worn away, she became pensive, and then, as if suddenly awakening as from a dream of girlish fancy, she hastened to assume the matronly character. The crape of her hair was combed out, the love lock gathered to its sister tresses and the whole head covered with a long lawn mob cap, the

[11] Marginal notation: "ten pages."

ruffles of which were, to be sure, rather fuller and deeper and the ribbon rather smarter than those generally worn by the married dames of Shingletrees, but where affectation has once swelled the female heart it may be discovered to beat in its latest pulsation. Her brocaded negligee was deposited in her trunk and her pocket hoop and plumpers in the garret from whence they were only occasionally brought to set the country damsels agape with admiration or provoke them to array themselves in the fantastic attire and hoyden about the room for the amusement of the rustic circle, while my mother would produce from a small compartment in her tent stitch pocketbook the fly cap and excite fresh peals of laughter at the smallness of the top and the broad expanses of the bottom fashions. Her high heeled shoes were exchanged for flat [...] heels, she no longer sang "Dear Ally Croaker" to sooth the empty noodles of Boston beaux but reserved its plaintive notes to lullaby me into repose while she knit her husband's worsted hose and rocked my cradle.

In fine she became an excellent housewife, was expert in all the mysteries of the dairy and superintended her household with such economy and decorum that she obtained the respect of all her neighbors and her husband's entire confidence. He used to observe that if all my mother's three thousand pounds old tenor was thrown into the sea and as much more after it, he should still consider that he bettered his fortunes by his marriage. Certainly Boston women make the best wives in the world—there the soil of the female heart is rich and fertile, its surface may be choked with the idle weeds of folly and frivolity, and marr'd by the pernicious culture of the fashionable education—but there is at the bottom a stratum of good sense which when brought into activity by experience seldom fails to produce a golden harvest.

Education is the apprenticeship children serve to mature life—the season in which they learn or should learn those ornamental and useful arts which they are expected to practice when they are out of their time and set up for themselves the business and trade of life. In the application of this simple axiom to the process of modern education how much might it abridge or divert the female studies—the main object of which is to fit the interesting tyros to become exemplary matrons. I am sensible that there is, especially in female youth and among the daughters of the oppulent what Blackstone calls an "awkward interval," but why fill this interval with what is seldom practiced in married life?

Are there not many accomplishments taught young ladies which seem rather designed to captivate good husbands than adorn good wives? Why is thrumming the piano forte held so indispensible to polite education and the poor girls drilled into a mechanical use of the instrument without any regard to a musical ear or taste—which can only be surpassed in absurdity by some new freak of fashion which shall drill the whole female youth into poets. How soon is the instrument abandoned while the new married lady is learning housekeeping and the culinary arts from her own domestics. How many, like my good mother, in their egress into married life have to commence their education anew and to substitute the useful for the ornamental. But what then is to be done with that same "awkward interval"? May it not be filled up with something practicable, with something which may prepare the pupil to sustain the character of the meet companion to a sensible man or to bear the infirmities of a weak one—to become, in a word, a good wife and mother which comprehends all that is excellent in the female character. All ears are not adapted to the harmony of sweet sounds but all female hearts are alive to the concord of family affection.

"All heads can reach it and all hearts conceive."

Let the opulent then fill this "awkward interval" by teaching their daughters geography, history and chronology (without which history cannot be profitably understood), English grammer and chirography, the belle letters and *practical,* not the *critical* piety—and perhaps it will do the young ladies no harm if they sometimes stray from the boarding school into the kitchen and obtain some insight into the domestic arts that they may know how to direct others, if their condition in life should continue such as to place them above the necessity of washing, ironing and cooking themselves.[12] The young lady may then fill her

[12] Marginal notation: "twenty six [*pages*]."

station in domestic life respectably tho' she may not be deeply versed in zoology, chemistry, botany, phrenology, mnemonics, and even tho' she might be ignorant of the Latin tongue.

CHAPTER II

I WAS BORN in the vicinity of Boston in the town and parish of Shingletrees, for so I choose to call the place of my birth although the ignorance of certain geographers have given another name to it on the maps.[1] I would conceal the topographical name of my native town, but that I write like all other authors, great and small, for posterity, and I anticipate the time when the towns of New England will like the seven cities of Greece who visited the blind singer Migrela with contempt while living and when dead contended lustily for the honor of giving him birth—and I foresee a day of fame, when time shall have mellowed the tints of my sketches and they are shrouded with the mantle of antiquity, that Hingham, Bellingham, Dedham and Slaughterham will, like Mytilene, Scios and the other shrivelled cities of Greece contend for the glory of making my cradle. It would be merciless in me to deprive the literati of those towns of the gratification of such a contest, and so I am resolved to cast no invidious light on the subject and the reader must be content that I was born in Shingletrees.

Good old Mother Britain seems, like some character I have read about, for I believe the character is not indigenous in the United States, who having been a reigning toast in her day is loth to resign the sceptre of beauty and becomes preposterously jealous of the expanding charms of her own offspring, would confine her marriageable

---

[1] Since Chapter I tells of the marriage of Updike's parents and Chapter III concerns itself with his schooling, Chapter II must have dealt with his birth and early childhood. The following two short fragments, however, are all that remain of Chapter II. The first paragraph (Fragment 5a) exists on a single unnumbered piece of paper with no heading. The other paragraphs come at the beginning of the small pamphlet containing miscellaneous sections of the novel (Fragment 3).

daughter to the nursery or the boarding school lest her stately form in spite of Mamma's cosmetics should betray the crowsfeet of her features, but all will not do, nature will have her course. The youthful belle in her day is destined to attract the admiration of her contemporaries. How much more becoming and respectable in the Old Dame would it be to *pride* herself in the graces, accomplishments and charms of her blooming child, and when Miss was conquering all hearts in the ballroom of life to exclaim, "Observe that young lady in the new robe and transatlantic coiffure—that is my own dear daughter—don't you think her charming, my Lord?"

I was born on the 22nd of February 17—and—. But upon mature consideration I have left the precise year a blank for several cogent reasons which, as like Roscoe and Kotsbue, I mean to have no secrets with that dear and confidential friend, my courteous reader, I will mention.[2] In the first place, there is a very pretty widow whose estate is contiguous to mine, who is for some reason I cannot comprehend extremely desirous of knowing the true day of my birth.

So far from having any desire to conceal it, if I were accounted worthy I should be willing to have my birth inserted in the almanac in capital letters like the sovereigns of Europe, but as I have a great regard for my fair neighbor I am loth to annihilate so copious a source of her enjoyment, for what is curiosity when once gratified? What a delightful thing is a riddle, a rebus, a charade or a conundrum, what guessing and conjecturing and concluding it is this or that, while we are in the dark? But no sooner are we possessed of the solution that the same riddle has lost all its interest and becomes as flat and wearisome as one of Mother Goose's melodies. No! I cannot find it in my heart to destroy the gratification she takes in puzzling and pondering on this momentous subject. It would absolutely deprive her of one of

---

[2] Tyler himself was born on July 18, 1757, at Boston. William Roscoe (1753–1831) is now remembered for his nursery classic in verse, "The Butterfly's Ball and the Grasshopper's Feast" (1806) and his biographies of Lorenzo de' Medici (1796) and Leo X (1805). In connection with *The Algerine Captive* Tyler may also have read Roscoe's poem, "The Wrongs of Africa" (1787) and his pamphlet, "A General View of the African Slave Traffic" (1788). August Friedrich Ferdinand Kotzebue (1761–1819) was a German dramatist, poet and historian.

the most sparkling topics of her conversation, would dissipate those pretty "forsooths," from the prettiest lips in the world, with which she has teazed herself and her acquaintances for these several years past.

"Not that she cares forsooth anything about the Doctor or his age, but one would like to know as a mere matter of curiousity."

But I confess I have a less gallant reason for thus concealing the day of my birth. I here lay a little trap for the critics. As I propose to sketch the manners, customs and opinions of a particular period, some crusty reviewer, more anxious to display his own accuracy than to detect my want of it, may sagaciously observe that such a fashion, habit, custom or opinion was not the mode at the time I have specified but certainly some ten or twenty years before or after. I then triumphantly bid Mr. Reviewer revert to my blank. The fixture of my birth proves to be a moveable feast, which by sliding backwards or forwards in the grooves of a whole century I can certainly comprehend the fashion, within the period pointed out by critical sagacity and Mr. Reviewer is fairly on his back.

CHAPTER III

I N MY CHILDHOOD I was sent as is customary to a woman's school in the summer and a man's school in the winter and made great progress in such learning as my preceptors dealt in.[1] About my twelfth year Mr. Priest, the priest of our parish, a gentleman of great influence in our town, attended an examination of our district school. My master, who esteemed me his best scholar, as I possessed great strength of lungs, a loud voice and read right onward without minding emphasis, stops or paragraphs, set me to read a lesson from Dilworth's spelling book,[2] which I performed in a tone that contrasted

[1] Fragment 3d is all that remains of Chapter III. It recounts some of Updike's schooling and leads directly into Chapter IV.

[2] Thomas Dilworth (d. 1780), author of *A New Guide to the English Tongue: in Five Parts*. It was a widely used school text of the mid-eighteenth century.

so advantageously with the whining monotony of my fellow students that I attracted the attention of the priest, who soon after visited my father to *dicker,* as it was called, about some cattle, and not finding my father sharp for a bargain changed the subject, observing how much he was pleased with my performance at school and what a pity it was that such a genius should not be encouraged.

"Mr. Underhill, you must put Updike to learning."

My father did not readily accede to this proposal. "I rather think," said he, "that a good substantial forehanded farmer is the best calling to insure a man independence and comfort through life, and besides, I look forward to the time when Updike shall be qualified to take charge of the farm and relieve me from all care so insupportable in the decline of life."

Just then my mother, who the reader is informed, had a great taste for letters, lifting her eyes from her knitting, joined the priest in observing, "With my good will, sir, Updike shall have learning, if I work my fingers to the bone to procure it for him. I make no doubt when he comes to preach he will be as much run after as ever the great Mr. Whitefield was.[3] I always thought the boy was a genius and always intended he should go to college. He certainly has two most striking marks of a great genius about him: he hates work and loves books. He has often read Valentine and Orson, Parismas and Parismanus, and Robinson Cruso, and I went the other day to borrow Pilgrim's Progress for him and he has read it through already, aye, and understands it too.[4] Why he ran a squewer thro' Apollyon's eye to help Christian beat him."[5]

[3] Rev. George Whitefield (1714–1770) is commonly regarded as the most persuasive personality of the Great Awakening. Although the religious upheaval had already started, it was Whitefield's preaching and the resultant theatrical conversions which stimulated and gave force to the burst of evangelical activity. The Great Awakening was covered by his second and third visits to America, 1739–41 and 1744–48.

[4] *The History of the Renowned Princes Valentine and Orson* was a popular children's chap book of the period. The tale was originally a French medieval prose romance written between 1475 and 1489.

Emanuel Ford (*fl.* 1607) was the author of *The Most Famous, Delectable and Pleasant History of Parismus, the Renowned Prince of Bohemia.* The second part contained "the adventurous travels and noble chivalrie of Parismenos, the Knight of Fame."

[5] The discourse between Christian and Apollyon in the Valley of Humiliation is

My father was so far convinced by my mother's cogent arguments that it was finally settled that I should go to learning under the care of the Reverend Mr. Priest (although he still protested against my going to college). As a sketch of the biography of this gentleman may display the character, mode of living and many of the common incidents in the life of country clergymen of those days, I must be indulged in detailing it in the next chapter.

found in *Pilgrim's Progress*, Part I.

CHAPTER IV

He was a man of passing merit,
Imbued with the true Christian spirit;
With meekness, candor, charity,
The fruits of genuine piety.

His Sunday's precepts you might seek
In his example thro' the week;
His daily conduct seemed to teach,
"This is the sum of what I preach."

His faith and works you might discover,
Reflected light on one another;
And shewed his flock a saint-like picture
Worth folios huge of notes on Scripture.

THE REVEREND Ammi Rhuhamah Priest was lineally descended from Diggery Priest,[1] one of the first settlers of Plymouth Colony of whom honorable mention is made by Doctor

---

[1] The first part of this chapter exists as a separate gathering in Tyler's hand (Fragment 6). In fragment 3 there is a short section entitled "Part of Chapter IV." It appears the author intended to work it in somewhere about page 5 of the rough draft where there is already one insertion (Fragment 5b). The end of the chapter is duplicated at the beginning of what remains of the novel's final draft as copied by Mrs. Tyler (Fragment 7).

Prince in his Chronology[2] and by Secretary Morton in his Memorial:[3] in that the said Diggery on the third day of December O.S., A.D. 1621-2 went up a hill and *thought he saw an Indian*.

Young Priest passed that routine of education which was considered requisite to accomplish a youth for the sacred ministry, that is, in early youth he attended the district school where he learned spelling from Dilworth, arithmetic from Hodder[4] and the Accidence from Cheever,[5] and writing from some one who had a proper respect for the second command of the Decalogue. As he advanced in years he was placed under the care of a neighboring clergyman who eked out a slender stipend by fitting boys for college.

At the age of eighteen, after passing a thorough examination in the Latin and Greek classics, he was admitted a student at Cambridge College, poor in purse but rich in learning. And by serving as butler's Irishman, ringing the bell for prayers, meals and recitations, by attend-

The records of the Plymouth Colony, including those of Prince and Morton cited below, mention that Digory (or Digery) Priest was one of the original Leyden contingent which came to the new settlement at Plymouth. Priest was a signer of the first compact of Government on Nov. 11, 1620. He died in bed of the "general sickness" on Jan. 1, 1621, and seems to have escaped the fatal encounter with the Indians ascribed to him by Tyler.

Digory was married to a widow, Sarah Allerton Vincent, and they had two daughters, Mary and Sarah. There is, however, no record of a son and the Rev. Ammi Rhuhamah Priest seems to be a fictional character created by Tyler.

[2] Thomas Prince (1687-1758), theologian, bibliophile and scholar. He was a friend of the Mathers and a noted preacher and author of theological tracts. He is best remembered for his *A Chronological History of New England in the Form of Annals,* published in 1736. The first citation of Section I is as follows: "1621. January 1, Monday. The People at Plymouth go betimes to work; and the year begins with the death of Degory [*sic*] Priest."

[3] Nathaniel Morton (1613-1685), Pilgrim father and author. Came to Plymouth on the *Anne* in 1623. He was secretary to the Colony from 1647 to 1685. His *New Englands Memoriall* was issued in 1669 at Cambridge. Digory Priest is mentioned therein on p. 16.

[4] James Hodder (*fl.* 1661), author of *Hodder's Arithmetick*. This popular manual, first published in 1661, went through 27 editions in the following decades. Its publication in Boston by J. Franklin in 1719 made it the first arithmetic printed in America.

[5] Ezekiel Cheever (1615-1708) was a noted educator and classicist. After teaching in New Haven, Ipswich and Charlestown he became master of Boston Latin School in 1670. His textbook, *Accidence, a Short Introduction to the Latin Tongue* was called the "wonder of the age."

ing as waiter at Commons and by the further aid of some exhibitions with which the college had been endowed by the liberality of its patrons, he passed through college with reputation, and on Commencement Day flourished his syllogisms in Bocardo and Baralipton[6] with all the assurance and pertinacity of a senior Wrangler in the University of Oxford.

During the first years of his baccalaureate he was a resident graduate at the college and was called "Sir Priest." The two remaining years he studied Divinity with a venerable father of the church and was licensed to preach. He then filled the office of tutor, instructing the students on weekdays and the people on the Sabbath. At length, after preaching some time as a candidate, he received and accepted a call from the church and congregation in Shingletrees in the vicinity of Boston upon a salary of £60 L.M. per annum, to be augmented five pounds annually as his family increased until it should amount to the handsome sum of one hundred pounds. To this was added a settlement of £80 with which, and some money he had saved while candidating, he purchased a small farm in the parish with a comfortable house and out buildings, and marrying the daughter of a reputable clergyman, well educated in all the arts necessary to the accomplished madam of a country parish, he commenced his career as pastor of the town and parish of Shingletrees.

The sermons of our pastor were moral and practical and wonderfully adapted to the circumstances and comprehension of the great majority of his hearers. It was his private opinion that the Christian religion disseminated in its early stages by illiterate men to many equally as illiterate, must in its essence contain much for daily practice, much to better the condition of man here as well as to prepare him for happiness hereafter. He accordingly recommended charity, self denial, a due observance of and affectionate conduct toward each other in all the relative duties of social life.

---

[6] A reference to Issac Watts' *Logick*, Part II, Sec. 3, "Of the Moods and Figures of Simple Syllogisms." Bocardo and Baralipton were two of the Latin terms used to illustrate these moods.

His favorite text was "By this shall men know that ye are all my disciples because ye love one another." Wise sermons were delivered in pure English, for altho' the divisions and subdivisions of the discourse, according to the fashion of the times somewhat marr'd its elegance, yet what it lost in arrangement was amply compensated by its terseness.

It is worthy of remark, when we observe the English literati fixing the standard of pure English in the reigns of Elizabeth and James the First, speaking with rapture of those pure wells of undefiled English which flowed so copiously in those reigns, that those are the very periods when our ancestors, having imbibed copious draughts from those rich fountains, first emigrated to New England and this rationally accounts for the uncorrupted English so universally spoken by our clergy. The English reader may smile perhaps contemptuously at the intimation that his native tongue is spoken with greater purity in New than in Old England. But my dear friend, if you with your hundred dialects flatter your countrymen with the belief that they alone are masters of the English language, will you not permit us with one dialect, and that dipped in the pure wells of Elizabeth and James, to flatter the self complacency of our citizens with a similar belief.

It was thus our worthy pastor continued to preach for some years, but at length the elders of the parish began to yearn for some of the profounder doctrines of their creed and to whisper somewhat about "milk for babes" and "the *pap* of the word." This coming to the knowledge of the parson he resolved to gratify them with some strong meat, and announced his intention to preach a series of sermons at lectures to be held every Friday evening.

The sermons were accordingly delivered and the learned pastor ingeniously contrived, by numerous citations from all languages living and defunct, by splitting of hairs in long desultory illustrations and by wrapping the whole in a fine web of metaphysical science, to confound all criticism and comprehension. The writings of the Scotists and the Thomists, the wrangling disciples of the subtle Dunscotus and the angelic Thomas Aquinus were plain as a pike staff in comparison.

These sermons completely silenced all gainsayers and the pastor was henceforth held to be a man profoundly learned in school divinity who in his usual ministrations kindly condescended to adapt his discourses to the capacities of the unlearned.

At the period of which I am speaking there was little or no controversy among our clergy. It was a time of quiet repose of the religious and the dawn of that political controversy which terminated in our glorious revolution. The clergy were all of one creed, as to doctrine and discipline all possessing the same faith and all presumed equally orthodox. Indeed, now and then a treatise on antipedobaptism would seem to provoke opposition but as the Baptists of that day agreed in fundamentals with the Congregationalists these ebulitions of sectarianism were suffered to be read unanswered for the edification of those of that communion.

However, during the third year of our pastor's ministry a certain bold innovator preached and published a sermon of the obnoxious doctrine of good works. He held that genuine Christian faith and good works were inseparable, that he who possessed genuine faith would necessarily do the works of righteousness and insinuated—for even this bold man dared not assert openly—that he who was in the habitual exercise of charity, loving kindness, temperance, humility and chastity with all other Christian graces might be a better Christian than he imagined himself to be.

How was this horrible heresy to be met?

The leading clergymen read the discourse and considerately concluding that an ounce of prevention is worth a pound of remedy and that it was far better to prevent the people from reading a heretical book than to trust to their judgement after they have perused a reply, they resolved if possible to adopt such measures as should prevent it being read.[7]

[7] This marks the end of Fragment 6. However, the last phrase of this sentence and the first part of the following one are found at the beginning of Fragment 5b, indicating Tyler's desire to place that section at this point in the manuscript. Fragment 3e entitled "part of Chapter 4th of the Bay Boy" was also meant to be added here. Fragments 5b and 3e, therefore, have been combined to provide the complete insertion as the author probably intended it.

Previous to proceeding to harsher means it was deemed advisable to attempt procuring from its author something that might at least *savor* of a recantation and by the clergy be construed into an abandonment of his heresies. To effect this a Boston clergyman, noted for the suavity of his manners, and a particular friend of the Rev. Mr. B. (author of the heretical sermon) was deputized to wait upon him, which he soon did, and after the common civilities of society were reciprocated the following dialogue ensued.

Friend. "I have perused your sermon with the attention due to its ingenuity. I am not prepared to controvert its doctrines but you will suffer me to express a doubt of the expediency of publishing it at the present time. There are many of our brethren who think with you who deem it not best to preach or publish their private opinions. I do not mean by this to impute to them any prevarication unbecoming their character. They do not preach against your principles but only pass them over in silence, as controversial subjects unessential in the Gospel system. You well know that the Episcopal clergy are generally *Arminian* while the Congregational divines are Calvinistic. We cannot be too careful to maintain this line of distinction between us."

Rev. Mr. B. "If they are correct why should we oppose them?"

Friend. "For this simple reason that there must be a line of demarkation and he who abandons his outworks, however defenseless, will soon find his theological citadel taken. It is with this view that some of your particular friends wish you to explain your sentiments in a second sermon."

Mr. B. "When I wrote this sermon I endeavored to express my sentiments in such plain language as could not be and I believe is not misunderstood. Any illustration, therefore, would only serve to obscure what is now sufficiently clear."

Friend. "I am grieved to find you in this temper and can only repeat, the great body of the clergy are greatly aggrieved by your sermon."

Mr. B. "I can truly sympathise with them for I have been many years greatly aggrieved by what they esteem their more orthodox discourses."

Friend. "I see I shall not prevail with you. Indeed, I scarcely expected it but I had hoped that the opinion of your brethren as to the expedience of publishing this offensive sermon would have so far prevailed with you that you might be induced from respect to them and some consideration of the peculiar exegencies of the times, when the Episcopal clergy are so sedulously attempting to proselyte and every proselyte to the Church is a convert to Toryism, I say, I had hoped that you might publish something, which if you did not con-consider retraction, might by others be considered as such."

Mr. B. "Indeed, my worthy friend, I do not wish to be misunderstood or misconstrued."

Friend. "Suffer me to make one more proposition which cannot in any way impeach your steady adherence to your principles but which may serve as an argument to your friends against the charge of your Arminism."[8]

Mr. B. "What is that?"

Friend. "Your wife, my good cousin, has recently presented you with another son. Suppose you should name him Calvin?"

Mr. B. "I certainly should have no objection to any name you should propose but there is one obstacle to this *given* name. You must

[8] Tyler was well acquainted with many of the liberal Congregationalists who had put aside the Calvinist doctrine of predestination and believed, as did the Dutch theologian Arminius, that man's actions on earth could have a bearing on his salvation.

For example, John Adams was known for his Arminian views and Tyler may have imbibed them while he was reading law in Adams' office. Of equal significance is Tyler's acquaintance with Ethan Allen, the noted Vermont political and military leader. In his controversial philosophical work, *Reason the Only Oracle of Man* (1784), Allen argued strongly that man had free will and was not subject to a predestination ordained by God.

In 1787 Tyler became friendly with Allen during the former's pursuit of the Shays Rebellion fugitives in southwestern Vermont. Proof that they discussed religion as well as politics is borne out by a letter from Allen to Tyler, dated Aug. 28, 1787, from Bennington, Vt. For further details on this episode and the full text of the letter see Marius B. Péladeau, "Royall Tyler and Ethan Allen's Appendix to *Reason the Only Oracle of Man*," *Vermont History*, XXXVI, No. 3 (Summer, 1968), 155–58.

For a recent discussion of the relationship between Puritanism and the Arminian controversy, see Gerald J. Goodwin, "The Myth of 'Arminian-Calvinism' in Eighteenth-Century New England," *New England Quarterly*, XLI, No. 2 (June, 1968), 213–17.

excuse me but I cannot call it a *Christian* name. My eldest boy has got a little snarling cur dog named Calvin. Now if we have two Calvins in the house the boy and the brute will be at a loss as to which we want when we call 'Calvin, Calvin.' If, however, you wish to have the babe bear the name of some eminent Christian, I am willing to call him Servetus[9] which name always reminds one of the charitable Calvin."

His friend, finding Mr. B. thus incorrigible soon retired, lamenting that theological controversy, even when advocating liberal principles, is still embued with the same inflexible spirit of pertinacious adhesion to its own opinions and of uncharitableness toward the opinions of others.

He soon after made report of his unsuccessful mission. The orthodox clergymen considering that no further delicacy ought to be used toward the heretic adopted a more efficacious mode of combat. They resolved to annex to the sermon an epithet equally ridiculous and disgusting. The sermonizer having strenuously insisted upon the necessity of the practice of all the moral virtues, which his opponents held to be the sure badge of self righteousness, in allusion to Isaiah 64:6 they styled his sermon "the filthy rag discourse."

Now what man or woman of common decency would read such a dirty work? Few, as was anticipated, perused it and poor Arminius with his filthy rags shrulked into neglect amidst the hisses and derision of the populace in the same manner and probably with similar sensations as some awkward booby, who has thrust his needlesome phiz into the precincts of the cookmaid, retires from thence with a dishclout pinned to his posterior shirts.[10]

If at any time they resolved to answer a heretical book they always employed some more uninformed brother to reply to it, who unrestrained by a thorough knowledge of the subject might proceed floundering on with his argument with a clear conscience affirming

[9] Michael Servetus (1511?–1553), Spanish theologian and physician who in 1553 discovered the course of the blood through the lungs. His bold speculation on matters of faith made him unpopular with both Catholics and Protestants. Servetus was tried at Geneva and burned alive in October, 1553. There was severe criticism of the active role John Calvin played in his trial.

[10] Conclusion of the insertion composed of Fragments 5b and 3e.

or denying positively whatever appeared to militate against the tenets he defended.

In more modern times a different course has been persued. Some learned doctor or some man eminent for his talents and learning has been selected to reply to the heresies of the day. But he having an established reputation for learning to preserve is ashamed to defend positions which, he is sensible, and the learned world will know have been abandoned as untenable by the venerable English divines of his sect;[11] and the reader of such reply is shocked to find that positions which he had hitherto deemed the strongholds of his doctrine abandoned by his own champion and thence is led to doubt the soundness of the remaining ground he maintains, and thus more scepticism is inculcated by such learned reply than by the heretical treatise which occasioned it. But to return from this digression to our more immediate subject.

I would be doing manifest injustice to the affectionate munificence of his parishioners and give a very deceptive estimate of the pastor's means of supporting his family, were I to suffer my readers to imbibe the impression that his resources accrued entirely from his salary. The greater work of his farm was all done gratuitously by his parishioners. At early dawn in the hay season the grating sound of the riffle and the ripple of the mowers' sythes might be heard in his meadows; about noon when the meridian sun had evaporated the dew the neighboring boys with their biforked sticks were seen turning the new mown grass and with the sportiveness of childhood tossing the half-made hay over their heads in many a wanton giration. Nor were the early and latter harvests forgotten. The English grain was reaped and shocked, the plumy stalks of the Indian corn were cut and stacked thro' out the field, each crowned with a cap to defend them from rain and in due season the staple grain of New England was husked and placed in the garner.

When the snow path was well troden [there] might be seen a long train of teams dragging a handsome load of wood for the family fuel,

---

[11] Marginal notation: "ten pages."

preceded often by ten or fifteen yoke of sturdy oxen with flag handkerchiefs waving from poles rising from their yokes and all attached
to an enormous load of wood piled on skids constructed for the
occasion, which was bourne with triumph and shout into the parson's
wood yard, where it was suffered to remain for some days until its
bulk dimensions had elicited the admiration of all who beheld it. The
succeeding weeks a party of athletic young men with bandanna
handkerchiefs encircling their brows, and with their keen, polished
axes in hand with many a sturdy blow cut and split the wood for
domestic use depositing as much under cover as the pastor's woodsheds
would contain, and arranging the residue in long chorded piles in the
open air—the very sight of which seemed to communicate a comfortable warmth to the half chilled observer.

But at the gathering in the harvest and the annual slaughter of the
cattle, sheep and swine designed for the winter consumption the cor-
nucopia of good things was especially overflowing. Niggardly must
that man have been who did not contribute some choice bit of the ox,
sheep, swine, or some selected fowl from the poultry yard. The shelves
of the pastor's pantry literally creaked and groaned under the weight
of the elymosynary provision—sirloins and [. . .] bones, brisket and
rattlerands, rump pieces and rounds, stake cuts and shine bones seemed
collected from the cattle of a thousand hills; while spare ribs and chine
bones, hands and hams, feet and ears for source, trout and petty tose
[sic], lard and sausages evidenced the annual slaughter of the well
fatted swine.

Nor were the carcasses of the petted sheep displaying a tempting
red and white to the epicure forgotten, nor the saddle of venison or the
delicate hind quarter of the cub bear. Turkeys, geese, barndoor fowls,
with now and then a brace of partridges shown conspicious. While
the broad earthen milk pan was redulant [sic] with honey and honeycomb and the yellow lumps of butter and fine new milk cheese
crowned the whole. While madam, the priest's lady in her grograin
gown and fluted apron, creased by the flat iron into regular compartments, stood ready to receive and acknowledge every gift, now point-

ing out with her knitting pin the excellency and delicacy of every present and now declaring that none but Deacon Singletary's folks could produce such beef or make such butter and cheese as Doctor Dose's wife.

But madam herself received her more appropriate presents. In due season on some appointed day might be seen groups of young maidens accompanied by their younger brothers bearing on their shoulders spinning wheels great and small, the distaffs of the latter well replenished with well hatchetted flax, and with hand reels and clock reels and all other appertenances of the spinning bee. Soon in every apartment of the house was heard the buzz of the small and the mimic thunder of the great woolen wheel, every damsel animated with the design of compleating her skein or run in time to present it to madam before supper.

Toward sunset appeared the matrons of the parish, everyone bearing a basket of crockery including various delicacies for the table, not omitting the nut cakes, cymbals which bear a homelier name, the apple and plum tart, custards, whitpot and the indispensable pumpkin pie. Suddenly the ample table was spread, covered with a profusion of rural dainties, but ere the repast began the fair spinners presented madam with the produce of their labors and while receiving from her the tribute of well earned praise the delighted mothers stood by eyeing with complacency the manufacture of their daughters which gave such certain presage that they in their day would be fitted to fulfill the duties of good wives. The repast was then eaten with abundance of kind criticism on the production of the bee, while each of the young women as they retired from the table crossed her hands upon her apron string and making a low curtsey gravely thanked madam for the goodly treat, and the knot of provident matrons in a snug corner in committee were discussing ways and means to have the yarn bucked, woven, bleached, and prepared for family use.

But there remained for the good madam other occasions of benefiting by the liberality of the parishioners, when she prepared biennially to add another olive branch to the family table: then all the needles in the parish, sharps, blunts and betweens and white chapple were in motion and madam's bureau drawers were filled with such abundance of caps and cap roses, bibs, tuckers, mufflers, frocks, petticoats and pinners, diapers, frills, cradle blankets and swaddling bands as might have well furnished a lying-in hospital. And on the more interesting occasion there was such junketing and gossiping, but I forbear as this scene, like the mysteries of the Bona Dea should not be exposed to vulgar eyes.

When the traveling guest visited the family which was not unfrequent as the clergy of that day seldom sojourned at the taverns, fearing lest the polluted atmosphere of the bar room might pollute the purity of the clerical robe, and accordingly on their journeys passed from one parsonage to another, ever courteously received and hospitably entertained especially when they rested over the Sabbath and occupied the pulpit where often on due intimation they suggested many beneficial things to the congregation which the stated pastor deemed it not prudent to say himself; and when such traveling brother was accompanied by his wife such was generally the case as the clergy of that day were not only exemplary men but the best of husbands, deeming all enjoyment worthless which was not shared by their wives.[12]

When the arrival of such guests was known in the vicinity then might be seen in the dusk of the evening some solicitious neighbor, slipping slyly into the back door bearing under her apron some nice addition to the tea or breakfast table, while at the same hour her anxious spouse was inspecting the stables to discover if aught was lacking to the confortable accommodation of the traveller's horse. On such occasions all those neighborly aids to good cheer were made and done without the parson's privity or observance. He used to relate a jocular incident to his college friends which had severely taught him not to burn his fingers by meddling with women's matters.

On a certain time when an unexpected guest had arrived, one of the

[12] Despite rewriting this sentence Tyler still did not end up with it grammatically complete.

neighboring women had joined the party, the parson noticing on the table a pye whose crust might vie with a babalonian brick for hardness could not refrain from observing to madam, "My dear, I am persuaded our visitors are sensible they have caught us unprepared and will make all due allowances but really this pye is too bad to offer them."

It was in vain that madam winked, nodded and attempted to turn the conversation from the unlucky pye; the parson persisted in his apology, nor did he discover till within the close covert of the curtains that the contributor of the pye sat next to him at the table.

In those good times the hospitality of the parsonage was identified with the character of the parish, and it would have been deemed a sin and a shame to suffer any traveller to be inhospitably entertained or shabbily accommodated.

At times too our pastor was in his turn the subject of the like hospitality.[13] He commanded a showy equipage in which he and madam paid annual visits to their parents or the neighboring clergy. This equipage merits a more minute description for the edification of the unborn antiquary. It consisted of a chaise or gig, suspended between stiff wooden shafts, which disdained all elasticity; the body somewhat resembling a coffin set on end without a lid—shallow in front and defended from storms by curtains of green hariteen, the flooring sunk so low that as you stepped over the shaft your feet descended into a box, admirably calculated to prevent madam's foot stove from falling out and for the occasional reception of a bag of grain when this admirable machine, quitting the loftier business of parade and show, conveyed the good pastor to mill or transported his benevolent lady on her parochial visits.

This body hung on huge thorough braces of leather, attached in front to an unyielding crossbar and suspended behind to a similar bar and secured by enormous brass buckles, and so ingeniously contrived as to pass the same thorough braces below the axle-tree. The harness

[13] These closing paragraphs of Chapter IV and all of Chapter V are duplicated in the rough draft Fragment 6 and the final version Fragment 7, with minor textual variations, starting with Ms. p. 58.

was resplendent with brass ornaments; while before the body of the carriage two iron stanchals stood erect and from the apex of each a seat of interlaced leather straps, supported the body of Cuff, the Priests' black boy who drove his master and mistress on the great occasions of weddings and funerals. On those solemn seasons when the priest by letters missive was invited to attend an ordination of council, the family carriage was seldom occupied, as the good Divine, as perpetual moderator in church meetings, had the nominations of lay delegates and generally named some opulent member of his church who prided himself in providing his own carriage for the use of his revered pastor and bearing his expenses on the road.

Thus aided and assisted he was enabled to educate three boys at college and portion off two marriageable daughters, giving to each two beds, one suit of cotton curtains on which the blue grape vines, bearing scarlet sunflowers and green holyocks wantoned luxuriently over the vallance and testor and crowned the arbor of domestic repose, crockery, glass and culinary ware, a table, chest of drawers, great and small spinning wheels, a clock reel, a cow with calf by her side and a quarto Bible containing family records.

Thus happily were the days of the years of his pilgrimage wearing away (for Massachusetts was then as it is now the paradise of the New England clergy) altho' it is true that the revolving seasons presented occasional impediments to family happiness. The parson's wig was considered too smart in the side curls when he returned from Boston after election or madam's new bonnet was garnished with too many ribbands, Dick's chanel pumps were too peaked at the toes or the red top knots of Charity and Mercy were adjudged to be too flaunting. But with habitual discretion these deviations from the parochial taste were speedily corrected and thus might the even and pleasant course of his happiness have continued until he was gathered to his Fathers. But also, "Man is born to trouble as the sparks fly upward." An event now happened which no human foresight could prevent or discretion avoid, which drove our happy pair from paradise and cast them upon the wide world to earn their bread by the swet of their brow.

CHAPTER V

Oh what avails grave wisdom's voice
Or circumspection's cautious tread
To man; his wisest, wariest choice
Oft brings destruction on his head.

Shrouded with clouds, and darksome night,
The path of life, no gas-light shows
And he who boasts the keenest sight
Can't see an inch beyond his nose.

The Pleasures of Pain
By the Author.

THE EASTERN part of the town of Shingletrees was intersected from north to south by a deep swampy morass, about one mile in length and about three quarters of a mile in breadth, impassable except in the winter season.[1] In the early settlement of the town this swamp presented no very serious obstacle to the intercourse of the few scattered inhabitants who occupied either end but when in process of time the population multiplied a good path of communication became greatly desirable. Two passages were contended for, the one leading in a direct line through the swamp, the other taking a sinuous direction round its northern border. The latter would be less expensive as there had long been a bridle road there, passing in its rout near several farms, among the rest the parson's, but the direct road through the swamp, although it could not be made without great present expenditure, appeared best calculated to accommodate the public and would probably be permanently advantageous to posterity. But Deacon Singletary in his celebrated speech delivered at the town meeting convened on the occasion very pertinently observed that—

"There was much clatter about *posterity*—we must do this and do that and submit to be harassed with taxes, all for the sake of *posterity*.

---

[1] In Fragment 6 this chapter follows without a break after Chapter IV. The headnote verse is found alone in Fragment 3f. The entire chapter, in final form, is in Fragment 7 commencing with Ms. p. 60.

Forsooth, why all this fuss about *posterity?* For my part I should like to know what *posterity* has ever done for us?"

Nevertheless the selectmen of the town were authorized by a vote of the meeting to survey and stake out the proposed road in and through the place, which in their discretion they should judge the most suitable. And after due deliberation they concluded that it was advisable to avoid the expense of making the direct road—to open and repair the bridle path and in concurrence with Deacon Singletary leave *posterity* to shift for itself. Accordingly the road was laid on the northern margin of the swamp.

But this act of the selectmen gave no satisfaction to the advocates of the direct road who appealed from their doings to the Quarter Sessions, and the next March meeting these selectmen retained their seats at the board by a majority of only one vote, which evidenced how equally the inhabitants were divided on this interesting subject. Indeed, never was a small community so agitated or so obstinately attached to the opinions they had formed. Families were divided, females ceased to visit, the quilting match and spinning bee were suspended, for who could bear to associate with those who talked and acted so foolishly!

Men who had known each other from infancy, who had shared together the hardships of settling a new country, and whose intrinsic worth, integrity and sound judgement had been proved by long experience in the true spirit of party were led to view each other as fools and knaves. Never did the "Guelps and Gibbelines" of Germany, the "Hats and Caps" of Sweden, or the "Hits and Devotees" of Italy excite such party zeal.

During the rage of this controversy, their good pastor with admirable discretion avoided all interference in the dispute and kept his own opinion private. But when all of his parish were engaged one side or the other and each inquired into his sentiments, he repeatedly assured them he had formed no decisive opinion on the subject, if the parish would suit themselves they would suit him. It was in vain the clamorous and violent endeavored to elicit his opinion but it was more difficult to withstand the moderate and the candid.[2] They observed, with some plausibility, that as the pastor had with admirable prudence kept aloof from the dispute he was well situated to become an arbitrator between the contending parties, that such was his influence in the parish that an early demonstration of his opinion would most probably have prevented this fatal division—that it had now certainly become his duty as he valued the peace of the parish to interfere and to express his individual sentiments, which let them favor either side would be received with candor, and it was believed, as the people were so equally divided and both sides weary of contention, restore harmony to the whole.

Thus addressed and thus advised by those he esteemed his friends and fervent supporters on both sides of the question, in an evil hour, with manifest reluctance he consented, not to disclose his opinion, that was far from his intention, but to deliver a sermon upon the subject of the existing difficulties. The lecture to be held on the ensuing Friday evening was announced from the pulpit the next Lord's day.

I have omitted to notice that the *parties of the paths* had during the irritation of the contest imposed names on each other. The advocates for the bridle road, in allusion to its deviations from a straight line, occasioned by the protrusion of several sloughs from the main swamp, were jeeringly called the *Wanderers* while they gave to the advocates for the direct road the appelation of *Midites*. I ought further to notice that the appeal to the Quarter Sessions from the decision of the selectmen had been hung up from term to term, probably with the expectation on the part of the justices that this protracted contest might be amicably settled and certainly without any injury to the pockets of the eminent council engaged on either side. And that in the interim the partisans of the direct road, apprehensive that the case might finally issue in the affirmation of the judgement of the selectmen had, by a voluntary subscription of money and labor, by draining and ditching, by pole bridges and stone causeways, contrived to force a broad road

---

[2] Marginal notation: "twenty nine pages."

directly through the swamp. When this was completed it was of
course traveled by the *Midites* and even the *Wanderers,* finding the
road made without any *inroad* into their pockets or purses, soon
traveled there also—and the bridle road was nearly abandoned except
by a few who prided themselves on consistency of conduct and rather
preferred traveling half a mile to taking a direct path which might
seem to imply an abandonment of preconceived opinions.

Matters were thus circumstanced when our good pastor by his
occasional sermon attempted to reconcile all difficulties and restore
harmony to his distracted parish. He selected his text from Proverbs,
Chapter 3d, 17th verse: "Her ways are ways of pleasantness and all
her *paths* are peace."

The sermon according to the fashion of the English Divines in the
reigns of the first James and Charles was divided and subdivided into
general heads and doctrines with corollary reflections, general and
particular, a general improvement, and special application and a brief
exhortation.[3] It began with a view of human life, which however
protracted is still brief and its tenure uncertain, that this world is a place
of trial, the passage through it rough and thorny, that the travellers
thereon are prone to fall out by the way and this perhaps not so much
owing to faults in individuals as to the universal depravity of our
common nature and a necessary concomitant to that state of sin and
misery into which our first parents by their disobedience fell. That it
was a matter of consolation, that even in this vale of tears there was
one *path* provided, namely, that mentioned in the text, on which all
may travel, not merely with comfort, but with pleasantness and
peace! How unwise then are those who forsake this pleasant way
which leads to life and spend the brief space allotted to them here in
contending about the crooked paths and byways passed by us in the
ordinary occupations of this wretched world, which leads but to the
grave, and concluding by exhorting his hearers, as well as pressing it
home upon his own conscience, if he, or they erred from this way of
wisdom to return to the same and travel on it with alacrity, remember-

[3] The sermon which Tyler delivered on Christmas Day, 1793, follows closely this
formal outline. See below, pp. 177–90.

ing that our stay here is short but the state to which the *path* we may select leads is never ending.

It was generally believed, at least it was confidently asserted, that our good pastor had so well timed his discourse that the object might have been attained if it had not been for the unfortunate selection of the hymn which he gave out at the conclusion of the lecture. I dare say the good man deemed it, as probably any reader may, quite appropriate to the subject matter of the discourse, but be that as it may, the words were:

> "Broad is the way that leads to death
> And many thousands travel there;
> But wisdom seeks a narrow path
> With here and there a *wanderer*, etc."

This verse had so manifest and pointed an allusion to the contested paths and disclosed such an obvious preference to the bridle path that the *Midites* were all in an uproar, nor were the *Wanderers* better pleased to hear it acknowledged from the pulpit that the swamp road was so generally occupied.

The pastor's character was assailed on all sides. His temporizing prudence was called gross procrastination. The next hay season the joyous ripple of the parishioners' sythe was not heard in the meadow and on the ensuing winter the annual supply of fuel was deteriorated to a few scattered loads of wood. The goodly sirloins and spare ribs were as sparse in the parson's pantry as the *wanderers* in the bridle road and the industrious hum of the spinning bee had ceased.

After a season of uncharitable altercation a council was summoned according to the platform to endeavor by their advice and mediation to heal the differences and restore peace. But there was no peace. And soon after it being generally admitted that however blameless the parson's conduct, yet his usefulness as a minister in that parish was entirely destroyed. A council of dismissal was by mutual consent called, who in their result, without censuring the church, gave the pastor an excellent character and warm recommendation to the sister churches. And thus the Reverend Ammi Rhuhamah Priest returned into private life, leaving a salutary lesson to the Congregational clergy of Massachusetts,[4] to wit, that the less they have to do with *mundane paths* the better for them and the people committed to their charge.

After the dismission of Mr. Priest some few of his more attached parishioners offered to build a new meeting house and to renew their engagement with him, but he declined doing anything that might cause further division in the parish. He, however, occasionally supplied some vacant pulpit in the vicinity and frequently prayed at the funerals of departed friends. But such was his deportment in private life that he was universally respected, several times represented the town in the general court and by his piety, candor, sincerity and gentle demeanor so effectually restored the peace of Shingletrees it was thought by many that his private example wrought as much good to the people as had been produced by his public ministration. Thus, I have attempted to sketch the life and character of this worthy Divine and in him will be found a faithful representative of the Massachusetts clergy of his day. And we may fairly challenge the world to exhibit an order of men who by their example of piety, moral conduct, urbanity of deportment, liberality of sentiment and candor towards those who differed from them in doctrine, and by keeping themselves unspotted from the world, adorn better the religion they profess than the clergy of that, and, I may add with pride, of the present day.

To this good man, a few years before his dismission from his pastoral charge, I was sent for instruction.[5]

(N. B. The anecdote of the pastor and the wild pigeons omitted. To be inserted if wanted to swell the work.)[6]

---

[4] The word "Congregational" occurs in Tyler's early version of the manuscript but it was pointedly omitted by Mrs. Tyler when she recopied it.

[5] Marginal notation: "thirty eight pages" and "Bay Boy."

[6] This note, found in Fragment 6, provides a clear illustration of the author's anecdotal method of composition. The episode mentioned is not among the surviving fragments of "The Bay Boy."

CHAPTER VI

Says Jonathan to learned Joe
What are those words you bring so pat in?
For I can't guess you well may know.
Quoth Joseph, "They are Greek and Latin."

'I talk in Latin and in Greek,
'Dear Jonathan, to show my knowledge
'That every time you hear me speak
You'll cry, "How grand to go to college."

Says Jock, "I count, beyond dispute,
Why boys are kept at college dreaming,
It is to talk so crabbed cute
That nobody can know their meaning."

WITH THE WORTHY Mr. Priest I studied several years, my studies being almost exclusively confined to Greek and Latin, to the former of which my preceptor was enthusiastically attached, he having delivered an oration in that language at the commencement at Harvard College when he took his first degree.[1] My poor brain of course became so tinctured with Greek and Latin and my imagination so saturated with ancient story and glorys that all the Greeks and Romans did, said and thought were to me the standard of perfection. I despised modern times and viewed with contempt the vulgar vernacular of my own family, in brief I became as absolute a pedant as ever enjoyed a fellowship at Gottengen or Oxford.

My folly was confirmed by my preceptor's associates. By his direction I committed to memory about four hundred of the most sonorous lines in Homer, which I was called to repeat before the members of the clerical association which assembled annually in our parish. These gentlemen were all educated at the same college and all imbued with the same taste for Greek and Latin. They were ever ready to express

---

[1] This chapter exists completely in Fragment 7 starting with Ms. p. 68. A preliminary draft of the first four paragraphs comprises Fragment 10.

astonishment and admiration at my literary acquirements. One of them prognosticated that I should be a great military chieftain from the fire and force with which I recited Homer's battles of the Greeks and Trojans. Another predicted that I should rival James Otis and Josiah Quincy in eloquence from my repeating the speeches of the heathen Gods with such accurate attention to the caesura, a third was sure I should become a Davis[2] in pulpit fame from the pathos with which I declaimed Jupiter's speech to all the Gods.

In fine these reverend gentlemen considered the classics the source of all valuable knowledge. With them dead languages were of more value then living and little more necessary to accomplish a young man for all that is profitable in life than a profound knowledge of Homer. One of them gravely observed that he was sure that General Wolfe must have had a competent knowledge of Greek and would never have ascended the heights of Abraham if he had not taken his plan of operation from that of Ulysses and Diomede seizing the horses of Rhesus as described in the fourth book of the Iliad.[3]

Thus flattered by the learned I gulped down daily portions of classic lore during four years. At length my father considering that I must by this time have acquired useful knowledge enough to qualify me to assist him in the work and care of the farm took me home but soon began to suspect that what I had learned was not the best adapted to the business of agriculture. My mother, however, was delighted for she *loved learning* and could not be persuaded that what she could not comprehend was consequently useless.

But while my father was perplexing himself about turning my learning to advantage a worthy Divine settled in Boston, passing through our town, called at our house and told him in a private con-

---

[2] John Davis (1737–1772). A graduate of Philadelphia College, he attracted wide attention because of his eloquence while ministering in Delaware. He was called to the pastorate of the Second Baptist Church in Boston. Davis was appointed agent of the Baptists in the Colony to represent their grievances under the exclusive laws then in force in Massachusetts. He took the ground that the charter granted religious equality and that Congregationalism was not the established religion of the Commonwealth.

[3] Tyler made a mistake. This incident occurred in the tenth book of the *Iliad*.

versation that all the Latin and Greek I had acquired was of no other use than fitting me for college. My father was astonished.

"Pray, reverend sir," says he. "Do they not learn this Greek language at college? If so, why do such wise men as the governors of colleges teach boys what is intensely useless? I thought that the sum of all good education was to teach youth those things they were to practice through life."

"Learning," replied our enlightened visitor, "hath its fashions and like other fashions of this world they pass away. When our forefathers founded the college at Cambridge critical knowledge in the mazes of school divinity was all the mode. He that could give a new turn to an old text or detect a mistranslation in the version was more admired than the man who invented printing, discovered the magnetic powers or contrived an instrument to abridge the labors of the husbandman.

"The sacred books of our faith and the voluminous commentaries of the Fathers, being originally written in what are now called the dead languages, the knowledge of these languages was then necessary for the accomplishment of a fashionable scholar. The moderns of New England have ceased to interest themselves in the disputes whether a civil oath may be administered to an unregenerate man or whether souls existing only in the contemplation of the Deity are capable of actual transgression. Fashion has given a new direction to the pursuits of the learned. They no longer soar into the regions of infinite space but endeavor by the aid of true religion and natural and moral philosophy to amend the heart and better the condition of man: and the universities of Oxford and Cambridge may be assimulated to an old beau with his pocket holes under his armpits, the skirts of his coat to his ankles and three gross of buttons on his breeches looking with contempt on the more easy garb of the present day for deviating from what was fashionable in his youth."

"But," inquired my father, "is there not some valuable knowledge contained in those Greek books?"

"All that is useful in them," replied our visitor, "has been already translated into English and more of the sense and spirit may be imbibed from these translations than most scholars would be able to extract from the original, even if they availed themselves of such an acquaintance with that language as is usually acquired at college."

"Well," replied my father, "do you call them *dead languages,* for it appears to me now that confining a lad of lively genius to the study of them for five or six of the most precious years of his life is like the ingenious cruelty of those tyrants I have heard of who chained the living and the dead together. If Updike went to college I should wish him to learn not *hard words* but *useful things.*"

"You spake of governors of colleges," continued our visitor. "Let me observe, as an apology for the concern they may be supposed to have in this error, that they are moral, worthy men who have passed the same dull routine of education and whose knowledge is necessarily confined to these defunct languages. They must teach their pupils what they know, not what they do not know. That measure which was measured unto them they mete out most liberally unto others."

"Should not the legislature, as the fathers of the people, interfere?" inquired my father.

"We will not talk politics at this time," replied his visitor.

My father was determined now that I should not go to college. He concealed this conversation from me and I was left to be proud of my Greek. The little real advantage this deceased language has since been to me has caused me sorely to regret the misspending of time in acquiring it. The French make it no part of their academical studies. Voltaire, d'Alembert and Diderot, when they completed their education, were probably ignorant of the *cognata tempra* of a Greek verb.

It was now resolved that I should labor on my father's farm, but alas! a taste for Greek had quite eradicated a love for labor. Pouring so intently over Homer and Virgil had so completely filled my brain with heathen mythology that I imagined a hamadryad in every sapling, a naiad in every puddle and expected to hear the sobbings of the infant as I turned the furrows. I gave Greek names to all our farming tools and cheered the cattle with hexameter verse. My father's hired men after a tedious day's labor in the woods, inspecting our stores for refreshment, instead of the customary bread and cheese and brandy, found Homer's Iliad, Virgil's Delphini and Schrevelius's Lexicon[4] in the basket.

After I had worked on the farm some months, having killed a fatted heifer of my father's (upon which the family depended for their winter's beef), covered it with green boughs and laid it in the shade to putrefy in order to raise a swarm of bees after the manner of Virgil (which process, notwithstanding I followed closely the directions in the Georgics, somehow or other failed), my father consented to my mother's solicitations that I should renew my career of learning.

I accordingly renewed my studies under my worthy preceptor and it was decided that I should enter college at the next commencement.

[4] Cornelius Schrevel (1608–1664), Dutch scholar whose *Lexicon Manuale Graeco-Latinum* was a standard text of the period. It was published in 1645. The first London edition appeared in 1676.

CHAPTER VII

Oh happy he, whose mind is richly stored
With Science. He who proudly nobly scorns
Basely to barter intellectual wealth
For fame.—But on the uncultured soil
Of youthful minds, his mental treasure pours
Profusely.—On him like flowerets, moisten'd
And refreshed by vernal showers, the young
Shall smile; and the delighted parents pay
Their debt of gratitude, with ceaseless praise.
                                     The Path of the Pedagogue
                                     By the Author.

A S THE REVIEWING my studies did not occupy but a few months, with that economy which was characteristic of the times, which sought to turn every moment to advantage, by the recommendation of our minister I was engaged to keep a school in a neighboring town as soon as our fall work was over.[1]

How my heart dilated with the prospect in the tedious interval previous to my entering upon my school! How often have I stood suspended over my dung fork anticipating my scholars, seated in awful silence around me, my armchair and birchen sceptre of authority! There was an echo in my father's sheep pasture; more than once did I repair there alone and exclaim with a loud voice, "Is *Master* Updike Underhill at home? I would speak with *Master* Underhill!" for the pleasure of hearing how my title sounded. Dost thou smile, indignant reader? Pause and recollect if these sensations have not been familiar to thee at some time in thy life. If thou answerest disdainfully—no— then I aver thou hast never been a corporal in the militia nor a sophomore at college. At times, however, I entertained less pleasing but more rational contemplations on my propects. As I had been once most unmercifully whipt at school for detecting the master in a false concord I resolved to be mild in my government, to avoid all manual correction and doubted not by these means to secure the love and respect of my pupils.

In the interim of school hours and in those peaceful intervals when my pupils were engaged in study I hoped to indulge myself with my favorite Greek. I expected to be *overwhelmed* with the gratitude of their parents for pouring "the fresh instruction o'er the minds" of their children and teaching their "young ideas how to shoot." I anticipated independence from my salary, which was to be equal to *four dollars* hard money per month besides my board. And expected to find amusement and pleasure among the circles of the young and to derive information and delight from the classic converse of the minister of the parish.

In due time my ambition was gratified and I [*was*] placed at the head of a school consisting of about sixty scholars. Excepting three or four overgrown boys of eighteen, the generality of them were under seven years of age. Perhaps a more ragged, ill-bred, ignorant set never were collected together for the punishment of a poor pedagogue. To study

¹ The entire chapter is found in Fragment 7, starting with Ms. p. 74. The introductory poem is found in Fragment 10 following Chapter VI.

in school was impossible. Instead of the silence I anticipated there was an incessant clamor. Predominant among the jarring sounds were, "Master, may I go out?" "Sir, may I spell?" "Master, may I read?" "Will Master mend my pen?" "Sir, please to rule my copy," etc. And what with the pouting of small children, sent to school not to learn but to keep them out of *harm's way,* and the gruff surly looks of the larger ones I was half distracted. Homer's *poluphloisboio thalasses,* roaring sea, was a whisper to it. My resolution to avoid beating them induced me to invent small punishments which often have a salutary influence upon delicate minds but they were insensible to shame. The putting a fool's cap on one and ordering another under my great chair only excited mirth in the school, which the very delinquents themselves often encreased by loud peals of laughter. Going one frosty morning into the school, I found one of the larger boys setting in my armchair by the fire. I gently requested him to remove. He replied that he would when he had warmed himself; "Father finds wood, and not you."

To have my throne usurped in the face of the whole school shook my government to the center. I immediately snatched my two foot rule and laid it pretty smartly across his back. He quitted the chair, muttering that he *would tell father.* I found his threats of more consequence than I apprehended. The same afternoon a tall raw-boned man called me to the door, immediately collaring me with one hand and holding a cart whip over my head with the other, with fury in his face, he vowed he would whip the skin from my bones if ever I struck Jotham again. Aye, he would do it that moment if he was not afraid I would take the law of him. This was the only instance of the *overwhelming* gratitude of parents I received. The next day it was reported all over town what a cruel man the master was. "Poor Jotham came into school almost frozen and near fainting, master had been setting a whole hour by the fire, he only begged him to let him warm himself a little when the master rose up in a rage and cut open his head with the tongs, and his life was despaired of."

Fatigued with the vexations of my school, I one evening repaired to the tavern and mixed with some of the young men of the town. Their conversation I could not relish, mine they could not comprehend. The subject of race horses being introduced, I ventured to descant upon Xanthus, the immortal courser of Achilles. They had never heard of 'Squire Achilles or his horse but they offered to bet two to one that Bajazet, the old roan, or the Deacon's mare, Pumpkin and Milk, would beat him and challenged me to appoint time and place.

Nor was I more acceptable among the young women. Being invited to spend an evening after a quilting I thought this a happy opportunity to introduce Andromache, the wife of the great Hector, at her loom; and Penelope, the faithful wife of Ulysses, weaving her seven years' web. This was received with a stupid stare until I mentioned the long time the Queen of Ulysses was weaving, when a smart young woman observed that she supposed Miss Penelope's yarn was rotted in the whitening, that made her so long, and then told a tedious story of a piece of cotton and linen which she had herself woven under similar circumstances. She had no sooner finished than to enforce my observations I recited about forty lines of Greek from the Odyssey and then began a dissertation on the *caesura*. In the midst of my harangue a florid faced young man at the further end of the room, with two large prominent foreteeth remarkably white, began to sing,

"Fire on the mountains! run, boys, run!"

And immediately the whole company rushed forward to see who should get a chance in the reel of six. I was about retiring, fatigued and disgusted when it was hinted to me that I might wait on Miss Mima home, but as I could recollect no word in the Greek which would construe into *bundling* or any of Homer's heroes who *got the bag,* I declined. In the Latin it is true that Æneas and Dido, in the cave, seem something like a precedent. It was reported all over town the next day that *master* was a *papish* as he had talked French two hours.

Disappointed of recreation among the young, my next object was the minister. Here I expected pleasure and profit. He had spent many years in preaching for the edification of private families and was settled in town in a fit of enthusiasm, when the people drove away a clergyman respectable for his years, piety and learning. This he was pleased to call an *awakening*. He lectured me at the first onset for not attending the conference and night meetings, talked much of *gifts* and decried human learning as carnal and devilish. And well he might, he certainly was under no obligations to it, for a new singing master, coming into town, the young people by their master's advice were for introducing Doctor Watts' version of the Psalms.[2] Although I argued with the minister an hour, he remains firmly convinced to this day that the version of Sternhold and Hopkins[3] is the same in language, letter and metre with those psalms King David chanted in the city of Jerusalem.

As for the independence I had founded on my wages, it vanished like the rest of my scholastic prospects. I had contracted some debts. My request for present payment was received with astonishment. I found I was not to expect it until the next autumn, and then not in cash, but produce; to become my own collector and pick up my dues, half a peck of rye or corn, in a place. I was almost distracted and yearned for the expiration of my contract, when an unexpected period was put to my distress. News was brought that by the carelessness of the boys the schoolhouse was burned down. The common cry now was that I ought in justice to pay for it, as to my want of government the carelessness of the boys ought to be imputed. The beating of Jotham was forgotten and a thousand stories of my want of proper spirit circulated. These reports and even the loss of a valuable Gradus ad Parnassum did not damp my joy. I am sometimes led to believe that my emancipation from real slavery in Algiers did not afford me sincerer joy than I experienced at that moment.[4]

[2] Isaac Watts (1674-1748) published his *Psalms of David* in 1719. Watts' psalms were very popular in the United States.

[3] Thomas Sternhold (*d.* 1549) and John Hopkins (*d.* 1570), authors, with others, of the famous first metrical version of the psalms in English published in 1549. More than 600 editions appeared between 1549 and 1878.

[4] Chapter VII of "The Bay Boy" is composed of Chapters VII and VIII of *The Algerine*

I returned home to my father who received me with kindness. My mother heard the story of my discomfitures with transport; as she said she had not doubt her dream of my falling into the hands of savages was now out.[5]

I abode at home the remainder of the winter. It was determined that I should persue one of the learned professions; my father, with parental pride and partiality, conceiving my aversion to labor, my inattention to farming business and the tricks I played him the preceding season as the sure indication of genius. He now told the story of the putrefied heifer with triumph as he had read in the newspapers that playing with paper kites was the foundation of Doctor Franklin's fame, that John Locke, who dissected the human mind and discovered the circulation of the soul, had in the full exercise of his understanding played at duck and drake on the Thames with his gold watch while he gravely put the pebble stone which he held in his other hand into his fob, and that the learned Sir Isaac Newton made soap bubbles with the funk of a tobacco pipe, and was ever after so enamoured with his sooty funk as to make use of the delicate finger of a young lady he courted for a pipe stopper.

I was allowed the choice of my profession. To discover the bent of my genius, by the advice of a friend, my father put into my hands what he was told were some of the prime books in the several sciences. In Divinity I read ten funeral, five election, three ordination and seventeen farewell sermons, Bunyan's Holy War, the Life of Colonel Gardner,[6] and the Religious Courtship.[7] In Law, the Statutes of Massachusetts-bay and Burns' Justice Abridged.[8] In Physic, Buchan's

---

Captive. Tyler neglected obviously to tell his wife to eliminate this reference to the earlier novel when she recopied the manuscript.

[5] This phrase is meaningless in "The Bay Boy" since Tyler did not use this episode which originally appeared in The Algerine Captive at the beginning of Chapter IV. Updike's mother had dreamed her son would be set upon by Indians.

[6] Col. James Gardiner (1688–1745), noted English cavalry officer, killed at the battle of Prestonpans, details of which are included by Alexander Carlisle in his biography. The volume, The Life of Colonel James Gardiner, was by Philip Doddridge (1702–1751).

[7] Daniel Defoe's Religious Courtship, or Marriage on Christian Principles.

[8] Richard Burns (1709–1785), authored the legal classic, The Justice of the Peace and

Family Physician,[9] Culpeper's Midwifery,[10] and Turner's Surgery.[11] The agreeable manner in which this last author related his own wonderful cures, the lives of his patients and his remarkable dexterity in extracting a pound of candles from the arm of a wounded soldier, and the neat little saddlebags, the spirited horse and tipped bridle of our own doctor determined me in favor of Physic. My father did not oppose my choice.

It was, therefore, decided that after passing through college I should become a physician, altho' my father dryly observed that he did not know what pretensions our family had to practice Physic as he could not learn we had ever been remarkable for killing any but Indians.

Parish Officer. First published at London in 1755, it achieved wide circulation. A Boston edition of 1773, *Abridgement of Burn's Justice of the Peace and Parish Officer,* was considered the bible of the Colonial peace officer.

[9] William Buchan (1729–1805) wrote *Domestic Medicine, or the Family Physician* in 1769. The first work of its kind in England, it went through 19 large editions, amounting to about 80,000 copies, during his lifetime. It was even more popular in America and on the European continent than in England.

[10] Nicholas Culpeper (1616–1654) gained his fame in medicine and astrology. His *A Directory for Midwives* appeared in 1651.

[11] Daniel Turner (1607–1741), physician and surgeon. His volume, *The Art of Surgery* (1721), although popular in his age, is of little worth now.

CHAPTER VIII

To fall in love—I hate the phrase;
'Tis so ignoble, flat, and base.
When I am touched by Cupid's flambeaux
Which oft will make both belle and man go,
When that sly gunner of the graces,
His lint stock tipped with pretty faces,
Lights his gay torch at some bright eye
And whirls his flaming port-fire high
And then applys the hottest part
To the gun-powder of my heart;
Then may I bounce, and hiss, and fly

Like Congreve rocket through the sky;[1]
And if the fair unyielding prove
And I go hang myself for love;
Howe'er the gentle passions end
Let me not *fall*, but still ascend.

Doggeral Romaunt
By the Author.

I AGREE entirely with the grave and enlightened poet above cited.[2] I too abhor the phrase *falling in love,* it seems like slipping into Bunyan's Slough of Dispond. I really wonder where this tumble-down phrase was coined, probably in some monastic mint where the Franciscan essay-master fell from his cell into the company of some superannuated nun in the dormitory.

When I am in love I mount, ascend, sublimate and to cap the climax in the best possible style, *I get up* into love. How I first ascended to this garret of the graces the reader shall be informed.

One Sunday, when I was in my seventeenth year, as I sat in our pew endeavoring to commit the text to memory, that I might repeat it to my mother, my eyes were suddenly attracted by a person whom I had never seen before[3] as the congregation had been recently *reseated* by the committee and families advanced or degraded as their age or circumstances rendered proper. A beautiful cherry cheeked girl now sat opposite to me whose sparkling black eyes gave animation to a round face and rather exuberant person—her dress such as might well have befitted a nymph in Gays's Pastorals. I could not keep my eyes from her all the service and when it concluded I watched her egress on the green. Oh, how I envied her brother when he spurred the old mare up to the horse block and received her on the pillion behind him! But

[1] Sir William Congreve (1772–1828) invented a rocket for use in warfare about 1805. The rockets were first employed in a naval attack against the French at Boulogne in 1806.

[2] In Fragment 7 this section is numbered Chapter VIII, starting with Ms. p. 81. In Fragment 10 this chapter follows immediately after Chapter VII.

[3] At this point in the manuscript Tyler placed an asterisk. There is, however, no explanation for it. He probably intended to identify the person to whom Updike was attracted but never got around to doing so. On the other hand, Tyler might have planned to expand the manuscript at this point to puff up the episode.

when she sprang upon the seat and put her arm round his waist, inserting her chubby fingers in his waistcoat button hole, my heart thumped like a basedrum.

I returned home, lost my memory and my appetite, sat down to a dinner of roast goose and apple dumplings. The first mouthful of goose stuck in my throat, could no more swallow than if a whole dumpling was sticking in my gullet, could not think what ailed me, never suspected I was in love. My father, honest man, never having been infected with this heartrending malady, was equally at fault, attributed my want of appetite to sick headache, recommended eating freely of parched corn. All would not do, could not taste of my mother's mince pie although made on purpose to treat me and hitherto a great favorite. Several successive Sabbaths went to meeting, never able to commit the heads of the sermon or even the text to memory, kept my eyes riveted on the same enchanting object and like Dryden's Alexander the Great when

> Lovely Thais by his side
> Sat like a blooming eastern bride
> In flower of youth, and beauty's pride,
> I sigh'd and look'd, sigh'd and look'd,
> Sigh'd and look'd, and sigh'd again.

What would I not have given to have heard one sweet sentence drop like honey from the honeycomb of her lips, it would have wrapt my soul in Elysium!

By some significant glances, since recollected, between my mother and Aunt Tabitha, I conclude they both more than suspected the cause of my doleful ailment. Women have a wonderful discernment on such subjects, almost intuitive. They took their measures accordingly: one pleasant morning my mother ordered Sambo to bring the horse and chaise to the door and with my aunt announced their intention of paying a few visits of business, but just as they were about stepping into the carriage my aunt suddenly recollected she had promised to toe off a stocking that very morning and declined going. I was invited to accompany mother in a careless way which seemed to intimate that I should not offend or disappoint her by declining.

We drove to the weavers to enquire about a web in the loom, to the clothiers to look after another on the tenterhooks, to the widow Twists to see if her daughter Linda would come and do our spinning and to several other places on domestic business so necessary to be effected in order to preserve the economy of a well regulated family. At length my mother, looking at the sun, observed that she had intended to call at Ensign Gander's but apprehended we should not have time and directed me to turn the mare's head toward home.

Now Ensign Gander's was the very house I wanted to visit for the Ensign was father to the attractive maid of the meeting house and my heart beat the double, double ruffle of love as we approached the head of the lane which led towards his domicil. I looked at my watch, then at the sun, then put my watch to my ear and looked at the sun again, and finally stammered out an opinion that we had full time enough to call at Ensign Gander's if my mother's business made it necessary. She appeared to hesitate. I stopped the mare. At length to my great relief she concluded that we might possibly have time to make a short call. I quickly drove to the door, handed my mother out of the carriage and while she entered the house busied myself in fastening the horse to a *willow* tree. How rapidly did a succession of contending reflections rattle through my percranium. Mahomet's flight to the seventh heaven which, I recollect, he performed in time to return and save every drop of water in a pitcher he overset at his departure, was a snail's pace to the rapidity of my thoughts. I was now at the very threshold of the temple of my idolatry. At one time I actually resolved against going in and went towards the goose pond to wear away the time of my mother's visit in suitable cogitations; then again I mustered all my courage and determined to approach my divinity although I should die before her shrine: your true lover always makes his first advances towards his mistress with trepidation and awe and I was indeed a true lover. I brushed my hat, dusted my shoes, adjusting my neckcloth, gave two stout "hems" to settle my resolution and then practicing all the way my best dancing school bow I entered the Ensign's spacious kitchen where "O horribeli dictu!" the first object that struck my astonished sight was my divine charmer.

"Fallen, fallen, fallen from her high estate" and wallowing in her grease. She was seated all in a heap in a low chair, her short gown striped with copperas dye slightly fastened with one pin at the waist, a blue and white checker'd handkerchief thrown carelessly over her shoulders, a linsey woolsey apron well lubricated with oil serving to protect her homespun skirt from the contact of a pair of wool cards with which she was carding into bats the annual produce of the sheep, her hair unkempt and the big drops of perspiration, occasioned by her labors, standing upon her forehead or trickling in dingy channels down her neck.

I stood appalled—"*Vox faucibus haesit, steteruntque comae.*" Mrs. Gander pointed to a chair.

"You may sit down, young man." I seated myself accordingly, viewing with evident disgust the object of my recent admiration.

My mother soon discovered the impression made by the interview and resolving that her maternal stratagem should have its full effect, after some confab with Mrs. Gander, turned towards the daughter with:

"I declare, Miss Dolly, you do credit to your keepers. Seems to me you gain flesh every time I have the pleasure of seeing you."

"Why yes ma'am so everybody says and I s'pose what everybody says must be true. Mother is always poking fun at me 'cause she says as how my arms look as plump as our big horn'd heifer just afore she calves and I tells her maybe my arms will soon calve too, don't you think so, ma'am?" holding up her arms with an arch look as much as to say, "*Ain't I cunning?*"

The charm of *first love* was broken. I hastened home, ate a whole minced pie and the next Sabbath could remember the whole heads of the pastor's sermon with the doctrinal uses and improvements.

Such is the fastidiousness of a more refined education. Miss Dolly Gander was after all a comely girl when arrayed in her *go to meeting* attire and at the time of our interview she was industriously employed in suitable work and properly habited for the occasion. She caused many a young farmer's heart, like mine, to thump like a base drum, was a town toast and no girl in the town of Shingletrees could dance a jig or trundle a reel of six with more spirit—or had slyly thrown into her lap more red ears at the husking of Indian corn.

On our drive home my mother took no notice of what had happened and I to be sure was equally silent. That evening, however, I overheard my mother and Aunt Tabitha making very merry at my expense as the latter in a snug coterie chuckled over the narration my mother gave her.

The enchanting Miss Dolly Gander has since made an excellent wife to a substantial farmer, brought up a large family of children and one of her sons has since represented the district of which Shingletrees is a part in the Congress of the United States. Happy country! wherein the honors and emoluments of government are within the grasp of all its citizens, where integrity and talents may attain the most exalted station without the aid of opulence, and without being depressed by the policy of state or the more oppressive weight of hereditary aggrandizement.[4]

Soon after this incident I proceeded in company with my worthy preceptor to Cambridge, was by him presented to the president for examination and having passed it decently was admitted a member of the freshman class in Harvard College. I omit an account of my collegiate life. There is a sameness in the occupations of all students at the same university. The same studies are pursued, the same rivalship excited, the same jealousies fostered and the same college tricks played as the classes, like the generations of men, pass away. And an old and intimate friend has kindly communicated to me the unfinished manuscript of a novel called "*The Autobiography of the Boston Boy*" in which

[4] This marks the end of the chapter in Fragment 10. The following two paragraphs are incorporated into the chapter as it is found in both Fragments 3c, 11 and 7. A reading of these two paragraphs will show why there is some question as to whether or not Tyler planned to include them into "The Bay Boy." In any case, they are inserted here as found in the manuscript.

are delineated the manners and customs of the good people of Boston, divided into several epochs from the eviction of Blaxton, the first settler, to the Battle of Bunker Hill, with notices of many surprising and interesting events and memoranda of the conversation and correspondence of the principal persons concerned therein, which I understand is to be published as soon as arrangements can be made with certain London booksellers. That autobiography embraces a view of the interior of the college from the presidency of the venerable Oakes,[5] when the students were horsed, whipt and called *boys,* to that of the good Holyoke[6] when fines were substituted for flagellation and the students were *young gentlemen.* I omit, therefore, all detail of my college life and refer my reader to the *Autobiography of a Boston Boy* where he will find ably delineated a lively picture of those classic scenes which, were I so disposed, I could only trace a faint outline.

It must be remembered that Harvard College had not then attained that unrivaled preeminence which now renders that university the pride and delight of the northern wing of the Union. I shall, therefore, simply state that after taking my bachelor's degree it was determined that I should commence the study of physic and surgery in Boston.

[5] Urian Oakes (c. 1631–1681), poet, clergyman and president of Harvard. His disappointment in not being named president of the college on the death of Charles Chauncy led to his leading those who wrecked the administration of Leonard Hoar. After Hoar's departure Oakes became acting president and finally president in name (1679–1680).

[6] Edward Holyoke (1689–1769). A 1705 graduate of Harvard, he became a tutor in 1712, fellow of the corporation in 1713 and president in 1737. Although he first commended George Whitefield on his convention sermon in 1741, a year later he felt called upon to publish a pamphlet attacking Whitefield as a "deluder of the people."

CHAPTER IX

The zephyrs fear to breathe, the morning gales
Flit o'er the dewy flowers with noiseless wing;
The early birds chirp forth their matin song
With modulated cadence, while the bright
God of day restrains his panting steeds lest
With their sparkling houghs they trampling beat
Their sapphire path with rude concussion.
Now all above, beneath, around is quiet;
Peace and holy rest. The Sabbath comes.

SUNDAY IN BOSTON IN THE YEAR 17—.[1]

ARRANGEMENTS having thus been made I entered upon my noviciate as pupil to the celebrated Dr. G., physician and surgeon.[2] It is a peculiarity with the people of New England, like the ancient Romans, to combine various arts and sciences in the same professor who not infrequently excels in all. The doctor was a gentleman of deep reading in the sciences he professed, of admirable judgement in detecting the latent locality of disease, affable in manners, frank, liberal and candid in his opinions on all subjects save religion and politics. He was a zealous Episcopalian and staunch Loyalist[3] but

[1] This line is found in the rough draft version of the chapter, Fragment 12.

[2] In Fragment 12 this section, which combines Chapter IX and X together without a break in continuity, is unnumbered. In Fragment 7 it is numbered Chapter VII although Tyler had already both a Chapter VII and VIII. From the transition, however, it is obviously meant to be Chapter IX.

There are more changes in vocabulary and phraseology between the rough and final drafts of this chapter than in any up to this point. It is clear Tyler spent a great deal of time over this section, updating the sentence structure and using more current words.

The "celebrated Dr. G." is Dr. Silvester Gardiner (1707?–1786). See above, pp. 32. A distinguished physician and surgeon, he was also engaged in mercantile ventures and owned extensive real estate in the District of Maine. Feeling that drugs were improperly dispensed in Boston, Dr. Gardiner established his own apothecary shop at Winter and Tremont Streets. Further details on Dr. Gardiner are contained in James Thacher, *American Medical Biography* (Boston, 1828), I, 24. A brief outline of early Massachusetts medicine is found on p. 14ff. See also Chapman, p. 75.

[3] Dr. Gardiner was both a Tory and devoted Episcopalian. He had been both a warden and vestryman of King's Chapel for many years and was one of those instrumental in raising funds for the famous "Stone Chapel" which is still standing in

even these aberrations from the prevailing sentiments of his fellow townsmen were not generally obtruded where they might give offense but were always chastened by habitual politeness and only manifested themselves in certain occasional acerbities of remark illicited by the conduct of those who held contrary opinions: opinions which he held in utter contempt as resulting from ignorance and an undue estimate of the powers of the British government and the purity of the Church of England.

The first few days of my abode under the doctor's roof were spent as may be readily imagined in familiarizing myself with the house and its inmates; with the study, library, surgical instruments and drugs and in receiving occasional directions from my master as to the course of my future studies. On Saturday afternoon I found the first leisure moment to look into the streets.

The sun was about half an hour high, the empty market carts were rattling their retreat through the streets, the day laborers were return-ing to their dwellings shouldering their tools and here and there one bearing in his hand a basin suspended in a blue checkered handerchief containing probably cold meats or other elymosynary provision bestowed by some charitable employer.

As I looked up and down Marlboro' Street[4] I observed the sideways as if by some previous concert were filled with parti-colored troops, prepared with broom and brush to sweep away the filth of the week in preparation for the ensuing Sabbath. Before every dwelling house the servants, black and white, were thus engaged while the spruce apprentice, with his muffeties on his wrists and a green serge apron 'round his waist, was employed in the same manner before the shops. For the apprentices of Boston in that day of decorum did not consider it any degradation to perform those menial offices and no condescen-

Boston. He held pews 7 and 8 in the church. As an ardent Loyalist his property was confiscated at the outbreak of the Revolution and he fled to Halifax, New York and finally England. He returned to Newport, R.I., after the war.

[4] This further confirms the attribution of "Dr. G." Dr. Gardiner's home was on Marlborough Street. (Marlborough Street in Tyler's era has been renamed Washington Street. It is not the present-day Marlboro Street in the Back Bay area of Boston).

tion to be seen, like the great Franklin,[5] occasionally trundling a wheelbarrow through the principal street. The good old maxim, "First learn to serve and then you will know how to govern" was frequently repeated by the merchant to his clerks and apprentices.

These busy polishers of the pavement soon retired and suddenly returned with vessels of water. Every pail, pot and pudding pan seemed put in requisition and all proceeded to watering the streets, some with watering pots but more with pails and tin dippers, while the active apprentice brings forth his bullock's horn filled with water and perforated at the tip, sprinkling the pavement with many a crincle-crankled libation.

At the same eventide, in what my master called the *Puritanic* families, the female domestics were as busily employed in paring, washing and preparing the vegetables for the pot, in trussing the meat for the spit, compounding the Indian or plum pudding, airing the Sunday attire and combing and washing the children, while the scullion was blacking and polishing with his elbow grease the shoes and turned pumps of the family. In brief, all were busily engaged in abridging as far as possible the labors of the approaching day of devotion and rest.

At length the sun descended in majesty, tinging the fleecy clouds with all the soft and varied radiance of an Italian sky. The streets were now deserted, nothing was seen except the tardy footsteps of the belated laborer or the cautious tread of the conscientious beau who was returning from the barber's shop under the shade of the projecting pent house with his chin smoothly shaved, his toupee nicely craped, his side curls neatly bound with leaden wires and the whole as white as the powder puff and castor could make them. At length the old South clock struck eight and all was silence.[6]

I arose early on Sabbath morning and looked out of my window but not a person appeared to interrupt the solemn stillness of the

[5] Tyler and Dennie criticised Franklin in a "Colon & Spondee" essay in *The Port Folio* (Feb. 14, 1801), 53. Tyler, however, did have kind words for Franklin in *The Algerine Captive,* Chapter XXIII.

[6] The Old South Church steeple clock was installed in the spring of 1770 by Gawan Brown.

streets. Immediately after breakfast, which from respect for the town habits we took in a back parlor, the doctor assuming one of his most affable smiles accosted me thus:

Doctor G. "Well, young gentleman, where do you attend public worship? I conclude you are aware it is as much as a young man's reputation is worth to absent himself from church in this puritanic town and time."

Author. "I can't say, sir, that I have determined where I shall attend permanently; had thoughts of taking a seat for this day in Grandmother Anvill's pew in Brattle Street."

Doctor G. "Ha! What? Hear silver tongue?[7] Must say you discover some taste. Fine man that, perfect gentleman in his manners, refined literary taste, eloquent elocution. Great pity such talents are devoted to a conventicle, often wished he was in holy orders, was going to offer you a seat in my pew at Trinity Church[8] but perhaps your parents have forbade your going to church, or you may have your own prejudices."

[7] Rev. Samuel Cooper (1725–1783). In 1743 he was elected pastor of the Brattle Street Church, the fourth church of the Puritan order to be established in Boston (1699). Cooper was noted for his eloquence, fluency and presence. He was active in the cause of freedom and had to flee the city in 1775 to avoid arrest by the British. Cooper was a friend of Dr. Gardiner and often dined at his house, together with such diverse company as Gov. Hutchinson, John Hancock, Gen. Gage and John Singleton Copley.

[8] Stretching his memory back more than 45 years caused Tyler to confuse King's Chapel (the oldest Anglican Church in New England) and Trinity Church (the third Episcopal Church in Boston). The relationship of the various members of the Gardiner family may also have contributed to this error.

Dr. Silvester Gardiner had been warden and vestryman at King's Chapel before the Revolution. His son, John, a lawyer, had been a prime mover in transforming King's Chapel, of which he too had been a vestryman, into a Unitarian Society. Furthermore, Dr. Gardiner's grandson, Rev. John Sylvester John Gardiner, D.D., had been rector at Trinity from 1805 until his death in 1830. He was also a founder of the Boston Athenaeum.

The result is that Tyler made the mistake of assigning Dr. Silvester Gardiner to Trinity instead of King's Chapel and associating with Trinity the rector serving at King's Chapel during Dr. Gardiner's service as warden (see footnote 9 below). For details of the Gardiner family role in the churches of Boston see Henry W. Foote, *Annals of King's Chapel* (Boston: Little, Brown & Co., 1882–1896), I, 547; II, 18–19, 44–48, 79–81, 118–19, 147–50 and 353–62. Tyler's grandfather, father and brother, John Steele Tyler, are all buried in King's Chapel graveyard.

Author. "My parents have said nothing to me on the subject and I am well persuaded would not attempt to influence me in this particular."

Doctor G. "Ha! What? Well, that is more than I expected from them. The fever of fanaticism is not apt to be intermittent. Well, suppose you should accept my offer. I need not add that as a member of my family it would be peculiarly agreeable to me."

Author. "I shall accept your offer with gratitude, hoping you will permit me to spend Thanksgiving day with my Grandmother."

Doctor G. "By all means. That Yankee festival is not in our calender. Eat your pumpkin pudding where you please. I hope, however, you will take your Christmas pie with me."

Author. "With great pleasure. I have a sweet tooth and shall relish both."

Doctor G. "Professional duties keep me from church oftener than I wish. When there, as church warden I am confined to an official seat but son John will shew you your seat. Think you will be pleased with Dr. C.;[9] not a Tillotson, a Sherlock or a South,[10] but will give you a good sound moral discourse, teaching us how to conduct ourselves toward each other here as men, Christians, and above all, as *good churchmen* without puzzling our heads about our destination hereafter. Short and sweet, never above fifteen or twenty minutes in his sermon, but then he reads the service elegantly with *true* piety and fervor. You never read the Book of Common Prayer, hey?"

Author. "Never, sir."

Doctor G. "Great pleasure to come. Pay attention to it while at

[9] Rev. Henry Caner became rector of King's Chapel in April, 1747. A Loyalist, he left in March 1776, when the British troops evacuated Boston. Dr. Gardiner had been one of the wardens welcoming Rev. Caner to King's Chapel in 1747.

[10] John Tillotson (1630–1694), divine and chaplain of Charles II. Like other churchman he became embroiled in the religio-political conflicts of the period.

William Sherlock (1641?–1707), Dean of St. Paul's succeeding Tillotson. His defense of the Trinity involved him in the Socinian dispute.

Robert South (1634–1716), churchman, chaplain to Charles II. In 1693 he published a pamphlet attacking Sherlock's support of the Trinity. Tillotson referred to his reputation for humor in the pulpit.

church. The oftener you hear it repeated the more you will be delighted with it. Never was there a human composition, if human it can be called, so calculated to lead the devotions of the real Christian. Such beauty, harmony and elegance of style, the homelies so instructive, the scripture selections so well arranged, litany so fervent and affecting, the prayers so admirably adapted to the wants and desires of every worshiper, so fervid without fanaticism, concise without obscurity and devoid of that disgusting familiarity with diety that so often disgraces the puritanic orisons. But I forbear, attend and judge for yourself."

Accordingly I took my seat in the doctor's pew in Trinity Church, I must confess the service was very imposing. The kneeling posture, the engagedness of the worshipers, the part which everyone bore in the exercises, the energy and conciseness of the prayers, the humble confession of unworthiness and continued ejaculation for mercy, the frequent repetition of the Gloria Patria, the vestments of the priests and the rich tones of the organ softening by its full diapason the harsh discord of the voluntary choristers were all highly calculated to impress a stranger with reverence and awe and enkindle in his bosom every latent spark of devotion. It is true I at first thought there was too much getting up and sitting down and was repeatedly foiled in my attempts to find the prayers and collects, but from this dilemma I was fortunately relieved by a maiden lady in the next pew, who observing my embarrassment arose from her hassock, first attempting to aid my search with the tip of her fan and finally with admirable facility finding the required passages in her own prayer book and interchanging with mine as often as occasion required. Thus assisted and by attending to the sonorous intonations of the clerk and the gentler modulations of my courteous assistant, I soon began to enter into the spirit of the service and to make my responses with freedom. The sermon was far superior to what my master had taught me to anticipate.

The assembly was in due time dismissed and we retired from the church, stepping lightly to an animating voluntary from the organ.

Perhaps there is no scene more delightful and interesting than a

Christian community returning home from their several places of public worship on the Lord's day. As we passed through Summer Street a view of our own congregation was interesting but when we entered the main street[11] and joined the full flow of population continually increasing by the addition of other congregations of worshipers pouring in from every lane and avenue we passed the effect was absolutely enchanting. Young men and maidens, old men and babes all neatly arrayed in their Sunday attire, the young beauties sporting the newest fashions, the youthful couples in the pride of early paternity supporting between them the tottering footsteps of their earliest pledge of love, followed by the sober matron who ever anon eyed askance her blooming daughters with maternal delight. There the young beau with his buckskins neatly stitched with white silk and as fine as a roll of list and buff ball could make them. There some town-born polemic, regardless of finery and fashion, musing on some knotty point of divinity or attempting in vain to unravel the snarl of metaphysics with which his favorite preacher had enveloped his doctrine, all walking with measured step and every countenance chastened by the sanctity of the day, excepting here and there as we passed some avenue a knot of young blades were seen lingering at the corner to catch a glymps of passing beauty and fashion, until frightened from their perch by the distant approach of some austere personage in the shape of parent, master or guardian—when they skulked into the passing crowd and graduated their features by the sober standard of the season.

I hastened home and dined upon plum pudding and roast beef, the standard Sunday dishes of the family. The afternoon service was more brief and I thought not so interesting as the morning. However, I continued to feel more and more interested in the church service. Soon after the parson had named his text and the excitement of the devotional exercises had subsided, the soporific influence of my dinner began to operate: my eyelids became heavy, I nodded, rubbed my

[11] Marlborough Street was the main thoroughfare.

eyes, fixed my attention on the parson, nodded again, and soon found myself sliding in airy curves from the pinnacle of one lofty building to another, suddenly falling from the craggy top of some jutting precipice and only saved from being dashed to pieces by landing safely on the cushioned seat of my pew. From this stupor I was relieved by the staid maiden in the next pew who handed me a bottle of pungent salts. Grateful for the favor and resolved to shew my gratitude, I suddenly drew the cork and applied the bottle to my nostrils. Whap went my head against the wall and my eyes filled with tears. This excited a smile in those near me in which my courteous neighbor joined with such complacency that I could not but imagine her mischievously inclined when she presented me the sal volatile.

As I had no further intention to doze and to avoid the glances of certain young ladies in my vicinity who were endeavoring to suppress a titter while they peered at me through the sticks of their fans, I stood up and took a survey of the congregation and discovered I was not the only one who felt the influence of a Sunday's dinner. It seemed as if some severe blast had blown through the church. Every pew exhibited drowsiness in all its dozing attitudes. The minor children were comfortably extended on the cushions and screened from the buzzing insect by the maternal handkerchief while the sober matron, after ineffectual recourse to her snuffbox, nodded over the fan with which she attempted to keep herself awake. And the wily maiden slept serenely under the covert of her hat or bonnet unconscious that her waving plumes, by their abrupt noddings, betrayed the secret she so artfully attempted to conceal, while the plethoric church warden sounded his own requiem from his elevated seat.

The sermon concluded, the clerk gave out the psalm and the lethean influence fled. The sleeping little varlets were lifted from the cushions and fanned and coaxed into recollection and we quitted the church, some I trust refreshed by an excellent sermon and certainly some by a comfortable nap.

On my return home I found my worthy preceptor, who had been absent on professional business all the forepart of the day, seated in his elbow chair, in his night-gown and slippers, smoking a T.D. pipe eighteen inches in length filled with Kidder's best Virginia.[12] He appeared highly gratified with the account I gave of my favorable opinion of the church service, when as if suddenly recollecting himself he directed me to open one of the folding doors of the beaufet on the inside of which I found a slate on which a pencil and sponge were attached, and upon which I learned it was the duty of some one of the family to note the residence of all applicants in his absence with such notice of their disease as could be procured. He took his spectacles from their shagreen case and proceeded to read, making such comments as occured in his own peculiar style.

"Mr. Kidder, two doors south of the Two Palaverers,[13] requests Dr. G.'s attendance at his house to consult with Drs. Pecker, Kast and Warren[14] on the case of his servant girl threatened with a tympany."

"Ha! What, young Warren called to a consultation. Bright youth that, promising talents, soon get into business, great favorite with the old ladies, sure prognostic of extensive practice. Pity, great pity a young man of his abilities should associate so familiarly with the crack-brained politicians of the day."

"Mr. John Trott, Black Horse Lane, crippled with the gout in both

---

[12] A tobacconist on North Street. (See below footnote 13.)

[13] The Two Palaverers, also called the Salutation Tavern, stood near the corner of North and Salutation Streets. There met the famous North End Caucus, a political club made up of Dr. Joseph Warren, Samuel and John Adams, Church, Young, Eddes and others who plotted for the overthrow of the British Colonial government.

[14] Dr. Thomas Kast (1750–1820), physician and surgeon, practiced in Boston from 1774 until 1804. Tyler may have known him personally since Kast received his M.A. from Harvard in 1774 while Tyler was still a student there.

Dr. Pecker, a contemporary of Dr. Kast, was also a Boston physician. Both are mentioned in Thacher, I, 25, 433–35. Dr. Warren was Joseph Warren (1741–1775), patriot and physician, killed at the Battle of Bunker Hill. Tyler had good reason to hear of Dr. Warren's talents. He had been the family physician of Joseph P. and Elizabeth Hunt Palmer, Tyler's parents-in-law. Mrs. Palmer, in her manuscript memoir, p. 8, relates Dr. Warren's visit to the Palmer household the night before the battle. He predicted he would not return alive.

The 14pp. memoir, entitled, "Reminiscences of Mrs. Jos. P. Palmer, née Betsey Hunt, from Ms. of her Grandson, Rev. T. P. Tyler, taken down at her dictation" [c. 1830], is appended to "MPT Memoir." See also GTB, pp. 43–44.

feet and one arm, forgot to consult the doctor during his last visit whether old Port or Madeira is best to keep the gout from the stomach. N.B., if the doctor does not visit him before sunset shall with his leave take a bottle of his old long corked Anno Domini."

"Mrs. Diaway, head of Scarlet's Wharf, wishes to see the doctor immediately, positive she can't survive this night through. Total loss of appetite, violent palpitation of the heart, begs the doctor to bring a box of her favorite pills. Last evening her nervous system was so shattered she could not compose herself without taking all the pills she had in the house which the doctor supposed would last a fortnight."

"Poor lady! These pills must be compounded without delay. Do step into the study, bring the glass mortar, a bottle of rose water, a phial of bergamot or any other essense you can find and then direct the house-keeper to send me a thick slice of brick loaf."

With these ingredients the pills were soon made.

"Now, Underhill, look into the pages of Paracelsus, otherwise called Auraelus Philippus Theophrastus Bombastus de Succo Metallorum with marginal notes by Carpus[15] and there you will find some gold and silver leaf. Cover half the pills with the former and half with the latter. Deposit them in two handsome boxes. I will attend the good lady as soon as I have smoaked my pipe. But ha, what have we here?"

"The doctor is desired to come immediately to the young man in Pleasant Street who broke his leg in jumping from the upper gallery of the old South during the great fright when Mr. Whitefield was preaching;[16] bandages loosened, leg bleeds."

"Aye, aye, this comes of your new fangled notions about *New*

[15] Philip Aurelius Theophrastus Bombastus von Hohenheim (c. 1490–1541), Swiss physician and alchemist, took the name "Paracelsus" to denote his superiority to Aulus Cornelius Celsus (1st Century A.D.), the great Latin medical writer. Paracelsus, who was the first public professor of chemistry in Europe, established the role of chemistry in medicine.

[16] Whitefield preached in Boston in 1743 and his diary entry for Sept. 22 recounts how five persons were killed during the excitement generated by his visit. (The diary is quoted in Foote, *Annals of King's Chapel*, I, 507.) Whitefield also preached at Boston's Old South Church on Aug. 19 and Sept. 3, 1770.

Light. The Boston clergymen were highly tickled when they first found this stray sheep from the fold of the church, let him into their pulpit and now he has preached them out of all their popularity and many of them I dare say, when they heard of this poor young man's misfortunes, wished heartily that the Methodist had leaped after him. Right enough too. All this comes from being dissenters. These fungi and excrescences grew out of the Mother Church in that hotbed of fanaticism during the great rebellion which brought the royal martyr Charles of blessed memory to the block and peopled New England with cant and hypocrisy. Tell Scip to harness the horses, I must attend this young man and you must carry these pills to Mrs. Diaway."

Author. "I shall be happy to obey you, sir, but do you not think these powerful pills will be as efficacious tomorrow as today?"

Doctor. "Ha! What? Now I dare say you imagine I am playing the quack. No such thing. I assure you the whole pharmacopia cannot furnish a medicine better adapted to her care. As you are to be the bearer it is proper you should know the whole ground. Attend to me. Mrs. Diaway is the widow of an eminent merchant who dying childless left her the whole of his large property. Our dissenters inherit from the English Puritans a taste for the retired and the comfortable. Their enjoyments are principally confined to the family circle and their pleasures to the gratifications of the table. Their daughters are therefore taught to become excellent housewives, they are nice semptresses and exquisite cooks, comprehending the arts of pickling, preserving, potting, collering, coddling, bottling, brewing and baking. They can furnish a dinner or a supper in good style, preserve economy among their domestics, keep their own attire neat and pride themselves on the purity and elegance of their husbands' linen but few of them know anything of intellectual pleasures.

"Such had been the education of Mrs. Diaway. During the lifetime of her husband her domestic accomplishments were daily brought into active exercise. His engagements as a merchant obliged him to keep an open table to which his supercargos, captains, masters, agents, as well as strangers were frequent guests. But his decease deprived her at once of her habitual employments. She retired into the recesses of the old family mansion, drank copiously of strong Bohea[17] to raise her spirits and soon sunk into lassitude and despondency. She made, however, many ineffectual attempts to regain her health and unfortunately by the recommendation of some silly gossips submitted herself to the direction of an imprudent empiric who passed himself upon the credulous Bostonians under the sounding title of the *High German Doctor*. By the injudicious application of tonics and frequent alteratives her whole system was so deranged that she became, I fear, a confirmed hyperchondriac.

"At length she was prevailed upon to consult me. I gave her my opinion, frankly and candidly recommended air and exercise and constant occupation. As to fresh air she declared it would be her death, she felt the least breath of wind blow through and through her and come out at her back. And how should she exercise who had not strength to walk? And as to occupation she found sufficient in marking the operation of her medicine and the progress of her disease. I found her dressing table covered with phials, pillboxes, galipots filled with stimulants and laxatives. The first object was to wean her from these pernicious drugs. How was this to be effected? Had I ordered ex cathedra the whole mass of tonics, sodorifics, cathartics, julups and cathotocans to be thrown out of the window I should probably have been thrown after them. Naught remained but to substitute in their place some harmless succedeneum and to convince her of its superior efficacy. I accordingly prepared these pills and the quack prescriptions were soon consigned to the vault. The application of these pills are attended with still greater advantages. When she suffers from repletion (for the good lady has at times an inordinate appetite) I then under pretence of regulating my prescriptions direct her to take a few silver pills after fasting several hours and not to take anything but cooling delutants for several hours more. In time her digestive powers acquire some tone which she kindly attributes to the wonderful efficacy of her favorite pills.

[17] A preferred tea of the day.

"So you see, young man, that if this is deception it is at its worst a *pia fraus*. But I perceive Scip is leading out the horses. Carry the pills as directed and mind your cue. You must be prepared to undergo a pretty rigid examination by the patient who has teazed me for months to communicate the ingredients of these pills. You can readily parry her inquiries by answering her in language she cannot understand and the best mode to effect this is to talk so as not to understand yourself. A word to the wise is sufficient. You may proceed."

I advanced toward the door.

"But hark ye, Underhill, should you be stopped by the wardens you have only to produce your pillboxes and tell them you live with me and are carrying medicine to a patient."

"Wardens, sir, who are they?"

"I had forgotten you are a stranger in town. The wardens are certain officers chosen by the town to keep order on the Sabbath. They perambulate the streets in their several wards and clear the streets of all loiterers or loungers, gentle and simple."

"How shall I know them, sir?"

"Their official insignia is a slender wand about half an inch in diameter and seven or eight feet in length. You must treat them with marked deference and respect for the greater part, I may say all of them, are gentlemen of the first respectability who for a puff of popularity condescend to humor the pranks of puritanism. Hasten to your business. Remember, however, that it is holy time and *festina lente,* hasten slowly."

I sallied into the streets. All the doors and the window shutters on the ground floors were carefully closed or all insight into the dwellings effectually interrupted by closed curtains or blinds of canvas painted with landscapes very *unlike* those of Claude Lorrain. The scene brought forcibly to my imagination the petrified city so beautifully described by the fair Zobieda in the Arabian Nights entertainments. All was solitude and silence excepting ever and anon the ear was struck with the sonorous hum of family worship, or now and then caught a sentence from "Matthew Henry's Exposition of the Bible,"

"Flavel's Token for Mourners," or the "More Last Words of Richard Baxter,"[18] or perhaps the fa, la, sol of some musical family uplifting a psalm to the tunes of Mear, Old Hundred, Bangor or St. Martins,[19] the counter of which was sung in the genuine chromatic style approved by the first amateurs, that is, it was sounded thro' the nostrils of an ancient dame whose nasal organ was obstructed by the collapse of a pair of horn spectacles kepit astride on the nose without the aid of temple bows. Whatever the Handel and Haydn Society may think their ancestors possessed a refined taste in sacred music.

As I passed down Marlboro' Street I could observe here and there in the windows of the second story a fair arm protruded beyond the half closed shutter or curtains with book in hand and frequently *guessed* I caught a glimpse of the bright eyes of the reader wandering from the sober page and shooting inquisitive glances through the crevice at the passing stranger.

I passed down Cornhill through Market Square by the foot of Cross Street and the flat conduit into Ann Street where my attention was forcibly attracted to the third story window of a lofty house[20] at the window of which two ruddy faced boys of the ages of twelve and fourteen, with hair tied behind with stiff paduasoy ribbon, combed

---

[18] Matthew Henry (1662–1714). His milestone five volume work, *Exposition of the Old and New Testament,* appeared between 1708 and 1710.

John Flavel (1630?–1691). Tyler could have been acquainted with Flavel's *A Token for Mourners; or, The Advice of Christ to a Distressed Mother.* The first Amercan edition was issued at Boston in 1729.

Richard Baxter (1615–1691), Presbyterian divine and prolific theological and devotional writer. His *The Dying Thoughts of the Reverend, Learned and Holy Mr. Richard Baxter* was printed in 1683.

[19] Mear, a common meter tune, is hymn no. 3 in *The Hymnal for Use in Congregational Churches* (Boston, 1897), Old Hundred is one of the most familiar tunes for a metrical psalm in the world and appears in almost every hymnal, often with the words, "Praise God from whom all blessings flow." St. Martin's is another well known 18th Century metrical psalm tune in common meter. Bangor refers to the antiphonary written at the monestary of Bangor, Ireland, between 680–691. It contains canticles, metrical hymns and versicles. Tyler must have been familiar with all these tunes since he had mentioned them earlier in his play, *The Contrast,* III, i.

[20] The author may have been describing his own boyhood home. The Tyler family home stood near the foot of Ann Street not far from the harbor. (Details on the house's location are in "TPT Memoir," p. 65.)

slickly over the forehead and cropped in a straight line from temple to temple, seemed mightily delighted as they leaned from the open sash and cast their eyes upwards.

I turned mine in the same direction and discovered in the attic story, at a luthern window, a black boy who was repeatedly thrusting his woolly pate and flat nose through the casement, twinkling his white eyeballs and exhibiting his pearly teeth through his black lips. As I approached I discovered that he had converted a string of pack thread into a fishing line by appending to it a crooked corking pin with which, by casting it over the eaves of the house and lowering it until it reached the window beneath, he angled for such fish as young masters could provide, who after hooking on sometimes a quarter of an apple or pear, at others a bunch of raisons or a fig feasted Pompey to his heart's delight.[21]

Just as I came opposite the house a sudden whim seized them and they fastened on an old shoe. How the young rogues twittered as Pompey drew up slowly his prize but when it peered over the eaves into his view the very idea of Pomp's disappointment tickled them so much that they brust out into a full peal of irrepressible laughter, which was soon echoed by Pompey who enjoyed the joke and joined cordially in the merriment.

Soon the commanding voice of the austere master of the mansion was distinctly heard from the foot of several flights of stairs, bawling, "Boys, boys, Pomp, Pomp, I say, what is that unseemly noise on the Lord's Day?"

"Nothing, massa, only old Tom de black cat, catch him mouse behind de meal chist."

"Ah, you rascal, I guess there are some other black cattle engaged

[21] This is reminiscent of one of Tyler's own youthful pranks while at Harvard. He had dropped a baited book on a line from his dormitory window trying to catch one of a litter of pigs in the college yard below. Tyler failed to notice the approach of the college president until he was close to the dangling hook. The line was pulled up with a sudden jerk in the hopes it would not be seen. Unfortunately, the hook caught the president's wig. As a result of this episode Tyler and his roommate, Christopher Gore (later Governor of Massachusetts and United States Senator), rusticated in Maine for several weeks on the order of the college authorities.

in that hubbub. Let me hear no more of it, and Pomp, Pomp, I say, when the old South clock strikes five do you and your young masters come down and say your catechism, and tell them I expect they will give a better answer to what are the reasons annexed to the fourth commandment, and Pomp, I expect you will be able to tell what is effectual calling better than you did last Sabbath."

"Yes, massa, me larns all about 'fectual bawling."

Silence now prevailed and I passed on.

CHAPTER X

Upon the pantry's luscious shelves,
Have you not seen those whisker'd elves,
The felon mice, with gormand nibble,
Amidst the huswives' dainties piddle,
Now sip the cream, now knaw the cheese,
Now rove from syllabub to pease,
Now climb the wheaten loaf on high,
Or burrow in an apple pie—
Still on the furtive sweets repleting
As if they thought life made for eating;
But e'er they close their stolen dinners,
Sly puss, the dread of all four leg'd sinners,
With tail erect and fiery eye,
Pounces among the nibbling fry:
No more on stolen sweets they riot,
Each seeks his hole and all is quiet.
So when the Magistrate Gramalkin,
On municipal grandeur stalking,
Comes purring forth with rampant paws
To mouse for crimes against the laws,
The idle, vicious and the base,
Those vermin of the human race,
Who still with petty crimes are piddling
And on the moral cheesecake nibbling,
All scamper from the warden's sight
And seek their safety in their flight.
                              Doggerel Romaunt.

A S I APPROACHED the drawbridge over the mill creek I observed approaching me a formidable personage, advancing with measured step his wand of office.[1] Imagine to yourself, reader, a handsome portly man, fair complexion, Roman nose, high forehead and bright hazel eye, his head covered by a full bottomed wig in the nicest buckle surmounted by a new beaver hat, in form midway between the smart dashing nivonai cock of the militia captain and the modest roll of the clerical brim. From his shoulders depended a flowing cloak of bright scarlet broadcloth confined beneath the chin with a silken loop, the graceful folds thrown open by the act of walking, discovered beneath a coat of silk alapine whose ample cuff occupied more than half the forearm, slit at the lower part and adorned by many a button and false buttonhole. The waistcoat of Genoa cut silk velvet, the pockets descending halfway down his thighs, and into the breast of which was carelessly tucked his many folded cravat of the finest cambric, besides the deep ruffle. Small cloaths of the same material as the coat and fastened at the knees by silver buckles richly chased, silk hose and shoes of the highest polish secured by buckles of the same pattern as those at the knees, and rounded at the toes so that the wits of the day asserted his shoemaker adapted a butter box for a last. One hand was covered by a high stiff topped kid glove from which dangled by one finger the unoccupied glove, while the other hand held the insignia of his office.[2] *This was the warden.*

As I approached him he accosted me with, "How come, young man, that I find you sauntering about the streets at this unseasonable hour?"

With pillbox in one hand and hat in the other, profoundly bowing, I offered my apology.

Warden. "Live with Dr. G., ahem, one would imagine the doctor

[1] Although Tyler already had a chapter numbered eight, he duplicated himself and called this also Chapter VIII. However, the transition from the previous chapter is obvious and he undoubtedly meant it to be Chapter X. Furthermore the chapter as it exists in Fragment 12 follows directly without a break after Chapter IX. In Fragment 7 this chapter commences with Ms. p. 105.

[2] Marginal notation: "thirty pages at this mark." This total was arrived at by running together Chapter IX and X in the rough draft Fragment 12.

prescribed to his patients weekly doses and selected the Sabbath for the day of distribution. You are, however, within the exceptions to the enacting clause, 'Excepting physicians, surgeons, nurses and others engaged in such like or similar acts of necessity or mercy; provided moreover and nevertheless that no persons engaged as aforesaid shall continue to appear in the streets, lanes or alleys of said town during the season aforesaid, for any longer space of time than shall be found absolutely necessary to carry into effect said acts of necessity and mercy, any pretext or pretence to the contrary notwithstanding.' Yes, yes, you are excused by the act. How long have you been with the doctor?"

Author. "Only a few days, sir."

Warden. "Let me caution you, young man, to avoid these errands as far as practicable on the Lord's Day unless especially commanded by your master (for servants must obey their masters, as it is written), to accomplish your business as soon as convenient, to return to your dwelling by the shortest route and to avoid too critical a survey of the contents of the windows and signposts as you pass the street. And permit me, young man, to give you a piece of advice which you may live to think upon with gratitude or regret you had not followed. A young man's success in life, I care not what his business, depends materially upon the reputation he may acquire for sobriety and industry in the opinion of the wise and prudent. Do not tarnish yours by the *appearance* of idleness and folly even though the reality may not exist. You may proceed."

I bowed, passed on, and soon arrived in sight of the stately mansion of Mrs. Diaway. Opening an iron gate and passing through an avenue flagged with white marble and lined with lime trees clipped by the gardener into many a grotesque shape I ascended a flight of stone steps where the front door with its enormous brass knocker presented itself. I knocked several times gently and receiving no answer I gave several violent raps which seemed to shake the old building by their echo. I soon heard from the chamber above a silver toilet bell ringing violently and a female voice screaming at the top of her breath:

"Betty, Betty, tell Zack to go to the front door. Some awkward booby is shattering my poor nerves to atoms." Zack quickly made his appearance to whom I told my business and was shewn into a spacious parlor and there left to my contemplations while it was communicated to his mistress. Having never inspected one of these rooms, even then the reliques of an elder time, I was attracted by the furniture. The windows were scooped out of the wall, each side of which the often folded shutters were concealed in recesses, the mahogany window seats were occupied by squab cushions and the whole shaded by the drapery of ample curtains of blue damask. A heavy broad slab of variegated marble, supported by gilt iron standards terminating in eagles' claws, occupied the space between the windows. High backed chairs with narrow seats worked with gold and silver tissue and encased in linen covers to preserve them from dust surrounded the room. An enormous desk surmounted by a bookcase with mirror panels stood on one side of the room, opposite to which my attention was drawn to a capacious semicircular fireplace, perhaps four feet deep and five feet between the jambs, the insides of which were faced with Dutch tiles so curiously matched and arranged as to display a scene from the Apocrapha to great advantage.

On the left were Bell and the Dragon with the idolatrous priests skulking off with the idol's supper, unconscious of the prints of their footsteps in the ashes. On the right were Susannah and the two libidinous elders. I could not but remark that if the Dutch limners had hit off the likenesses of the Jewish elders with tolerable accuracy the chastity of the fair Susannah was not exposed to any very violent temptation. From the middle of the ceiling, in the center of a circular department of stucco work, was depended a glass globe, the inside coated with quicksilver, and not far from either side two paper fly cages zigzaged into every shape angular and rotund.

But before I had half compleated my survey I was summoned to my patient. As I ascended the vast staircase, the walls of which were covered with smoak dried pictures, and arrived at the first landing place I met a man drooping under a weight of years with a striped cotton cap on his head and a pipe stuck into a side apperture in his frieze breeches. I stopped for him to pass down but he not moving I surveyed him more narrowly than the light admitted through the high curtained windows had first permitted and soon discovered it to be one of those ornamental figures once so common in houses fashionably furnished, painted on canvas attached to a board which humored the shape. On the next landing was an old woman of the same family with a birch broom in her hand apparently sweeping the stairs.

I well recollect an anecdote which may demonstrate the imposing appearance of the figures. A good woman from the country was passing from house to house peddling the produce of her spinning wheel. She walked into a spacious hall or entry occupied by one of those wooden domestics. There is a trait in the manners of the New England people which seems to have escaped the observation of the English traveller. They uniformly complain of our obtrusive inquisitiveness but do not appear to have discovered that a genuine, well-educated Yankee female can carry on both parts of a conversation in the presence and without the aid of the respondent, so as to obtain all the information requisite to the right understanding of the colloquy. This is one of those nice shades of character which are found among every people and which can never be detected by a foreigner but by a long residence among them.

The good woman described above entered the area and seeing, as she imagined, a decent matron busily engaged in knitting, accosted her with, "You don't want any cotton or linen yarn, do you?"

After a brief pause, "Then I think you say you don't want any, good morning, ma'am," and exit, bobbing a curtsey.

I was soon ushered into the sick room, the suffocating effluvia of which was readily accounted for by the listed doors guarded by sandbags at their bottoms, by the fire on the hearth, the curtained windows and the folding screen half encircling the fireplace. I found the good lady seated in a full cushioned easy chair enveloped in a silk wrapper lined with sable, her head covered with mob caps tier over tier and the whole surmounted by a cambric handkerchief which she occasionally shifted, as if to guard against the rude contact of some wandering zephyr. On her left side was a chamber stand on which were placed her silver bell, a gold repeater[3] of the size of a saucer, appended to an equipage whose jointed compartments were terminated by a large hook by which in former days it was suspended to her apron strings, and from the sides of which hung many a seal and key besides a curious little enameled receptacle for perfumes. Her porcelain saliva pot compleated the furniture on the left.

On her right stood a table covered with a damask cloth bearing the fragments of a plentiful meal. A china dish had contained a brace of partridges well stuffed and larded, the bones of one deposited in a silver bowl and the breast of the other gone, flanked by a castor on the silver labels of whose cruets soy, ketchup, chian and many other provocatives were visible; the remains of a dish of custard, some glasses of calves feet jelly, a mince pie, an apple tart, part of a rich plum pudding, some prunes, preserved pineapples and highly seasoned blancmange, all of which had been liberally partaken of.

As I entered she ordered the servant with a shiver to close the door quick behind me, then languidly pointing to a seat, said,

"I understand you come with a message from my physician, Dr. G. Are you studying with him?"

"Yes, madam."

"Very skillful man that; the only physician who ever understood my constitution. Entire loss of appetite, such a craving void here at the pit of my stomach and then such a palpitation of the heart—throb, throb, throb. Do sit nearer to me, doctor."

Blessings on her, the good old lady. She called me *doctor*. Only think after only a few days study to be dubbed *doctor*. Sounded even better than *Master Updike Underhill*. The College of Cambridge may have conferred higher honors but they never caused such a throb of delight with all their M. D.'s and L. L. D.'s.

"You have brought a supply of my favorite pills; any particular directions?"

[3] A watch or clock which can be made to strike the hour (or, sometimes quarter-hour) it has struck last.

"The doctor advises, madam, that after fasting six hours you take three golden pills, after which you may take a little white wine whey."

"Pray, doctor, can you tell me of what these wonderful pills are composed?"

"Now comes the examination," thought I, "but I am prepared for it."

"As I have been but a short time with the doctor, madam, I cannot be presumed to understand the profound mysteries of the profession." Well parried, thought I.

"I have sometimes suspected they contain mercury."[4]

"You may rest assured, madam, there is not a particle of mercury in their composition."

"Indeed! And pray, young gentleman, if you are so ignorant of what they are composed how can you be so positive they contain no mercury?"

"Blisters on my tongue! He that sets his wits against a woman's, sick or well, must learn something more than is taught at college.

"Positive, madam? O no, not really positive, but I think I know the principal ingredient which is never combined with mercury."

"Well, what is that called?"

"I believe, madam, the Edinburg Dispensatory calls it the *Becculum vitia*."[5]

"French, I suppose, doctor. Be so good as to English it."

"Cannot say, madam, am not particularly conversant with the French tongue."

"This won't do, doctor. You must know and I insist upon your telling me or I shall not sleep a wink tonight."

"Since you insist upon it, madam, I believe it is called the *Magnificum Arcanum,* administered with so much success by the great and

---

[4] The use of mercury by New England physicians was widespread from about the first quarter of the eighteenth century onward. Its popularity, however, depended upon the ability of the medical profession to conceal its use from the public due to the considerable public prejudice against it. See Thacher, I, 27–8.

[5] Updike was following Dr. Gardiner's instructions. "Becculum vitia" is pig latin.

learned Sydenham to the most delicate females in Greenwich Hospital."[6]

"Surely, doctor, you must be mistakened in the hospital. Captain Swearagain, who sailed so long in my husband's employ, told me Greenwich Hospital contained only superannuated seamen. I am apprehensive you are imposing upon me, young man."

"By no means, madam. Greenwich did I say? I certainly meant— I mean—."[7]

But I was unexpectedly relieved from this dilemma by the entrance of a beautiful girl, introduced to me as Miss Charlotte Love, niece of the old lady.

It may be well for those readers who take an interest in my humble adventures to be made acquainted with this young lady. Miss Charlotte Love, a combination of all that is divine and dulcet in the female character, was then in her sixteenth year. I will attempt to give a sketch of her person and dress, for he who knows these knows half the female character; the third part consists entirely in the management and display of these, and the fourth embraces her temper, disposition, intellectual acquirements and virtues and above all that retiring modesty which sheds a bewitching luster over them. These will be better known by a development of her conduct than by any description, being as Burke says of taste, "too valuable to bear the chains of a definition."

This young lady was of the exact height and size of the Venus de Medicis though undoubtedly much handsomer, with an oval face rather inclining to the rotund, a fair complexion, bright blue eyes, Grecian nose, coral lips admirably calculated to display two even rows

---

[6] A "magnificum arcanum" would have been a great secret, mystery or remedy. Thomas Sydenham (1624–1689), after a distinguished military career, entered the practice of medicine, specializing in the study of epidemic diseases. He was a friend of John Locke.

Greenwich Hospital for naval pensioners was designed by Christopher Wren and on its completion was the largest twin-domed baroque edifice in England. It could accommodate 2,700 patients. Opened in 1705, it was closed in 1873 and the building became the home of the Royal Naval College.

[7] Marginal notation: "50 Pages."

of pearly teeth, a cloven chin and cheeks flushed with roses which seemed as if she had freshly returned from a game of romps with her cousin Hebe. This beautiful countenance was adorned by hair of light auburn whose ringlets fell luxuriantly down her shoulders or wantoned carelessly over her polished brow. On the back part of her head was pinned a cap of blue satin resembling in form the pileus or Roman cap of liberty, covered with a white silk netting, while a tight vest with long sleeves and short skirts, called a Shepherdee, displayed the symmetry of her form to exquisite advantage. A skirt of Mersaeles quilted with double rows of fringes at the bottom and white satin shoes clasped with French paste buckles compleated the lovely contour.

"Pray, doctor," continued the old lady, "are not disorders of the heart considered by the faculty as always in the end proving fatal?"

"Galen and Hippocrates among the ancients and Garth and Akenside[8] among the moderns, madam, seem to be of that opinion. They however think that no deleterious consequences are to be apprehended for patients in advanced life but admit they are often very injurious to adult people."

"I have often been apprehensive, doctor, that my niece would take some of my disorders. She has at times alarming symptoms. Do observe how her cheeks are flushed. Is not the palpitation of the heart catching, doctor?"

"If I should judge, madam, from my own experience I should fear it is."

"You alarm me, dear sir. When were you seized with a palpitation?"

"I believe it was just as your lovely niece first entered the room."

Reader, do you believe in eye shot wounds? I do. Did you ever

[8] Sir Samuel Garth (1661–1719), physician and poet. A pioneer in urging the establishment of dispensaries or out-patient clinics for the poor. His work was praised by Alexander Pope.

Mark Akenside (1721–1770), poet and physician. His great didactic poem, "Pleasures of Imagination," was published in 1744 on the urging of Pope. Although he had a large medical practice he shocked some of his contemporaries by his roughness and cruelty to the poor.

feel, not see, that some person was looking hard at you? If you are skeptical on this point pray hand the book to that lovely girl, your sister or cousin, or some one dearer than either. But if you think with me and Lord Verulam[9] that one experimental proof is worth a hundred plausible theories you will credit me when I say that with my eyes fixed on the old lady's gold repeater and not dreaming of any harm or hostility, I received a blow on the corner of my left eye which made me start and almost with Phutatorius ejaculate, "Zounds!"

I turned my face and saw two bright blue eyes ambushed behind some of the most enchanting ringlets in the world shooting such disdainful glances that I cowered before them. Aye, these same sparklers spoke too, in language not to be misapprehended.

"Sir, I understand you. But you are mistaken if you imagine that playing on the credulity of my aunt is the way to gain favor with her niece."

She soon after rose, observing, "You will excuse me, my dear aunt. I believe it is time for me to attend to catachising the servants."

Then, with rather a stately step, her lips adjusted to an enchanting pout, she dipped a disdainful curtsey as she passed me and retired. I soon found the suffocating air of the room became intolerable and I took my leave. Thus ended my first clinical visit. I have been more particular in recording it for the benefit of young students of the medical school, who if they understand the dissection of the human heart, not after the manner of Hunter[10] but of Addison may possibly make some discoveries in this science which may prove profitable.

As I again approached the draw bridge[11] on my return home I perceived at a distance the same warden coming toward me and at the same time heard from the north the rattling of a chariot's wheels. Conscious that I had grossly neglected his advice and ashamed to meet him I escaped into an arched way which led to Stoddard's wharf and

[9] Francis Bacon was raised to the peerage as Baron Verulam on July 12, 1618.

[10] Dr. John Hunter (1728–1793), a noted physician, surgeon and anatomist married to the poetess Anne Home Hunter.

[11] There was a swing bridge near Boston harbor next to the old triangular warehouse.

fairly ensconced myself between two empty rum puncheons and a sugar hogshead, through the apertures of which I could see and hear what passed.

The warden and chariot approached each other. Aye, thought I, here comes one of those overgrown flies which buzz through the cobwebs of the law. We shall see whether Mr. Warden will lecture him. Persons in several windows within sight, if one might judge from their extended necks and listening attitudes, seemed to have similar impressions.

The carriage and warden met directly opposite to where I found a lurking place. The check string was pulled, the horses stopped, the window glass was let down and discovered a short plump personage dressed in black. His head was adorned with a bobwig from which depended a huge black silk bag, the ribbon roses of which appeared conspiciously under his ears. Several courteous salutations were exchanged.

Warden. "I hope I have the pleasure of seeing your Excellency in usual health."

Sir Francis.[12] "Very well, I thank you; hope Mrs. T. and your family are so. I went this morning to the King's Chapple, heard an excellent sermon from T., but there is something so excessively ponderous in your Sunday air immediately after service I rode over to my little box at Jamaica Plains, sent to Logan and we drank His Majesty's health in a fine bumper of claret. On my return to town I ordered Frank to drive to Winnesimmet and am now returning to the Province House.[13] Astonishing how still your streets are, have not met a single

[12] Sir Francis Bernard (1712–1779). Following a couple of years as Colonial governor of New Jersey he was commissioned in the same position for Massachusetts in January 1760. His final years as governor were turbulent ones. Although an able man, of liberal temperament and awake to the plight of the colonies, the problems he faced were beyond his power to solve. He regarded the Stamp Act as inexpedient but as the representative of the home government was required to carry out its policies. He became most unpopular and following the publication of some of his letters to officials in England he was recalled in 1769.

[13] The governor's mansion, Province House, stood near the junction of Cornhill and Marlborough streets close to their intersection with Milk Street.

soul. When I was a resident Fellow at Oxford we imagined we preserved tolerable order on the Sabbath but not all our beadles and proctors ever kept the populous in such subjection. It is truly admirable! Burnet[14] taught me to expect something of the sort but this exceeds all anticipation."

Warden. "Our attention to order, especially on the Sabbath, I know has been branded as pharisaical but it is obviously attended with great advantages."

Sir Francis. "Will you permit me to say a word to you in confidence?"

Warden. "Most happy to attend to any communication from your Excellency."

Sir Francis. "The treasurer informs me that he has received an intimation which is also confirmed by the secretary that Otis and Sam Adams and others of the Junto are preparing a declaration of the chartered rights of the Colony which they mean to tack on as a rider to the bill making the appropriation for the payment of my salary and that of the other provincial servants of His Majesty. Do you know anything of it?"[15]

Warden. "Since I have had a seat at the Board I know very little of what is passing in the Lower House."

Sir Francis. "I do not blame your friends for seeking popularity although it is to be deplored that it cannot be obtained but at the expense of their loyalty. Every man desires popularity. When I first landed in this country it was with a fixed determination to render myself as popular as your old charter Governors Winthrop and Leverett.[16] It is for the interest of the Colonies that there should be a good understanding between us. His Majesty's colonial governors have it in their power by their communications with ministers to

[14] Gov. Bernard may have been referring to either Thomas Burnet, D.D. (*d.* 1750), rector of New College, Oxford, or William Burnet (1688–1729), colonial governor of New York and New Jersey until he was appointed governor of Massachusetts in 1728.

[15] Marginal notation: "58 Pages."

[16] John Leverett (1616–1679), served as governor from 1673–1679. John Winthrop (1587–1649), was the Massachusetts Bay Colony's first governor.

meliorate commercial restrictions and to do many other beneficial acts to the Colony. Occasion for dispute between them should not be sought. Besides, your friends should consider that a provincial governor is delicately circumstanced. Hillsborough[17] watches them with a jealous eye and thinks no popularity can be obtained by them but through the sacrifice of the royal prerogative. I stand well with him at present, do not let us by futile altercations wake the sleeping lion."

Warden. "The Bay Colonists have inherited from their ancestors a strong attachment to their chartered rights and should not be blamed for shewing that attachment on every suitable occasion. Indeed they go further. They think themselves *entitled* to all the privileges of Englishmen for they cannot conceive how their crossing the Atlantic, still paying a voluntary allegiance to the same sovereign, can have divested them of the rights of Magna Charta. I am convinced if put to the test they would resist unto blood."

Sir Francis. "Some centuries hence perhaps."

Warden. "That may depend on the pressure of commercial restrictions."

Sir Francis. "You cannot seriously imagine that the Colonists would dare brave the power of the mother country? The idea is too preposterous. If the people of the several provinces are jealous of the royal prerogative they are more jealous of each other—they can never be brought to unite in opposition to the Crown. And if they could, with your sparse population what stand could they make against the veteran troops of England? The idea of opposition above a few paper resolves is too preposterous! You will have the goodness to mention my suggestions in the proper place?"

Warden. "Certainly."

His Excellency's chariot moved on while the warden with admirable gravity, waving his wand as if ordering a barrier to be opened, exclaimed loud enough to be heard from the adjacent windows:

[17] Wills Hill, Earl of Hillsborough (1718–1793). In 1768 he was appointed secretary of state for the colonies, obtaining most of his information from Sir Francis Bernard. He was strongly opposed to any concessions to the American colonies.

"Well, Sir Francis, since your excuse seems reasonable I shall permit you to pass but hope no repetition of such conduct."

Bostonians, such were the arts by which your ancestors governed the populace and obtained for the town the name and praise of being the most orderly, best regulated and freest from tumult, riot and petty crimes of any town in the Colonies.

You will perhaps smile at the duplicity of the magistrate and the cullibility of those who could be governed by it. In this day of greater light I am sensible you manage matters much better. When there is a vacancy in a city office several candidates are brought forward. Their friends, not content with exhibiting the qualifications of their respective favorites to the best advantage, endeavor to give him a *comparative* preference by belittling his opponents by all kinds of vituperation so that the successful candidate is on his induction into office (in the opinion of a respectable minority) sure to be the most unsuitable person who could possibly have been elected. Nor does the opposition stop here. The fever of election does not suddenly subside, those in the opposition think themselves pledged to watch for his haltings to magnify every little aberration from the strict line of duty and on all occasions, before all kinds of people, to hold him up to ridicule and contempt. It is true the wise and discerning know how justly to estimate all this vituperation. They know that it is the office not the incumbent that is to be respected. But do the base part of society on whom such officer's authority is made to bear argue thus wisely? Your present municipal officers, I doubt not, are as well qualified and as upright as those of your ancestors but I much doubt whether your whole board of aldermen, with your excellent mayor at their head, could carry that weight of official authority as did the warden I have described. The opulent and discerning honored him because they knew that in supporting him they protected their own property and enjoyments. Wheresoever the lower orders of society heard him spoken of by their superiors it was in terms of the most profound respect. His discernment, inflexible justice, his power and personal respectability were everywhere magnified. Vice, folly and idleness fled before him and the petty depredator trembled in his lurking place and was often frightened from crime by the dread of that eye which he was taught to believe could pierce into every recess. Your present magistrates have probably more authority than the municipal officers of your ancestors but it is *naked authority* divested from the causes above mentioned of the engrossing charm of universal respect.

How I wish you could have seen this venerable officer. Sirs, there was irresistable authority in the very creak of his shoe leather! Pardon the garrulity of an old man who loves to prattle of the sunny days of his childhood and who, like Goodman Dogberry, the municipal officer of Messina, can find in my heart

"To bestow all my tediousness upon your worships."[18]

But to return: when, in Yankee phrase, the coast was clear I stole from my retreat and hastened home.

An anecdote which has excited much merriment amongst the thoughtless may serve to illustrate the state of public feeling on the due observance of the Sabbath in those days.

A member of the general court, while residing in Boston during the winter sessions, observed the admirable order and quiet preserved there on the Sabbath and pretended to wish for that reason to extend the appointment of wardens, which depended on a bylaw of the town, to all parts of the Commonwealth, and for this purpose he introduced a bill into the House. The knowing ones, however, suspected that the object of the act was the correction of an abuse of the Sabbath in the vicinity of Boston.

Upon the seashore a few miles from town was a delightfully sequestered spot open to the sea prospects and breezes. Here several scattered farm houses afforded shelter to a few invalids who repaired thither for the benefit of sea bathing and to mitigate the oppressive heat of the dog days. Here they were supplied with fresh butter, strawberries and cream in their season and syllabub warm from the cow at all times. But where the sick resort for quiet and health the gay

---

[18] *Much Ado About Nothing*, III, v, 22–5.

and the idle will soon repair for pleasure and amusement.

Accordingly, this sweet sequestered spot soon became a place of fashionable resort *especially on the Sabbath* and received from its gay visitors the Asiatic name of Tinian. Now it so happened (as the story book says) that the halfway house from Boston to Tinian was an inn kept by a man of great influence in his town and who made vast gains from the passing and repassing of travelers. It was hoped by the wise legislators that the appointment of wardens in all the towns would put an effectual stop to this unseemly breach of the Sabbath. The act was accordingly passed and every town directed at their annual March meeting to appoint two wardens whose duty it should be to stop all unnecessary travelling on the Lord's Day. Many towns complied with the act, not so the town in which the halfway house was situated. By the influence of the landlord, then one of the selectmen, no wardens were elected.

At the next session of the legislature a resolve passed requesting the King's Attorney to file ex officio information against all towns who neglected to comply with the act but this officer upon examining the act assured the House such prosecution would be altogether nugatory as the act omitted to assign any penalty to the breach of it. The act was now amended and a penalty of five hundred pounds lawful money was inflicted on any towns neglecting to elect wardens. The selectmen of the refractory town were now put to their trumps. The wardens were therefore elected, their names published among other town officers in the newspapers, which was received as the amend honorable to the general court. Still the Sunday excursions did not cease, many a robust invalid slipped out of town on the Sabbath morning under pretense of taking an airing and did not return until sunset.

At length it was discovered that of the two wardens elected by the refractory town *one was stone blind* and the other had been *bed ridden for fourteen years.* The truth is that the men who *then* governed in the town and gave currency to its habits and opinions were among the last of the race of Puritans who founded it while the rising generation was beginning to evince that love of pleasure and impatience of wholesome discipline which have since obliterated the sober footsteps of its pious forefathers, charged them with hypocrisy and bigotry[19] and exposed them to unmerited ridicule and contempt.

I observed that these were the last of the good old Puritans who *governed* the town but there are still remaining many private families who follow their laudable practices. Who keep their children and domestics within doors on the Sabbath, teach the assemblies catechism, read portions of holy scriptures or expositions of them by the learned and devout and lift the voice of praise and pour forth the fervent prayer in family worship.

Indeed, the present orderly appearance of the city on the Lord's Day may be traced to the sober habits of their progenitors. The general attendance on public worship, the chastened deportment of the citizens passing to and from church and the quiet of the streets, like the shrivel'd coat, the vapid taste and the faded color of the preserved pippin remind us strongly of the plump rind, ruddy tints and the rich flavor of the autumnal fruit.

When I reached my lodgings the sun was fast declining and shot its departing rays upwards, sporting with golden effulgence on the attic panes and imparting a more brilliant hue to the gilded vane or weathercock.

I could now observe many an eye watching from a half open turret door the sinking luminary. At length it disappeared and the streets soon began to fill with gay groups hastening to the mall to enjoy the evening breezes. But these embraced but a small section of the inhabitants. The greater part still preserved that respect for the day enforced by its solemn services.

A wide difference of opinion prevailed as to the hour when the Sabbath commenced. Some held it to be on the going down of the sun the preceding Saturday (which was the statutable time), others were for begining the holy time at twelve o'clock on Saturday night and consequently extending it till twelve on Sabbath night, and some unresolved as to the precise meaning of the text,

---

[19] Marginal notation: "68 pages to this mark."

"And the evening and the morning of the first day,"
wisely resolved to keep them both.

Thus terminated my first Sabbath in Boston. (End of this chapter.)[20]

[20] This closing phrase is found only in Fragment 12 together with the notation: "seventy pages."

CHAPTER XI

Was *Milton* blind, who pierced the gloom profound
Of lowest Hades—thro' seven-fold night
Of shade with shade compact; saw the arch fiend
From murky caves and fathomless abyss
Collect in close divan his fierce compeers:
Or with the mental eye, thro' awful clouds
And darkness thick, unveiled the throne of *Him*
Whose vengeful thunder smote the rebel fiend?
Was *Saunderson?*[1] who to the seeing crowd
Of wondering pupils taught (sightless himself)
The wonderous structure of the human eye.

                        Author's Manuscript Poems.

IN THE COURSE of a few weeks I extended my acquaintance in town and was upon a familiar footing with a worthy family rendered peculiarly interesting by the blindness of the heir and hope of his parents.[2] It was with unfeigned pleasure that I was summoned to attend an operation to be performed upon the eyes of this youth, an account of which may not be unacceptable to the lovers of natural research.

[1] Nicholas Saunderson (or Sanderson) (1682–1739), mathematician. Although he lost his sight at the age of 12 months from smallpox, he became a proficient lecturer of mathematics and accomplished flutist. A disciple of Newton, Saunderson was created a Doctor of Laws by George III.

[2] This chapter was lifted by Tyler primarily from material he had employed previously in *The Algerine Captive* (Chapters IX, X and XI) but only after making significant and extensive improvements in vocabulary and phraseology. In Fragment 7 this section starts with Ms. p. 124. It is also rough draft Fragment 14.

This young man was twenty-two years of age, of a sweet disposition, amiable manners and oppulent connexions. He was born stone blind; his blindness, however, in some measure compensated by the attention of his friends and the encreased power of his other organs of perception. His sisters enriched his mind by reading to him in succession some hours every day from the best authors. His sense of feeling was astonishingly delicate and his hearing not less acute. His senses of taste and smelling were not so remarkable. After the customary salutation of shaking hands with a stranger he would know a person by a touch of the same hand, several years after, though absent in the meantime.

He could read a book or newspaper newly printed tolerably well by tracing with the tip of his finger the indents of the types,[3] having acquired a knowledge of the alphabet early from the prominent letters on the gingerbread alphabets of the baker. He was master of music and had contrived a board, perforated with many gimblet holes, and with the assistance of a little bag of wooden pegs shaped at top according to his directions, he could prick almost any tune upon its being sung to him. When in a large company who sat silent he could tell how many persons were present by noting with his ear their different manner of breathing. By the rarity or density of the air not perceivable by those in company he could distinguish high ground from low and by the motion of the summer's breeze, too small to move the lightest leaf, he would pronounce whether he was in a wood or open country.

He was an unfeigned believer in the salutary truths of Christianity; he had imbibed its benevolent spirit. When he spoke of religion his language was, "Love to God and good will to man." He was no zealot but when he talked of the wonders of creation and redeeming love he was animated with a glow of enthusiasm.

"You observed the other day as we were walking on this plain, my friend" (addressing himself to me, as I was intimate in the family),

---

[3] In this context it is interesting to note that Louis Braille (1809–1852) had not yet worked out his six dot code system of embossed letters for the blind. His efforts were first published in 1829.

"that you knew a certain person by his gait when at so great a distance that you could not discern his features. From this you took occasion to observe that you saw the master hand of the Creator in the obvious difference there is between man and man: not only the grosser difference between the Indian, the African, the Esquimeaux and the white man but that which distinguishes and defines accurately men of the same nation and even children of the same parents. You observed that as all the children of the great family of the earth were compounded of similar members, features, and lineaments how wonderfully it displayed the skill of the Almighty Artist to model such an infinite number of beings and distinctly diversify them from the same materials. You added that the instance you noticed gave fresh occasion for admiration, for you were convinced that even if all men had been formed of so near resemblance as not to be discerned from each other when at rest, yet, when in motion from their gait, air and manner, they might readily be distinguished. While you spoke I could perceive you pittied me as being blind to a wonderful effect of creative power. I too in my turn could triumph. Blind as I am I have discovered a still minuter but as certain a distinction between the children of men which has escaped the touch of your eyes. Bring me five men, perfect strangers to me; pair [*i.e. pare*] the nails of their fingers so as to be even with the fingers' ends. Let me touch the tip of my finger the nails thus prepared, tell me each person's name as he passes in contact before me, bring the same persons to me one month afterward with their nails paired [*pared*] in the same manner and I will call every one by his right name. For be assured, my friend, that *Great Artist* who hath denied to me the thing called sight hath opened the eyes of my mind to know that there is not a greater difference between the African and the European, than what I could discover between the finger nails of all the men of this world."

This experiment he often tried with uniform success. It was amusing in a gayer hour to hear him argue the superiority of the touch to the sight.

"Certainly," said he, "the feeling is a nobler sense than that you call sight. I infer it from the care nature has taken of the former and her disregard of the latter. The eyes are comparatively poor puny weak organs. A small blow, a mote or a straw may reduce those who see with them to a situation as pitiable as mine, while feeling is diffused over the whole body. Cut off my arm and a sense of feeling remains, completely dismember me and while I live I possess it. It is coexistent with life itself.

"The senses of smelling and taste are but modifications of this noble sense, distinguished by the inaccuracy of men by other names. The flavor of the most delicious morsel is felt by the tongue and when we smell the aromatic it is the effluvia of the rose which comes in contact with the olfactory nerves. You that enjoy sight inadvertently confess its inferiority. My brother the other day honing his penknife passed it over his thumb nail to discover if the edge was smooth. I heard him and inquired why he did not touch it with his eyes as he did other objects. He confessed that he could not discover the gaps by sight.

"Here the superiority of the most accurate seat of feeling was manifest. To conclude," he would archly add, "in marriage, the most important concern in life, how many miserable of both sexes are left to deplore in tears their dependence on this treacherous thing called sight.[4] From this damage I am happily secured," continued he, smiling and pressing the hand of his cousin who sat beside him, a beautiful blooming young woman of eighteen who had been bred with him from childhood and whose affection for him was such that she was willing, notwithstanding his blindness, to take him as partner for life. They expected shortly to be married.

Notwithstanding his accuracy and veracity upon subjects he could comprehend there were many on which he was miserably confused. He called sight the touch of the eyes. He had no adequate idea of colors. White he supposed was like the feeling of down and scarlet he resembled to the sound of martial music. By passing his hand over the porcelain, earthen or plaster of Paris images he could easily conceive

---

[4] Tyler wrote several poems on the drawbacks of picking a wife merely from external appearances. See *Tyler Verse*, pp. 48–9, 67, 79–81, 158–64.

that they represented the human form or that of animals, but he could have no idea of pictures. I presented to him a large portrait of his grandfather with oil colors on canvas; told him whose resemblance it was. He passed his hand over the smooth surface and mused. He repeated this, exclaimed, "It is wonderful!" looked melancholy but never asked for the picture again.

Upon this interesting young man my preceptor operated successfully. I was present through the whole process although few were admitted. Upon the introduction of the couching instrument and the removal of the film from the retina he appeared confused. When the operation was completed and he was permitted to look around him he became violently agitated. The irritability of the ophthalmic muscles faintly expressed the perturbation of his mind. After two-and-twenty years of total darkness to be thus awakened to a new world of sensation and light, to have such a flood of day poured on his benighted eyeballs overwhelmed him: the infant sight was too weak for the shock and he fainted. The doctor immediately intercepted the light with the proper bandages and by the application of volatiles he revived.

The next day the dressings were removed. He had fortified his mind and was more calm. At first he seemed to have lost more than he had gained by being restored to vision. When blind he could walk tolerably well in places familiar to him; from sight he collected no ideas of distance. Green was a color particularly agreeable to the newborn sight: being led to a window he was charmed with a tree in full verdure and extended his arms to touch it though at ten rods distance. To distinguish objects within reach he would close his eyes, feel for them with his hand and then look earnestly at them.

According to a preconcerted plan, the third day his bandages were removed in the presence of his parents, sisters and friends, and of the lovely amiable girl to whom he was shortly to be married. By his request a profound silence was to be observed while he endeavored to discover the person of her who was the dearest object of his affections. It was an interesting scene, not a finger moved or a breath aspirated.

The bandages were removed and when he had recovered from the confusion occasioned by the instant effusion of light he passed his eye hastily over the whole group. His sensations were novel and interesting. It was a moment of importance for aught he knew he might find the bosom partner of his future life, the twin soul of his affection, in the fat scullion girl of his father's kitchen or in the person of the toothless, palsied, decrepit nurse who held the basin of gruel at his elbow.

In passing his eyes a second time over the circle his attention was arrested by his beloved cousin. The agitation of her lovely features and the evanescent blush on her cheek would at once have betrayed her to a more experienced eye. He passed his eye to the next person and immediately returned it to her. It was a moment big with expectation: many a finger was raised to the lips of the spectators and many a look expressive of the silence she should preserve was cast towards her. But the conflict was too violent for her delicate frame. He looked more intensely, she burst into tears and spoke. At the well known voice he closed his eyes, rushed towards her and clasped her in his arms. I envied them their feelings but I thought then, and do now, that the sensations of my preceptor, the skillful humane operator were more enviable. The man who could restore light and usefulness to the darling of his friend and scatter light in the paths of an amiable young pair must have known a joy never surpassed, except, with reverence be it spoken, by the satisfaction of our benevolent Savior when, by his miraculous power he opened the eyes of the actually blind and made the dumb to sing and the lame and impotent leap for joy.[5]

Mentioning this subject many years afterwards to the celebrated Dr. Henry Moyes[6] who delivered, although blind, a lecture upon

[5] At this point ended *The Algerine Captive* Chative IX. Chapter X starts with the following paragraph.

[6] Tyler was personally acquainted with Dr. Moyes who had come to Boston and boarded with Tyler's future in-laws, the Palmers. Mrs. Tyler said her husband "was very much interested in his [*Dr. Moyes'*] wonderful operations and used to assist him at his Public lectures." See "MPT Memoir," pp. 43–7 and 107; and *GTB*, pp. 83 and 95–7.

A similar operation on the eyes of a blind person had been carried out a few years optics and delineated the properties of light and shade to the Bostonians in the year *1785,* he exhibited a more astonishing illustration of the power of the touch. A highly polished plane of steel was presented to him with the stroke of an etching tool so minutely engraved upon it as not to be visible to the naked eye and only discoverable with a powerful magnifying glass. With his fingers he discovered the extent and measured the length of the line.

This gentleman lost his sight at three years of age. He informed me that being overturned in a stage coach one dark rainy evening in England when the carriage and four horses were thrown into a ditch, the passengers and driver with two eyes apiece were obliged to apply to him who had none for assistance in extricating the horses.

"As for me," said he, "after I had recovered from the astonishment of the fall and discovered that I had escaped unhurt, I was quite at home in the dark ditch. The inversion of things was amusing. I, who was obliged to be led like a child in the glaring sun, was now directing eight persons to pull here and haul there with all the dexterity and activity of a man-of-war's boatswain."[7]

I passed my time very pleasantly with my preceptor although I could not help being astonished that a man of his acknowledged learning should not sometimes quote Greek. Of my acquirements in that language I was still proud. I attributed the indifference with which it was received in the town where I kept school to the rusticity and ignorance of the people. As I now moved in the circles of polished life I venturned sometimes when the young ladies had such monstruous colds that they could not be prevailed on by the most earnest solicitations of the company to sing, and when it had been frequently observed that it was Quaker-meeting, to sprout a little Greek. It is true they did not interrupt me with

"Fire upon the mountains, run, boys, run!"

earlier by Jacques Daniel (1696–1752), the originator of the modern treatment of cataracts by the excision of the lens.

[7] This marked the end of *The Algerine Captive* Chapter X with Chapter XI commencing immediately after.

but the most sonorous lines of the divine blind bard were received with the cold approbation of politeness. One young lady alone seemed pleased. She would frequently ask me to repeat those lines of *Wabash* poetry. Once, in that sublime passage in the Odyssey of the hero Ulysses hanging fifty young maidens with his own hands, I heard the term *pedant* pronounced with preculiar emphasis by a beau, at my back.

If I had taken the hint and passed my Greek upon my companions for Indian they would have heard me with rapture. I have since known that worthy, indefatigable missionary to the Indians, the Rev. Mr. K., the modern Elliot, entertain the same company for whole evenings with speeches in the aboriginal languages of America as intelligible to them as was my insulted Greek.[8]

I was so pleased with the lady who approved the Greek heroics that I determined to make my first essay in metre in an ode addressed to her by name. I accordingly mustered all the high sounding epithets of the immortal Grecian bard and scattered them with profusion through my ode. I praised her golden locks and assimulated her to the ox-eyed Juno, sent her a correct copy and distributed a number of others among her friends. I afterwards found that what I intended as the sublimest panegyric was received as cutting insult. The golden tresses and the ox-eyed epithet, the most favorite passages in my poem, were very unfortunate as the young lady was remarkable for very prominent eyes which resembled what in horses are called wall-eyes and her hair was what is vulgarly called carrotty. Its unfashionable color she had long endeavored in vain to conceal by the daily use of a lead comb.

[8] Most likely Samuel Kirkland (1741–1808), missionary to the Oneida Indians for more than 40 years. The founder of Hamilton College as an academy for Indian youths, he was a tireless worker for better relations between the colonists and the Indians.

CHAPTER XII

"FIRST THEATRICAL REPRESENTATION
IN BOSTON"

> Come, Thalia, with thy comic smiles,
> Thy quirps and cranks and wanton wiles,
> And with thee bring thy doleful sister
> And let the tearful maid, now twist her
> Sad tragic phiz and mouth so pretty
> Into all shapes to move our pity;
> And let her bring her cup and dagger
> And start and weep and die or stagger
> Till she make hearts as hard as pumpkins,
> Grow soft as pates of city bumpkins.
> She comes, I know her by her moaning,
> Her deep drawn sighs and heavy groaning,
> Her ah's and oh's! her starts and throbs,
> Her buskined toes and tearful sobs;
> Yet fly, O fly, this Yanky land
> Where Puritans note high command.
> Hence, bear away thy tragic groan,
> They love no sadness but their own;
> This Yankee town can surely be
> No place, Melpomene, for thee.
> I guess if you yourself don't hide well
> You'll act a moving part in bridewell.[1]
>
> The Doggerel Romaunt
> *By the Author.*

I NOW BEGAN to extend my acquaintance among the young people, introduced by a classmate who was also a medical student.[2] I became member of a club consisting of merchants' and lawyers' clerks, with some fellow students in physic. Here I became acquainted

[1] Bridewell was once a notorious prison in a section of London by the same name.

[2] Tyler entitled this chapter "First Theatrical Presentation in Boston" but gave it no number. In the final draft (Fragment 7) as copied by his wife it comes immediately after Chapter XI and so is here logically considered to be Chapter XII. The section commences with Ms. p. 133.

with Charles Brightly, a young gentleman of liberal education, handsome in his person, captivating in his address and ever entertaining in
his conversation: he was what the world calls a genius. He could
achieve everything he attempted with wonderful facility, comprehended the whole contents of a book by merely skimming the title
page, was foremost in all parties of pleasure, a great favorite with the
young ladies, and even many of the old ones prognosticated he would
make a steady man when his wild oats were sown. His talents seemed
so various that in Dryden's language,

> "He seemed to be,
> Not one—but all mankind's epitome."[3]

The dark side of his portrait exhibits him as devoid of the common
principles of economy and to this, with a certain pliability of disposition which could never decline any proposal either for fatigue or
pleasure, may be attributed that continued state of vexation and embarrassment in which he worried through life. To me he seemed a
superior being. As a new acquaintance he attached himself particularly
to me and appeared sedulous to add to my gratification by every
means in his power.

By him I was informed under the strongest injunctions of secrecy
that a play in which he was to perform a principal part was to be acted
privately. Now there were no entertainments public or private which
were received with such abhorrence by the Puritans as stage plays, and
indeed with reason. The players during the licentious reign of Charles
the Second were the peculiar protegees of his libidinous court. The
plays then enacted cannot now be read in any decent family. Jeremiah
Collier's Philippic against them was generally read and highly approved.[4] In addition to the general objections to these licentious

---

[3] This quotation is from John Dryden's "Absalom and Achitophel," Part I, ll. 545–
6.

[4] Jeremy Collier (1650–1726), leveled his attacks on the corruptions of the stage in
the *Short View of the Immorality and Profaneness of the English Stage* in 1697–8. Partly
because the public sentiment was with him the publication was a marvelous success.
Rebuttals came from William Congreve, Sir John Vanbrugh, John Dennis, James
Drake, and others.

representations of libidinous manners of that day the Puritans were often introduced in the persona of the drama, and their piety, their religious conversation, their precise habits and what was justly held as a greater abomination—the doctrines of their sect—held up to public scorn and ridicule. Can we wonder then that the early colonists, having recently sheltered themselves in the wilderness from the profane obloquy so plenteously bestowed upon them in the "Cutter of Colman Street"[5] and other dramas by the wicked and courtly wits of that day, should have held the stage in utter abhorrence? Or that some of their feelings should have been transmitted to their descendants and should have caused that sturdy opposition to theatrical exhibitions which happened some years subsequent? And that among the first acts of legislation under their charter they should have enacted a law against the introduction of stage plays into the Colony and annexed severe penalties to the breech of it? That they should have made it penal in the sexes to wear each other's attire, a practice then and since but too common on the stage? That in their private converse they should have represented the playhouse as a receptacle of all uncleanness, a place where voluptuous assignations were made, the passions inflamed, debachery encouraged, in fact where the grand adversary of mankind held his court, for the destruction of all that is religious and the ridicule of all which is pious.[6]

Amidst this general abhorrence of dramatic writings there was one play suffered to be read, and those austere men who would rather have had a pack of cards in their house than a volume of Shakespeare still suffered their children to read Addison's Cato. This is a Whig play and though better adapted to the closet than scenic representation it contains so many fine passages about liberty and evinces such a hatred to despotism that it was a great favorite notwithstanding Cato was but a

[5] *The Cutter of Coleman Street* was written by Abraham Cowley (1618–1667). It was performed Dec. 16, 1661, at Lincoln's Inn Fields with Pepys in attendance. For other indications of Tyler's interest in Cowley see *Tyler Verse*, pp. 84–6.

[6] The act to prevent stage plays in Boston was passed by the Massachusetts General Court in March, 1750. For the text of the decree and details on the restrictions to acting during this period see William W. Clapp, Jr., *A Record of the Boston Stage* (Boston, 1853), pp. 1–4.

droll kind of Republican, killed himself like a very pagan with Plato's Phaedon in his hand, written espressly against suicide. But it was a Whig play, and those were liberty times, and every little boy who could mouth a passage of blank verse was inquiring

> Whether there was not some hidden curse,
> Some chosen thunder midst the stores of heaven,
> Red with uncommon wrath to blast the man
> Who owes his greatness to his country's ruin?[7]

meaning the Earl of Bute or Lord North[8] as repeated at different eras.

It was this popular drama that was to be performed by certain young clerks, principally of the club I have mentioned. The theater was an empty store, excepting one or two counters and several empty hogsheads, barrels and boxes which served as pit, box and gallery for the spectators. The inhabitants usually retired about ten in the evening and the actors all retired with the family but no sooner were Mater, Pater or guardian asleep when each softly stepped down stairs and joined their friends at the rendezvous.

The front door of the store was closed and every crack and keyhole carefully stopped with paper or cotton that no glimmering light might alarm the passing watchman. The entrance was through a bye lane into a door in the backyard, and such was the caution observed that but one person was admitted at a time, while two, one at each end of the lane, were on the watch to see if the person to be admitted had been noticed. No knocking was permitted but a slight scratch announced the approach of the initiated.

---

[7] *Cato,* I, i, 22–5. The play had been produced in this country at Williamsburg in September, 1736 (see the *Virginia Gazette,* Sept. 10, 1736), at Philadelphia, August, 1749, and at New York, March 5, 1750, and July 8, 1751.

[8] John Stuart, third Earl of Bute (1713–1792). Through his close friendship with George III he became prime minister in fact although not in name. He fought with Pitt over foreign policy and following the unpopular terms of the peace with France and Spain in 1763 was forced to resign.

Frederick, Lord North (1732–1792), Named First Lord of the Treasury in 1770. Although he carried a resolution in February, 1775, which said that there would be no other taxes levied on the American colonies if they taxed themselves with the consent of the King and Parliament, this concession came too late since the battle of Lexington in April made peace impossible.

Well did the wise man say "Stolen waters are sweet." For my own part I am ready to declare that tho' I have since proceeded openly to the theatre and taken my seat without dread of violating the law or my reputation, I have never since chuckled with such animated delight as I felt while sneaking under the shadow of the houses. I stole toward the prohibited stage with as much circumspection as if I was joining a gang of counterfeiters. At length I approached the door, scratched, was admitted and took my seat upon an empty overgrown hogshead.

The theatre was not, to be sure, quite so well decorated and furnished for scenic representation as some I have since seen. There was no curtain to provoke by its tardy rising the impatience of the audience, no side or back scenes to supply by their admirable deceptions the want of wit and interest in the play acted, no box, but sugar boxes and empty of the sugared loveliness of female beauty, no pit to contain the snarling critics or upper gallery with its worse vociferation to interrupt the attention of the audience by hissing, or crying "off, off," or calling for Yankee Doodle, and no orchestra to rosin their bow strings for the vulgar taste. But the actors seemed, as indeed they were, a company of amateurs acting under the criticism of a circles of cognoscente. It was near the witching time of [mid]night before the whole select party were assembled.

At length, to my great gratification the play began by the entrance of Marcus and Portius from behind the counter where they had been perched perdu on some reversed half bushels—

> The dawn is overcast. The morning lowers
> And heavily in clouds brings on the day,
> The great, the important day
> Big with the fate of Cato and of Rome—[9]

But ere the accomplished actor had in a stentorian voice delivered his first speech the hoarse voice of the watchman was heard bawling from the end of the bye lane,

> "Past twelve o'clock—and a cloudy morning."

[9] *Cato,* I, i, 1–4.

A panic seized the whole assembly. Marcus and Portius sneaked behind the counter, the lights were extinguished or put under a bushel, but the voice of the watchman as he chanted his midnight ditty distancing as he passed on, we took new courage and the play proceeded.

I do not recollect the performance very accurately but I well remember we all thought there was an astonishing display of fine acting. As Dennis[10] says the plot thickened. And Sempronius entered disguised as the Numidian Prince, with the design to bear off the pretty deer he had tracked to her covert, was met by Juba, an encounter ensued which terminated in favor of Juba who shot Sempronius with a horseman's pistol and left him a corpse with head muffled for the inspection of Cato's daughter, Marcia, who very naturally, in the person of a small apprentice boy dressed in his sister's hooped petticoat and plumpers, issued from behind the counter for the express purpose while Juba retired to listen.

After Marcia had lamented over the body of Sempronius, which she imagined to be that of Juba, we all looked anxiously for the reappearance of the Numidian Prince who was probably struck stiff with exhilarating astonishment to find, as Dennis says, he was not going to be cuckolded by a dead man, when suddenly the hogshead on which we were seated began to shake and roll and forth came Juba heels foremost. How he got in there undiscovered it is impossible to say and must be left to be settled by those great naturalists who account for the introduction of insects into amber. At any rate Juba was in the hogshead with his ear applied to the bung hole in the attitude of listening, and soon retrograded into view, in the person of a scrawny Scotch lad who had about this period rendered himself conspicuous and popular by publishing several essays in favor of the Sons of Liberty. As soon as he recovered the use of his limbs from his crippled attitude, in his broad natural accent he exclaimed,

---

[10] John Dennis (1657–1734), critic, poet and dramatist. He answered Collier's attack on the stage in *The Usefulness of the Stage to the Happiness of Mankind, to Government, and to Religion* (1698).

"And dost thou love, thou charming maid—"
Marcia.   "And dost thou live to ask it"[11]

Indeed the acting was very fine. I wish the admirers of your Cookes, Keans, Kembles and Coopers[12] could have seen it. Soon, however, we approached what the great Esq. R_____ calls the final Cata-stroph of such peg-entry. Cato, the patriotic republican, Cato with his bane and antidote both before him appeared. Here was exhibited the glory of the representation. Cato was habited with the most scrupulous attention to the Roman costume: a large full bottom'd wig covered his head, a night gown of silk plaid bound round the waist by a militia captain's scarlet sash enveloped his person, and tho' "Pent up in Utica" he looked the Roman senator.

It would be unfair to attribute this display of antiquarian science in the habiliments of Cato to our young Racii.[13] The truth is the dress of Cato was copied from that of Booth, who originally personated the self immolated patriot in the presence of Addison.[14] If you aim to excel do not copy copies but apply directly to the standard of taste. It must be confess'd that the managers of English stage display unrivalled excellence in the accurate adaptation of the side and back scenes, the paraphernalia of the actresses, the habiliments of the actors and the

[11] These two lines are a summation of the action at the close of *Cato*, IV, i.

[12] George Frederick Cooke (1756–1812). After an apprenticeship in Dublin, Cooke joined Covent Garden in 1800 where his reputation in tragedy rivaled Kemble's. He came to the United States in 1810 where he made a considerable impression.

Edmund Kean (1787–1833). He rose to fame at Drury Lane in 1814. Kemble's retirement in 1817 left Kean the master of the London stage. He made tours of the United States in 1820 and 1825.

John Philip Kemble (1757–1823). He made his London debut as Hamlet in 1783 at Drury Lane. He also played Cato in that first season. Kemble moved to Covent Garden in 1803 and played Cato there in 1816.

Thomas A. Cooper (1776–1849). Although he never reached great heights of fame in England, Cooper was an instant success after he came to the United States in 1796. He was one of the first authentic stars of the American stage. He helped secure Cooke's appearance in this country. For Tyler's favorable impression of Cooper's appearance in Boston during the 1805–6 season see *Tyler Verse*, pp. 133–41 and 150–4.

[13] This reference has not been located.

[14] Barton Booth (1681–1733). His impersonation of Cato in 1713 at Drury Lane brought him to the front of his profession.

arms and furniture of the stage, to the age in which the play acted is laid.

I have since been present at the performance of the Rival Queens in an English theatre[15] and observed with admiration that in the feast given by the mayor and common council of Babylon to Alexander the Great, the table was furnished with double flint decanters, while Clytus got pot valiant with brown stout poured from black glass bottles into beer glasses, undoubtedly bearing an exact resemblance to the flaggons, goblets and Chian wine of antiquity. But it was not only in these inanimate objects that the resemblance of ancient times was copied. The actors themselves seemed begrimed with the crust of antiquity and Clytus untwisted the wire and drew the cork of his porter bottle with a twang never surpassed in ancient Macedonia. Pardon this digression, gentle readers, and suffer the desire to do ample justice to the taste of a refined people to serve as my apology.

To return to Cato and our stage. Scarcely had the Roman patriot, his eyes in a fine frenzy rolling, got plump into

"The war of elements
The wreck of matter and the crush of worlds"[16]

when one would have thought the contemplations of Cato were suddenly realized. The thumping on the front and back doors by the staves of the constables, the authoritative demand for admittance in His Majesty's name, left little doubt who were the assailants. The whole dramatis personae skulked and scampered in all directions. I luckily made my escape thro' a back window as did some others who occupied the stage box with me. But several of the actors and spectators were apprehended and carried to the house of a Justice of the

[15] Tyler might have seen this play in Boston but he never saw it in England as he says since he never left American shores.

From Updike's description which follows it appears that he is talking about Colley Cribber's parody of Nathaniel Lee's heroic tragedy, The Rival Queens, or the Death of Alexander the Great (London, 1677). Cribber's play, The Rival Queens, with the Humours of Alexander the Great, was acted at Drury Lane in 1710 and published at Dublin, 1729. The banquet scene described by Updike occurs in Act IV, ii, of both plays.

[16] Cato, V, i, 30-1.

Peace with whom were several other magistrates. But upon viewing the party and especially noting the Scotch Juba, and finding some children of zealous Whigs engaged, the magistrates deemed it most prudent to accommodate the affair privately, lest as they afterwards observed the prosecution might be misconstrued as if levelled against the sentiments of the popular play rather than against the actors engaged in it. Besides it would have been too great a triumph for the Torys and would have made too conspicuous a paragraph in Mein and Fleeming's paper[17] where the sober Scotch patriot would have been exhibited for the amusement of the Loyalists. The magistrates therefore concluded to communicate the affair to the parents of the young actors who might punish the delinquents privately and then dismissed the theatre corps with a severe reprimand—and exeunt omnes.

Reader, you attend the theatre. You have acquired a correct taste for the drama. You have sat amidst a blaze of light and of beauty, have had your ears stunn'd with the noisy voices and still more noisy feet of the gods in the upper gallery, and your hearts thrilled with the animating or dying tones of the orchestra, while you sat gazing at stars of the first magnitude, and you imagine you have enjoyed a play. You are mistaken.

I too should have been deceived if I could have forgotten the first performance of a play in Boston, that felicitous period when all was fresh and ravishing, when no surly canons of criticism forbade me to relish what my taste approved, when passions within and terror without, scenery and the charm of doing that which was forbidden gave a zest to the performance. Be assured that a public theatrical exhibition is in comparison stale, flat, and unprofitable. Could I once again assist at such a private theatrical I would give more for a ticket even on the steps than was ever bid at vendue for a seat in the stage box on the appearance of Cooke or Kean.

---

[17] *The Boston Chronicle* was established Dec. 21, 1767, by John Mein and John Fleeming as a weekly. On Jan. 2, 1769 it was enlarged and issued as a semi-weekly. The paper was discontinued in June, 1770.

CHAPTER XIII

I SOON FOUND from some kind friends that the pretty Charlotte Love amused a large tea party with a minute description of my person, dress and address which she pronounced to be mean, unbecoming and absolutely insufferable.[1] This provoked all my ire and I would have given up all my hopes of professional eminence to be revenged on the insulting little gypsey. Now your true lover from time immemorial, whether pleased or angry, is wonderously apt to jingle his feelings into rhyme. I accordingly composed the following fable which I caused to be inserted in the poet's corner of the Spy, a newspaper just then published by Isaiah Thomas in support of the cause of the Sons of Liberty.[2]

THE WOLF AND WOODEN BEAUTY
An Old Fable new Vamped[3]
O Pulcrum Caput—Sel-Fab. Æsopi.

Once on a time a wolf did pop
His head into a Carver's shop
And there espied a bust of wood
Made to resemble flesh and blood;
With eyes so black and skin so fair,
And arched brows and curled hair;
With pouting lips and bosom's swell,
Cheeks painted like a modern belle;

[1] This unnumbered chapter, in Tyler's hand, is placed at this point in the narrative because of internal evidence. It has to come before Fragment 8, "Thanksgiving and Christmas Days," since the latter mentions the subject of this chapter: Charlotte Love's abuse of Updike's dress and speech. This is Fragment 9.

[2] The *Massachusetts Spy* was started by Zechariah Fowle and Thomas on July 17, 1770. With the dissolution of the partnership in October of that year Thomas carried on alone until April, 1775, when he moved the newspaper to Worcester. This allows us to date Updike's contribution to the paper as between October, 1770, and April, 1775, the dates when Thomas published the paper by himself in Boston.

[3] This long didactic verse was published separately by Tyler in *Polyanthos*, V (May, 1807), 127–32. See *Tyler Verse*, pp. 160–4. This illustrates how Tyler was using items he had written years before in assembling the novel in the years before his death in 1826.

Features in the most tonish style
Which simpered a perpetual smile.
He took her for bright beauty's goddess
With cestus round her Paphian bodice,
But the poor beast did never rove
O'er the bright charms of *Charlotte Love*.
For had he known the lovelier Charlotte
He'd thought not on that heavenly harlot.
"O Jove," he cried, "What pangs I feel,
How handsome, dashy and genteel.
If such her outward form I find
What are the beauties of her mind!
Sure she that's so divinely pretty
Must be supremely wise and witty."

He bowed and scraped, first at a distance,
But finding she made no resistance
And to his flatteries all the while
Kept up the same enchanting smile,
Like brisk gallant whose roguish trade is
To steal the hearts of simple ladies
Who when he hopes to gain their favor
Still takes his cue from their behavior,
And still applies his arts ensnaring
Till frowns repulsive check his daring,
So Isgrim made more bold advances
Lured by his timber love's kind glances.
At length he dared assail her honor
And claped his brutal paw on her,
But when he found her made of wood
In dumb perplexity he stood,
Then pawed the soulless beauty o'er
And finding her a horrid bore
He thus exclaimed: "Ah what a bite,
This comes from loving at first sight.
Thy features, mien, and tonish dress
Seem formed a lover's heart to bless,
But ah, within thy pretty skull
How mean, how empty and how dull!
Beauty 'tis true all hearts enflames,

But what is beauty without brains?"
He said no more, but with a hop,
Growling contempt he left the shop.

"What have we here?" the Cynick cries,
With frowning brow and critick eyes.
"What childish prattle 'tis to tell
Of talking beast and wooden belle!
A nursery tale and only meet
To lull a brawling brat to sleep.
Shall we in this enlightened age
Quit the delights of Shakespeare's page,
Leave plays and novels, and romances
For such poor mawkish childish fancies?
In schoolboy days we had enough
Of Æsop's tales and such like stuff."

But stop, my snarling, pride puffed Cynick,
This tale has got a moral in it:
And this same moral may apply
Perhaps to boys of six feet high.
Have you not seen? Come, tell me truly
(I know they're scarce as frost in July)
Some female heads, no matter where,
Perhaps in Maine or Delaware,
In Narraganset or Patucket,
Or Martha's Vineyard, or Nantucket,
For wheresoe'er you did accost one
We know 'twas not in town of Boston,
For there the gentlemen will sware
The ladies are as *wise* as fair.
Have you not seen some female noodles
As beautiful as Grecian models,
Made perfect by the hand of nature
With nicest symmetry of feature,
With spangled combs, or gay egretts,
Or frizled, jewelled, smart frizletts,
With essence, curling and pomatum,
Made fine as barber's art could make them;

Faces that might with Venus vie,
Or give to Helen's charms the lie,
Eyes which sparkled with love's wiles,
Cheeks dimpling with perpetual smiles,
And coral lips which ope'd beneath,
Not to converse, but to show pearl teeth;
Have you not seen?—Zounds, stop your pen,
Yes, I *have* seen—and pray what then?

Then if you seek to choose a wife
To comfort, stay, enliven life,
Not the companion of a day,
But helpmate on life's weary way;
Not she who thinks that life was made
For dress and flutter and parade;
Who scorning sweet domestic duty
Sighs for the sovereignty of beauty,
And at the concert, mall or ball,
Though bound to one, would conquer all;
But She, who fills with nobler pride
That female throne, the fire side;
Who with her bridal dress, lays by
The whims of girlish vanity;
And in their stead with pride embraces
The modest matron's solid graces;
Who seeks alone the toilet's aid,
To keep the conquest she has made—
And makes—and seeks to make alone
Your interest, cares, and joys her own.
And should life's olive branches rise
To bless your fond paternal eyes,
She who with all a mother's care
The nursling plants will fondly rear;
The excrescent shoots with firmness prune,
Each noxious weed with care consume,
Till nurtured by her fostering hand,
The rising plants grow and expand,
Bud, blossom, bear, while each survives,
The ripened fruit of virtuous lives.
Or should misfortunes dire assail

And friends look cold and credit fail,
She who thro' each disturbing scene
Is prudent, constant, and serene;
Who, when woes cluster, and the frown
Of wealth unfeeling weighs you down,
With sweet affection's kindly power
Sustains you in that trying hour,
Or, on her fond and faithful breast,
Lulls all your sorrows into rest.
When sickness comes (as come it must
To us weak children of the dust;
For life when all its joys we have
Is but a turnpike to the grave,
And fever, cholick, stone, and gout
Are but mere guideposts on the rout)
When sickness comes, and fever dire
Awakes its slow consuming fire,
Or when enraged the tyrant reigns
Triumphant in your mantling veins,
When watchers fail and nurses tire
And hope seems ready to expire,
She, who with ever ready hand,
Takes by your side her patient stand,
With velvet step draws nigh your bed,
The pillow smooths beneath your head;
Cools your parched tongue with proffer'd sweets;
Tho' oft repulsed, with kindness greets,
With languid smile can still sustain
The wayward petulance of pain,
Echo your groans, your sighs renew,
And seems to suffer more than you.
   Come youthful bachelors, be candid,
Nor use me as that cynick man did—
An honest answer I require:
Is this the wife that you desire?

If so, before you rashly wed,
Muse on the simple tale you've read;
Before you tie the fatal knot
Think on the wolf and carver's shop.

But scarcely had the printers' boys circulated my satire than I bitterly lamented its publication, for with the waywardness of youthful love, the gall of my satire was suddenly converted into the very treacle of loving kindness and she who in the morning I would have broken on the wheel of vituperation, the same afternoon became again the goddess of my idolatry.[4] I bundled all the Massachusetts Spys within my reach to the wanton destruction of the essays of the Catos, Aristides, Epaminondas's, Phocions and other champions of colonial rights and privileges[5]—condemned the rhymes as stale, flat and worthless and boldly denounced their author a fool and the fable nonsense. While I was disquieting myself with a thousand abortive resolutions of more dire revenge on the presumptuous fair one, my good master returned from his early professional visits and accosted me with:

"Well, Underhill, I have visited our friend, Mrs. Diaway. You are a great favorite in that quarter, I find; thinks you will be an ornament to the profession. Gives you great credit for intelligence and suavity of manners; wants more pills and requests that you may be the bearer of them. So make up a parcel and carry them to her directly. You may expect another examination and perhaps you had better be a little careful how you people Greenwich Hospital with hysterical ladies. She, however, attributes your mistake to the embarrassment caused by my previous injunctions to you."

I soon prepared my pills, hastened towards Scarlet's warf, venting imprecations all the way on the saucy baggage who had contumeliously arraigned my person, dress and address, resolving and re-resolving that if I encountered her, which I hoped would not be the case, I would repay scorn with scorn.

On my approaching the house I was received by Zack who informed me that Betty was making some arrangements in her mistress's chamber previously necessary to the introduction of even a medical

[4] At this point in the manuscript there is an asterick but Tyler did not explain why it is there.

[5] Here Tyler made an insertion into the manuscript of the phrase immediately following. He reworked this section rather extensively and deleted several paragraphs he thought unsuitable. For him, such large cancels were unusual.

visitor and was ushered by him into a back parlor where I found the charming Charlotte seated at her spinet. She rose and received me with such affability, ease and politeness that when I observed the Massachusetts Spy on its lid with the vile Poets' Corner exposed to view, I began to wish that all the [. . .] and corners of poetry were at the bottom of the Red Sea. Every trace of her pristine scorn was obliterated and she conversed with that easy familiarity which inspired confidence and self complacency. She spoke with tenderness and intelligence of her aunt's unhappy indisposition and readily accepted the apology I made for humoring her fancies as the necessary adjunct of professional skill. And when at my entreaty she reseated herself at the instrument and ran her fingers over the ivory and ebony notes I could but imagine that she intended something peculiarly appropriate to our situation when she accompanied with her voice the air and words of the old song:

> Forever fortune wilt thou prove
> An unrelenting foe to love,
> And where we meet two mutual hearts
> Step in between and bid them part;
> Bid us sigh on from day to day
> And sigh and hope our years away
> Till youth and all its joys are flown
> And all the life of life is gone.

I paid a short visit to the aunt—passed a brief examination and was accompanied to the front door by the divine Charlotte who at parting kindly hoped that it would not be long ere I renewed my visit to her dear afflicted aunt. I went home treading on ether, building a thousand castles in the air in every one of which the charming Charlotte sat embowered like the loveliest dames of ancient chivalry.

Happy, thrice happy is the Eden of youth, the loss of which is but poorly compensated by the adult knowledge of good and evil which forces conviction of the austere realities of human life. Happy, thrice happy days of youthful credulity and cullibility, when pleasure and pain, anticipation and disappointment, canter thro' the imagination like so many parti-colored jockies on a race course, when the sunshine and the cloud alternately enliven and shadow the April morn of existence, when the gloom of vexation or the thunder gusts of anger and revenge are rapidly succeeded by the bright beams of hope which reflect their glittering rays on the watery bubbles that hang pendent from every shrub and spray in the youngster's horizon.[6]

[6] Marginal notation: "20 Pages."

CHAPTER XIV

"JEALOUSY"

> Shakespeare, who's taste is never doubted,
> In a fine passage often spouted
> (I think it is in his Othello,
> Where that besotted Negro fellow
> About a 'kerchief took such fright
> And put out Desdemona's light),
> Tells us that jealousy, I ween,
> Has ghastly eyes—he calls them green;
> But save with deference to sweet Willy
> I think his green eyes rather silly,
> For jealousy, I am inclined,
> Has not green eyes but is stone blind;
> Blind as a beetle when his flight
> Goes blundering on—a summer's night,
> Into the fire or candle's light,
> And burns his nose—to mend his sight.
>   Doggerel Romaunt
>   *By the Author.*

HAVING CITED as a motto to this chapter a few jingling rhymes from a doggerel poet who has rather irreverently affected to dissent from Shakespeare, I cannot resist the temptation to hazard my opinion of the genius and writings of this mighty master of the scenic art.[1]

The English pride themselves on Shakespeare. They enthusiastically admire his plays and challenge the whole world to produce a dramatic writer of such universal preeminence. The French wits, with Voltaire at their head, have been disposed to deny to the Bard of Avon this supreme eminence and attribute the English opinion of his merits to national prejudice and to an incorrect if not a barbarous taste. No umpire has yet appeared well qualified to decide between them.

I conclude on reflection we Americans may be deemed properly qualified. Familiar with the language in which Shakespeare wrote, free from the imputation of national prejudice, and if our judgement is in any way bias'd from the not yet forgotten resentment occasioned by our revolutionary struggle and the irritation of a more recent war[2] and the vulgar aspersions of her travellers and reviewers, it surely is not inclined to English pretentions. We, therefore, seem well suited to decide upon the claims of the dramatist and we think we ought and shall be credited when we say that the English do not estimate the genius and dramas of the immortal bard too highly.

That their enthusiastic admiration of his plays does not proceed from national prejudice or incorrect or barbarous taste, but simply from a familiarity with their vernacular tongue in which he wrote. That Shakespeare's brilliant imagination by which he repeopled the earth with the offspring of his own fancy or the splendid and noble passages so often quoted from his writings and so often vainly attempted to be translated, are but minor excellences and by far exceeded by that admirable facility and familiarity with which he penetrates the bosoms of the persons represented by his dramatis personae,

[1] This chapter, unnumbered but entitled, "Jealousy," marks the end of the revised draft of "The Bay Boy" recopied by Mrs. Tyler (Fragment 7). The remainder has been lost. From a reference at one point in the manuscript it is obvious that an intended previous chapter is either lost or was not written, while another reference at the end of chapter makes it clear that it is supposed to preceed Chapter XV ("Thanksgiving and the Christmas Days").

[2] This mention of "a more recent war" clearly refers to the War of 1812. This fragment, therefore, would have been composed post–1815.

making every one, whether the inmates of the palace or the cottage, of the ocean, the wilderness or the cavern, whether surrounded by domestic comforts or cast forth roofless and abandoned to bide the "peltings of the pitiless storm," whether actuated by passion or bereft of reason, whether grave or gay, drunk or sober, wise or witty, in love or in debt, pedantic or foolish, conduct just as a deep knowledge of human nature would make us conclude persons so situated would naturally act, think and talk, and frequently by some brief and unobtrusive speech making them develop a whole life of character. And all this effected in a manner so simple, so natural, and with such apparent lack of effort that the reader of his dramas is often tempted to withhold the merit of invention from the bard and to conclude it impossible for people similarly circumstanced to talk and act in any other way than they did. No, the English with all their self complacency do not estimate the genius and dramas of Shakespeare too highly, and the foreigner who can not relish his plays, tho' he may peruse the production of other English poets with pleasure, may rest assured he is still but imperfectly acquainted with the English tongue.

I had now become almost domesticated in Mrs. Diaway's family. She preferred my visits to those of my master, not that she was weak enough to place any reliance upon my medical skill but I was the best listener to her complaints, a subject which she could converse with one upon with perfect propriety. My master did not discountenance my frequent visits as the old lady had manifested her preference for me and insisted that he should charge them at the same rate as if he gave his personal attendance. Thus circumstanced scarcely a day passed in which I was not an inmate of her sick chamber, excepting those hours when she took her daily nap when I was consigned to the charge of Charlotte in the lower back parlor where we read together and said and looked a thousand interesting things which appeared appropriate enough at the time but which might look mightly silly upon paper. Perhaps some of my fair readers may supply this deficiency by recollecting some delightful passages in their youthful life.

Charlotte having mentioned our readings the old lady directed us to bring the book into her chamber. We accordingly relieved each other by wading thro' the deep water of Sir Charles Grandison.[3] We execrated Sir Hargrave Pollexfen, rejoiced when Sir Charles knocked out his butler's teeth with the pommel of his sword, bowed gracefully on the noble ladie's hand with the hero, and sympathised with the exalted Clementina and nodded over the long conversations of the Byron family.

There was an incident which happened about this time that made me a great favorite with the domestics of Mrs. Diaway. At nearly sun setting on the Commencement Day of Harvard College I had strolled for exercise towards Charles's ferry. My attention was soon arrested by a mob of vulgar-looking white men who had gathered near the ferry way and appeared to be watching the approach of the boat. No sooner had it struck the ways than the mob impetuously rushed towards it and entering the boat, to my astonishment, seized upon two Negro females who were returning from Cambridge dressed in all their holiday finery and plunged them into the water where it was near three feet deep and were proceeding to throw a Negro man after them. I hastened towards this scene of unmanly outrage and soon heard a familiar voice calling to me in apparent distress, "Massa doctor, Massa doctor, don't let poor Negro be abused."

It was Zack who was driven to desperation in defense of a comely young Negress whom the brutal assailants were attempting to drag into the water. In a moment I was by the poor fellow's side and with my hickory cane menaced the mob into something like attention and then attempted to shame them out of this conduct, begging them to consider that these poor slaves out of the three hundred and sixty-five days of the year had but two or three which they were permitted to call their own, that the frolic of these festival days were the only sweet drops in the bitter cup of servitude, that it was unmanly and even

---

[3] *Sir Charles Grandison* by Samuel Richardson must have been a favorite of the Tyler-Palmer families. It was the first book Joseph Palmer (Tyler's father-in-law) gave to his fiancée, Betsey Hunt, during their courtship. (See "Reminiscences of Mrs. Jos. Palmer," p. 4, and *GTB*, p. 17.)

barbarous to abridge their little hour of enjoyment, that in fine it should not be done while I had an arm to defend them.

"Who is this spark?" cried several ragamuffins.

"I know him," replied one in the rear. "He lives with that old Tory, Dr. G."

"A Tory—a Tory—a Tory," was the general cry.

"Tar and feather him!" cried some.

"Cart him up to the Liberty Tree!" cried others.

Just as they were pressing upon me to carry their threats into execution I was unexpectedly relieved by the appearance of several constables with a magistrate and some reputable gentlemen known as true Sons of Liberty at their head.

It seems that the leading men in Boston now anticipated the contest with the Mother Country as certain and deemed it advisable to put down all domestic feuds in order that we might present an undivided opposition to ministerial measures. These gentlemen, therefore, sensible that the custom of ducking the Negroes on their return from Commencement would be pursued, resolved to abolish it by the authority of the magistrate and the still greater authority of men who were held by the populace as the principal chiefs in the cause of liberty.

On their approach I was immediately released and commended for my interference and resistance to the mob, who were not severely treated on this occasion. None were apprehended by the magistrate but all dismissed by a speech from Mr. M., a popular orator of the day, who in certain blind terms well understood by the populace intimated that as our rights and privileges were endangered and we might soon have to contend for them (he did not say with whom) up to our knees in blood, it became us as true Sons of Liberty to behave well among ourselves. That while we were contending for our own rights we ought not to infringe those of the meanest among us, that their conduct it was true was sanctioned by an old custom which we had learned from our English ancestors from whom no good to this land of liberty ever came. The populace gave the orator three cheers and all retired peaceably.

I confess it is with some hesitancy that I have introduced this humiliating scene, so discreditable to all engaged in it. I would rather, like the children of Noah, have gone backwards and thrown a garment over our fathers' nakedness—"sed magna vis veritatis"—and I am compelled to add that hitherto had this barbarous custom been considered so amusing that it was not uncommon for the children of respectable families to make parties, and for the windows of the house adjacent to the ferry ways to be crowded with well dressed females who came from remote parts of the town to see the Negroes ducked on Commencement Day. I do not agree with orator M. that we owed this custom to our English ancestors. I believe this to be one of the few bad customs which was purely colonial.

When it was understood from the orator's speech that ducking the Negroes was inconsistent with the character of true Sons of Liberty the general sentiment suddenly turned in favor of the poor blacks. The dripping females were taken into the houses and accommodated with dry clothes. Zack, after accompanying his sallow partner home, returned to his mistress and vociferated my praises first in the kitchen and then thro' the whole house. How very easy it is to do an act of common humanity and how sure to be followed by the best kind of popularity. It seemed as if my defense of Zack was communicated as if by magic to the whole African race. The very next day as I passed the street every Negro I met, both male and female, evinced by doffing their hats, their low obeisances and by their officiousness in removing any obstructions in the way that they had heard of the defense of Zack and viewed me with gratitude as his champion. I observed that I became a favorite with Mrs. D.'s domestics, and the youthful suitor who is popular in the kitchen, and that popularity obtained by good conduct rather than by profuse liberality, may proceed to the parlor under the happiest auspices. There is a wonderful discernment in the lower orders of the people, their prospective is undazzled by the brilliant polish of refined society and their opinions of men never restrained by the decorum of more exalted life. Their influence over their superiors tho' always despised is often irresistible.

Some weeks previous to the twelfth night mentioned in my last chapter,[4] while I was reading to Mrs. Diaway in presence of Charlotte, she requested me to lay aside my book and to our great surprise observed that we were sensible by how slender a thread her life was suspended, that she had frequently reproached herself with being too selfish, too regardless of the happiness of others who were dear to her.

"I am always persuading Charlotte," she continued, "to go into company and the good girl has done so at my request. But she receives no visits except an occasional call in return, for who can be expected to visit the family of a poor dying woman? Now I have been thinking that Charlotte shall give a ball and supper. The dancing may be in the old dining room where it will not disturb me and when the worst comes to the worst the doctor can slip upstairs and give me an opiate. You, doctor, must act as a brother to Charlotte and invite the young gentlemen and Charlotte shall send out her cards to the young ladies."

It is needless to say the proposal was joyfully accepted. The cards were sent out, the invitations given, and among my friends invited was Charles Brightly. The old lady had now something to occupy her mind, suited to her earlier taste, and in directing the servants to put the house in order in preparation for the supper, in decorating the old dining room with all the old fashioned splendor she could recollect she forgot her infirmities and I believe she did not take more than half a box of the doctor's gold and silver pills in three weeks.

I hastened home and informed the doctor, who observed that the occupation of her mind would do her more service than even the wonderful pills. With a view to procure an invitation for some young ladies, daughters of particular friends, he invited Charlotte to his party on the twelfth night.[5]

[4] Unfortunately, there is no trace of the event "mentioned in my last chapter." Either Tyler neglected to compose this episode or it is not now extant.

[5] The doctor's twelfth night party is the subject of the following fragment. This allows us to determine the proper order of these two chapters.

CHAPTER XV

"THANKSGIVING AND CHRISTMAS DAYS"

'Tis autumn now, and all around
The teeming earth's with plenty crown'd;
Now, now prepare both great and small
To hail New England's festival,
Thanksgiving Day—oh day of joys;
To capering girls and hungry boys
Thanksgiving comes, and with it brings
The savory flavor of good things;
Plumbpudding, turkeys, roast and boil'd,
Brant, fowl and geese both tame and wild,
Custards and tarts and whips froth'd high,
And last not least the pumpkin pie.
Old Christmas in the rear is seen,
Deck'd with all sorts of evergreen;
Welcome to me old Christmas merry,
Welcome thy mince pie, port and sherry;
But yet more welcome in my sight
Is the rich cake of the twelfth night.
Ah lucky damsel who is seen
To draw the slice with hidden bean;
That sure prognostic she shall be
A bride before the year shall flee.
Now Yankeys, let not self intrude
But shew the fruits of gratitude;
Eat of the fat and drink the sweet
And hungry poor with portions treat.
 'Tis evening—and with merry shout
In rush the merry antic rout—
With mask and grotesque dress and mien
To act the ribald comic scene,
To dance or fight or laugh or cry
As suits their mimic comedy;
Pleased with the dole of some few pence,
The mansion's master may dispense;
Sure never was the Thespian trade
So briefly done or so poorly paid.

O N THANKSGIVING DAY I was invited to dine at my
Grandmother Anvill's with a family party consisting of my
father, mother and Aunt Tabitha, the old lady's children and grandchildren, several sons in law and some young men who were considered as betrothed to sundry of her blooming granddaughters.[1]

On my return from worship I entered the front door and immediately opened a door which led to a closet under the stairs' case, and
carelessly threw my hat on a shelf, my usual place of depositing it. I
did not recollect it was Thanksgiving Day! Crash went a whole
server of custards, and whipt syllabubs, besides oversetting a bowl of
apple sauce, crushing the top crust of two puffpaste plum tarts and
marring the crust figures which adorned a pumpkin pie, which looked
ruefully at me as if resenting the insult on this day of its glory.

I snatched up my unlucky hat and proceeded to a parlor on my
right hand, and was just on the point of demolishing a score of calves-
feet and currant jellies which were under a cloth on a marble slab. I
peeped into every closet and beaufet. All were filled with good cheer,
even the bureau drawers seemed pregnant with minced pies. Having
with some difficulty and with great precaution found a spot to deposit
my hat and gloves, I ventured into the sitting room where I found a
large party assembled round a blazing fire, and the Negro servants
busy serving them with lemonade sangree and punch while one or
two of the seniors were partaking of a foaming mug of flip which they
professed to drink on no other day, but that Thanksgiving would not
seem like Thanksgiving without it.

After some impatience was exhibited the folding doors were thrown
open and we seated at a long table richly replenished with dainties,[2]
in the center of which arose a stately pyramid formed by several glass
servers, diminishing in size, placed on their pedestals one above another and the apex crowned with a copious goblet containing a yellow

[1] This chapter (Fragment 8), titled, "Thanksgiving and Christmas Days," must come
after both Chapters XIII and XIV because of the references to it in those earlier sections.
This manuscript fragment is in Tyler's hand.

[2] This point marks the start of an insertion tipped onto the margin of the manuscript.
The place of the insertion was indicated by an asterisk.

sea and floating island of froth, while the servers tier above tier exhibited jellies and syllabubs of all colors, and from its sides were suspended little glass buckets of sweetmeats.[3] An enormous plum pudding seemed to preside over the feast. Turkeys roasted, boiled turkeys and oyster sauce, hams and neats tongues, brant, ducks and geese, chickens boiled and roasted, chicken pie, spare rib and apple sauce, venison pastry and roast pig, with cheese from my mother's dairy which, in the true spirit of patriotism, was preferred to the English. Indeed, if our good father Adam had been seated at my grandmother's table and taken a survey of the courses he might have named all the beasts of the field and the fowls of the air without leaving his seat.

When, as Virgil says, the "rage of hunger" was abated, the principal repast concluded, thanks returned, the damask tablecloth removed and the green covering spread with walnuts, almonds, raisons, oranges, filberts and chestnuts, apples and pears, with saucers of nollipops, including dainty devices about love and matrimony for the amusement of the young ladies and sundry decanters of red and white wines were exposed to view, my venerable grandmother, seated in her armchair at the head of the table, drew the attention of the company by a gentle tap with the haft of her three prong'd fork on the table and thus address'd us:

"My children and friends, we have just returned thanks to the beneficent giver of the good things of which we have partaken. I trust we are sincerely thankful for these and all other of his favors during the past year, and indeed in the course of our lives but it is very natural to feel grateful while filled with his bounties, but our gratitude it should be remembered is best shewn when tempered by resignation and when returned for his smallest blessings in days of distress and deprivation. Then may we imitate that of our ancestor Gov. Carver, who when the last bache of bread was in the oven composed chiefly of bran, and his family had just dined on a dish of clams dug from the beach and the colonists were exposed to starving, in the outpourings of his

---

[3] The end of the insertion.

grateful heart he returned thanks to the beneficent giver of every good
and perfect gift that he gave them to such of the abundance of the sea
and of treasures hid in the sands. And while we feast on the bounties
of Providence so liberally provided in this goodly land remember,
my children, that it would be the height of ingratitude to the muni-
ficent donor should we surrender these blessings to foreign domina-
tion. I do not much approve of toasts but it is customary. Fill your
glasses to the health of our Sovereign, George the Third. May he in
whose hands the heart of the King is, incline his to the way of righteousness and peace."

Thus, early in every family was resistance to the oppressive acts of
the Mother Country inculcated by those whose precepts were considered venerable by the fighting portion of the community. To the
good old lady's toast succeeded the health of Mr. Pitt, Earl Temple,
Coln. Barry[4] and other friends of colonial rights and privileges, and
the whole concluded with "Prosperity to the American provinces—
united we stand, divided we fall."

Good eating, altho' certainly a very pleasant occupation, and as
Sancho Panza said of sleep, "blessings on the man that invented it,"
whatever may be said of good drinking, it is not very promotive of
converse. The company as soon as tea was over split into parties, the
seniors to talk politics and patriotism, the old ladies to detail domestic
gossip. The little ones were dismissed to another room to play blind
man's bluff, puss, puss in the corner or hide and seek, while the young
folks in their teens amused themselves with "What's my thought like,"

[4] William Pitt, Earl of Chatham (1708–1778), the "Great Commoner." As secretary
of state under George II he was the architect of England's victory over France in North
America.

George Grenville (1712–1770). A strong exponent of the right of Parliament to tax
the colonies, his ministry was responsible for the imposition of the Revenue, or Sugar,
Act of 1764 and the Stamp Act of 1765, both of which were strongly resisted in
America.

Col. Henry Barry (1750–1822). As lieutenant, his regiment, the 52nd, was engaged in
the American colonies during the Revolution. He acted as aide-de-camp and private
secretary to Lord Rawdon, later Marquis of Hastings. The 52nd was at Bunker Hill,
Brooklyn, White Plains and Fort Clinton. Barry became colonel of the regiment in
1793 and later served in India.

"questions and commands," or the more interesting game of forfeits. At ten the company broke up. I took leave of my parents, promising to call the next morning and breakfast with them on broiled plum pudding which my good grandmother assured me was much better than when eaten hot from the oven.

On Thanksgiving Day all secular business was suspended by the Congregationalists and their stores and shops closed of course. Those of the Episcopalians were also shut, as they gave out, to teach the Dissenters a lesson of civility, but the latter who were ever distrustful of the former rather insidiously attributed the closing of the Church-men's stores to the lack of customers. However, on Christmas day the congregationalists did not return the compliment. All the shops and stores were open and the townspeople engaged as usual on weekdays, while here and there might be seen a solitary shop or store with the windows and doors closed which indicated that the owner had gone to church.

On Christmas eve, when a small party of friends were assembled in Dr. G's parlor, the kitchen door was suddenly thrown open and in rushed a party of lads grotesquely dressed, their faces masked, several of them armed with wooden swords and daggers, who notwithstand-ing the opposition of the cook maid, immediately began to enact a little farce or comedy. This brought all the family and visitors into the kitchen and the doctor suffered them to proceed. I have not a very correct recollection of the performance of these antics, as they were called, but I well remember that two of the party soon quarrel'd and engaged in deadly combat but the why and the wherefore would be as difficult to comprehend as it often is in a recounter between real duellists. One of the masked combatants soon fell, and to appearance expired, and suddenly there was as great a demand for a doctor as ever Cooke made for his gelding in the character of the tyrant Richard.

"Five pounds for a doctor," "Ten pounds for a doctor," was vociferated on all sides.

Soon the son of Galen appeared: "I am a doctor."

"You, a doctor! What can you cure?"

"The itch, the stitch, the cholic and gout,
The pains within and pains without;
I can take an old woman of ninety-nine,
Wrap'd up in pitch, tar and turpentine
And then with what lays on the point of this knife
Quickly I'll bring the old lady to life;
And for the price of a half pistereen
Can make her dance like a girl of sixteen."

The wonder-working medicine which seemed to have all the virtues of Dr. Solomon's Balm of Gilead was soon applied to the deceased, who jumped up and declared himself as sound as a roach and presented his cup for the contribution of the company. The largess was given, the masque retired and we could hear them rush into the neighboring mansions. This is all I can recollect of the performance of the antics. I thought the custom merited a memorandum as evidencing singular anomali in the habits of our ancestors, that bitterly opposed as they were to everything that savored of popery they should have suffered this forlorn fragment of monkish mysteries to pass unnoticed among them.

On Christmas Day I attended church, admired the evergreens with which the church was decorated, sung the Christmas carols, heard an excellent sermon and returned to my master's where I found a large party assembled. The feast rivaled Thanksgiving in plenty and sumptuousness. However, New England people may differ in religion and politics they are all uniformly orthodox in the creed of good eating and drinking.

After dinner the health of His Majesty, George the Third, King of France, Defender of the Faithful, etc., etc., was full loyally drunk in bumpers of old Madeira. Then the Queen, the Princess Dowager of Wales, and all the branches of the royal family; then health and prosperity to the Earl of Bute and Sir Francis Bernard, governor of Massachusetts, and lastly confusion to those who would bring confusion into the colonies. Being of a Whig family I did not enter fully into the spirit of this lavish loyalty. Sometimes, when in the course of conversation, I heard the Sons of Liberty vituperated and their certain downfall confidently predicted I chewed my mince pie rather hard and drank off my bumper toasts with mental reservation.

Since the Revolution I have often reflected on this Tory entertainment. The company embraced men of integrity and sound judgement in all the ordinary concerns of life, of men who, I am persuaded, had what they imagined to be the welfare of the Colony at heart. But they were so impressed with the power of the Mother Country and many of them so firmly believed that under the sanction of the royal prerogative and the right of Parliament to bind the colonies in all cases they should live to see the Church established as national in New England, that they were anxious to see that power exerted, tho' accompanied with the awful and bloody consequences of an unsuccessful rebellion. But they lived to discern that they were false prophets and many of them when they returned to this country after the Revolution toasted as serenely prosperity to the United States as they ever tipped a loyal glass to His Majesty, George the Third.

On the Twelfth Night my good master resolved to display his attachment to the Church and her festivals. He accordingly sent out invitations to a supper and ball and authorized the juvenile members of the family to invite their particular friends. I availed myself of his permission and invited Charles Brightly. The doctor had previously visited Mrs. Diaway and given a personal invitation to Miss Charlotte Love, and her aunt's permission was obtained upon the doctor's promise that I should see her to his house and home again at an early hour.

The long anticipated night, tho' in the opinion of most of us young folks creeping at a snail's pace, at length arrived. I waited on the fair Charlotte to the doctor's and observed with delight that she was the best dressed and by far the prettiest girl in a very large company. Dancing soon commenced and after going down "Beans well buttered and hot as toast" and "Peas upon a trencher" with her, I presented Charles Brightly to my partner who immediately engaged her hand for the next two dances. My heart misgave me as soon as I introduced him to her. How could I be so imprudent, or rather why did I invite him at all? Brightly was all life and Charlotte all animation. They attracted all eyes.

At the conclusion of the contra dances the floor was cleared and they danced a minuet tho' the season for minuets, which always preceded the contra dances, was long past. They invited all eyes. "What a lovely couple" was whispered round the room but when the slow time of the minuet was exchanged for the quick measure of a reel, which she danced with castinets, admiration was changed into rapture. When she was seated by her partner all her acquaintance gathered round to congratulate and to praise. I attempted a compliment altho' I thought I never saw her dance so ill, but as I approached her my heels seemed loaded with lead and my fine compliment stuck crossways in my throat. What was the matter with me? Can you tell Miss—? I could not then but have suspected since.[5]

We were summoned to the supper table, Charlotte escorted by the gay Charles Brightly. And I, what did I do? Why I acted like a fool. Passing over several pretty girls with whom I had danced, I singled out the same staid maiden who had so kindly aided me in my devotions at church. Miss Prudence Sweeting was just at that age when she had lost all apprehensions that any one would attempt to steal her heart. She therefore withdrew her watch over it and busied herself in watching the affections of others. She was the most candid lady I ever knew. Whenever she gave a stab to your own peace or wounded the reputation of others like the theological controversalist, she would oil her dagger with professions of good will. She rarely obtruded an opinion or a story but excited your curiosity to know what she longed to tell and obliged you to blame yourself for the unpalatable communication.

After I had heaped her plate with delicacies and she had arrived at that period when a word could get out without being jostled by what was continually going in, she turned to me and said:

[5] Marginal notation: "Seventeen Pages."

"Pray, who is that pretty girl who is so mightily tickled with the civilities of young Brightly?"

"Miss Charlotte Love."

"What, the niece of that old frump, Mrs. Diaway, who is always dying and lives only for the benefit of her physician, 'tis a pitty."

Now whether the " 'tis a pitty" alluded to Mrs. D., the fair Charlotte or young Brightly, I longed to know, and, "Pray what is a pitty, madam?" said I.

"Pitty did I say? O now I recollect, it is a pitty the doctor's cook did not put more anchovies in this oyster sauce. I say nothing, pray favor me with the sauce boat." I sat with my piece of mince pie suspended half way between my mouth and my plate pondering on " 'tis a pitty."

"Pray Dr. Underhill, do you know Brightly?"

"He is a particular friend of mine."

"Of that I have no doubt. He has a thousand friends, everyone is his friend who can serve his turn, but I say nothing. Come hob and nob, which do you prefer—white or red? Come, here is real *friendship* and *genuine love*. I say nothing but if somebody who shall be nameless is not disappointed in his expectations of wealth I am greatly mistaken, but I say nothing."

"Pardon me, Miss Sweeting, but you intimate if not say a great deal."

"I—I say nothing—indeed nothing is necessary to be said to a young gentleman of your discernment. Report says that Charlotte is to be heiress to the old invalid, and they call niece and aunt, but you assuredly know they are related only by Adam, but I say nothing."

"Indeed I did not."

"No, then I am sorry I asked the question for you will recollect I did not say it was so. On reflection I am glad I have been so prudent on this occasion and said nothing and more than glad I did not inquire of you what is Charlotte's real name. But that is of no importance. Brightly can furnish her with a name. But I say nothing."

And nothing more would Miss Prudence say altho' I strove with all my address to draw some explanation from her. I once indeed imagined I had brought her to the point, but she broke a sugar nol-lipop and read from the little point scroll,

"Your money and your darling Kate

Trust not with a thief or rake, but I say nothing."

This table tete-a-tete was interrupted by the removal of the cloth, when our attention was undividedly attracted by a large dressed plumb [sic] cake on the center of the table, on the ample top of which might be seen the sugar huntsmen and hounds pursuing the stag thro' groves of box twigs tipped with gold, while the center was covered by a large royal crown with G. R. flaming in gold on its fillet. This cake had been ingeniously severed into slices, held together by its top. In one of its compartments it was understood that an almond, commonly called a bean, was concealed and the young lady who was fortunate enough to select that piece was according to the tradition of our English ancestors pretty sure, if a suitable offer was made in due season, to become a bride before the next Christmas holydays.

Who drew the interesting prize I could not at first discover as I could not perceive that she who drew it blushed deeper than those who missed it. I however soon learned that the fortunate adventurer was pretty well known among the young ladies and amidst their smiling, giggling, bridling and talking, sundry questions were put to me, which seemed to imply that Charlotte had drawn the bean, and I as a favored lover was to assist in the accomplishment of the augury. One young lady was very solicitous to know when I commenced practice for myself, another wished to know whether Mrs. Diaway would be prevailed upon to part with Charlotte and another thought it would be an admirable plan for me to reside with the old lady, when she would have all she wanted on earth—a physician and nurse in her own family. Sundry other questions were put and as my replies indicated a period before or beyond the next holydays they were received with a mock condolence or gracious nod, which seemed to say, "Aye, that will do. The bean will tell the truth this time."

After a renewal of the dances, I waited upon Charlotte home. I was

dull, if not sullen, she delighted. She spoke of Brightly in flattering
terms, alluded to his handsome person, easy address and elegant dancing, and said he was the life of the company. Every word was a dagger
to my heart. I restored the old lady's darling to her and took my leave.
Alas, how little did I then know of the female heart. I had yet to learn
that the woman who praises a man openly is not in love with him
secretly, and that Charlotte's abuse of my person, dress and address
after our first interview augured more in my favor than all her commendation did in favor of Charles Brightly. But as my dear Miss
Prudence Sweeting said, "I say nothing."

A Sermon and Prayer for Christmas Day

IN THE YEARS immediately following his graduation from Harvard, Tyler admittedly remained uncertain in the choice of a career. For some time he wavered between the legal profession, teaching and the ministry. In his later years he wondered out loud whether or not he had made the right choice or whether he should have become a minister.[1]

Few religious congregations in Vermont and New Hampshire at the end of the eighteenth century could attract or afford a resident minister and so men of the cloth, like painters, lawyers and others who had to make a living in a sparsely populated region, "made the circuit." In the intervals when a minister was not available, services would be conducted by the deacons, elders, or other prestigious members of the congregation.

Naturally, a college-educated man would have been in great demand, especially if, like Tyler, he had an established reputation as an earnest and fervent orator. The parishes in Charlestown and Claremont, New Hampshire, during the fall of 1793 invited Tyler to give a series of Sunday sermons and conduct the scripture readings.

His efforts were so appreciated that he was asked to return and lead the services on Christmas Day. *The Eagle* of Hanover, New Hampshire, reported Tyler's sermon at Claremont as follows:

> We hear from *Claremont,* that at their late CHRISTMAS CELEBRATION, a learned, serious, and pathetic discourse was delivered by ROYALL TYLER, Esq. before a numerous and respectable assembly, from this text: *And suddenly there was with the angel a multitude of heavenly hosts, praising* GOD, *and saying,* Glory to GOD *in the highest, and on earth peace, good will towards* MEN.
>
> The composition, tho' extemporaneous, was considered by the audience, as a masterly combination of elegance, and ingenuity, and the performance, a perfect model of pulpit eloquence. A HYMN, composed for the occasion, shall appear in our next.[2]

The "Christmas Hymn" by Tyler was printed in *The Eagle* on January 6, 1794.[3] On December 25 Tyler also journeyed to Charlestown and de-

---

[1] "MPT Memoirs," p. 114. Also, in a letter of March, 1799, to Joseph Nancrede, Tyler made brief mention of how he had, in his youth, tutored young children and probably given serious thought to entering the teaching profession. The letter is quoted in "TPT Memoir," pp. 143–4.

[2] *The Eagle,* I, No. 24 (Dec. 30, 1793), 3.

[3] See *Tyler Verse,* pp. 18–20.

livered the same Christmas sermon, as well as a short prayer, at the Episcopal Church there. The manuscripts of these, carefully revised, were found among his papers.[4] Mrs. Tyler, in her manuscript memoirs, provides us with some of the circumstances surrounding the composition of the discourse. Unfortunately, the other sermons which she mentions her husband composed have not survived:

> . . . he had been invited by the Warden and Vestry at Charlestown . . . to read the Episcopal services in their Church on a certain sabbath; they having no clergymen there then, they were in the habit of having Lay reading. It was just before Christmas, and the Court *had* been sitting there, or *were* to sit soon after, I forget which. There were many Lawyers there and the Judges—and many more respectable people congregated in the little Village—some of whom were Lovers of the [*Episocopal*] Church and her beautiful Liturgy, and he was solicited by all such to consent to officiate. And did so, and so far as the Prayer Book and scripture lessons went; there was nothing uncanonical in his doing so. But he also read a sermon of his own composition which *was* uncanonical, which I now have, in the house. A most beautiful sermon—and orthodox enough for any body. It was in an evening gathering of sober folks, that he had let it be known to some, that he had written several sermons. Of course he was solicited to read one—perhaps no one knew any better for the Church was a Stranger in this part of the world then. But the sermon was so much admired that he was solicited to read again on the approaching Christmas—and having written *for Christmas*—altho' some time before, he was persuaded again, and again loaded with praise and approbation from all.[5]

Although an Episcopalian by upbringing and inclination, Tyler could be very accommodating to other faiths, as the tone of his sermon indicates. In 1795 members of the Congregational Church in Guilford, then the only parish in that community, requested Tyler to compose and recite a series of discourses during the Christmas season while their pastor, the Reverend Elijah Wollage, was temporarily absent.

Tyler wrote three or four sermons, including one for Christmas Day. Another of the discourses was based on the New Testament parable of the raising of the widow's son at Nain (Luke 7:11–17). The sermon took the following lines:

[4] The two comprise Ms. No. 115 in the "RT Collection." Charlestown, the site of old Fort No. 4, was one of the earliest and most strategic settlements in that region. It is only 35 miles from Guilford where Tyler had settled and 13 miles from Claremont, making it practical for Tyler to conduct morning and evening services in the two communities on the same day.

The pulpit of the Claremont Episcopal Church had not been filled regularly since 1791 and the Episcopal Church of Charlestown had also not had a full-time rector for several years.

[5] "MPT Memoirs," pp. 113–4.

Besides a vivid description of the scene, and remarks upon the benevolent nature of our Lord's miracles, with the singularly simple style of the evangelist's record of them, without a single attempt at rhetorical ornament or oratorical amplifications, he applies his knowledge of the principles of evidence to this case; noting the impossibility of collusion [*between the various witnesses*] ... thus establishing, as far as human testimony can, the truth of the event.[6]

Still another sermon written at this time was based on the Biblical admonition, "Judge not, and ye shall not be judged" (Luke 6:37 and Matthew 7:1). Although stating this was primarily in reference to the final judgement, Tyler also pointed out "the evils resulting from rash and hasty judging, in this world, as the cause of quarrels in neighborhoods and families; of scandal, heartburnings, and the like."[7]

None of these manuscripts survive and the sermon and prayer delivered on Christmas day in 1793 remain as the sole examples of Tyler's skills in this field of endeavor.

A SERMON

THAT PORTION of this Blessed Book which I have chosen to introduce the observations upon this solemn festival may be found recorded in the second chapter of the Evangelist St. Luke in the 13th and 14th verses—

"And suddenly there was with the Angel a multitude of the heavenly host praising God, and saying, 'Glory to God in the highest and on earth peace, good will toward men.' "

This, my friends, was the joyous salutation with which the Angel of the Lord, amidst a multitude of the heavenly host, nigh eighteen centuries ago usher'd in the morn of that glorious birthday, the anniversary of which we are now assembled to celebrate. During these

---

[6] "TPT Memoir," p. 124. When writing the memoir in 1873 Tyler's son mentioned that there was, at one time, a manuscript of the Guilford Christmas discourse but he had not seen it for at least 40 years.

[7] *Ibid.*, pp. 124–5. This outline was also taken from a rough draft of the sermon among Tyler's papers. In the intervening years it has been lost.

revolving ages thousands and tens of thousands myriads and millions have enjoyed the efficacious influences of the birth of the Saviour of Mankind, and language itself would want numbers should we attempt to enumerate that great company of the redeemed who are now in the mansions of bliss, perhaps accompanying the angelic messenger in our text and the multitude of the heavenly host who visited the earth with him on that happy day—in singing Hallelujah's to the Lamb and reiterating the blissful hymn of "Glory to God in the highest, on earth peace, good will toward men."

'Tho no man is more opposed than the speaker to invidious distinctions among churches and 'tho truly sensible that the good, the wise, the pious and the worthy are to be found among all denominations of Christians who differ perhaps more in mode and form than in essentials, yet if our Episcopal Church has anything whereby she may glory above other religious societies I think we may, with true Christian candour and charity, say that it exists in the respect we pay to the birthday of the Saviour of the world.

Without doubt it is highly becoming, and our civil rulers merit the highest commendation, when by public authority at the close of the year they set apart a Day of National Thanksgiving for public and private mercies; and surely we do well, when according to the pious custom of our ancestors, as one people on one public day with united voices we offer up our unfeigned thanks to God the Creator by whom we live, move and have our being; who is the Father of all things and whose tender mercies are over all his works. But when we consider, my friends, whose birthday it is which according to the Ordinances of our Holy Church we celebrate, that it is the natal day of the Lord our Saviour who is not only the author and giver of all our temporal enjoyments but who by his amazing love, his condescending birth, his bitter sufferings and cruel death has saved us from an eternity of agony and woe, and secured to us eternal portions of felicity in the world to come; surely we have more occasion of thanksgiving and joy than when our corn, our wine and our oil are increased. Surely we ought to rejoice with exceeding great joy.

'Tho we may have no positive injunction in scripture for the observance of the solemn festival, yet while we have one spark of gratitude as men, or one ray of hope as Christians we are bound to commemorate it. We do well with our wives and our families, our children, domestics and friends to go up to our temples upon the anniversary of His birth and to speak and declare unto the congregation of the people the good things which the Lord our Saviour had done for us.

Shall we think it much to spend one day of sacred joy on the birthday of Him who spent a life of sorrow for us?

Will you not rejoice a few hours for Him who wept many agonizing days and nights for you?

Will you not devote a small pittance of your lives to the celebration and remembrance of His nativity who laid down even His most precious life for you?

Will you not consecrate one day in many days to Him who after having tasted death for your sakes is ascended into Heaven and sitteth on the right hand of God the Father where He continueth to make intercession for you?

My friends, if you have any gratitude think on these things and on this day rejoice! Be grateful! Be exceeding glad! Let me call upon you all, high and low, rich and poor, old men and maidens, young men and children to join with me in repeating the benevolent ascription in our text of—"Glory to God in the highest, on earth peace, good will toward men. For behold I bring you good tidings of great joy which shall be to all people. For unto you was born this day in the city of David a Saviour which is Christ the Lord."

To improve this day profitably, my friends, let us confirm our faith by recollecting that gracious promise made by God unto mankind immediately after the primeval transgression of our first parents, even that "the seed of the woman should bruize [sic] the Serpent's head," upon which the plan of our redemption by Jesus Christ is founded. Let us recite some of those principal prophecies in the accomplishment of which we are assured and believe that our Lord Jesus was sent into the world as the fullfilment of this inestimable promise to mankind.

We know that our Saviour was sent as the accomplishment of this promise by the preaching of John the Baptist, who pronounced him to be the Lamb of God—"For John, seeing Jesus coming unto him, saith unto him, 'Behold the Lamb of God who taketh away the sin of the world.' "[8] While John the Baptist's own coming and manner of life was foretold seven hundred years before by the Prophet Isaiah and four hundred years before by the Prophet Malachi—"Behold [I will send my messenger and he shall prepare the way before me."[9] [and] "As the voice of him who crieth in the wilderness, prepare ye the way of the Lord, make straight in the desert a high way for our God."[10]

We know that our Saviour was the Messiah from his miraculous conception and birth which was foretold by the same inspired writer seven centuries before—"Therefore the Lord himself shall give you a sign; 'Behold a virgin shall conceive, and bear a son, and shall call his name Immanuel.' "[11]

The manner of his life was also foretold, that he should be a man of sorrows and acquainted with grief.

And lastly the circumstances of his death, for we read, "And with him they crucified two thieves, the one on his right hand and the other on his left; and the Scripture was fullfilled,"[12] which was the prophecy of the same Isaiah and saith, "He was numbered with transgressors."[13]

Time will not admit of adding more prophetic proofs of the divinity of our Saviour's mission. Whoever peruses the prophecies with candour and attention must be astonished at the exactitude and precision with which so many centuries before our Saviour's birth, life and

---

[8] Jn. 1:29. Throughout the sermon Tyler placed the citations of the Biblical quotations and paraphrases in the margins of the manuscript, indicating that he might have had thoughts of publishing it at some future date. The citation form has been changed here to conform with modern usage.

[9] Mal. 3:1.

[10] Is. 40:3.

[11] Is. 7:14.

[12] Mk. 15:27-28.

[13] Is. 53:12.

circumstances and manner of death were described; and can leave no doubt on the mind that He was indeed that Son who was to be born, that Prince who was to be given, who[se] name should be called Wonderful, Counselor, The Mighty God, The Everlasting Father and The Prince of Peace.[14]

The time of our Saviour's appearance on earth affords an additional argument to the learned of His heavenly mission. We read, "When the fullness of time was come Christ came into the world." Here profane history lends its friendly aid. We learn from hence that Christ's birth was at that period when the Temple of Janus was closed by Augustus Caesar as a sign that war had ceased throughout the world, and that men being relieved from the disquietude of war might be better prepared for the reception of the Gospel of Peace. Whoever turns the historic page will see that no time since the creation of the world was more suited to the advent of the Great Prophet, who was to bring life and immortality to light through the gospel, as mankind at no age were [sic] ever more debased in their religious ideas; the whole world, some few philosophies and the Jews excepted, bowing down to sticks and stones or paying lewd, impious and abominable rites to imaginary deities created by their own depraved fancies who, if they did really exist, could only boast a pre-eminence over their worshippers in the magnitude of their follies and vices. Even the wiser heathens themselves at that period looked earnestly for some great religious reformer, and no sooner was our Saviour preached to the Gentiles than many of them believed in Him.

Do we in this enlightened age need any further proof of the divine mission of our Saviour?

Then let me call your attention to the scene of the Angels' appearance to the shepherds from whence our text is taken. To the appearance of the emblematic luminary, the New Star which shed its infant beams upon His birth.

To the declaration of the Wise Men from the East who pay'd Him homage with all the pomp of Eastern magnificence.

[14] Is. 9:6.

To the miracles which He wrought. To His bitter death when the vail of [*the*] Temple was rent in twain, when the sun hid his face in darkness, when the sheeted dead mingled with the living and the earth trembled from her centre or to the great article of his glorious Resurrection and Ascension into Heaven—all these afford irrefragable proof that He is indeed Christ the Lord.

No, my friends, a doubt cannot arise in our minds but that glorious personage whose birth we now celebrate is the promised Messiah of whom "God spake by the mouth of his Holy Prophets which have been since the world began to give knowledge of salvation unto His people by the remission of their sins."[15]

It is a mispense[16] of time to prove it elaborately. Let us rather employ ourselves in recollecting those actions of His blameless life which may incite us to imitate Him in all His imitable perfections—and here, my friends, the bright examples of His spotless life rush so fast upon the mind that we know not where to begin or where to end. Well did St. John the Evangelist say, "That if all the things which Jesus did were noted in a book the world itself would not contain the books which would be written."[17]

All ranks, ages and conditions of men may find something worthy and not impracticable to be imitated in His spotless life.

Shall I refer my young friends, the children of this assembly, to the childhood of our Divine Master; there they will see a most perfect pattern of submission and duty to their earthly parents. For we read that He, even the Lord of Heaven when on earth was subject unto His parents, and even in His expiring moments gave a tender instance of filial affection by recommending His mother to the care of a beloved disciple.[18]

Would my young friends know the value of learning and the advantages of forsaking juvenile amusements and consorting themselves with the wise and the aged? Let them view the Divine Jesus in

[15] Lk. 1:70, 77.
[16] The word "waste" was written in by Tyler above the original word "mispense."
[17] Jn. 21:25.
[18] Lk. 2:51 and Jn. 19:26–7.

the Temple at "twelve years of age sitting in the midst of the Doctors both hearing them and asking them questions when all that heard Him were astonished at His understanding and answers."[19]

The discernment of those of maturer age render it in some measure unnecessary to point out to them those actions of Him whose whole life was a priceless lesson of whatever is due to God or Man.

Give me leave, my friends, however, to observe that if you have ever suffered from the sallies of an ungoverned temper, if you are too irritable in your dispositions, too apt to resent insult or proffer abuse, you learn from our Divine Master the most admirable government of your temper, for He, when under all the poignant woundings of insult, ignominy and bodily pain, held his peace. He was as a sheep dumb before his shearers, He opened not His mouth and when He was reviled He reviled not again; when He suffered He threatend not but committed Himself to Him who judgeth righteously.[20] Would you wish to attain the noble virtue of disinterested friendship? Behold our Lord weeping the tears of friendship at the grave of Lazarus, when even the hard-h[e]arted Jews exclaimed, "Behold how He loved Him."[21]

Would you learn sympathy for the distressed? See Him comforting the disconsolate Widow of Nain at the funeral of her only Son: "For when the Lord saw her He had compassion on her and said unto her, 'Weep not.'"[22] Would you learn submission to civic rulers? See Him paying tribute unto Caesar.[23] Would you learn the generous virtue of forgiveness? Hear Him pray for even His murderers, "Father forgive them for they know not what they do."[24]

Lastly, would you learn resignation to the will of God in the allotments of His providence, would you even prepare yourselves for the solemn hour of death itself? View our Divine Master in the Garden of Gethsemane when in the agony of His soul the sweat ran as it were drops of blood from His sacred face, and He prayed to His Father

[19] Lk. 2:46–7.
[20] 1 Pet. 2:23.
[21] Jn. 11:35–6.
[22] Lk. 7:13.
[23] Mt. 22:21.
[24] Lk. 23:34.

saying, "Father if thou be willing remove this Cup from me, but nevertheless, not my will but Thine be done."[25]

All these divine examples should be carried as valuable lessons for man. For in our Saviour's school we learn lessons for time and eternity.

Although we may expect to reap the rich fruits of our Saviour's birth more especially in another world yet we should remember that all power is committed unto Him by God the Father and that He moves the wheels of universal providence.

It is by our Saviour's goodness that the sun pursues its annual course and sheds upon the earth light, heat and vegetative life. He causeth the season to revolve and each season to come laden with its peculiar blessing to man. He giveth the former and the latter rain. It is His dew which drops marrow and fatness in all our paths. He thundereth in the Heavens but in the midst of His thunder His mercy is seen for it is His lightning which refreshes the air. He cloatheth the earth with snow as with a garment and He tempereth the wind to the shorn lamb.

To Him was given the heathen for His heritage and these uttermost parts of the earth for His possession. He led our forefathers over the tractless ocean. He caused the plains, the valleys and the hills to rejoice in their produce and this American wilderness to bud and blossom as the rose.

He supported us in the great political contest for the birth-right God gave to us as men. He secured our independence as a people and gave us a name and a seat among the nations of the earth, and it is He who hath set us on high as the great day star from whence civil light and liberty is dispersed into all the benighted empires of the old world.

It was our Saviour who raised up a Washington for our leader. He gave him wisdom for council, He taught his hands to war and his fingers to fight and shielded him in the day of battle. And when He had returned him to his home in peace, He inspired him with patriot energy to come forth from the bosom of his family, and from a most honourable retreat to take upon the reins of our government and made

[25] Lk. 22:42.

him the uniting link that should bind the citizens of these United States in one federal bond of amity and peace.

It was our Saviour who brought this, his Holy Episcopal Church into America, and 'tho upon its first introduction into this land it met with some opposition from other persuasions of our fellow Christians which we would rather charitably impute to the narrow zeal and bigotry of the times in which they lived than to a perverseness of heart, yet he has caused this His Church to increase and daily additions are making to it of such as we trust shall be saved. It is our Blessed Saviour who has caused His day spring of religious liberty from on high to visit us and that we may now worship every man according to the dictates of his own conscience. This very building in which we are now assembled should be a lasting monument of gratitude to our Saviour to all those who worship within its walls. Consider, my friends, that it is scarce a century ago and even within the memory of some of you who now hear me that this spot whereon it is erected was covered with the tall trees of the forest and almost impenetrable shed its awful gloom over the place whose silence was only interrupted by the wild ravings of the beasts of the desert and by savage man more fierce than they.

On this very spot perhaps some time or other the Indian prepared his horrid war feast. Here he kindled his merciless flames. Here with cruel ingenuity he protracted and augmented the torments of his hapless prisoner and here he sated himself with the horrid banquet of human blood.

No Christian voice was then heard here, except the cries and mournings of the captive mother who was dragged with her husband and children from her friends and home at the heels of her barbarous conqueror to suffer hunger, thirst, fatigue and the inclemencies of a winter's sky. She indeed raises her voice but it is in wailings for her husband sunk beneath the tomahawk of the Indian or in shrieks for her tender infant dash'd by the inhuman savage against the rocks.

This picture is not too highly painted. Many of you have known from your ancestors that these things are true. Contrast this barbarous scene and be grateful! See the country attaining the perfection of agriculture. See the numerous happy families, convenient buildings and fertile farms. View the very appearance of the inhabitants who crowd this church from the vicinity, and on this spot once dedicated to war, rapine and cruelty a temple erected to the God of Peace. Instead of the cries of the captive and the savage war song there now ascend acclamations of gratitude and songs of praise to the source of eternal love.

There is not one blessing, my friends, great or small, public or private but you owe to [our] divine benefactor.

Are you prospered in your worldly affairs? Hath God set an hedge about you, are your garners full and have your flocks increased? Is your table spread with the fat of the land and does your cup overflow? Have you friends who are kind? Have you children and do they conduct themselves worthily? Be grateful and remember that Christ the Benefactor gave you all these blessings richly to enjoy them.

Have you been preserved from bodily accident, from fire, famine or pestilence (or that deadly contagion which has so lately ravaged our sister state). Then, my friends, be grateful to our Lord the Savior, for he [. . .]

Have you met with misfortune, is poverty your lot? Do you ever go sorrowing all your days? Still be grateful! And remember that afflictions are often blessings in disguise and that these light afflictions which are but for a moment often work out a far more exceeding and eternal weight of glory.

Have you been bereaved of near relatives or dear friends by death, have you lost the husband or wife of your youth, or the son and daughter of your best hopes? And when you have been bowed down with sorrow and clouds, and thick darkness are round about you and when ready to faint and despair you have found yourselves surprizingly supported [by] a ray of hope suddenly springing up within you, succeeded by an unexpected serenity of soul, then be grateful to the

Lord your comforter. For it was this good Samaritan, this true friend and neighbor to mankind, whose birth we this day celebrate, who poured the oil and wine of His consolation into your wounds and bound up the bruizes of your broken heart.

Let us not waste our time and thoughts in fruitless inquiries, after the manner of some, into the extent and number of those who finally reap the benefits of our Saviour's birth. But rather, let every man look to his own conduct and by imitating the example He hath set us by faith and patience endeavour to make our own calling and election sure.

It becomes us all, however, to speak with the highest reverence to the extent of our Saviour's redeeming love. He killeth and maketh alive according to His own good pleasure and who shall say unto Him who thundereth in the Heavens, "What doest thou!?"

Doubtless, my friends, there are many saints in glory who if they had been judged by some of their fellow men would have been con-demned to regions of unutterable woe. For aught we know, my friends, the savage original of this country who disgraced this land and human nature by the most atrocious cruelties has in some way unknown to us felt that all efficacious power of the divine spirit and is now arrayed in white robes of innocence and righteousness and chanting forth the praises of the author of the Gospel of Peace, and perhaps lifting his voice with ours in this solemn festival and singing, "Glory to God in the highest, on earth peace, good will toward men."

Perhaps the Deist may cavil and the weak-minded Christian when he turns the page of history and sees the world filled with war, con-tention and tumult and nation rising up against nation since the birth of our Saviour, when he turns his eyes toward Europe in the present day and sees the numerous armies of man collected to ruin and murder each other, when he views the fertile land of France made fat with the best blood of its own citizens he may inquire where is that peace on earth, that good will toward men with which the Angel of the Lord hail'd mankind upon the natal day of our Saviour.

These men err as the Jews erred before them. They consider not that our Saviour's kingdom is not of this world. The true Christian knows that there is this peace on earth and feels the effect of this good will toward men. He finds a peace, a serenity within his own bosom which those who do not feel it cannot conceive and those who do want words to express. It is that peace of God the Saviour which according to the energetic language of inspiration, "passeth all understanding."

And the genuine Christian shall possess this peace amidst all the contentions of mankind. He shall possess it amidst the din of arms, amidst the confused noise of the battle of the warrior and amidst garments rolled in blood. He shall possess it on earth and when these Heavens above us shall pass away with a great noise, when the elements shall melt with fervent heat and this earth and the things therein shall be burnt up.[26] And he shall possess it when the mighty Angel of the Lord shall lift his hand towards Heaven and swear that time shall be no more.[27]

Although, my friends, this peace is amply sufficient for us, yet we have a sure and certain word of prophecy, 'tho we may not live to behold its fullfilment, that the time shall come when the gospel of peace shall extend from the rising to the setting sun and from the rivers to the ends of the earth. When all men shall know the true God, when every knee shall bow in adoration to our Saviour and every tongue shall confess him to be Lord, to the glory of God the Father. When even on this earth nation shall no more rise up against nation but they shall beat their swords into ploughshares and their spears into pruning hooks and learn war no more. When every man shall sit under his own vine and own fig tree and have none to disturb him or to make him afraid. When the wolf shall dwell with the lamb and the leopard shall lie down with the kid and the calf and the young lion and the fatling together, and a little child shall lead then. When the suckling child shall play on the hole of the asp, and the weaned child shall put his hand in the cockatrice's den. When they shall not hurt nor destroy in

---

[26] 2 Pet. 3:10.   [27] Rev. 10:5–6.

all my Holy Mountain, saith the Lord, for the earth shall be full of the knowledge of the Lord as the waters cover the sea. Hasten this Blissfull Day.

Amen Halleluia Amen.

Now unto Him who loved us, who condescended to take upon Him our nature and on this day to be born of a woman, who suffered that we might be happy, who died that we might live forever, and who hath arose from the dead and hath ascended to the right hand of God the Father, where He continueth to make intercession for us through Him to God, His and our common father, be all glory and honour, might, majesty, dominion and power, world without end, Amen.

A PRAYER AFTER SERMON
ON CHRISTMAS DAY

GRANT, O MOST MERCIFUL God, that the feeble attempt which we have this day made to celebrate the birth of thy beloved Son, which we have heard with our outward ears, may not be like that seed which fell by the wayside and was choaked; but being accompanied by the mighty power of thy blessed spirit may sink deep into our hearts and so far as they are agreeable to thy holy word and will may take root there; and of the peace[a]ble fruits of love, gratitude and obedience may bring forth some fifty and some a hundred fold to the happiness of mankind and the glory of thy Holy Name.

Dismiss us from this thy temple with thy blessing. Go with us to our several places of abode, meet us and bless us there. May we feed on the fruits of thy bounty without sin. May we break our bread with thankfullness, drink our wine with a merry heart and send portions unto them who are needy.

May we temper our mirth with discretion, may we be gay with innocence and may the employments of this evening bear the reflections of thy memory. May all mankind remember that they are brethern and that thy family is a family of love. As we are all journeying to one heavenly country may we not fall out with our fellow travellers by the way.

If the source of war be necessary may we not destroy one another in the midst of the peace. May the rights of conscience be free, may all who differ in modes and forms of worship still be united in one bond of charity and love. And as thou hast seen fit to beautify the fields of thy natural world with flowers and fruits of various dies, so in they moral world may the prayers of thy numerous votaries, approaching thee under various modes and forms, but all centering their adoration in thee their common father, rise and ascend unto heaven in a rich and variegated profusion of incense to thy praise.

Be gracious unto our friends, our neighbors, our relatives, our acquaintances, our country, our land, the whole world of mankind and universal nature. Variate thy mercies unto them as their several exigenc[i]es may require and do unto them whatsoever seemeth good in thy sight for we know and are assured that whatever is from thee is right. Pity the sons and daughters of affliction, protect the widow and the orphan and hear the sighing of the captive, the prisoner and the broken hearted. And in blessing them bless *us,* even us O our Father also. And when we shall no more celebrate the nativity of thy beloved [*son*] here on earth may we be all fitted and prepared to drink new wine at those eternal festivals of joy which He has prepared in mansions of bliss for those who love Him.

These our imperfect petitions, as we merit nothing of ourselves, we humbly proffer in the name and for the sake of thy son Christ Jesus, our Saviour, whose birth we this day celebrate whom thou hearest always; in whose worthy name and in the words He hath taught us would we sum up all our petitions, addressing thee as—Our Father &c.—

The "Spondee" Essays

THE ESSAYS and anecdotes by Tyler that were written as part of the "Colon and Spondee" partnership with Joseph Dennie make up the largest gathering of prose in this volume outside of "The Bay Boy." Light and topical in content they show Tyler at his most engaging.

The aim of the column was basically satirical. The two partners set out to comment upon and lampoon contemporary American and foreign politics and life in both verse and prose. The column resulted in immediate fame for both partners from the time it was started in 1794 until it ended in 1811. Throughout the eastern seaboard, especially in population centers as Worcester, Boston, Philadelphia, New York and Hartford, the reputation of "Colon and Spondee" as accurate spokesmen of the Federalist point of view on politics and as commentators on American culture, literature, morality and life in general grew daily.

Imitation has been called the supreme form of flattery. If this is the case, Dennie and Tyler were the period's most copied columnists. In other newspapers and periodicals there surfaced such competitors as "Messrs. Dactyl and Comma," "Quip, Crank and Co.," "The Shop of Messrs. Anapoestic and Trochee," "The Manufactory of Bite 'em Slyly," "Jonathan Dactyle," "Messrs. Verbal and Trochee" and others. Naturally, none of them could vie with Tyler and Dennie. The breath of the joint talents of "Colon and Spondee" allowed them to far outstrip their competition.

It appears that the originator of the column's concept was Tyler. Joseph T. Buckingham, who was on intimate terms with both men when he served as a printer's devil at Walpole, said that "the original idea of this fictitious Shop of Colon & Spondee, was the offspring of Tyler's prolific brain; and the first public manifestation of it was made in the Eagle. . . ."[1]

"The Shop of Messrs. Colon and Spondee" was opened by Tyler and Dennie in Josiah Dunham's *The Eagle: or, The Dartmouth Centinel* on July 28, 1794. The newspaper had been established by Dunham in July, 1793, at Hanover, New Hampshire. It was evident from the start that the publisher desired to give his paper a decided literary cast.

Until January, 1795, "Colon and Spondee" contributed on a fairly regular basis a wide variety of prose and poetry to *The Eagle*. As had been predetermined, Dennie was the author of most of the prose while Tyler was

---

[1] *Specimens of Newspaper Literature*, II, 203.

to take care of the verse.[2] This division of duties, however, did not always hold true in future years, and although Dennie was not a versifier the more talented Tyler often contributed anecdotes and essays.

During the seven month sojourn of "Colon and Spondee" with *The Eagle* there was only one prose item by Tyler (signed "Spondee"). Entitled "Prime Pumpkin," it appeared on January 26, 1795. It was published simultaneously in Robert Treat Paine's *Federal Orrery* in Boston and Isaiah Thomas reprinted it in his *Massachusetts Spy* in Worcester on February 18, 1795, under the title, "Story of a Vermont Pumpkin."

One of the reasons Tyler and Dennie probably decided to leave *The Eagle* at the beginning of 1795 was Dunham's inability to increase the space devoted to literary contributions.

There is no doubt that Dunham himself was inclined to improve the cultural tone of the paper but his rural subscribers indicated their preference for fewer frills and more hard news. In February, 1794, Dunham issued in *The Eagle* proposals for publishing a combination literary-political magazine.[3] A week later he elaborated on this plan, stating that the new publication would be called "The Minerva; or, Rural Magazine." It would appear monthly, contain 48 pages per issue and would roll off the presses as soon as sufficient subscribers were obtained.[4]

Four months later Dunham admitted that public response to the new venture was poor and a search through the pages of *The Eagle* turned up no further mention of "The Minerva."[5] It is probable that Dunham had planned to retain Tyler and Dennie to furnish the bulk of the new magazine's contents and the failure of subscriptions to materialize by late summer was a deciding factor in the partners' decision to leave *The Eagle* and seek greener fields elsewhere.

"Colon and Spondee" broke with *The Eagle* in February, 1795 (the last column, signed "C." appeared in the paper on Feb. 23, p. 3). The partners felt that their talents might be better recognized among Boston's larger audience than in the smaller more provincial towns of northern New England.

[2] This division of duties and the assignment of the pseudonyms "Spondee" to Tyler and "Colon" to Dennie has been well documented. See *Tyler Verse*, p. xli-xlii, for full citations on this point.
[3] *The Eagle*, I, No. 30 (Feb. 10, 1794), 4. Dunham also issued his proposals in *The Newhampshire and Vermont Journal*, I, No. 45 (Feb. 14, 1794), 3. For a biographical note on Dunham see H. Milton Ellis, "Joseph Dennie and His Circle," *Bulletin of the University of Texas*, No. 40 (July 15, 1915), 63.
[4] *The Eagle*, I, No. 31 (Feb. 17, 1794), 3.
[5] *Ibid.*, I, No. 47 (June 9, 1794), 4.

Their friend, Robert Treat Paine, had started the *Federal Orrery* in Boston on October 20, 1794. His entreaties that "Colon and Spondee" should try their fortune in the "literary emporium" of Boston were apparently convincing. For over two months—from January 22 to April 2, 1795—Tyler and Dennie used the *Orrery* as an outlet for their efforts.[6] All the "Colon and Spondee" contributions, in 12 issues between January and April, are signed with Dennie's initial "C." except for one essay signed "Spondee," and two prose pieces and one poem which are unsigned.

Since the vain Dennie, who was in Boston at this period, was wont to take all the credit possible for the "Colon and Spondee" pieces, it is assumed that the unsigned poem and two prose efforts were submitted from Guilford by the more modest Tyler. The signed "Spondee" essay on the Vermont Pumpkin shows that Tyler was very much active in the "Colon and Spondee" collaboration at this time.

The first unsigned Tyler piece appeared on January 22, while the other one was published by Paine on March 5. Dennie submitted six other columns after this latter date and the last "Colon and Spondee" piece in the *Orrery* appeared on April 2. Tyler was becoming more and more occupied with his growing law practice and Dennie was involved in establishing his own literary magazine, *The Tablet*, in Boston.

The Tablet, started in May failed to attract either sufficient contributors or subscribers. It lasted for only thirteen issues and permanently passed from the scene in August.[7]

There is no doubt that the partnership was in a very unsettled state in early 1795. Dennie's over optimism about *The Tablet* and his depression at its failure was one contributing factor. Another was the physical separation of the pair—one in Boston, the other in Vermont.

For months the partnership tossed and turned without either Dennie or Tyler in a position to pull things together. Even while committed to Paine's *Orrery* during the opening months of 1795, "Colon and Spondee" still considered contributing to a rival Boston newspaper, the *Columbian Centinel* published by Benjamin Russell.

In the February 21, 1795, issue of the paper Russell inserted the following Editor's Note: "We acknowledge the favour of an original from the Shop

[6] Paine had published Tyler's poem, "Occasional Prologue," in the *Orrery* on Dec. 29, 1794, but it was not a "Colon and Spondee" production. The paper was also to reprint much of Tyler's work after "Colon and Spondee" left for Walpole. The publishing history of the *Orrery* is found in Clarence S. Brigham, *History and Bibliography of American Newspapers, 1690–1820* (Worcester, 1947), I, 296.

[7] The background of Dennie's establishment of *The Tablet*, its patrons and its publishing history are contained in Ellis, pp. 73–83.

of Messrs. *Colon* and *Spondee,* it shall appear." The attempt by the partners to play the *Orrery* against the *Centinel* in competition for their column apparently was aborted, for at no time during the remainder of the year did the "Colon and Spondee" masthead appear in the *Centinel*. Whatever was the original contribution which Russell received, he decided not to publish it.[8]

Following the last appearance of "Colon and Spondee" in the *Orrery*, the column disappeared from the public eye for a year. From April, 1795, until April, 1796, no fresh material came from either partner's pen. Dennie was trying to re-establish his morale after the failure of *The Tablet*. He removed from Boston to Walpole in the fall of 1795 and gave thoughts to becoming an attorney.

Tyler, on the other hand, had both personal and professional problems to occupy his time. He had been appointed State's Attorney for Windham County and his own law practice was growing rapidly. His reputation as a successful pleader for the downtrodden and unfortunate filled his docket but not his pocketbook.

Since May, 1794, when he had married Mary Palmer in a secret ceremony at Framingham, Massachusetts, Tyler had been attempting to bring his young bride to live with him in Vermont. In early 1795 he tried to make the voyage but poor sleighing that winter forced him to leave her and their new-born son, Royall, in Framingham for another year. Tyler continued, however, to make several trips between Framingham and Guilford during the spring and summer of 1795 and these journeys, together with his legal duties, partly explain why he was unable to resume the "Colon and Spondee" column.[9]

Nevertheless, by the end of the summer both partners independently thought it was time to attempt a rebirth of the column. On October 2 Dennie wrote to Tyler from Walpole:

I propose residing here for some time. This information may induce you to descend from the mountains, to cooperate with your friend. . . . I am here, more afloat than at any time since I first navigated the ocean of life. . . . I want your advice. . . .[10]

[8] In the very next issue of the *Centinel* (Feb. 28) there appeared an article on Jacobin Clubs under the title, "Intelligence Extraordinary." It is a subject on which both Tyler and Dennie were to write but since it is an unsigned column it is impossible to state definitely it is the "Colon and Spondee" piece which Russell announced he had received.

[9] For details of Tyler's courtship and marriage of Mary Palmer see "MPT Memoirs," pp. 52–3, 67–8, 82–4, 109–14, and 127–39; and *GTP*, pp. 73–6, 104–7, 169–80.

[10] The letter, dated Oct. 2, 1795, is included in "TPT Memoir," pp. 90–2 and reprinted in *The Letters of Joseph Dennie*, pp. 150–2.

Before the letter reached Tyler he sent off a note to Dennie, dated October 7. He suggested that the two get together to resurrect the "dead Babe of Boston," an apparent reference to the short and fruitless stay of "Colon and Spondee" with the *Federal Orrery*. To whet Dennie's appetite, Tyler further said, "I have a little plan for you—come and hear it."[11]

Each others' letters apparently made Tyler and Dennie think seriously of returning to their joint literary endeavors, although nothing concrete took place until April, 1796. Tyler had been working on several projects. He had commenced *The Algerine Captive* in early 1795 and in the same year he had tried to complete a comedy, an opera and a book of poetry. Dennie mentioned these projects in his letter of October 2 and the rumors were given additional weight by the following "Literary Intelligence" in *The Newhampshire and Vermont Journal* on December 8:

A poet of Vermont, whose easy and classical lines have always ministered delight to the admirers of sprightliness and simplicity, it is expected, will soon gratify the public by a volume, entitled "THE PROLUSIONS OF ALI."—If the trustees of the Boston Theatre should so far "delight to honour" the theatrical works of their own country . . . a Dramatick and American writer, who has set a Newyork audience in a roar by his *wit,* and stole softly on musical ears with his *song,* will present to the manager an Opera and a Comedy, which, having their basis in domestick scenes, may interest a patriotick audience . . .[12]

No record exists that Tyler completed "The Prolusions of Ali" and the opera, but by early 1796 he was at least far enough advanced on *The Algerine Captive* that he could heed Dennie's plea of resurrecting "The Shop of Messrs. Colon and Spondee." His home life was more settled (he had finally brought his wife to Guilford in February) and his law practice had achieved some semblance of order.

Since residing in Walpole Dennie had become increasingly familiar with the merits of *The Newhampshire and Vermont Journal: Or, The Farmer's Weekly Museum,* published by Isaiah Thomas, the noted Worcester, Massachusetts, publisher and printed by David Carlisle of Walpole. Thomas provided the capital while Carlisle was, in reality, shop manager. Ever since its establishment as a weekly in April, 1793, the newspaper had grown in both reputation and circulation. Besides reflecting the Federalist political

[11] The original Ms. letter, dated from Guilford, Vt., Oct. 7, 1795, is at the New Hampshire Historical Society, Concord.

[12] *The Newhampshire and Vermont Journal,* III, No. 140 (Dec. 8, 1795), 3. For possible identity of the comedy mentioned see Péladeau, "Royall Tyler's *Other* Plays," *New England Quarterly,* XL, No. 1 (March, 1967), 53–5.

viewpoint, it also entertained its readers with a lively literary section.[13]

These factors, plus the closeness of Walpole to Guilford, contributed to the decision by Tyler and Dennie to ally themselves with *The Newhampshire and Vermont Journal*. The newspaper had reprinted several of their columns from *The Eagle* and the *Federal Orrery* in previous years and both men were well known in the paper's immediate circulation areas on both sides of the Connecticut River. (In 1794, Tyler, Dennie and John C. Chamberlain, another young attorney, had collaborated on an original column entitled, "Saunterer," which was printed in *The Newhampshire and Vermont Journal*.[14])

On March 29, 1796, Thomas dissolved the partnership with Carlisle and in the next issue on April 5, Carlisle notified his subscribers that the newspaper would be continued as before with himself as sole owner. He promised several changes and improvements in the appearance and content of the publication. In his front-page notice he said specifically that the paper's readers would soon be able to enjoy "*small parcels* of the fancy goods of Mess. COLON and SPONDEE."[15]

Over the next two and a half years—until the end of 1799—Tyler and Dennie contributed more than 80 different "Colon and Spondee" columns to *The Newhampshire and Vermont Journal* and its direct successor, *The Farmer's Weekly Museum*.[16]

On assuming sole ownership of the newspaper in April, Carlisle had made Dennie editor, and from that time forward he made certain that the paper's literary content took on increasing importance. By the end of 1796, however, Tyler's contributions to the "Shop" had declined drastically. In an

---

[13] For a fine biography of Thomas see Clifford K. Shipton, *Isaiah Thomas, Printer, Patriot and Philantropist, 1749–1831* (Rochester, 1948). Thomas' troubles with Carlisle are put forth on pp. 61, 76–8. See also *The Letters of Joseph Dennie*, pp. 171, 178, and Ellis, pp. 84–5. The publishing history of *The Newhampshire and Vermont Journal* is in Brigham, I, 186–9.

[14] For the "Saunterer" essays attributed to Tyler see below, pp. 322, 332–45.

[15] *The Newhampshire and Vermont Journal*, IV, No. 157 (April 5, 1796), 1. A discussion of the break between Thomas and Carlisle is in Ellis, pp. 86–7.

[16] The change in name came with the issue of April 4, 1797. These years marked the peak of the paper's reputation and circulation. For details see Ellis, pp. 92–4.

Of the 79 original pieces during 1796–99 there were 55 essays, anecdotes or other prose items and 24 verses. A number of miscellaneous pieces, such as reprints of works by other authors, push the total number of "Colon and Spondee" contributions to more than 80. The annual breakdown is as follows: 1796—seven prose and three verse items; 1797—20 prose and 11 verse; 1798—11 prose and three verse; and 1799—17 prose and seven verse.

effort to goad him back to work, Dennie humorously announced his demise on January 24, 1797 in the following manner: "The heirs of 'SPONDEE' are informed, by the *surviving* partner, that he shall soon take out letters of poetical administration and exhibit an inventory of the goods and estate of the defunct."[17]

Although Tyler returned to the "Shop," his contributions became more irregular. Partial reason for this is given by a notice in the July 24 issue of the paper which said that "the elder partner in the shop of Mess. Colon and Spondee, is preparing for the press, a collection of Fugitive Pieces, wrought in his own loom . . ."[18] What these "fugitive pieces" were is not known and the volume never appeared. Besides all these miscellaneous literary projects which caused Tyler to neglect temporarily his responsibilities as "Spondee" was the overriding consideration that literature throughout his life was always an avocation and that it could be and was put aside when the duties of his legal career pressed upon him.

Everything went smoothly at Walpole and Guilford through 1797 (*The Algerine Captive* rolled off Carlisle's presses in August) and into the next year. But by the end of 1798 another crisis arose which, although it turned out to be temporary in nature, foreshadowed the physical parting of the partners a little more than a year later. Tyler had been complaining that his literary responsibilities were occupying too much of his time and detracting him from his legal career. Dennie, on the other hand, had reached the point where he felt he had accomplished all that he could in Walpole and should try to achieve a wider and financially more remunerative fame in a larger metropolitan area. With both men so distracted, the literary quality of the paper showed a marked decline.

"The Shop of Messrs. Colon and Spondee" voiced their dissatisfaction with the outlook for the future in November, 1798:

Business is rather dull at "The Shop of COLON and SPONDEE." Customers are few, and Mr. WEISER, the old tenant, rings his bason about their ears. He tosses about his powder with such an air of gracefulness, and brandishes his keen razor with such dexterity, that the partners think seriously of quitting the premises.[19]

---

[17] *The Newhamphire and Vermont Journal*, IV, No. 199 (Jan. 24, 1797), 3.

[18] *The Farmer's Weekly Museum*, V, No. 225 (July 14, 1797), 3.

[19] *Ibid.*, VI, No. 191 (Nov. 5, 1798), 3. Mr. Weiser (also spelled "Wiser") was a Hanover, N.H., barber in whose establishment "Colon and Spondee" had first opened their "shop" in 1794. Even though they had since moved to Walpole the partners continued to retain their old "residence" in Hanover. See below the original advertisement for "The Shop of Messrs. Colon and Spondee," pp. 202–04.

A reason for their dissatisfaction with the paper was its shaky financial condition and their joint distrust of Carlisle's business methods. However, Carlisle was able to persuade the two that the financial and literary fortunes of *The Farmer's Weekly Museum,* in great measure, were tied to the reputation lent it by Tyler and Dennie. So, for a little longer the pair were placated; Tyler promised to write as time allowed and Dennie remained in Walpole as editor, although in a reduced capacity.[20]

At the beginning of 1799 Dennie was again forced to exhort Tyler to contribute further essays and verses. His continual prodding bore fruit for in February he announced: "We are glad to hear again from our dear old friend on [sic] the Green Mountains. His laugh exhilerates every reader of the Museum. We have had the strongest reason to lament, that Comus and he should be so long 'Comates and brothers in exile,' from the purlieus of this paper."[21]

The year 1799 was a productive one for the "Shop." As if they planned to exit in the proverbial "blaze of glory," Tyler and Dennie outdid themselves. Both qualitatively and numerically 1799 was one of the high points in the careers of both men.

They continued and improved upon their series of paragraph criticisms of different authors called "Shreds of Criticism," and they opened a new department entitled "An Author's Evenings." These columns consisted of short reflections on subjects of contemporary interest with emphasis on literature, both American and foreign, illustrated by extended extracts from various authors' works. By the end of the year there had appeared 11 "Author's Evenings" essays. The majority were from Dennie's pen, although a number of excellent ones were also contributed by Tyler.

But by September the end was in sight. Dennie was even more vocal than in the past about his dissatisfaction with being caught in "the backwash of fame." Talented, but also vain, egotistic and ambitious, he desired more than being the mere editor of the finest newspaper in New England. He wanted to immerse himself in the political and literary world and this could be done only in Boston, New York or Philadelphia.

Tyler, too, had his own personal reasons for ending the partnership, most of which evolved from his increasing duties as state's attorney and the possibility of his election to the Vermont Supreme Court. (He did serve as a Supreme Court judge from 1801 to 1807 and as Chief Justice until 1813, being elected to the bench a total of 12 times.)

[20] An expression of the dissatisfaction with Carlisle is found in Ellis, pp. 104–5. Thomas returned as publisher of the paper on Feb. 20, 1798.

[21] *The Farmer's Weekly Museum,* VI, No. 306 (Feb. 11, 1799), 3.

In August, 1799, Dennie thought seriously of running for Congress but the opportunity did not materialize. Failing in this, he sought political office through the patronage of his Federalist friends. After several false starts he finally succeeded in being appointed private secretary to Timothy Pickering, the U.S. Secretary of State. He was also offered the editorship of John W. Fenno's *Gazette of the United States*. By the end of September Dennie had packed and left for Philadelphia, then capital of the young nation.[22]

With the rather sudden dissolution of the partnership in August and September there were a number of loose ends left hanging untied. Tyler had completed a couple of "Spondee" contributions which he did not want to send to Carlisle. One of these essays he apparently gave to his friend, Benjamin Smead, then publisher of *The Federal Galaxy* in Brattleboro. Whether or not Smead hoped for other pieces from "Spondee" is unknown, but the column which appeared on September 9, 1799, is the only one which he published.[23]

In 1801 Dennie was offered the editorship of a new literary magazine, *The Port Folio*, to be published in Philadelphia. He was to make the publication the finest such effort to appear in the United States up to that time and was to remain its editor until his death on January 7, 1812.

Although several hundred miles separated the two men and there is no record Tyler and Dennie ever saw each other again during the last 12 years of Dennie's life, the mails allowed the two to remain very close friends. In the early years of *The Port Folio* the struggling editor called upon Tyler several times to fill his columns with original verse. "The Author's Evenings" essays, which "Colon and Spondee" had started in Walpole, were continued in the Philadelphia magazine.[24]

In 1816 Harrison Hall, then publisher of *The Port Folio*, used documents,

[22] Ellis, pp. 105, 108–33. That the partners separated on friendly terms is borne out by the praise Dennie continued to lavish on Tyler. In the *Gazette of the United States* early in 1800 Dennie in an editorial note described Tyler as "A native American, though not an American *native*, nor altogether a True American; yet a gentleman who writes verses; and who having a certain facility or *knack* (like a naughty varlet) of infusing sense, genius and wit into his compositions, lies buried amongst ironworks and implacable bores, in the polished state of Vermont."

[23] Although the piece is not signed, it is known that Tyler was an intimate friend of Smead's, while Dennie was not. It is, therefore, assumed that if anyone was to give Smead a "Colon and Spondee" column it would have been Tyler. Smead did print some of Tyler's other efforts, notably the full text of *An Oration on the Death of George Washington* in the June 28, 1800, issue of the *Galaxy*. See below, pp. 269.

[24] The Tyler poems in *The Port Folio* are found in *Tyler Verse*, pp. 110ff. Dennie's years in Philadelphia are well put forth in Ellis, pp. 135–214.

letters and manuscripts at his disposal to annotate a complete run of the magazine. In the margins he identified many of the contributions by various authors who had written for *The Port Folio* under initials, pseudonyms or otherwise anonymously. These annotations provide the basis for definitely assigning three "Author's Evenings" and two other columns in 1801 and 1802 to Tyler.[25]

They are the final known contributions by Tyler under the masthead of "Colon and Spondee," although Dennie was to continue the "Author's Evenings" essays himself until 1811. The partnership had lasted from 1794 to 1811. It had been amazingly productive and had provided both men with a matchless platform for their literary productions.

For Dennie, the column had served as a vehicle by which he amassed great contemporary reputation as editor of *The Farmer's Weekly Museum* and *The Port Folio*. For Tyler, with no overriding desires for literary fame, the"Spondee" essays, poems and anecdotes gave him an outlet for his muse without unduly interfering with his career as attorney and jurist.

Each man contributed his own personality and style to "The Shop of Messrs. Colon and Spondee." The talents of one complimented the other's and although very different in character and outlook they enjoyed and were stimulated by each other's company. Time, distance and separation never interfered with a deep friendship. The duration of such a fruitful partnership for so many years attests to this.

The following collection of "Spondee" pieces by Tyler includes separate works of all types written between 1794 and 1802. Attribution of some of these can be made through the existence of the manuscripts among Tyler's papers. Others are assigned to Tyler's canon by means of the annotated copy of *The Spirit of the Farmer's Museum* now at the Boston Public Library.

Following the departure of Dennie and Tyler in 1799, the literary columns of *The Farmer's Weekly Museum* suffered from a lack of original material of quality. Carlisle, however, wanted to take advantage of the fine

---

[25] The annotations have been discussed by Randolph C. Randall in "Authors of the *Port Folio* Revealed by the Hall Files," *American Literature*, XI (Jan., 1940), 379–416. Hall made no pretense that he knew the identity of all the anonymous authors and many pieces, some of which may be by Tyler, are not attributed to anyone. Only those which can be definitely assigned to him, therefore, are included here. Of the five appearances of Tyler in *The Port Folio* the three "Author's Evenings" essays are original, the piece entitled "Logic" first appeared in *The Farmer's Weekly Museum* on June 12, 1797, and the notice, "Messrs. Colon and Spondee to Their Kind Customers" in the same paper on April 1, 1799.

For a brief note on the fate of *The Port Folio* after the death of Dennie, and the names of the editors who followed him, see Ellis, pp. 214–5.

literary reputation which the paper had established over the years and in 1801 he issued an anthology of the best pieces. The book, entitled *The Spirit of the Farmer's Museum,* contained a wide selection of the biographies, anecdotes, epigrams, essays and verse which had appeared in the paper.[26]

The Boston Public Library copy of the work, annotated by Dennie, together with the annotations made by Hall in *The Port Folio,* is invaluable in attributing the majority of the "Spondee" pieces in this volume to Tyler. In the margins of *The Spirit* which Dennie presented to his Philadelphia friend, The Reverend James Abercrombie, he wrote next to the majority of the selections the initials or surnames of those who had authored them under various literary disguises.[27]

[26] Carlisle issued proposals for the anthology in *The Farmer's Weekly Museum,* VIII, No. 382 (July 28, 1800), 3. Thomas carried the proposals in the *Massachusetts Spy,* XXIX, No. 1431 (Sept. 10, 1800), 3.

[27] A discussion of the annotated copy of the book is contained in Tanselle, "Attributions of Authorship in 'The Spirit of the Farmer's Museum' (1801)," *The Papers of the Bibliographical Society of America,* LIX, No. 2 (April–June, 1965), 170–76. Tanselle casts some doubt on the reliability of the annotations. He mentions that the marginal notes are in more than one hand and in both pencil and ink. The implication is that not all of the annotations are by Dennie and, therefore, may not be valid.

While admitting the former the latter does not necessarily follow. Dennie, in presenting the book to his friend, the Rev. James Abercrombie of Philadelphia, probably made the majority of the attributions himself. But Abercrombie, wishing to know the identity of every author, could have asked Dennie for further information. Dennie could have verbally made these further attributions and Abercrombie have written them in the margins himself. This would explain the two different handwritings and the use of both pencil and ink.

Thus, the attributions would still be valid. They are, in any case, contemporary to the book's issuance and are for the purposes of this volume considered legitimate.

TO THE *LITERATI.*

Mess. COLON & SPONDEE,

WHOLESALE DEALERS IN
VERSE, PROSE, & MUSIC,

Beg leave to inform the PUBLIC,
and the LEARNED in particular, that
—previous to the ENSUING
COMMENCEMENT—

They purpose to *open* a fresh Assortment of
Lexographic, Burgersdician, & Parnassian

GOODS,

SUITABLE FOR THE SEASON,
At the Room on the Plain, lately occupied
by Mr. Frederic Wiser, *Tonsor,*[28]
if it can be procured—

—Where they will expose to Sale—

Salutatory and Valedictory Orations, Syllogistic and Forensic Disputations and Dialogues among the living and the dead—Theses and Masters' Questions, Latin, Greek, Hebrew, Syriac, Arabic and the ancient Coptic, neatly modified into Dialogues, Orations &c. on the shortest notice—with Dissertations on the Targum and Talmud, and Collations after the manner of Kennicott—Hebrew roots and other simples—Dead Languages for Living Drones—Oriental Languages,

[28] The barber shop of Mr. Wiser faced the Common adjoining Dartmouth College in Hanover.

with or without points, prefixes, or suffixes—Attic, Doric, Ionic, and Æolic Dialects, with the Wabash, Onondaga, and Mohawk Gutturals —Synaloephas, Elisions, and Ellipses of the newest *cut*—v's added and dove-tailed to their vowels, with a small assortment of the genuine Peloponnesian Nasal Twangs—Classic Compliments adapted to all dignities, with superlatives in *o,* and gerunds in *di, gratis*—Monologues, Dialogues, Trialogues, Tetralogues, and so on from *one* to *twenty*-logues.

ANAGRAMS, ACROSTICS, ANACREONTICS;

Chronograms, Epigrams, Hudibrastics, & Panegyrics; Rebuses, Charades, Puns and Conundrums, by the *gross,* or *single dozen.* Sonnets, Elegies, Epithalamiums; Bucolics, Georgics, Pastorals; Epic Poems, Dedications, and Adulatory Prefaces, in *verse* and *prose.*

ETHER, MIST, SLEET, RAIN, SNOW

Lightning, and Thunder, prepared and personified, after the manner of Della Crusca, with a quantity of *Brown Horror, Blue Fear* and *Child Begetting Love,* from the same Manufactory; with a pleasing variety of high-colored, *Compound* Epithets, well assorted—Farragoes, and other Brunonian Opiates—Anti-Institutes, or the new and concise patent mode of applying *forty letters* to the spelling of a monosyllable —Love Letters by the Ream—Summary Arguments, both *Merry* and *Serious*—Sermons, moral, occasional, or polemical—Sermons for Texts, and Texts for Sermons—Old Orations scoured, Forensics furbished, Blunt Epigrams newly pointed, and cold Conferences hashed; with *Extemporaneous* Prayers *corrected* and *amended*—Alliterations artfully allied—and periods polished to perfection.

AIRS, CANONS, CATCHES, AND CANTATAS

—Fuges, Overtures, and Symphonies for any number of Instruments

—Serenades for Nocturnal Lovers—with *Rose Trees* full blown, and *Black* Jokes *of all colors*—Amens and Hallelujahs, trilled, quavered, and slurred—with Couplets, Syncopations, Minims, and Crotchet Rests, for female voices—and *Solos,* with *three* parts, for hand organs.

CLASSIC COLLEGE BOWS, CLEAR STARCHED,

lately imported from Cambridge, and now used by all the topping scientific connoisseurs, in hair and wigs, in this country.

ADVENTURES, PARAGRAPHS, LETTERS FROM

Correspondents, Country Seats for Rural Members of Congress, provided for Editors of Newspapers—with Accidental Deaths, Battles, Bloody Murders, Premature News, Tempests, Thunder and Lighting, and Hail-Stones, of all dimensions, adapted to the Season.

CIRCLES SQUARED, MATHEMATICAL POINTS

divided into quarters, and half shares; and jointed Assymptotes, which will meet at any given distance.

SYLLOGISMS IN BOCARDO, AND BARALIP-

ton; Serious Cautions against Whoredom, Drunkenness, &c. and other coarse Wrapping-Paper, *gratis,* to those who buy the smallest article.

☞*On hand a few Tierces of Attic Salt—Also, Cash, and the highest price, given for* RAW WIT, *for the use of the Manufactory, or taken in exchange for the above Articles.*

*   *   *   *   *

Miscellany.

GREENFIELD, JAN. 8.

PRIME PUMPKIN!!

MASSACHUSETTS *Beat—with a Black*
Eye for Connecticut.

Whilst puny Nature, on her sea beat shore,
Prides in the dwarfish race the shivering bore,
More genial suns our inland upland warms:
Vermont shall rule in Pumpkins as in arms.

R. LA MOILE. P.L.V.

EXTRACT of a Letter from Colonel Samuel Hide, dated
Smooth Plains, Vermont, December 3, 1794.

"MR. JOSEPH MILLER, a very polite farmer of this town, raised a pumpkin vine, which grew from a seed casually dropped into a water trough in the front eves of his house, which ran over the house down the back side, and from thence in a right line 763 feet three inches and three fourths, by Gunter.[29] It is probable, as it was a fine season, it would have run much further, if Mr. Miller had not chopped it, to save a six year old orchard from being choked by its exuberance; as another branch of the same vine had already destroyed a fine maple sugar place, from which he used annually to make 400 lbs. of sugar. The vine, nevertheless, produced 83 pumpkins (being one for each soul in the town, according to the late census,) the largest of which weighed 497 lbs. without the seeds and guts; and, when removed home by the neighbors, with levers and handspikes, who made what is called a bee for this purpose, half of it being neatly scooped out, and

[29] Edmund Gunter (1581–1626), English mathematician and inventor of several useful measuring devices.

the hollow turned down, it serves as an excellent stye for a sow of Mr. Miller's, weighing upward of twenty stone, with thirteen pigs, of the Chinese breed; and may be seen any day by the curious in pumpkins.

Col. HIDE adds, I am sensible that this account will not be thought worthy of publishing by my neighbors, as they have seen nature, on their own farms, produce still more exuberantly. But I was piqued for the agricultural honor of the state, when I read in the Greenfield Gazette, of Nov. 27th, a pompous display of some PUMPKINLINGS, raised in the town of *Reading,* and state of Massachusetts."[30]

SPONDEE.

* * * * *

From the Shop of messrs. COLON & SPONDEE

Amid the festivity of the *christmas* holidays, we feel a peculiar desire to congratulate our countrymen, upon the decay and downfall of democratic clubs and the Pittsburg insurrection. The whiskey spirit has fairly evaporated *in fumo,* and dr. J*RV*S, and BEN A*ST*N[31] are compelled to stay at home vending *julups* and twisting *ropes* for unfortunate patients, instead of mountbanking the stalking horse of government, or impeding, with *fine spun yarn,* the public proceedings.

* * * * *

[30] The article which elicited this "Spondee" column can be found in the *Greenfield Gazette,* III, No. 44 (Nov. 27, 1794), 3.

[31] Dr. Jarvis and Benjamin Austin were both strong, outspoken Republican politicians. Austin, especially, was merciless in his attacks on Boston Federalists.

President Washington had to call out the militia in the summer and fall of 1794 to put down the Pittsburgh Insurrection, an uprising of citizens dissatisfied with the funding act, the excise law, the Bank of the United States and unfair taxation.

From the Shop of Messrs. COLON & SPONDEE.

Although to the man of reflexion, as well as to those, who, in the words of Mandeville, are "damned to hoes and spades," the prolixity of congressional orators may appear disgustful, yet their consequence merits all our praise. The compilers of the British annual register furnish us with the most brilliant speeches of the members of both houses of parliament; and, with over-weening admiration, describe the lucid order of Loughborough, the rapidity of Fox, the metaphors of Burke, and the Ciceronian suavity of Mansfield. But, on examination, cis-atlantic readers are compelled, fastidiously, to exclaim

One stuns the exchequer, and one dulls the rolls."

The law-lords, with sauces choaked by the dust of westminister hall, cannot be expected to "utter dulcet breath." Pregnant in the terms of common justice, they may express with fluency the technicals of the law, but rarely, from a British pleader's gown, has oratory stretched her graceful land. The speeches of the chancellor of the exchequer are methodical and correct; but, like the comedies of Coleman, are tame in their interest, and never kindle an enthusiastic emotion. Mr. Burke undoubtedly commands the ready faculty of speech, and sometimes combines the glow of Bollingbroke, with the fertility of Rousseau, and the corrosion of Junius. Thurlow has a "saucy roughness" of words, which, aided by his "black scowl," and an imperious manner, has been dignified with the name of energy. But all these speakers are rather the idols of party, than orators, whose harrangues challenge the praises of the critic.

The fame of American eloquence rests on a more stable foundation. Speeches have been uttered, in our national assembly, which would rival Cicero's oration, pro domo. The erudite German professor, who instructed C. & S. in the elements of speech, would employ an hour, in descanting upon the whole alphabet; but it was reserved for a congress to employ four in settling the propriety of the first letter. Sterne has told us, that to an ingenious prelate, "Cappadocia, Phrygia, and Pontus," is a text sufficiently fertile. What manner of persons then must our public speakers be, whose rapid invention can suggest brilliant topics upon an insignificant particle. The funding system, a foreign war, or land tax, in future, shall not waste the precious moments of a southern spouter. Give him an adverb or a conjunction, and with the promptitude of redoubtable Hudibras,

——————— "He shall not ope
His mouth, but out will fly the trope."

* * * *

FROM THE SHOP OF
Messrs. COLON & SPONDEE.

BETWEEN YOU AND I.

How I came by the power of jerking myself unperceived into every private company, and, concealed by the cloak of invisibility, of noting the most private conversation, I won't tell you. But I heard

Gen. St. Clair whisper Gen. Harmar,[32] "Many a brave soldier has been sacrificed to savage barbarity—*Between you and I.*"

I heard Mrs. Limberham whisper her husband, after their divorce, "That was a very little affair, which made so much mischief—*Between you and I.*"

I heard Mr. GALLATIN whisper Mr. LIVINGSTON,[33] "That was a fine Jacobin speech on the treasury papers—*Between you and I.*"

I heard Miss Frisk whisper Mr. Brisk, "Last evening I was hugely tickled—*Between you and I.*"

---

[32] Arthur St. Clair (1736–1818), rose to the rank of Major General during the Revolution. After the war he was appointed governor of the new Northwest Territory (1787). Indian dissatisfaction with his handling of matters after the Treaty of Fort Harmar in 1789 led to a battle in which St. Clair and his troops were surprised and overwhelmingly defeated on Nov. 4, 1791, by a confederated Indian army under the Miami, Little Turtle.

[33] This is in reference to the comments in the House of Representatives by Edward Livingston, the Democratic-Republican Congressman from New York, on Albert Gallatin's *A Sketch of the Finances of the United States,* written in 1796. The pamphlet represented the views of the Democratic-Republicans on treasury matters.

I heard Ben Burgler whisper Capias, the deputy sheriff, "That was a cursed treaty—Between you and I, *and the post.*"

I heard Abraham Baldwin whisper General Gunn,[34] "That *challenge* was a ridiculous farce—*Between you and I.*"

I heard Moses Robinson[35] whisper Mr. Burr, "Thy will be done—*Between you and I.*"

I heard Israel Smith[36] whisper to a *mule,* "My dear cousin, there is a very close resemblance—*Between you and I.*"

I heard President WASHINGTON whisper Gov. JAY, "The salvation of the United States was secured from democratical rage—*Between you and I.*"

* * * * *

FROM THE SHOP OF
Messrs. COLON & SPONDEE.

The RUNNER, *or* INDIAN TALK

(Of Savage Nations, the polished European, and even American, speaks with contempt. We resort to them for examples of the sterner passions, un-

---

[34] Abraham Baldwin (1754–1807), statesman and U.S. Representative and Senator from Georgia. A pioneer in education, he is called the father of the University of Georgia. Politically he was a moderate Democratic-Republican.

James Gunn (1753–1801). As a captain of dragoons he participated in the relief of Savannah during the Revolution. Gunn was later promoted to the rank of brigadier general of the Georgia militia and served as United States Senator from 1789–1801.

[35] Moses Robinson (1741–1813). A colonel in the Vermont militia, he was at the head of his regiment on Mount Independence when St. Clair evacuated Ticonderoga. Upon the admission of Vermont into the union, he was elected as a Democrat to the U.S. Senate, serving from 1791 until his resignation in 1796. He was Vermont's Chief Justice for three terms.

[36] Israel Smith (1759–1810). He served in the U.S. House of Representatives and Senate, became Vermont Chief Justice and capped his career by being elected Governor in 1807. There is a mention of Smith's role in the contemplated establishment of a branch of the Bank of the United States at Rutland, Vt., in a letter from Tyler to U.S. Congressman James Elliot, dated from Brattleboro, c. 1807. (The correspondence is in the Elliot Papers, p. 103, Boston Public Library.)

conscious that we *too hate, and* we *revenge, but—in the silken garb of* civilization! *If such a novelty could be found, as a* Creek *or* Cherokee Press, *an* Indian *Editor might possibly publish a Paper like the following.*)

ADVERTISEMENT.

Mons. Bellisle, Hairdresser, Complectionist, and Perfumer, from Esquimeaux, at the Talapoose, dresses young men's heads for the War Dance, with or without Snakes and Feathers; he is master of the Cherokee cut, the Muskogee braid, and the Chactaw twist. He paints faces to admiration, with his genuine crow blacking; he raises the cheek bones, and affords the true rattlesnake cast to the eyes; he gives to the most squawfaced young man, that horrid manly look, so frightful to the enemy, and *so pleasing to the young women*. He has, at great expense, procured the genuine Hottentot, Cassrean Pease Bladder from the Cape of Good Hope.

N. B. Mons. Bellisle was body Hairdresser to Little Billy.

Vermillion, Red and Yellow Ochre, Lampblack and other Cosmetics; Deer's leg Oil, Esquimeaux Blubber, Bear's Grease, and other perfumery, wholesale and retail.

Extract from the White Men's Public Talk. *From the Great Council Town, on the Schuylkill.*

"The Old Beggar, who was found starved to death, on a dunghill, in this city, proves to have been a soldier, who served with reputation, during the whole war, in the late continental army."

"The body of a young woman was found in the water, near a wharf, in this city, with her throat cut from ear to ear. By other marks of violence, on the corpse, it appears this unfortunate young person had been first ravished by some villain."

From our Brethren of St. Tamany, at Newyork.

Yesterday were executed in this city, seven men for forgery, three for perjury, and ten for horse stealing.—As these sights are common, few persons attended.

"We hear from Black River, Northcarolina, that on Sunday, the day dedicated by white men, to the Great Spirit of Love, a set battle was fought, for forty one guineas, between Sawny Mc'Broughton, and Frank ap Dowse, to the infinite diversion of a numerous collection of gentlemen and ladies. Broughton, with inconceivable dexterity, broke the jaw bone of Dowse, and the odds were in his favor for twenty minutes, when Dowse gouged out both eyes of Broughton, from their sockets, which decided the battle. The parties shook hands, and drank a quart of whiskey together, to shew that they had no malice at heart."

From Charleston, Southcarolina.

"Last Sunday evening a duel was fought in this city, between Col. Carte and Lieut. Tierce, in which the latter was dangerously wounded, and the former immediately killed, by a pistol ball through his heart. These gentlemen were particular friends. The dispute arose about the character of an actress. The parties seemed inclined to adjust this difference amicably, but the rigid laws of honour prevented. They shook hands before they fired. The Colonel has left a widow, and five small children to lament his loss, which is the more inconsolable, as they depended entirely upon their deceased parent for their education and support.—But the seconds say, this affair was conducted according to the *strictest rules of* HONOUR.

From over the Great Pond.

"The young Sachem of the *Bull* tribe, over the Great Lake, owes seven beaver skins. His father, the *Mad Bull,* has offered to pay his debts, if the Bull Nation will give him, from their hunting stock, two beaver skins, every twelve moons, until the sun and moon shall be sunk in the swamp, without borders."

"We hear from France, that our ancient brothers, the French, the friends of the Hurons, have tomahawked their chief Sachem, and his squaw, and half starved the royal papooses.—They have scalped and tomahawked more men, women and children, than are in the Chickesaw, Chactaw, Creek, Missouri, and Five Nations, and all of their own tribe. It is said they made great canoes, and bound their brethren, their sisters, and their infants, with moose thongs, and then sunk them in the river, without allowing them time to sing their death song."

(Great Spirit! Those who give these accounts of themselves, in their public talks, are the people, who call thy red children, barbarians and savages;—*Indian Editor.*)

Shucwegee, who visited the Great Wigwam in Philadelphia, twenty and sixteen moons ago, says it is not true, as is commonly believed, that the Big Book of the white men teaches them all that deceit, cruelty, and ferocity, which they exercise one towards another; but that in one talk of it, they are expressly commanded to love one another, and even to love their enemies. Though we apprehend from the white men's doings, that Shucwegee, not well understanding their tongue, must have mistaken this talk. No—No—Doubtless their Big Book tells them to deceive, hate, gouge, scalp, tomahawk, and murder each other.

The MONITOR.

The first man, as the White Powwows say, was called Adam; because he was made of red earth, he was a red man. You, who are nearest to him in colour, are most excellent among his children. Do you act with the spirit of red men. The white men, who have been adopted among us, must not let the white of their faces sink into their livers; but shew the tribes, that it is possible for a white skin to cover an Indian spirit.

PUBLIC SALE.

To be sold, by Pine Knot, twenty piles of muskets, twenty bundles of pikes, twenty strings of great war horses, twenty heaps of camp kettles, taken at the fight of the Miamis, from the great white runner, St. C—r, with a curious crutch, supposed to belong to some great

Captain; also one bad horse, taken one day's journey, from the camp of the flaming warrior Wayne.[37]

BEN. SCALPUM.

Manufacturer from England, at Lake Erie, near the Miamis, makes and sells, cuttoes, scalping knives, and tomahawks, and has on hand, a large quantity of brimstone matches, and seasoned pine knots, for the tormenting of prisoners.

N. B. Wanted a young lad of good disposition, as an apprentice.

OBITUARY.

Gone to the World of Spirits, Talotheske; he was a great Cherokee warrior, had twenty scalps in his wigwam, and the cup he drank his black drink from, was the skull of a chief. His wife has dreamed twice that she has conversed with him, and is soon therefore to go to him; his wolf dog was sent to him yesterday.

Also, at Tuscorara, Fox Feet, the great Hunter; he killed more Wauppanaughs, than Frenchmen have Frenchmen; he would dive the falls and catch a salmon; he changed the religion of his father, because the Jesuit Powwow told him that St. Peter, his chief Sachem, was a good fisherman, and would teach him to take mummy chog in the lakes of the moon.

MARRIAGE.

Yesterday, deposited the shivers of the live oak, Ouabi, the son of the white chief, and Azakia, the daughter of Ouabi, the big warrior, who many moons ago rushed into the land of spirits, to demand of the Great Man, why he was not before called to his seat, beyond the woods and waters.

DOMESTIC TALK.

Last moon, a party of the big knife, of fifty young men, came upon

[37] The site of St. Clair's defeat by the Indian army under Little Turtle was on a branch of the Wabash River a day's march from the site of Ft. Wayne.

a Wabash family, consisting of an old man, his squaw, three young women, and four children, and barbarously murdered them.

Yesterday, thirty white warriors, supposed Yankees, by their trail of molasses, stole two horses from the banks of the Chataluithe. Same day, got an old Cherokee drunk, and stole his beaver pack.

Last moon, Natewego delivered an *Elegant Spirited* Talk, or *Oration,* in commemoration of the *Bloody Massacre* at Wyoming.

It is said, that at the Grand Council of the Missouri, a Shawanese chief, proposed to send a large number of canoes, to take possession of a certain savage Isle, in the Great Lake, called Rhodeisland, to bring away some of the inhabitants, to learn them their language, and then send them some warriors, to civilize them, and some powwows, to teach them the true religion.

When the white prisoners, taken at St. Joseph, were carried among the men of the Bear Nation, they would not allow them to be in the same rank of men with themselves. Doubtless, said they, their ancestors were red men; as we all come from one common stock; but these creatures are whitened by disease, like the decaying leaves of the woods. They therefore painted them with red earth and coals, to make their appearance supportable to the young men and women.

Published at Talapoosa, *one string of Wampum for Twelve Moons, and one Talk each Moon.*

* * * * *

FROM THE SHOP OF
Messrs. COLON & SPONDEE.

FINE COMB POINTS:

Or, a sovereign cure for the common disorders in the head.

Take a fine small tooth ivory comb, pass it through the patient's hair every morning before breakfast, in various directions, for about ten minutes; about once in two minutes it will be necessary to pass a stiff brush over the comb to clear the teeth or points from the magnetic or electrical fluid.[38] N.B. If the disease is obstinate, let the comb points be applied also in the evening, before the patient is put to bed.

By letters, which the inventor has received from several respectable clergymen, some eminent nurses, and other literati, the efficacy of the comb points is established beyond doubt. Here followeth a sketch of sundry remarkable cures.

An infant child of Mrs. Sarah Slattern had ever since its birth, been grievously afflicted with a certain disorder in the head, called by the learned, "the dander, or dandriff." The poor babe was in such a deplorable situation, that few of the neighbours could bear to look at it, while it pierced the HEART with its cries and shrieks; by the application of my fine comb points for only nine successive mornings, it is now as quiet as a lamb, and looks the picture of health.

The widow Slipshod had seven children afflicted with an epidemic disorder, which ran through the heads of the whole family. The poor children were in such distress, that they were obliged to have sometimes one, and sometimes both hands in their hair, to alleviate the pain. I earnestly recommended the fine comb points. Upon their being applied once a day for several successive days, the patients are so far recovered that the eldest, who was most diseased, eat a whole bowl of hasty pudding, without putting his fingers in his hair but three times.

Letter from a gentleman of the CLOTH, *to the* INVENTOR.

Sir,

Since the decease of his mother, my son had been afflicted with a cutaneous disorder in his head, which at length raged so violently as to run down the vertebrae of the neck. The poor boy could not even sleep quietly. By the recommendation of a brother at Boston, I tried Dr. Perkins's patent points, I am sorry to say without success, though we moved the tractors in every direction. But upon the application of

[38] Magnetic fluid was a hypothetical liquid thought to exist for the purpose of explaining the phenomenon of magnetism. Tyler also mentioned it in one of his poems. See *Tyler Verse,* p. 58.

your fine comb points, the child has entirely recovered. He now reposes so quietly, that he actually slept during one of my shortest sermons. It is true he has several times relapsed, but the renewed application of the comb points, never fails to give him ease.

Yours, &c.

SAVAGE THEOLOGY.

The savage state is rude, but marked with strong lines of character, action and expression. These distinct indentings are effaced, by the polish of society. If we would admire the bold exertion of Roman virtue, we must not peruse the polished era of the Caesars, but recur to the age of the elder Brutus. The nervous laconism of the Lacedemonian was uttered, when Sparta contained a horde of savages.—In our day, whatever a young orator of the federal house may think, if we would admire nervous expression, we should do well to turn our attention from the committee of the whole on the banks of the Skuylkill, to the Indian orator on the borders of the Miamis.

I lately had occasion to hear the rhetoric of both. The former I honour, the latter I admire. I purpose, one day, to draw a parallel between them, after the manner of PLUTARCH; in which I shall contrast the irritability, the clamour, the impatience of civilized debate, with the savage sedateness of an Indian council. The Indian is not merely an orator in council; but if conveying our ideas in the fewest words, and those the most happily chosen, be the perfection of elocution, the Indian is ever eloquent. The attributes of Deity continually convince man of their incomprehensible nature, by the difficulty he finds, in attempting to clothe them with human language.

Pray, said I to an old Sachem, what are your ideas of God? He is a great spirit, he replied, who is the father of all good. He gives us refreshing showers and clear sunshine; health and good hunting seasons. But there is evil in the world. True, replied the Sachem, the evil spirit sends that; he makes bad crops, springs the beaver trap, blows winds and tempest, and disease. Which is the strongest of these spirits, said I? Oh the good spirit, to be sure. Then why do you not pray to him to destroy the evil spirit, I resumed? The Sachem paused—and contemplated his God. His faith taught him that he was a good spirit, and mercy was his prevailing attribute. I pressed an answer. The savage cast an Indian look, and with an arch deliberation said, why does not the good spirit destroy the evil? "*He is so plaquey good natured, he won't hurt him.*"

The mercy of the Supreme Being has been expressed in loftier, but never in more forcible terms.

ON GRACE BEFORE MEAT.

Pray, my friend, do you ask a blessing, before you sit down to dinner? Your father did, our pious ancestors practiced this decent custom, and you yourself, if you were master of a family, before the war, used to call for the protection and blessing of the Author of every good gift, ere you partook of his common bounty. But this is a liberal age. France has abolished all religion; and once decreed there was no God; and some among us love to ape France. Still, I think the custom of graces was laudable, and though branded as superstitious, I find traces of the custom, even among the liberal ancients. It was customary among the polished Greeks and Romans to pour a small portion of liquor from the cup on the ground, as an offering to the Gods, before drinking. The courtly Horace, when in convivial hours at his villa with Macenas and Atticus, poured a libation to Bacchus, before he quaffed his Falernian. Socrates was so attached to this grateful habit that, when he was presented with the cup of hemlock, at his execution, he enquired if there would be a sufficient portion of the potion left, should he pour a libation to the Gods.

In the early annals of our country, who can read the blessing of the worthy Brewster, and not find his heart warmed with the fervour of his piety.

It was in the great drought, and consequent famine, which distressed our forefathers, soon after the settlement of New England, when the last batch of bread was in the Governor's oven, as Hutchinson informs us,[39] this pious elder rose at the head of his family, over a dinner of clams, and, in the fulness of a grateful heart, blessed God, *"who had given them to suck of the abundance of the seas, and of treasures hidden in the sand."*

* * * * *

FROM THE SHOP OF
Messrs. COLON & SPONDEE.

ARISTOCRACY.

I have looked into my Entick[40] and he says that it is a government by nobles. Heaven preserve us from aristocrats; they would cut all our farms into Lordships, and sell us for slaves. So says my neighbour Grumble, and he knows for he is what they call a dishonourary member of a Jacobin Club. But, pray, my dear jealous countrymen, are not all kind of ocracies, dreadful things—and are they not running rampant among us?

Yes—there is your

HOGOCRACY:

That is where an ignorant booby has blundered into a great estate, and has the riches, without the education, sentiments, or manners of a gentleman.—His pride and insolence form a horrid hogocracy over his poor neighbours. More happy is the Russian peasant, sold with the land he ploughs to his haughty Boyar, than the tenant, or dependent of such a hogocrat.

Then there is your

PIGOCRACY:

The pigocrat may be known by his long pig's tail, bound with six yards of ribband, his wheat meal and lard upon his head, and his shrill dolorous whine; with these he establishes a tyrannical pigocracy over the blooming generation of young ladies.

[39] Thomas Hutchinson (1711–1780), royal governor of Massachusetts. His *History of the Colony of Massachusetts Bay* in three volumes is still highly regarded.

[40] John Entick (1703?–1773), schoolmaster and author. His *Spelling Dictionary* appeared in 1764 and his *New Latin and English Dictionary* in 1771.

Then there is your

RIBOCRACY:

That is, when the married lady discards the bewitching drapery of the skirt, for the immemorable insignia of the man, and rules the conjugal roost, when she neglects the pie and pudding, and scolds politics at her husband's visitors; and, after having insulted the patience of the good man by day, awakes him by night to the refreshing eloquence of a curtain lecture. Such a woman has established a Da* * * * * *—I dare not at present say what—as, unhappily, my own dear rib now casts a loving look over my left shoulder.

N. B. My wife is a profound politician—I wish you could hear her talk upon liberty and equality.

Then there is your

MOBOCRACY.

But I beg pardon, this is only a species of Democracy—I say again, heaven preserve us from all ocracies.

* * * * *

FROM THE SHOP OF
MESS. COLON & SPONDEE.

De MINIMIS curat Lex.

That the will of the people should govern, is the essence of republicanism.[41] How this will shall be most advantageously manifested, is the grand desideratum. Some weak ones have fancied it is best declared by the voices of the majority. This is denied by those profound logi-

[41] Tyler had touched upon this subject before in *The Algerine Captive*, I, Chap. XXVIII. There is an argument between Thomas Paine and Peter Pindar and at one point Paine asserted "that the minority, in all deliberative bodies, ought in all cases to govern the majority." Naturally Tyler manages to have Paine loose the debate.

See also a letter from Thomas Jefferson to Baron Alexander von Humboldt, Prussian diplomat and naturalist, dated from Monticello, June 13, 1817. Jefferson said, "The first principle of republicanism is that the lex majoris partis is the fundamental law of every society of individuals of equal rights: to consider the will of the society enounced by the majority of a single vote as sacred as if unanimous, is the first of all lessons in importance . . ." (The Ms. letter is at the Library of Congress, Washington, D.C.)

cians, Colon and Spondee. The minority ought, in all cases, to carry the vote; and we prove it, with the clerical formality of the last age,

From Reason,
From Experience,
From Expediency, and
From Religion.

1st. From Reason.   The bulk of mankind are fools. The proportion of men of sense and integrity, to men ignorant and knavish, is, perhaps, as five to ninety-five. Now, in every collective body, consisting of one hundred, the ninety-five ignoramuses will vote wrong, and thus constitute a powerful majority. While the five knowing ones will vote correctly, and, therefore, let Dr. Watts deny it, if he dare, ought assuredly to govern.[42]

2dly. From Experience.   Look at the blunders of British ministers. You will trace them all to this absurd plan of implicit obedience to a parliamentary majority. Who passed the Boston port bill? Who voted the parliamentary right to bind the Americans, in all cases whatsoever? A majority in parliament. Ask Mr. Pitt why he subsidizes half Germany; and after reiterated defeat, and the loss of the United Provinces, he persists in forcing a government upon the French: he will answer, it is the will of the nation, expressed by the majorities in both houses. Who occasioned all the curses of the late war between mother and child? Invoke Lord North from the tomb of the Guildfords, and he will tell you, it was his uniform language that the majority in both houses forced him to make Howe and Burgoyne ridiculous in America. But, when the sensible minority took the lead, American independence was acknowledged.

To bring this matter home. I ask you, Mr. Democrat, what do you think of the majority in the senate, who voted the acceptance of the treaty? Ha! would it not have been better if the virtuous, sensible

[42] Watts' book, *Logic,* would have been familiar to Tyler since it was a standard text at Harvard.

minority had prevailed? That glorious brotherhood of ten, more renowned, at least by three, than the Seven Sleepers of ancient story.

And you, Mr. Federalist, what do you think of the mob majorities in Philadelphia, Boston and New York, who have condemned the treaty *in toto*? Would it not have been as well for those *august* bodies to yield to a minority? Is not deliberation better than bellowing, and a cool argument to be preferred to a flying brickbat?

3dly. From Expediency. It is well known that many, actuated, no doubt, by patriotic regard to the general weal, quit their labour, and, to the great injury of their private business, and perhaps distress of their families, hasten to town meeting, to swell the majority for the public good. Now, let minorities decide; and every good cit would be as anxious to stay at home, cherishing his wife, as he is now to make his escape from her clack, or her caresses. The merchant would then hurry his vessel to sea, with the same solicitude that now retards her lading, to keep his crew ready for an approaching election. If the meeting should, peradventure, be full and tumultuous, the popular orator, instead of belying his sentiments, as he now does, would express his real political creed, in order to be reckoned among the minority.—Thus, when the vote was called, one and all, aristos and demos, feds and antis; "blue spirits and white, black spirits and grey;" old whigs, new whigs, and hair wigs; night-men and jacobins; attorneys and ropemakers; negroes, and other politicians, bobtailed by the moderator, would rush out of the hall, and leave the clerk to record the votes of the philosophic few.

Lastly, the pre-eminence of minorities we prove

From Religion. The good book says, follow not the multitude to do evil.[43] And trow you not, fellow citizens, that, according to the most approved religious systems, the majority of mankind are reprobate in this world, and will be eternally dammed in the next.

* * * * *

FROM THE SHOP OF
Messrs. COLON & SPONDEE.

TO THE *PUBLIC*.

We yesterday read, with surprize, the following impudent advertisement in the Federal Galaxy;[43] *for the editor of which, we have, however, a high respect*—The only notice we shall render it is, to desire all lovers of good order, especially our brother mechanics, to attend to the advertisement annexed.

COLON & SPONDEE.

TO THE LITERATI.

JONATHAN DACTYLE,
Who has served a regular apprenticeship in the manufactory of Messrs. COLON & SPONDEE, *would inform his friends and the public in general, that he has opened a shop, on the west side of Connecticut River,*[44] *where he sells, by wholesale and retail,*

VERSES, Proses, and other piece goods; Heliconades, Pamionades, Aioniades, and Pimpliades, with Sonnets, Odes, Madrigals, and Ballads for lovers' and ladies' wear, Blank Verse by the sentence, member, parenthesis, apostrophe, single book or epic Poem, with Hexameters by the foot, Catches, Chorusses and Glees set to any midnight hour, with Bundling Airs and Catches set in all their parts, Newspaper Founts, Rills and Rivulets inundated by the season, and Shrubberies supplied with the freshest *artificial* Plants and Flowers equal to the *natural*; Quirks, Quibbles, Quillets and Quiddities for young Attornies; Love Letters, with Answers, prudish, coquettish or coming, assorted for city consumption; elegant Elastic Elegies, Patent Spring Sermons, which will suit any text or occasion; *Challenges to fight* and *murder,* approved by men of honour, Blunt ditto for *members of Con-*

[43] Tyler was pulling someone's leg. He was probably only having a joke at the expense of his good friend, Benjamin Smead, publisher of the *Galaxy*. No such notice appeared in the paper on July 7, 1797.

[44] A reference to the *Federal Galaxy* being published at Brattleboro, Vt.

gress, Parathesises, Rhetorical, Grammatical, or Taustical, with Circumflexes, Sliding and Stationary Puns, Jokes, Gibes, Witticisms, Bores, Hums, Charades, Conundrums, Riddles, Rebuffs, Acrostics, Elegies, Palinodes, Georgics, Lyrics, Bucollics, Anagrams, Epigrams, Epitaphs, Odes, Satires, Nuts, Strophees and Antistrophees, by the groce or single dozen; a few double washed, high polished Epithets for young poets, one doz. double twisted Satire Lashes, with or without Snappers, High proof Spirits and Attic Salt, by the Quantity.

Mr. Dactyle prepares, on the shortest notice, Speeches for Town Meetings, Congress and Courts of Law, handsomely decorated with "Mr. Moderator," "Mr. Speaker," and "May it please your Honours." He has on hand a few of the genuine shining black *Last Words* and *Dying Speeches,* for Malefactors and Members of Democratic Clubs.

With various other articles too tedious to mention.

French Assignats, Old Conti,[45] and other waste paper gratis.

Cash, and all kinds of *Brain Produce* received in payment.

ONE THOUSAND DOLLARS REWARD !
Stop Thief, Forger, and Runaway !!!

BROKE his indentures, and run away from the subscribers, an apprentice BOY, named *Jonathan Dactyle.* He may be known by a Roman nose, and hobble in his gait; being remarkable from his birth for taking a long step with his sore foot, and two hops with his hinder; had on when he went away a French cap of Liberty, and a Sans Culotte pair of sentimentals.

This villain of wit stole and carried away with him, from the shop of the subscribers, the following pieces of wit and wisdom:

Viz. Two unfinished Elegies, which wanted only the grief watering

------

[45] Louis Francois Joseph de Bourbon (1734–1814), Prince de Conti. Descended from a famous line of French nobility, after some military experience in the Seven Years' War, he made his name as a timeserver. Subservient to Louis XV's mistresses and an opponent of the suggested reforms of 1788, the Prince emigrated at the outbreak of the French Revolution. Returning to France he was found guiltless by the Revolutionary Tribunal and banished from the country in 1797.

to complete them: a doleful Elegy upon the departure of citizen Adet;[46] another upon the approach of citizen Thomas Paine.

Also, carried away with him, tied up on a tricoloured silk handkerchief, somewhat dirty and bloody, five Fables, without morals; a Pun on Antifederal Election Sermons; a French Directory Decree, and a Conundrum.

Also the following tools of trade and shop furniture:

Viz. Two Sonnet Moulds—one Steel Epigram Pointer—three Riddle Screws—one Sermon Vise—four Speech Burnishers—some Cerulean Emery, and Cyprian Rotton Stone—one Rhetoric Square and Compass, marked with the maker's name (Holmes)[47]—a small pair of Aeolean Bellows, and an Attic Retort—an injecting machine to smoke Hogs and Beaus—two Fool Tractors, one Brass the other Steel, and two Hum Points—seven Joke Punches—a Fun Bore, and Great Borer, and a pair of Satire Nippers—one Song Press, and Chorus Drawers, and an Italian Slur Riddle—one Comic File, and one Tragic Bow String—one Leaden Tragedy Mould, maker's name (Burke)[48]— three Rebus Twisters—one Charade Gig—one Conundrum Picker— a strong Argument Chain—a Reason Drawer—a Logic Trap—a Wit Stone, and a pair of Nut Crackers—a bunch of double twisted Speculating Contracts—two double gilt Lover's Promises—one pair of Cytherean Forceps, and a hank of Law Quirks—two Legislative Speech Echos, one with, the other without variations.

The said Dactyle also stole and carried away with him the following articles in the Perfumery and Cutlery line, patented according to the

[46] Pierre Auguste Adet (1763–1832). His actions as French minister to the United States greatly displeased the Federalists.

[47] Nathaniel Holmes (1599–1678), puritan divine noted for his preaching. Samuel Pepys recounts his visit to Whitehall to hear Holmes preach on Feb. 12, 1659/60. (*Diary*, I, 27.)

[48] John D. Burk (c. 1775–1808). Born in Ireland, he came to this country in 1796 and settled in Boston. Attempts to start newspapers both in Boston and New York proved unsuccessful. The year of this "Colon and Spondee" essay, Burk composed two dramas, *The Death of General Montgomery in Storming the City of Quebec* and *Bunker Hill, or the Death of General Warren*. The latter is noted as among the earliest portrayal of an American battle scene on the stage. It was played at the Haymarket Theater in Boston on Feb. 2, 1797, and at the John Street Theater in New York on Sept. 8, 1797.

ACTS of Congress:—one Carboy of sweet scented Address Drops—Lyon's veritable Court Plaister,[49] and Dayton's double tongued Member Latchets.[50]

Also the following Toys for Children:—One pretty Georgia Bubble[51]—one Dismal Swamp Ditto[52]—one pretty picture of a Canal from Connecticut River to Boston, H. K. Pinxit—one pair of Bridges, and one pair of Theatres, from the great Toy Shop in Boston—a Chicken Guillotine, a pretty play thing for Republican Children.

Whoever will apprehend the above named villain, and secure him in some one of the federal gaols, shall be entitled to the above reward, to be paid in due bills on sight, at the shop of the Subscribers.

N. B. All persons, especially authors, Booksellers and Printers, are forbid harbouring the said Dactyle, or they may depend upon being prosecuted to the utmost rigour of the law.

☞We will be accountable for no debts of his contracting after date.

It is strongly suspected that this miscreant has forged a draught on the bank of Helicon.

COLON & SPONDEE.[53]

*   *   *   *   *

[49] Tyler never missed an opportunity to get in a dig at Matthew Lyon, the controversial U.S. Congressman from Vermont. See *Tyler Verse*, p. 62.

[50] Jonathan Dayton (1760–1824). A delegate to the Constitutional Convention from New Jersey, Dayton was the youngest man to sign the Constitution. A Federalist, he served in both the House of Representatives and the Senate. Dayton was arrested in 1807 on the charge of conspiring with Aaron Burr on treasonable projects but was never brought to trial.

[51] The scandal over the Yazoo Purchase lands, which first arose in 1795, dragged on for decades.

[52] In 1790 an attempt was made to reclaim a part of the Great Dismal Swamp and to build a canal through the area. Periodic charges of improper dealings were leveled at these efforts.

[53] That this column was an attempt to excuse the recent infrequent appearances of Colon & Spondee is borne out by the following notice in the *Museum* of August 7: "The *Shop of* COLON & SPONDEE has been shut about fourteen days. Their business is a little embarrassed in consequence of the candestine departure of Jonathan Dactyle, who carried off many useful articles of the shop apparatus, particularly our double polished *sun* bores, the only good set which belong to the concern. Dactyle has, however, been apprehended, and most of the necessary articles are recovered. The shop will again be opened in a very short time, and business will be prosecuted as usual."

FROM THE OFFICE OF
Messrs. COLON & SPONDEE.

OILNUT, or BUTTERNUT.

Styled by the German Botanists, JUGLANS ALBA;
by the English, JUGLANS NIGRA; and, by the
Americans, JUGLANS CATHARTICA.

It is a well known property of this valuable tree, that its bark will dye twelve distinct colours, or shades of colours, one for each month, in which it may chance to be collected. This is noticed by Dr. Belknap, in his interesting history of Newhampshire; who observes, that it has "a quality of dying several shades of gray and black."[54]

It is reported that a farmer's wife, in this vicinity, has discovered a method of dying, with the bark of this tree, in such a manner as that the same piece of cloth, once well coloured, in the month of January, without further process, will assume a new distinct colour, as it passes through every succeeding month in the year; besides several agreeable shades, as it terminates one month, and enters upon another. This bids fair to open a wide field to American economics; as the young farmer, from his maternal loom and dyetub, will be able to sport to appearance twelve suits of clothes at the expense of one; and if he can only contrive to suit the joys and sorrows of life, to the colour in season, he may, without a new application to the tailor or trader, with his stock suit, be completely equipped for a dance, a military muster, or a funeral. Like all other great discoveries, this was said to have been made by mere accident.

This customary liquid of the dyetub, not readily being procured, the good woman infused, as it is conjectured, the root of the arum, or poke in water; and having dyed the cloth for her husband's coat, a handsome gray, put it away in the chest. Some months after, in look-

---

[54] Jeremy Belknap's *History of New Hampshire* was published in three volumes between 1784–1792. The quotation is from Vol. III, 102.

ing for the cloth to make up, she was surprized to find it missing, and a bright blue in its place. Her husband being an ensign in the militia, she concluded he had changed the gray for a cloth proper for regimentals. White lappels were applied, and the regimental made. It was in vain the ensign asserted, that he had swopped the cloth; his wife would not credit him, and he, himself, imputed the supposed exchange to some private bargin of his wife. Training day drew near; the coat was shewn to his brother officers, and all declared it was the brightest navy blue ever seen; and the ensign's ambition was much excited at the respectable appearance he expected to make on the parade. This was in the month of May; muster was in June; the drums and fifes came to salute their officer; his boots were black, his hair powdered, and the girl was sent up stairs for the regimental coat, when lo! to the bitter surprize of the family, down came not a blue, but a handsome olive coloured coat. The white lappels identified the garment in such a manner as obviated all doubt. The ensign was obliged to recur to his rifle frock. But his disappointment was compensated the next month; when, upon his grandmother's death, he found the changeable coat equipped him with a fine crow black for the funeral.

*   *   *   *   *

FROM THE SHOP OF
Messrs. COLON & SPONDEE.

To our constant CUSTOMERS *and the* PUBLICK.

Reputation is the life of trade—upon the favour of his customers depends the success of the mechanic; and, although we gratefully confess that few young tradesmen, in these *hard times,* have stood fairer with the public, or have been blest with a better run of custom, yet we have not entirely escaped detraction. Some transient dealers have decried our wares; not, however, as too highly priced, or of inferior quality, but as not suiting the *size* of those for whom they were intended.—Master Billy Bootee, of Boston, beau, in June last, applied to us for a Poetical Address, to be presented to a young lady with a bunch of strawberries. As the young gentleman was in love, and consequently generous, he bespoke a tasty, high priced address. We accordingly directed our journeyman, a prime workman, to prepare his lathe, and turn a delicate address. It was highly polished, after our best manner, and brighly spotted with our best Floss Epithets, wrapped in gilt paper, and presented to the gentleman; and all this for the moderate price of eight shillings.

About two months afterwards, Master Bootee came into our shop, threw the address upon the workbench, and swore, dem 'is soul, that he had been cheated, he meant to have bought a thing quite the tippy, and had presented it to the lady, who thought it a cursed bore, and had laughed at him ever since.

We returned the young gentleman his money, and sold the address to a magazine monger at half price. We learned since that the fault was not in our ware, but that Master Bootee, upon his return to town, finding strawberries out of season, after pondering between geniting pears and apple codlings, unluckily sent our address to the lady, accompanied with a basket of gooseberries. We do not wonder that the lady was not highly pleased with observing her temper compared with the taste, or her breath with the fragrance of the fruit; and though Master Bootee was displeased, we cannot condemn the lady for smiling when she was bid in the language of the address—

"In the ripen'd fruit to view
The blushes of her cheek."

A man from Boston, whose name we do not know, indeed we have been informed that many years he has palmed himself upon the public, with a specious false one. We observed, however, that he had lantern jaws and a meaching look. He talked much of the rights of man; and said the French nation were the most humane people on earth, that Tom Paine was a most excellent Christian, and another Tom Somebody was the man of the people; that a people could never be happy in a republican government, unless that had a great mob ready to huzza their Representatives when they pleased them, and to knock them down when they did wrong. He wanted to purchase a Newspaper Essay, "*on the blessings of a Free Government;*" and offered us payment in hemp, in which he said he dealt. We rather declined this barter trade, but politely observed to our new customer, that perhaps he had better keep his commodity for his own personal use, and those of his dear friends after the suppression of the next rebellion.—We immediately cast the Essay; but happening to mention the administration of the late President, the respect we had acquired and were daily acquiring among the nations of Europe, under the wise, firm administration of our beloved Adams, and just noticed the prosperity of our farmers and mechanics, and the contempt into which certain disorganizing incendiaries had fallen, that the miscreants who fired our cities were some of them hung, and their brethren, the Jacobin Societies, detected, and some other *obvious blessings* of our free government;—then our customer flew into a violent rage, called for tar and feathers, endeavoured to raise a mob, and fiercely swore he would employ one Doctor Tully to write against us in a certain obscure newspaper, we think he called it the Chronicle, but we are not certain, as we never took any of them in these parts.[55]

* * * * *

FROM THE SHOP OF
Messrs. COLON & SPONDEE.

In our last, we mentioned some disagreeables in the line of our trade— here follow more.

Mr. Vans Vander Von Thick, a young gentleman of sprightly fancy, at Newyork, sent us the letters of his mistress's name, and bespoke an elegant Acrostic. We sent him, per post, one of our prime, dovetailed Acrostics. Mr. Von Thick, when he returned it as unsuitable, should

[55] The *Independent Chronicle* of Boston was a noted Democratic-Republican newspaper. "Dr. Tully" is unidentified.

have been candid enough to have informed us, that he had inadvertently misspelled the Christian and Surname of the Lady.

Miss Dorothy Distich bespoke a song and sent us the chorus or burthen—

"I'd die for to please the dear man of my heart."

We fabricated the song in our hot press: it was returned, as having too much love, and such stuff in it. The City Gazette, Charleston, (S.C.) let us into the secret. It seems that the loving Dorothy had been happily married, and the honeymoon was well over before she received our unfortunate ware; and it was more to the Lady's taste to hum the old song,

"I wish, I wish, but all in vain,
I wish I was a maid again."

Miss Kitty Conundrum bespoke half a dozen of Riddles; we forwarded the requested number of our double twisted inexplicables. She returned them, and declared she was cheated; for she did not believe they had any solution. We then sent her the keys; she returned them again, and said, any fool might have found them out.

One of our customers requested an Ode in the style and manner of Philenia.[56] We begged the gentleman not to insist upon an imitation of what the world confesses to be inimitable.

* * * * *

---

[56] "Philenia" was the pseudonym of Mrs. Sarah W. A. Morton, the Boston poetess.

FROM THE SHOP OF
Messrs. COLON & SPONDEE.

TO OUR KIND CUSTOMERS.
Some months since we received the following letter.

Philadelphia, Chestnut Street,
July 16, 1797.

To Messrs. COLON & SPONDEE,
Wit mongers, and Verse makers, Walpole.

GENTLEMEN,
In a circle of young ladies and gentlemen, in this city, "The Looker
On,"[57] a British periodical publication lately republished for Mr.
Ormrod was introduced, and I, being a very good reader, (though I
say it, that should not say it) was requested to read some passages out
of it, for the amusement of the company. Among others, I read the
annexed Fable from No. 63, of that work.

EXTRACT

"Clarina was married to the most affectionate of husbands; and, it
appeared to the world, the love which she felt in return had never
been equalled in any tale or romance. Four months had not elapsed,
since their marriage, before the husband fell dangerously ill; yet the
poor Clarina was the object of the greatest compassion. It was judged
impossible for her to survive him; and so unbounded was her affliction, that no one thought she could live to close even the eyes of her
dying husband. "O Death! Death!" she cried, as she leaned weeping
over his emaciated body, "Oh death, if you are not altogether a
stranger to pity, make me your prey instead of my dear husband."
Death heard, and presenting himself at the door, demanded who
called? "The gentleman who lies in that bed," replied Clarina.

[57] "The Looker-On," published in London by "Rev. Simon Olivebranch," 1792–93.
Reprinted in 1794, 1795 and 1797.

This fable was much applauded, by one part of the company, and I happened unfortunately to observe that it would be still more striking if done into verse. As I am known to be somewhat of a poet, having writ an answer to a Rebus, in the Pennsylvania Museum, which met the approbation of Mr. Carey, the Editor,[58] and was pronounced "enchanting," by several old and young ladies, I was requested to turn the Fable into verse. This I have not found leisure to do, though I have attempted it several times. I once thought your advertisements a mere newspaper joke; but, being convinced to the contrary by several pieces of verse and prose, which now go about this city, with applause, to the supposed authors, though I know they were manufactured at your shop, I have to request that you would turn the above Fable into verse. I do not wish to be at the expense of highly polished poetry. The dimensions as per margin. Please to forward the poetry directed to Joseph B., Chestnut Street, Philadelphia, with your account, and I will forward the needful.

Yours,

JOSEPH B ———.

DIMENSIONS

No. of Verses, nine.
Lines in each verse, four.
Feet, eleven by eight, or by nine, commixed.

P.S. As it may save you some trouble I send one verse I made myself.

> Clarina the fair, lately chose for her mate,
> A husband as appears* the most affectionate,
> Her love in return had never been equall'd,
> In tale or romance, as appears by the sequel.

J.B.

P.S. I hope secrecy may be depended on.

[58] Mathew Carey (1760–1839), publisher of *The American Magazine, or Universal Magazine* in Philadelphia from January, 1787, to December, 1792.
* To the world. [*Original footnote.*]

Upon the receipt of the above letter, we immediately ordered a journeyman to cast the following version, which was forwarded as directed; but our employer, having quitted his attachment for the muses, to another stronger *attachment,* which arose from a land speculation, never took our packet from the office. By the urbanity of the Post Master General, it was returned to us per last post; and we now present it to our customers.

COLON & SPONDEE.

FROM THE SHOP OF
Messrs. COLON & SPONDEE.

THE TEST OF CONJUGAL LOVE.

Deprendi miserum est.—Hor. Sat.

On his fever burnt bed, quick gasping for breath,
    Lay Strephon, convulsed with pain,
While the wind in his throat shook the rattle of death,
    The *hot* blood rag'd through the swollen vein.

Large drops of cold sweat on his forehead did stand;
    The lustre was dim'd in his eye;
While the chill of his feet, and the chill of his hand,
    Pronounc'd that poor Strephon must die.

His neighbours all wept, and his kindred all cried,
    With handkerchiefs held to each eye,
While a boy and a girl sobb'd loud at side,
    To think that their father must die.

But who can describe the fond griefs of his wife,
    Her shriekings, her tears, and despair,
When she vow'd that same hour should end her own life,
    And tore off by handfuls her hair,

Oh death! thou fell monster, in anguish she rav'd,
   Oh spare my dear husband, Oh spare,
Throw thy ice dart at me, let my husband be sav'd,
   Or I sink in a whirl of despair.

Oh how shall I live, when my husband is dead,
   Or why this loath'ed life should I save,
Then haste, welcome death, take me in his stead,
   Or I'll go with my love to the grave.

The wind whistl'd high, the old mansion about,
   And rock'd like a cradle the floor,
When death in the entry stood knocking without,
   With his knuckle of bone on the door.

And he bursted the lock, and the door open'd wide,
   And in the slim spectre slow strode,
And he rattl'd his jaws and he rattl'd his side,
   As over the threshold he trod.

Who's here, cried the spectre, who calls loud for me,
   Who wants death? the thin spectre then said;
Why, who? cried the wife, why, who should it be?
   But the gentleman there on the bed.

*   *   *   *   *

FROM THE SHOP OF
Messrs. COLON & SPONDEE.

(As the Chronicle paragraphists are remarkably stupid of late, and as their lame imagination frequently makes the tour of Invention, without picking up a single incident in the laborious journey, we are willing to furnish said scriblers with a straggling body of volunteer LIES; and, conscious of the miserable state of democratical finances, shall not demand, in return, a single cent, by way of subsidy for our aid.)

PARAGRAPHS For The CHRONICLE
cidevant PRINTERS for the STATE.

The conduct of the Honourable Mr. Lyon is highly applauded by all *good Patriots.* His spitting in the face of Mr. Griswold, whilst it indicates him to be the firm friend of *the Rights of Man,* will undoubtedly secure his next election, by the *enlightened Freeman* of *his* district.[59]

Griswold's conduct, in beating Mr. Lyon, in the face of the House, whilst the *Patriot* was armed only with a pair of tongs, argues a most cowardly spirit; whilst Mr. Lyon's manly resignation shews the dignity of the ancient Brutus.

Yesterday the body of a drunken man was found, frozen to death, near the north battery of this town. Such accidents may be frequently expected, under the present iniquitous administration of this government. If the deceased had received a competent share of those funds, which are now possessed by British foreigners and British Americans, undoubtedly this innocent sufferer would have been above the com-

[59] In 1797 the Federalists in Congress taunted Lyon about his military service. This led to the famous fight in the House of Representatives between Lyon and Congressman Roger Griswold of Connecticut. For the testimony on the subsequent motion to expel Lyon and his defense, see *Annals of the Congress of the United States. The Debates and Proceedings in the . . . Fifth Congress* (Washington, 1851), pp. 955–57, 961–62, 964–68, 982–1029. The debate is expanded in J. Fairfax McLaughlin, *Matthew Lyon, the Hampden of Congress. A Biography* (New York, 1900), pp. 213, 220–23, 307, 409.

mission of intoxication, and would have long continued an ornament to his country. Those at helm should consider this matter seriously.

———

The Centinel Major should not be too lavish of abuse of Mr. Lyon, for spitting on Mr. Griswold; as Russell may recollect to his disgrace, it is not many years since he himself spit in the face of an honourable writer in this paper.[60]

———

Citizen Monge's[61] vessel for transporting the armies of Liberty to overturn the ancient tyranny of Britain, in undoubtedly one of the most stupendous displays of human invention. The editor has conversed with a citizen, who has inspected this new ark, which is to transport the republican Noahs to the new world of liberty. It is twenty two miles in hocogramme, or length, and twenty four in milagramme, or breadth. It will cross from Calais to Dover with three millions of land forces, besides cavalry; and it is to be victualled for a voyage of twelve decades. The Pilot is to be seated in the bow, and give his directions to the citizen, at helm, by means of a Telegraphe. Lest this glorious vessel should ground, upon the water leaving the British channel, citizen Monge has affixed to it three thousand pair of wheels, of a new construction: the axletrees being fitted to the tires of the wheels, which is a great saving in cart boxes; and should the bottom of the channel prove too rocky for wheels, it is to be transported through the air, by a ballon thirty feet in circumference, under the direction of Mr. Blanchard,[62] who has left this country for

[60] Comments on the Lyons-Griswold affair were carried in Benjamin Russell's *Columbian Centinel* of Boston on Feb. 24, 1798, p. 2; March 3, 1798, p. 2; and March 14, 1798, p. 2.

The allusion to Russell insulting a writer "in this paper" is unclear. However, if Russell had come to odds with either Tyler or Dennie at some time in the past it may explain why Russell never published "Colon and Spondee" columns as he had first intended back in 1795 (see above, pp. 193–94).

[61] Gaspard Monge (1746–1818), mathematician and creator of descriptive geometry. He served as Minister of Marine, 1792–93, and accompanied Napoleon to Egypt where he was active in cataloging the treasures found there. Russell's *Centinel* commented upon Monge's plan on March 3, 1798, p. 2; and April 7, 1798, pp. 1–2.

[62] Jean-Pierre Blanchard (1753–1809), French aeronaut who, with the American

that purpose. It will thus serve for land and water; and may land the army of the ocean in Bantry Bay, and serve as a bridge over the Thames, which river separates Great Britain from Scotland. When Billy Pitt saw a plan of this immense work, he was so daunted, that he immediately offered to resign his office in the treasury to the Master of the Buckhounds.

The effrontery of the aristocrats, in asserting the popularity of John Adams, is astonishing. His late visit to this town must convince every true republican to the contrary. It is a fact, that though he was attended to the aristocratical feast, by the governor, the judges, counsellors, senators, the clergy, and other hireling officers of this state, yet that citizen Prince Hall, citizen Cato Hancock, citizen Austin, and other sons of liberty and equality, never honoured him with one huzza!

Citizens Munroe and Blount[63] are honest men, they have deserved well of their country. The Aurora, edited by a grandson of the great Franklin,[64] is the vehicle of truth,—Porcupine's Gazette is a very foolish paper: he has three thousand subscribers, but they purchase, only to laugh at it.[65]

The degradation of the editor of this paper, from the office of

John Jeffries, made the first aerial crossing of the English Channel (1784–85), and the first balloon ascension in America (1793).

[63] William Blount (1749–1800), member from North Carolina to the 1789 convention to frame the Constitution. In 1790 he was appointed territorial governor of the area which, under his leadership, became the new state of Tennessee. He was expelled from the Senate for his attempts to arrange the transfer of Spanish Florida and Louisiana to Great Britain. Although impeachment proceedings were started they were later dismissed.

[64] Benjamin Franklin Bache (1769–1798), prominent Democratic-Republican journalist. In 1790 he founded at Philadelphia the General Advertiser (later known as the Aurora). He opened the columns of his paper to the French Minister Adet in 1796 and printed the four letters Adet sent to the U.S. Secretary of State, Timothy Pickering.

[65] Porcupine's Gazette was established March 4, 1797, in Philadelphia by William Corbett. He was forced to flee the city because of the yellow fever epidemic in August, 1799. After publishing for a while in a Philadelphia suburb, Corbett issued his last paper in New York on Jan. 13, 1800.

State's Printer, by the General Court, shews what *true patriots* are to expect from a *certain junto*.

By a late treaty of regenerated France, with the Swiss Cantons, the town of *Transylvania,* upon the river AMAZON, in HUNGARY, is to be erected into a free port. A republican fleet has sailed the 9th of Nimbose for that purpose.

It is said citizen Burroughs,[66] who was sentenced to hard labour upon the castle, by the Supreme Court of this state, *appealed to the people.* But the voice of the Patriot is not heard in these aristocratic days.

Notwithstanding the cavils of the aristocrats, citizen Thomas Paine's Age of Reason is unquestionably a masterly defence of the Christian religion; and his letter to General Washington shews citizen Paine to be a genuine lover of his country.

The price of hogs rose yesterday in the market to fourpence half-penny per pound—Another blessed effect of the aristocracy of the Federal Government.

There never was a more fortunate event happened to the Dutch republic than the capture of their fleet by Admiral Duncan,[67] as there can be nothing more ruinous to a nation, than the expense of a navy. —When the frigate Constitution stuck in her ways, all good citizens hoped this devoted country would be saved from a great naval expense.

* * * * *

[66] Since Tyler facetiously submitted this for insertion in the *Independent Chronicle* of Boston (see also above, footnote 55), this case would have been tried in the Massachusetts courts. Unfortunately, there are no published reports of Massachusetts Supreme Court decisions before 1804 and it is therefore impossible to learn more of the unfortunate Mr. Burrough's fate.

[67] Admiral Adam Duncan, Viscount Duncan (1731–1904), defeated the Dutch fleet under Admiral DeWinter on Oct. 11, 1797.

FROM THE SHOP OF
Messrs. COLON & SPONDEE.

REMNANTS.
Health and Fraternity. Thomas Paine and Judas Iscariot.

ONE AND INDIVISIBLE.

By the Redacteur, a Paris paper, under the immediate direction of the French Directory, we learn that Tom Paine is writing, under the patronage of Tallyrand, a "Vindication of the character of Judas Iscariot," wherein, with his usual plausibility, he endeavors to prove that Judas was a *bon patriote,* that he betrayed his master, upon principles of liberty and equality, and that the thirty pieces of silver, which he received, as the price of blood, was but a *Douceur,* which is countenanced by the proffers and proposals of X. Y. and a *Lady.*[68]

Among the many appropriate texts from Holy Writ, with which the venerable clergy have introduced their sermons on the national Fast, we cannot refrain from noticing that of the Rev. Mr. PRATT of Westmoreland, Judges, Chapter xvi. Verse 20, *"the Philistines be upon thee, Sampson."* We presume, from the talents and patriotism of this excellent pastor, that the subject was well applied. Surely much might be said of the French lady, the *Delilah* of the dispatches, who endeavored to shave the locks of our Envoys, though, thank God, our virtuous plenipotentiaries were superior to her enticements. We wist [*sic*] the Lord has not departed from the American Sampson; that he shall not become bound, by those traitorous Jacobins, who lie in wait, but that he shall yet arise in his strength and smite the French Philistines hip and thigh.

[68] President Adams had appointed Charles C. Pinckney, John Marshall and Elbridge Gerry as a commission to meet with the French in an attempt to prevent an open break between France and the United States over the former's harrassment of American shipping.

The "lady" is Mme. de Villette who contrived to put the Americans in contact with three agents (called X, Y and Z) of the French foreign minister, Charles Maurice de Tallyrand-Périgord.

FROM THE SHOP OF
Messrs. COLON & SPONDEE.

The laudable rage, for bringing science to the meanest capacity and purse, is a great consolation to the firm. Abridgements of Geography abridged; Treatises of Arithmetic, of the size of the adventures of Tommy Trip; and Grammers, as pleasing and as portable as Goody Twoshoes, have already enriched our literary land. By the kind invitation of some learned and sagacious Preceptors in New England, science, which used to cling to the hoary lock, and snuff up the midnight oil, now condescends to become a playfellow of our children, and to mingle her technicals with top and taw.

We pride ourselves in appreciating these learned labours; but though "much is done, yet much remains to do." Boys, who can scarce *run,* may now indeed read; and little Isaac Newtons, tiny Lowths, and lisping Sheridans, totter through our schools.[69]—But alas! the nursery is yet unexplored. By the same *cunning* process, which has so happily succeeded in levelling science to the brains of small boys, it may be further reduced to the occiputs of infants.—We purpose to have shortly ready for sale, at our shop, gilt, lettered, and faced with pellucid horn, an elaborate work, entitled

THE PAP OF SCIENCE;

Or GODDY B————'s NURSERY GIFT,
In Five Volumes Centesimo.

The first of which is styled GEOGRAPHICAL LULLABIES, in which the systems of Guthrie and Salmon[70] are rendered as *intelligible*

[69] Robert Lowth (1710–1787), Bishop of London, noted Hebrew scholar and sometime versifier.

Thomas Sheridan (1719–1788), highly regarded teacher of elocution. He was the father of Richard Brinsley Sheridan.

[70] William Guthrie (1708–1770), historical and politcal writer. Best noted for his *Geographical, Historical, and Commercial Grammer* (1770).

Thomas Salmon (1679–1767), author of *Modern History, or the Present State of All Nations . . . Illustrated with Cuts and Maps* (1739).

as *amusing,* and the abridgment of Morse,[71] made yet more simple.

Specimen of the Work.
Here we go—up! up! up!
And here we go—down-a, down-a,
What a sweet city is this?
Oh! dear!—'tis Boston town-a.

VOLUME SECOND.

Entitled, *CYPHER CANDY.* Comprehending Arithmetic, and containing all the fundamental rules of the Mathematics, from Sir Isaac Newton's principia down to a Table of Simple Interest.

Specimen of the Work.
"One two—come buckle my shoe,
Three four—shut the door,
Five six—pick up chips,
Seven eight—shut the gate,
Nine ten—a good fat hen!"

THIRD VOLUME.

BIOGRAPHICAL BON BON, or GOODY GOODIES; being the memoirs of little top i, written by itself.

Specimen of the Work.
"Oh my ducky, my ducky,
Oh my ducky, my ducky,
What a fat ducky am I—
ME looks like the Marquis of Granby."[72]

---

[71] Jedidiah Morse (1761–1826), the "father of American geography." His *Geography Made Easy* (1784) was the first such work in the United States. Tyler did not approve obviously of the many abridgments and condensations of Morse's volumes which were so popular during this era.

[72] John Manners, Marquis of Granby (1721–1770). During the Seven Years' War he distinguished himself upon becoming commander-in-chief of the British contingent in Germany.

FOURTH VOLUME.
THE HISTORICAL RATTLE BOX.

First Part.
On the French Revolution.

Specimen of the Work.
"Hie diddle! diddle! the cat's got her fiddle,
The FROG jump'd over the moon;
The little dog laugh'd, to see the sport,
And the dish danc'd after the spoon."

Second Part.
The pretty story of the United States, adorned with cuts. Picture of
a book containing the Federal Constitution; under it,
This is the HOUSE which Jack built.
Picture of the Treasury of the United States.
This is the MALT which lay in the house which Jack built.

VOLUME FIFTH.
THE POLITICAL SUGAR PLUMB.

Part First.
On the present rupture with France.

Specimen of the Work.
Tommy's bridge is broken down
Dance over my Lady Lea;
How shall we mend it up again?
Dance over my Lady Lea;
Little Georgy Logan shall mend it again,[73]
Dance over my Lady Lea, &c.

---

[73] George Logan (1678–1755). A supporter of the Hanoverian accession in 1745, he
advocated the defense of Edinburgh against the Jacobite army. Physically he was "a
little neat man."

Second Part.

Upon the French Directory.

> Miller—a miller—a musty pole,
> How many bags have you stole?
> One from the Dutchman, one from the Dane,
> And one from the big boy who lives down Federal
>   Lane.

Third Part.

Upon Antifederal Editors.

> See saw, Margery Daw;
> Honee still serves his old master;
> Give but the rogue a penny a day
> And Honee will fib the faster.

ANOTHER.

> Goody Bache she keeps a Dog,
> And he goes bow, wow, wow, &c.

FINIS.

———

In addition to the above work, Messrs. COLON & SPONDEE purpose to edite, by subscription, a CORAL and BELLS, which shall gingle all the dead and living languages, so that New England babes shall learn the tongues, whilst they are cutting their first teeth.

N. B.   Ample testimonials of the utility of the above works will be procured from the heads of our Colleges and other literati.

*   *   *   *   *

FROM THE SHOP OF
Messrs. COLON & SPONDEE.

Messrs. COLON & SPONDEE *to their kind* CUSTOMERS.

It has fared with the poet of the United States, as it has with the manufacturer of cloths; each has found a plenty of raw materials, each has made good homespun ware, and each has failed in raising that fine nap, and giving that brilliant colour to their manufactures, which strike the eye of people of fashion. As we may, without vanity, be presumed to be at the top of our trade, we have thought it our especial duty to examine, critically and scientifically, the most modish, literary manufactures of Europe, to discover the causes of their tonish superiority; and to avail ourselves of our discoveries, for the benefit of the fine writers, as manufacturers of our own country. The great Frederick of Prussia stole the art of making China from Canton, and the Englishman, Wedgwood, by a similar address, has caused the wares of Birmingham and Stafford to rival the porcelain of Potzdam, and the vases of Etruria.

We shall proceed to acquaint our brother tradesmen with our discoveries in order.

In our opinion, one of the principal causes of the fashionable superiority of poetry, woven in European looms, is the judicious use of epithets. These should be gorgeous, splendid, far fetched, and obnubulous; that is to say, almost unintelligible. The fault of the American Parnassian weaver is, that he makes both warp and filling of strong, plain, good sense, when the stuff will find a much readier market, if he will merely warp with sense, and fill with epithet. Doubtless, there is now on hand many a durable piece of American stuff, which would command a ready market, if tamboured with choice epithets, after the manner of those ingenious weavers, Mrs. CHARLOTTE SMITH, DELLA CRUSCA, and ANNA MATILDA.[74]

---

[74] Tyler wrote several poems satirizing Della Crusca and his followers. See *Tyler Verse*, pp. 51–4, 59–61, 65–6, 83–4.

Messrs. COLON & SPONDEE,

Have, at great expense, erected an Epithet Jenny, with which they card, spin, and twist all kinds of epithets; single threaded, double twisted, and long rolled epithets, by the hank, or pound. A few real gold and silver wire, and spangled ditto, for the manufacturers of epilogues and theatrical addresses. Ditto tinsel for songs.

N.B.   They may be sewed on old plain poetry, so that the seam cannot be discovered, through the best spectacles.

In seven words of New England poesy, in the New England Primer, are the following lines.

> The cat doth play,
> And after slay.

This happy description we have amplified, and bespangled with epithets, in the following manner of CHARLOTTE SMITH.

SONNET TO AN OLD MOUSER.

Child of lubricious art! of sanguine sport!
Of *pangful mirth!* sweet ermin'd sprite!
Who lov'st, with silent, *velvet step,* to court
The bashful bosom of the night.

Whose elfin eyes can pierce night's fable gloom,
And witch her *fairy prey* with guile,
Who sports fell frolic o'er the grisly tomb,
And gracest death with dimpling smile!

Daughter of ireful mirth, sportive in rage,
Whose joy should shine in sculptur'd bas relief,
Like Patience, in rapt Shakespeare's deathless page,
Smiling in marble at wan grief.

Oh, come, and teach me all thy barb'rous joy,
To sport with sorrow first, and then destroy.

FROM THE SHOP OF
Messrs. COLON & SPONDEE.

Although authors are too proud to acknowledge, with *us,* that fine
writing is a mere trade, that what, in school master dialect, is called
composition, requires the labour of the hands, rather than the head, yet
we observe that when our present fashionable writers publish their
prose and sing song, no Williamstreet or Cornhill shop keeper was
ever more solicitous to exhibit his etwees, his tinsel tassels, and his
spangles to advantage, through a pellucid glass case, than these men of
genius are, by a thousand handicraft tricks, to allure the eye of the
reader to notice their literary millenary. One author endeavours to
catch the eye with a luminous page, a hot pressed leaf and neat type.
A second aims to attract by a broad envelope, where "a rivulet of
text sportively meanders through a meadow of margin." A third, like
the learned John Graham, L.L.D.[75] decks his leaves with Morocco
leather, and, by a gilded exterior, aims, beau like, to compensate for
their internal insignificancy. But of all the tricks of authorship, to pass
a flimsy article, that of the profuse use of capital and italic letters,
asterisks, dashes, and notes of admiration, is most to be applauded, as
the cheapest, and the most likely to attract the reader's attention. Of
the sovereign efficacy and fascination of this press polish of dull works,
we have had ample experience, in the course of our trade.

No piece of stuff ever came from our looms, which we thought
better calculated to command a penny, than a collection of Sonnets,
after a patent pattern of Mrs. Charlotte Smith. These Sonnets were

[75] John Andrew Graham (1764–1841). Coming from Connecticut, he established a
considerable reputation as an attorney in Vermont before moving to New York. Tyler
is here probably referring to Graham's *Descriptive Sketch of the Present State of Vermont*
published in 1797, two years before this "Colon and Spondee" column.

Tyler did not think too highly of Graham. Resting from a session of Court at
Rutland in 1802, he told his wife in a letter that "Dr. Graham tells us all about London,
and lies with the most traveled taste." ("TPT Memoir," p. 165.) An examination of a
copy of the *Descriptive Sketch* (in the Brattleboro, Vt. Brooks Library) does show it to
have been a pretentiously bound and illustrated volume, with heavy gilt designs on
mottled calf and with an elaborately engraved frontispiece of Graham.

printed on a woven paper, hot pressed, silver type; were adorned
with an ample arrangement of ambient alliteration; were decked with
a profusion of obsolete epithets, freshly selected from Chaucer and
Spenser; were replete with pleasing melancholy, soft despair, blissful
woe, and heart rending happiness; and, in a word, were as impassioned, as uninteresting, and as unintelligible, as a young lady of the
most fashionable taste could desire. But alas! week after week, they
cumbered our shelves. We tried, in vain, all the laudable arts of our
trade, to get them off our hands. We exposed them in our bow window, among our most shewy articles. We slyly inserted them in every
new invoice; and vowed, upon the veracity of shop keepers, that they
were "fresh and new come in," and the tip of the taste in Philadelphia.
But, ah well a day, our customers passed over our Sonnets, with as
much neglect, as last Sunday's sermon, or last summer's bonnet. One
melancholy day, when we were taking an account of stock, and
gravely noting profit and loss, what is the reason these Sonnets do not
sell, said our elder partner to Tom Trochee, our youngest apprentice,
who by his chit chat has helped off many a stale commodity from our
counters? Why, master Colon, says Tom, I observe that when the
young ladies and gentlemen come a shopping they always pick out
those goods, which are printed, like this book, holding up a volume
of Della Crusca. We took the hint, ordered our compositor to reprint
the Sonnets, and set the types, solely from the large capital, and italic
letter cases. The whole impression went off, at an advanced price,
almost as quick, as a never failing cosmetic to remove freckles, and
smooth wrinkles.

ADVERTISEMENT.

Messrs. Colon and Spondee would now inform their kind customers, that they brighten the dullest compositions in prose and verse,
by the apt and judicious insertion of capital letters, italics, dashes,
asterisks, brackets, apostrophes, carets, hyphens, idiopathics, ichno-
graphics, ellipses, and synalephies, notes manual, digital, and astral,

with notes of interrogation, obnubulation, and admiration, by the gross or dozen.

   N.B.   They have some capitals of an uncommon large size, for the use of the female muse.

———

From Our Shew Board.

   Selected from the above mentioned collection of Sonnets, second edition, polished and burnished to the tip of the mode.

———

SONNET To The TURTLE DOVE.

SWEET CHILD OF WOE!!! who pour'st *thy love lorn lays*
On the dull ear! of PENSIVE night,
Who with THY *sighs* protract'st the pitying gale,
WHICH seeks with GOS'MER *wing* the INFANT LIGHT.

DAUGHTER OF SIGHS, whose plumy pinions wave
In ONE *dank circle* of despair,
WHO in the surge OF MISERY lov'st to lave,
And draw'st *rich solace* from the realms of CARE.

OFFSPRING OF GRIEF! child of EXTATIC woes!!
NOW *night* sheds soft her curtain'd sleep,
AND *greedy* wealth, and vulgar *bliss* REPOSE,
And only sorrow JOYS to wake and weep.

COME, CHILD OF WOE, and let Eliza join
In all your SORROWS, for your JOYS are MINE.

*   *   *   *   *

FROM THE SHOP OF
Messrs. COLON & SPONDEE.

STATE OF LITERATURE IN ENGLAND AND
AMERICA, AT DIFFERENT PERIODS.

Matthew Paris, speaking of the deplorable ignorance of the English, in 1601,[76] narrates a contest between the rector of a parish and his parishioners, respecting the duty of repairing the church pavement. The cause was carried into the King's Court, and the rector gained his suit by the following quotation from St. Peter—"Paveant illi, non paveam ego"—which he construed—"They are to pave the church yard and not I"—this was allowed by the judge to be good law, and accepted as a correct translation.

There is extant an act of the British Parliment passed so late as the year 1460, which enacts, "That noblemen, and the fellows of the university of Oxford, should be entitled to the benefit of clergy, *even though they could not read.*"

AMERICAN LEARNING, 1798.

A speculator, who had rapidly amassed a princely fortune, wishing to figure as a scholar, sent the following order to an eminent book-seller in Boston—

    sur

i wants to by sum Buks—as I am prodighouse fond of larnen—plese to send by the Bear here 5 hunder Dollars woth of the *hansumest* you have—   Yoors &c. — —

*   *   *   *   *

[76] Matthew Paris (*d.* 1259). Tyler's citation here is unclear. There was an edition of Paris' *Chronica Majora* in 1606 but none in 1601.

PURCHASED for the GALAXY,
At The Shop of
MESS. COLON & SPONDEE.

Parables have in all ages and nations proceeded from the mouth of the wisest men. They were the glory of the Roman forum, and the pride of the Grecian porticoes, and the Saviour of mankind illustrated the doctrine of salvation by parables.

Listen then!—Ye who seem insensible to sound argument and incapable of logical deduction, listen to a parable—and peradventure your dim optics, which cannot bear the strong light of reason, may see the application, which it should be presumed a child might readily discern.

What is the reason, said a poor Democrat, that you Federalists abandon the glorious patriotic principles of 1775? In all my attempts to impede the present government of the United States, I act only on the noble republican principles of '75; those principles upon which Washington and Adams then acted, though they have since deserted them.

Put on your spectacles, my dear Demo, and try to spell out this parable.

A PARABLE.

There was once a number of worthy people, with their families, confined in a huge Gothic stone prison—poor souls!—The flinty walls of their prison were not the greatest hardship they had to endure; they were tyrannized over by an inexorable merciless gaoler, who would strip their pockets of their last shilling without their consent, and upon the least wry look load then with shackles and throw them into the noisome dungeons of the prison. One day—I think it was in the year 1775—these good people arose, with one accord, to destroy their prison, and take vengeance upon their merciless gaoler: Some provided themselves with crow bars; some with pick axes, spades, hawkbills, and every other tool they could conveniently come at which were fit to destroy gaols and gaolers—and at it they went. It would have done an honest man's heart good to see them, one and all, fly, pell mell, at the old building—Crash went the doors—bounce went the windows—here the foundation shook, and there the roof rocked, till a short time down came the old prison, and not one stone was left upon another. As to the poor devil of a gaoler, he sought safety on the other side of the water.

No sooner was the hurly burly over, then these good people found they had pulled down one house without providing themselves another; they were exposed to the inclemency of the weather, and what property they had was liable to be stolen; every vagrant thief would pilfer from them, and every sturdy rogue insult them. But being a sensible people, they soon determined to join all hands and raise a new house, commodious and fit to receive them all; and agreed, to prevent disputes, that the plan of the new house should be drawn by the best architects, and submitted to all concerned, and if two thirds approved it, it should be adopted. Two thirds, and at length, the whole agreed to the plan, except a few wrong-headed people, who wished to have the cellar in the garret, and the back kitchen and cold hole made the best rooms in the house; some amendments were made, for the sake of concord, to please *even these wise builders.*

The new house was erected;—it drew the admiration of the traveller:—Indeed it was a beautiful edifice—elegant without—a good firm foundation, and commodious within—all our worthy people moved into it;—every one had room and to spare, for the comfortable accommodation of himself, wife, and little ones:—Our worthy builders soon grew rich;—every one had plumb pudding and roast beef in plenty, a good kitchen to cook them in, a handsome parlour to eat his meals, and good feather beds and convenient bed chambers for himself and family to lie down and sleep after a hearty supper.

One day, certain of those wrongheads whom I hinted at, who wished to have the cellar in the garret, raised a great mob, got fuddled with whiskey, worked themselves into a rage, seized the same tools which had done such excellent service in pulling down the old prison, and begun to pick away at the new building, like so many mad men;

one drove his crow bar through the panel of the great door—another dashed in a window—while a third was actually employed in digging away the foundation. The good sober people ran out, and begged them, for God's sake, to stop, and not destroy a building which had been erected with their joint consent and labour; at least to try it a few years; but they would not stop until some of the graver people called upon some of the more robust young ones, who soon, with a few hickory cudgels, reduced them to order.

When the confusion was over, one of these wrongheads, who had been very busy with his crow bar, hawkbill, and pick axe, was heard to exclaim, in surly soliloquy, "What is the reason, that *these here* tools, that did such excellent service in pulling down the old prison in '75, will not answer now? I am sure, in handling my crow bar, hawkbill, and pick axe, I act with the same spirit, and upon the same principles, I did in old whig '75: Our great men encouraged me then—ay, and worked as stoutly as the meanest of us—they have certainly changed their principles." An honest federalist, smiling at his simple stupidity, calmly replied—"Why, my dear *Honeè,* is there no difference between applying our crow bars and other destruction tools in destroying a prison in which we are ill at ease, and forced to inhabit —and flying in a rage with our crow bars, hawkbills, and pick axes, those glorious, handy tools of '75, to destroy a building, which we erected ourselves, and in which we enjoy every domestic comfort?"

MORAL.

Pray, Mr. Demo, do you see the application of this parable?—If not, in answer to your query, let me tell you in plain English, that the principles of 1775 were admirably calculated to pull down a government; and the men who incite you to act upon them now, wish to use them and you for the same purpose. But you really should make some distinction between destroying a monarchical government imposed upon us, and attempting to revolutionize a republican government erected by your own free consent.

* * * * *

FROM THE SHOP OF
Messrs. COLON & SPONDEE.
ATTENTION, HAYMAKERS.

Suspend your scythes—Lean upon your pitchforks—Stick your rakes in the
sod, and while the refreshing pitcher goes merrily round, listen to Neigh-
bour Winrow's advice upon drinking.

FELLOW LABOURERS,

WHEN we sweat most, we thirst most, and drink most abundantly—
You will all pronounce that liquor best, which makes you most strong
and healthy.

Then do not drink FLIP—The body in this sultry season being extremely heated, acts like a still, the Rum immediately flies off, and the
heavy, clammy dregs of the beer and sugar remain to clog the stomach,
render the labourer dull and weak, and often excite inflammatory
disease.

Do not drink Toddy or Milk punch, for the same reason.

If Rum, Brandy, Whisky, Gin, or other ardent spirits must be drank,
take half a gill at a time, unmixed, and immediately drink large
draughts of water after it. For the same reason, when a man is crack
brained enough to throw a fire brand into a magazine of powder, he
cannot do better than to throw water upon the burning coals as fast as
possible.

Drink Switchel—that is, Molasses or Maple sugar mixed with water.

Drink whey, or milk and water, two thirds water, spruce or small
beer.

Drink cyder. Not boiled—if you would be merry, but cyder and
water, if you would be healthy, happy and wise. The acid in cyder, is
the best preventative against all putrid disorders.

Drink vinegar and water for the same reason.

Drink PURE WATER—you have been told of many people whose
fat has been cooled, and who have died suddenly by drinking cold
water. Set the pail in the sun, half an hour before you use it; or rinse
your mouth three or four times with the coldest water, and you may

then drink freely from the coldest spring. If the water is much colder than your bodies it will then do you no harm; it will strengthen and quicken your animal functions, will make you sweat copiously and freely; your nap at noon, and slumbers at night, will be pleasant and refreshing, and you will need, at the next dawn, no other call to awake you, than the chirping of the early bird—you will arise to the next day's labour like a giant, refreshed with wine.

Do you doubt what I say, let the stoutest grog bruizer come and try a fall at wrestling with me, a temperate water drinker of sixty five years of age—or stake out an acre of fowl meadow, and see who will cut it first.

Fellow labourers, when you work for yourselves you will readily allow that the disuse of strong liquors will be a great saving to your purses. If you want to know how great, go and inspect your accounts at the traders; if not, listen to my calculation. Say the Hay Season lasts, taking the after growth into the calculation, one month, say that you have three hands to work—allow them each half a pint of rum each day. This will amount, by a rough calculation, to six gallons, which at twelve shillings a gallon for Westindia Rum, would cost twelve dollars, besides the expense of sugar. Newengland Rum, it is true, would be something less, but brandy something more. Now the sum of twelve dollars in these hard times, would do many valuable things for a farmer—it might purchase three Calves, which would triple in two years. It would pay the ministerial, the town, the county, or state taxes of a small farmer. It would buy many a comfortable matter for his wife when she blesses him with the rich present of a sturdy boy, or healthy girl. It might effect a valuable swop in oxen, or perhaps pay two or three small notes or accounts, or such part of them as may prevent the lawyer from making two or three bills of costs, each larger than the original debt, and so save the favourite mare, or the likely two year old, from being taken by the sheriff, and sold for half their value at the Post.

But some of you, fellow labourers, drink strong liquors when you work out as we do now, because you say they cost you nothing; and you are ready to call your employers stingy who wish to discountenance the use of spirits. You are mistaken, my friends, every gill of rum given to you by those who hire you, costs you much.

Sometimes it costs you a quarrel with your best friends, sometimes a bloody nose, or broken limb, and often a lawsuit, and bill of cost, or a fine upon confession, before a Justice of the Peace, for assault and battery; and oftener a long doctor's bill for a disorder, which you may not, but the physician knows arose from this very cause of strong liquors. Sometimes it costs you the respect of your townsmen; the regard of your children, and love of your wife. Sometimes your reputation in this world, and I fear, your happiness in the next. Are not these heavy costs, Friends?

Thus spake Jotham Winrow, to a gang of Haymakers, in my uncle Jotham's meadow. The whole gang immediately cried out, "Jotham Winrow has spoken wisely"—They club'd upon the spot, and sent a boy to the next grog shop for a humming pitcher of flip, and ordered half a pint more than the usual quantity of rum to be stirred into it, and all with one accord got tipsey by drinking the health of the wise Jotham Winrow.

IMRI RIFLE.

* * * * *

FOR THE PORT FOLIO
AN AUTHOR'S EVENINGS

From the Shop of Messrs. Colon and Spondee

To night, after my return from the theatre, into which I sometimes saunter, to smooth the wrinkles of my brow, to surrender myself to the illusions of imagination, and derive fresh spirits for my lucubrations, I could not help reflecting, in consequence of witnessing the new pantomine of *Obi,* upon the universal belief of the existence and potency of supernatural and malevolent beings. Magical rites and incantations; the charm and the cauldron, the loathsome reptile and the dragon's blood, have been successfully employed by the cunning, and implicitly dreaded by the timid, in every age. The striking similarity observable in most of the mummeries of superstitution, lead me to the collation of the *"charms"* of sorcery, as described in three different authors. The circumstances, on which this piece* is founded, are related in Dr. Moseley's Treatise on Sugar, and Medical Observations.[77] A revolted negro, named Jack, of gigantic strength and great intrepidity, took up his residence in the inaccessible parts of Mount Lebanus, in Jamaica, and by his boldness, bravery, and depredations, became the terror of the island. Many attempts were made to subdue him, but without success; in one of these conflicts with a negro, named Quashee, he lost two fingers, and thus acquired his nickname. He was dreaded by the negroes, on account of his supposed magical powers, and the influence of his *obi*. This obi consisted in a composition of dirty and disgusting materials; namely, *grave* dirt, ashes, the blood of a *black* cat, and *human fat,* mixed into a paste, kept in the end of a goat's horn, and worn about the neck. He had also in a bag, a dried toad, a pig's tail, and a slip of *virginal* parchment of kid's skin, inscribed with characters in blood. His repeated enormities, at length, induced the government to offer a large reward for killing him, which was finally effected by two negroes, Quashee and Sam; aided by a little boy. Before they set out on the expedition, the negroes took the precaution to be baptized, in confidence that by such means, they would be enabled to resist the effects of obi.

The following article contains some additional information touching this *African* magic.

Obi, or, as it is pronounced in the English West Indies, obeah, originated, like many customs among the Africans, with the ancient *Egyptians*. Obi, for the purpose of bewitching people, or consuming them by lingering illness, is made of grave dirt, hair, teeth of sharks

---

* "Three-Fingered Jack." [*Original footnote.*]

[77] Dr. Benjamin Moseley (1742–1819) published *A Treatise on Sugar with Miscellaneous Medical Observations* in London in 1799. A more recent account of this episode concerning Three-Fingered Jack is contained in Joseph J. Williams, Jr., *Voodoos and Obeahs. Phases of West India Witchcraft* (New York, 1932), pp. 182–3.

and other animals, blood, feathers, egg-shells, images in wax, the hearts of birds, liver of mice, and some potent weeds, roots and bushes, of which Europeans are at this time ignorant. A negro, who thinks himself bewitched by obi, will apply to an obi man or an obi woman for cure.

The next narrative of these baleful rites is to be found in Ben Jonson, who, in his *"Masque of Queens,"* has thus minutely described a noctural meeting of the hags of witchcraft. As this description is not generally known, as it is most wildly poetical, and of vivid interest, as the form of invocation is tremendous, and as it describes things "most fanciful and strange," we recommend it to the curious reader.[78]

> Dame, dame, the watch is set:
> Quickly come, we all are met,
> From the lakes, and from the fens,
> From the rocks, and from the dens,
> From the woods, and from the caves,
> From the church-yards, from the graves,
> From the dungeon, from the tree
> That they die on, here are we.
>
> The owl is 'broad, the bat and toad,
>   And so is the cat a-mountain,
> The ant and the mole both sit in a hole,
>   And frog peeps out of the fountain;
> The dogs they do bay, and the timbrels play,
>   The spindle is now a turning;
> The moon it is red, and the stars are fled,
>   But all the sky is a burning:
> The ditch is made, and our nails the spade,
> With pictures full, of wax and wool;
> Their livers I stick, with needles quick;
> There lacks but the blood, to make up the flood.
>   Quickly, dame, then bring your part in,
>   Spur, spur upon little Martin,

[78] "The Masque of Queens," Jonson's most finished example of this genre, was produced Feb. 2, 1609. This lengthly selection commences near the start of the production.

Merrily, merrily, make him sail,
A worm in his mouth, and a thorn in's tail,
Fire above, and fire below,
With a whip i' your hand, to make him go.
   O, now she's come!
   Let all be dumb.

   I have been all day looking after
A raven, feeding upon a quarter;
And, soon as she turn'd her beak to the south,
I snatch'd this morsel out of her mouth.

   I have been gathering wolves' hairs,
The mad dog's foam, and the adder's ears;
The spurging of a dead man's eyes,
And all since the evening star did rise.

   I last night lay all alone
O' the ground, to hear the mandrake groan;
And pluck'd him up, though he grew full low;
And, as I had done, the cock did crow.

   And I ha' been choosing out this skull!
From charnel houses, that were full;
From private grots, and public pits;
And frighted a sexton out of his wits.

   Under a cradle I did creep,
By day; and when the child was asleep
At night, I suck'd the breath; and rose,
And pluck'd the nodding nurse by the nose.

   I had a dagger: what did I with that?
Kill'd an infant to have his fat.
A piper it got, at a church aisle,
I bade him again blow wind i' the tail.

   A murderer yonder was hung in chains,
The sun and the wind has shrunk his veins;
I bit off a sinew; I clipp'd his hair;
I brought off his rags, that danc'd i' the air.

The screech owl's eggs, and the feathers black,
The blood of the frog, and the bone of his back,
I have been getting: and made of his skin
A purset, to keep Sir Cranion in.

And I ha' been plucking (plants among)
Hemlock, henbane, adders-tongue,
Night-shade, moon-wort, libbard's bane;
And twice, by the dogs, was like to be tak'n.

I, from the jaws of a gard'ner's bitch,
Did snatch these bones, and then leap'd the ditch:
Yet went I back to the house again,
Kill'd the black cat, and here's the brain.

I went to the toad breeds under the wall,
I charm'd him out, and he came at my call;
I snatch'd out the eyes of the owl before,
I tore the bat's wing: what would you have more?

DAME.
Yes, I have brought (to help our vows)
Horned poppy, cypress boughs,
The fig tree wild, that grows on tombs,
And juice that from the larch tree comes,
The basilisk's blood, and the viper's skin:
And now our orgies let's begin.
Dame Earth shall quake,
And the houses shake,
And her belly shall ake,
As her back were brake,
Such a birth to make,
As is the blue drake,
Whose form thou shalt take.

The sticks are across, there can be no loss,
The sage is rotten, the sulphur is gotten
Upto the sky, that was i' the ground.
Follow it then, with our rattles, round;
Under the bramble, over the brier,

A little more heat will set it on fire:
Put it in mind, to do it kind,
Flow water and blow wind.
Rouncy is over, Robble is under,
A flash of light, and a clap of thunder,
A storm of rain, another of hail.
We all must home i' the egg-shell sail;
The mast is made of a great pin,
The tackle of cobweb, the sail as thin,
And if we go through and not fall in. . . .

DAME.
Stay, all our charms do nothing win
Upon the night; our labour dies!
Our magic feature will not rise;
Nor yet the storm! we must repeat
More direful voices far, and beat
The ground with vipers, till it sweat.

Bark dogs, wolves howl,
Seas roar, woods roll,
Clouds crack, all be black,
But the light our charms do make.

Not yet? my rage begins to swell,
Darkness, devils, night, and hell,
Do not thus delay my spell.
I call you once, and I call you twice;
I beat you again, if you stay my thrice;
Through these cranies where I peep,
I'll let in the light to see you sleep.
And all the secrets of your sway
Shall lie as open to the day,
As unto me. Still are you deaf?
Reach me a bough that ne'er bare leaf,
To strike the air; and Aconite,
To hurl upon this glaring light;
A rusty knife to wound mine arm;
And as it drops, I'll speak a charm,
Shall cleave the ground, as low as lies

Old shrunk-up Chaos, and let rise,
Once more, his dark and reeking head,
To strike the world and nature dead,
Until my magic be bred.

Black go in, and blacker come out;
At thy going down we give thee a shout.
                    Hoo!
At thy rising again thou shalt have two,
And if thou dost what we would have thee do,
Thou shalt have three, thou shalt have four,
Thou shalt have ten, thou shalt have a score.
                    Hoo. Har. Har. *Hoo!*

A cloud of pitch, a spur and switch,
To haste him away, and a whirlwind play,
Before and after, with thunder for laughter,
And storms for joy, of the roaring boy;
His head of a drake, his tail of a snake.

About, about, and about,
Till the mist arise, and the lights fly out.
The images neither be seen nor felt:
The woolen burn, and the waxen melt:
Sprinkle your liquors upon the ground,
And into the air: around, around.

Our last quotation is sufficiently familiar, but it would be high
treason to the majesty of Shakespeare, to omit the subsequent passage
from his *"Macbeth."*[79]

Thrice the brindled cat hath mew'd,
  Thrice; and once the hedge pig whin'd.
Harp[*i*]er cries: 'tis time, 'tis time.
  Round about the cauldron go,
  In the poison'd entrails throw;
  Toad that under the cold stone
  Days and nights hast thirty-one

[79] *MacBeth,* IV, i.

Swelter'd venom sleeping got,
Boil thou first in the charmed pot.

Fillet of a fenny snake,
In the cauldron boil and bake;
Eye of newt, and toe of frog,
Wool of bat and tongue of dog,
Adder's fork, and blind worm's sting,
Lizard's leg, and owlet's wing,
For a charm of powerful trouble,
Like a hell broth boil and bubble.

Scale of dragon; tooth of wolf,
Witch's mummy, maw and gulf
Of the ravin'd salt sea shark;
Root of hemlock, digg'd in the dark,
Liver of blaspheming Jew;
Gall of goat; and slips of yew,
Sliver'd in the moon's eclipse;
Nose of Turk, and Tarter's lips;
Finger of birth-strangled babe,
Ditch deliver'd by a drab;
Make the gruel thick and slab;
Add thereto a tiger's chaudron,
For the ingredients of our cauldron.

* * * * *

MISCELLANY
AN AUTHOR'S EVENINGS
FOR THE PORT FOLIO

From the Shop of Messrs. Colon and Spondee

The London Monthly Magazine, conducted by Dr. Aikin, &c. and contributed to by Drs. Priestley, Beddoes, &c. contains much ingenious literary matter, whenever the writers choose to let church and state alone.[80] The following is a most exquisite piece of poetry, which the good taste of the above writers has snatched from oblivion. . . . The delightful images of every couplet will be eagerly gazed at by every lover.

"If I swear by that eye, you'll allow
Its look is so shifting and new,
That the oath I might take on it now,
The very next glance would undo.
Those babies that nestle so sly,
Such different arrows have got,
That an oath on the glance of an eye
Such as yours may be off in a shot!
Should I swear by the dew of your lip,
Though each moment the treasure renews,
If my constancy wishes to trip,
I may kiss off the oath, when I choose.
Or a sigh may disperse from that flower
The dew, and the oath that are there,
And I'd make a new vow ev'ry hour,
To loose them so sweetly in air!
But clear up the heaven of your brow,
Nor fancy my faith is a feather;
On my heart I will pledge you my vow,
And they must be both broken together!"

In the course of my reading I am never more pleased than when I meet some memorial of the versatile talents of Sir William Jones,[81] who had the rare good fortune to flourish among a liberal people; to

---

[80] The magazine was started by Dr. John Aikin (1747–1822) in February, 1796. He was assisted by Dr. Joseph Priestley (1733–1804) and Dr. Thomas Beddoes (1760–1808).

[81] Sir William Jones (1746–1794). British orientalist and jurist, he was a pioneer in Sanskrit learning and founder of the Bengal Asiatic Society. Jones rendered the language and literature of the ancient Hindus accessible to European scholars.

America took due notice of his importance. There is notice of his death in the *Federal Orrery*, II, No. 68 (June 11, 1795), 264, and an article entitled, "Eulogy on Sir William Jones," in the *Massachusetts Magazine*, VIII, No. 3 (March, 1796), 159–166.

be instructed by Parr and Sumner;[82] to possess all the gifts of mind; to challenge the boon of riches, and the shouts of praise, and to resist the sleep of sloth and withstand the blandishments of pleasure.

The British critics analizing one of his last literary labours, have thus justly praised this accomplished orientalist.

"But there is another circumstance, which recommends this work to our peculiar regard. It is among the last labours of a very eminent and industrious scholar, whose exertions in the cause of literature and of mankind, death has prematurely interrupted. That he has not left his equal behind him for genius and for diligence it may be thought extravagant to maintain. But where shall we look for his persevering courage and ardour of curiosity? The thirst for wealth has always excited, and will still continue to excite, thousands to brave the perils of the ocean, and the utmost severities of climate. It was reserved for Sir William Jones, and perhaps for him alone, to pursue knowledge with unabated ardour, and unexampled success, in defiance of the scorching suns of India, and the still more dangerous allurements of its pleasures."

I frequently turn over the charming odes of the Anacreon of Persia,[83] and suffer delighted Fancy to cross "the stream of *Rock-nabad*," or loiter in the gay "bower of *Mosellay*." The following is copied with a hope that the ingenious "*P. D.*" will give it a poetical dress. Not to mention a word of his tardiness of invention or the mediocrity of his rhymes, the "author" is too laboriously engaged in *reading* poetry to have any leisure to combine a couplet.

Ode from the Persian of Hafiz, translated by Sir W. Ouseley.[84]

I cannot relinquish the delights of love and a flowing cup; I have vowed a hundred times to forsake them; I *vow*, but I can do no more.

[82] Robert Carey Sumner (1729–1771), Master of Harrow and a friend of Dr. Johnson and of Parr and Jones.

Dr. Samuel Parr (1747–1825), scholar and contemporary of Jones at Harrow.

[83] Tyler was among the early admirers of Hafiz in the United States. For a discussion of this point and the poems Tyler composed in imitation of the Persian lyricist, see *Tyler Verse*, pp. 171–4.

[84] Sir William Ouseley (1767–1842), orientalist.

The garden of Paradise, the celestial shades, and the bowers of the lovely Houris are not equal in my opinion, to the mansion of her, whom I adore.

If, as 'tis said, angels are not affected with the power of love; I, a mere mortal, cannot conceive that which constitutes their felicity.

In the time of prayer, the graceful form of my beloved obtrudes on my imagination; and induces a mussulman to become a worshipper of an idol.

*   *   *   *   *

MISCELLANY
FOR THE PORT FOLIO
An Author's Evenings,
From the Shop of Messrs. Colon and Spondee

Imitatores Servum Pecus.

I sometimes relax among books, as well as men. After reading my accustomed portion of the sacred scriptures the last evening, I caught up a volume of Lord Chesterfield's Letters to his Son. The venerable volume I had laid by, is generally the last I take in hand, previous to my repose; but the courtly pages lay so temptingly by me, and . . . perhaps I had better confess the truth . . . some passages in the divine writings demanded so serious a consideration, that I resolved to think on those things, at some more "convenient season," and to amuse and divert myself from the melancholy which was pervading me, by the elegant instructions of his lordship. Here I was sure, at least, that if my heart was not cheered, my conscience would not be wounded.

Perusing the sacred and profane writers, in the same hours of retirement, gave rise to the following reflections.

UPON PROVERBS.

It is astonishing to reflect, how those pithy adages and brief sentences, which convey instruction to all conditions of men, in all circumstances of life, with such force and precision, which were so long the boast of the ancient sages, and the glory of men of wit and learning, should have so undeservedly fallen into disuse, been restrained to the pulpit, or degraded into the conversation of the illiterate. But, alas! even learning has its fashions, and, like other fashions of this world, they pass suddenly away; for those excellent wise sayings, which were the perfection of eastern literature, and the pride of the Grecian porticoes, of which kings were emulous to be esteemed authors, and which philosophers viewed as their brightest wreaths of immortality, are become like a garment, which is "waxen old."

The misfortune of proverbs has been that, from their obvious utility, they have been rendered common, and being once common, they have become contemptible. The wisest of the moderns, however, for many centuries, imitated, although they have never equalled, the more nervous ancients, in the use of adages and maxims. We find them scattered profusely in the writings of the Christian fathers, and everywhere adorning the pages of the philosopher; nor is it indeed until a century past, that they have fallen so generally into disrepute. At present, the polite and learned, of all countries, seem combined against them; and the late Earl of Chesterfield, who has analyzed politeness, and reduced good manners to a system, it is supposed has given them their fatal stroke, by noticing the entire disuse of them, as one principal criterion of polite conversation. But, if we of this age have indeed polished our style, by their disuse, I fear we have purchased the ornamental, at the expense of the useful; and I am apprehensive the noble author has, in this sentiment, evidenced rather a sickly than a refined taste.

If to express much in the fewest words, and those the most happily chosen, be the *perfection,* as indeed it is the modern definition of fine writing, what literary composition shall compare with the proverbial? It is not a little curious to observe, that the whole of this graceful writer's directions for his son's conduct in life, which are truly valuable, is but a commentary upon the proverbial sayings of the inspired writers. His modish disciple does not consider, that, whilst he is assiduously pursuing his lordship's directions, he is often rigidly obeying the wise admonitions of the son of Sirach. I contend, that the wisdom of Lord Chesterfield is the wisdom of Solomon, and his sententious admirers. Let his admirers seek a better origin for his follies, his frivolities, and duplicity. The only difference between the inspired penmen and his lordship, as to the truly valuable, is, that they give us at once, in their proverbial saying, the very essence of those sweets, which *he* presents us, diffused in copious baskets of flowers.

Does his lordship recommend a strict attention to instruction, and enforce his advice with examples of the uncourtly carriage of those, who neglect it? Does he spend pages to elucidate this? With what brevity has the proverb said, ages before, *Whoso loveth instruction loveth knowledge, but he that hath reproof is* BRUTISH.

Does he recommend the Suaviter in modo, the gentle way of effecting a purpose, or procuring friends? Has not the wise man taught us, that "*Sweet language will multiply friends, and a fair speaking tongue will encrease kind greeting*": and in the more familiar adage, "*Soft words turn away wrath?*"

Has he advised his son to associate with persons, older than himself? "*Stand in the multitude of the* ELDERS," says the proverb, "*and cleave unto him, who is wise.*" Does he recommend reserve and secrecy, in matters of importance, necessary to be concealed? The Solomon of ancient times has said, "*Open not thy heart to every man, lest he requite thee with a shrewd turn*"; and "*A fool uttereth all his mind, but a wise man keepeth in till* AFTERWARDS."

Does his lordship caution his son against trusting a man, with whom he has once been at variance? The proverb has before cautioned us, "*Never trust thine enemy, for, like as iron rusteth, so is his wickedness.*"

Has he at large recommended a certain regular, systematic mode of doing business to effect, and instanced very great men, who, with a life of fatigue, for want of attention to this mode, have brought little to pass? We read that "*There is one that laboureth, and taketh pains, and maketh haste, but is so much more behind.*"

Does he impose upon his son diligence in his political concerns, as a sure step to court preferment? The proverb says, "*Seest thou a man diligent in his business, he shall stand before kings.*"

Nor are the proverbs less the text of his lordship's directions, in those things, which more particularly concern the welfare of the body. Does he warn him of intemperance, as the sure destroyer of health? Are we not warned in the Proverbs, that "*Wine is a mocker, strong drink is raging, and whoso is deceived thereby is not wise?*" and "*Be not insatiable in any dainty thing, nor too greedy upon meats, for excess in meat bringeth forth sickness, and surfeiting will turn into choler?*" Nor these lesser instructions, which relate to his son's conduct in company. Is the youth cautioned of the folly of tedious and unseasonable stories? The proverb says, "*An unseasonable tale shall always be in the mouth of fools.*"

Is the young gentleman guarded against boisterous laughter? Is he directed by the courtly parent merely to dimple his features into a smile of complacency? Even for this he is indebted to the proverb, which says, "*A fool lifteth up his voice with laughter, but a wise man doth* SCARCE SMILE." And even an attention to those "*graces,*" which we meet with, almost as frequently as with the beauties of style in the letters of this elegant writer; even the minute attention to dress, address, and to the numberless decencies of carriage, feature, and person, which we are told mark the real gentleman with such precision, are recommended in these uncourtly proverbs, for the preacher saith, "*A man's dress, laughter, and gait, shew what he is.*" . . . And as this polished instructor drew so much knowledge himself from these ungraceful adages, it would have been well if he had commented upon one more proverb, in his letters to his son: "*Why wilt thou, my son, be ravished with a strange woman, and embrace the bosom of a stranger?*"

Much more might be added, but the printer's boy calls, and I much fear, by tracing the sentiments of this polite writer to so unfashionable a source, I may destroy that relish for his works, which gives the true zest to most of his readers.

T.

An Oration on the
Death of George Washington

TYLER WAS MUCH in demand as a public speaker. His reputation as an attorney, his position as a member of the Vermont Supreme Court, and his forensic talents resulted in his being called upon to mount the podium on both civic and religious occasions.

A humorous example of Tyler's participation in public celebrations occurred in April, 1808. The first bridge over the Connecticut River between Brattleboro and Hinsdale, New Hampshire, was completed and its opening to the public was a grand occasion. Tyler was retained as the orator and the Reverend Bunker Gay of the Hinsdale Congregational Church was to give the invocation. The two stood on a wagon in the center of the span which was packed from end to end with local townspeople. Reverend Gay had finished his prayer and Tyler had just started his discourse when creaking timbers gave notice the bridge was not equal to the weight of humanity. Everyone fled to safety and although the bridge did not fall then it did a short time later. Needless to say, Tyler's remarks on this occasion were not preserved.[1]

Tyler seems to have been especially in demand for Fourth of July celebrations. Usually his efforts were mainly to review the historical importance of the day, as in Brattleboro on July 4, 1798, when the local newspaper reported that "after music, a spirited and elegant Oration was pronounced, by Royall Tyler, Esq. in which he *strikingly* considered the feelings, the manners and principles which led to the great national event celebrated; and *conspicuously* displayed the present situation of our country, and its relation with other powers."[2]

In 1803 Tyler was requested to read the Declaration of Independence during the Fourth of July festivities at Castleton before the principal orator gave the main address. In a letter to his wife, Tyler recounted that the event was enlivened by a processional of a dozen young maidens "all dressed in white, with laurel crowns and branches in their hands." After reading the Declaration of Independence, Tyler said, "I could not let these little folks go without a word, and I knew that the orator had prepared no address to them

---

[1] The incident is recounted in "TPT Memoir," pp. 242-3.
[2] *Federal Galaxy*, II, No. 81 (July 17, 1798), 3.

in his oration. I therefore, ventured an extempory address to them; and, though very brief, it took surprisingly."[3]

Several verses which he delivered at patriotic feasts, such as the Fourth of July, have survived, but none of the orations.[4] The only formal speech which Tyler delivered which has come down to us is the eulogy of President Washington delivered at Bennington on February 22, 1800, a little over two months after Washington's death.

A letter from Tyler to his wife fortunately preserves some of the circumstances surrounding the delivery of the address.

I wrote you a hasty line this morning, while the audience were collecting in the meeting house. . . . If you have not received it, I should tell you I was invited, through a Committee of arrangements of this and the adjacent towns, to deliver an oration on the death of Washington. The spectators were numerous and my success—was what you might wish. I shall only say here, that the austere Democrats who came resolved to be displeased; down whose hard unmeaning faces ne'er stole a pitying tear—wept. . . .

One great inducement I had to deliver this oration was the hopes of making myself more known in this vicinity; and giving the people a sample of my speaking powers. I have found the good effects of my plan already. In one hour after I left the meeting house, I was engaged in three important causes; and I am told that I shall be in more . . . I am truly fatigued with the hurry and exertions of the day.

Your affectionate husband,
R. Tyler[5]

At this period, Tyler had been carrying on a correspondence with Joseph Nancrede, the prominent Boston publisher, about the publication of Tyler's projected collection of moral tales for children. On February 11, 1800, Nancrede wrote to the author:

The delightful Eulogy is exceedingly appropriate; and I only regret my inability ever to be revenged upon you for the tears its perusal surprised from me. Thus far for my

[3] The letter is quoted in "TPT Memoir," pp. 177–8. There is also mention on the same pages of several instances where Tyler spoke extemporaneously before school children, both in Brattleboro and Middlebury.

[4] For his Fourth of July poems see *Tyler Verse*, pp. 96–109.

[5] "TPT Memoir," pp. 128–31. The letter is dated from Bennington, Jan., 1800, yet the oration as printed states it was delivered in February of that year. Also, Tyler's letter to his wife indicates she was not present, yet in her memoir Mrs. Tyler says she did hear it delivered ("MPT Memoir," p. 53).

It is possible Tyler gave the eulogy twice, once at the end of December after Washington's death on the 14th or early in January, and again on Washington's birthday in February. It is likely that Mrs. Tyler heard it on the second occasion. This theory is reinforced by the fact that Nancrede received his manuscript copy of the oration in February and acknowledged its receipt on Feb. 11.

opinion of the manuscript as respects the question of its answering the purpose for which it was intended. . . .[6]

It is clear that the oration fulfilled Tyler's dual intentions— move his audience to tears over the loss of their beloved ex-president and stimulate his law practice in southwestern Vermont. There is no doubt that the death of Washington caused an emotional upheaval among the citizens of the young republic that is difficult to imagine in present frames of reference. One hundred and fifty years later, however, the strained romantic sentiments wrapped up in the stilted, formidable language and rhetoric of the age makes the entire oration sound false, overtaxed and unnatural.[7]

Tyler must have retained a duplicate of the manuscript for a carefully revised fair copy exists among his papers. Apparently the oration was a contemporary success. It was printed in a Brattleboro paper, the *Federal Galaxy*, on June 28, and on the special request of Vermont Governor Isaac Tichenor, was issued in a 16-page pamphlet from the Walpole press of David Carlisle.[8]

[6] "TPT Memoir," pp. 131–2. The remainder of the correspondence between the two men is discussed below, pp. 456–59. See also Tanselle, "Author and Publisher in 1800: Letters of Royall Tyler and Joseph Nancrede," *Harvard Library Bulletin*, XV, No. 2 (April, 1967), 129–39.

[7] For a discussion of Tyler's rhetoric see *Royall Tyler*, pp. 34–7.

[8] The manuscript is in the "RT Collection," Ms. No. 82. Copies of the pamphlet are at the University of Vermont, the American Antiquarian Society and the Henry E. Huntington Library. After being collated with the manuscript the printed version was used for the text in this volume since it contains some front matter not available elsewhere.

[*Obverse of Title Page*]

AN
ORATION
Pronounced At *BENNINGTON*, Vermont,
On the 22d February, 1800.
IN COMMEMORATION OF THE DEATH OF
General GEORGE WASHINGTON

———

By *ROYALL TYLER, Esq.*

———

WALPOLE, Newhampshire,
Printed For THOMAS & THOMAS,
By DAVID CARLISLE.

———

1800.

[*Reverse of Title Page*]

Bennington, *March* 3, 1800.

ROYALL TYLER, Esq.

DEAR SIR,

MANY *of the admirers of your Oration, delivered on the 22d ult. in commemoration of the Death of our late beloved WASHINGTON, request a copy for publication; this is at the special request of his Excellency Isaac Tichenor, the Hon. Supreme Court, and many other respectable citizens, with that of*

Your Most Obedient, and very Humble Servant.

AMOS PORTER.[9]

———

[9] Amos Porter (1742–1807), a member of Gov. Tichenor's staff, was one of the original purchasers and settlers of Brownington, Orange County, Vermont. A private in the Revolution, he migrated from Massachusetts to Vermont in 1799. He conducted the Brownington seminary for a short while.

GOD alone is immortal—Jehovah alone liveth forever.—Were immortality the lot of man; were it not appointed unto man once to die; could the practice of the sublimest virtues; could the prayers of the pious, or the blessings of a grateful nation have averted the stroke of Death; we should not, my fathers, friends, and fellow citizens, have met to mourn the death of our beloved WASHINGTON. We should not, at this time, have attuned our voices to mournful melody, or raised our prayers for comfort to the Great Source of consolation in this day of our sorrow. For our nation would yet have rejoiced in his life; and our children's children would have seen the man who gave them that liberty, which, I trust in a merciful God, our children's children will ever enjoy.

BUT never ending length of days are not the laurels, with which the Supreme Being crowns virtue; and WASHINGTON, the great and the good, is mingled with the clod of the valley. That voice, which inspired us with courage in the hour of danger, shall no more be heard in the land; and that invincible arm, so often raised for our protection, is laid low in the dust. But, though his voice is forever silent, yet he shall forever speak to us by his great example. Gather then ye children of our political father, around his tomb, and hear the instructive lesson of your parent's life.

TRUE, my friends, no children of his loins lifted their little arms and raised their suffused eyes around his dying bed, to catch a father's last blessing; but WASHINGTON was not childless; he was the father of his country, the parent of millions; and who is there so mean among you, that is not of the happy number?

ON this day, sacred to family sorrow, let every jarring passion be hushed; and let the tomb of WASHINGTON be the grave of political animosity. Often, fellow citizens, may we turn the historic page, often may we read lessons of virtue in the volumes of the moralist; but alas! a thousand volumes are too few to teach us what is virtuous and honourable. But the life of WASHINGTON is a compendium of instruction. His life is a practical treatise of the cardinal virtues. Would you learn how to live? Read his life. Would you learn how to die? Visit his dying bed.

HE taught us how to live, and oh! too high a price for human knowledge, taught us how to die. Point me out a virtue which adorns man, and I will shew it to you brilliantly illuminated in his life.

WOULD our youth learn that vigour of mind which incites to deeds of pith and moment, see the youthful WASHINGTON, in the dawn of life, pursuing alone his hardy career through the trackless desert, to avert the tomahawk of the savage from the vitals of his countrymen; or see him protect the baffled troops of the expiring Braddock on the banks of the Monongahela.

WOULD our fellow citizens be soldiers? Are they ambitious to command the armies of their country? View WASHINGTON on the heights near Boston, teaching the hands of the untutored yeoman to war, and his fingers to fight.

WOULD you possess that martial courage which commands success? Pass the Schuylkill with WASHINGTON, on that tremendous night, when, warring with the embattled elements and superior forces, he led in triumph the troops of Hesse.

WOULD you imitate that fortitude which sustains the hero in the dreadful hour of adversity? Follow WASHINGTON through the Jersies, at the head of his discomfited troops, when the last spark of American hope was coruscated from his steeled breast.

WOULD you learn that Christian, that divine grace of forgiveness to your enemies? See him save the youthful ASGIL from ignominy and a disgraceful death.[10]

WOULD you possess that dignified virtue of equanimity, in the

[10] In April, 1782, British Loyalists hanged an American captain in retaliation for his killing of a British partisan. Capt. Charles Asgil, a British officer captured at Yorktown, was chosen by the Americans to be executed in reprisal before it was discovered that Asgil was due protection because of the terms of Cornwallis's surrender which prescribed specific treatment for officers. Not wishing to carry out the planned avengement, Washington referred the case to Congress. After Asgil's mother interceeded with our French allies, Congress voted Asgil's release and Washington ordered it. (See: Douglas S. Freeman, *George Washington. A Biography* (New York, 1952), V, 414, 419–20, 425.)

possession of Dictatorial power, and humility in the resignation of it? Pursue WASHINGTON to the tented field, and read his Resignation of his high Commission of Commander in Chief of the armies of the United States.

WOULD you impress modesty, that seal of all the Virtues, upon all of your actions? Peruse his official Letters.

WOULD you entwine the laurels of glory round deeds like these? Then, like him, serve your country without pecuniary reward.

DOES civil life delight you? Are you ambitious of serving your country with reputation in the civil grades of Society? Remember that gloomy, distracting period, which succeeded the close of our War with Great Britain, when Americans knew not how to enjoy, in peace, that Liberty and Independence which their valour had won in war; when our nerveless general government could only recommend measures, and the States received their recommendations with indifference or contempt; when our American Government was trampled upon at home, and insulted from abroad; when the jarring States lost sight of the national good in their own individual interest; when all was tumult and confusion; then remember how WASHINGTON, like the fabled god of the Ocean, raised his majestic head amidst the political storm, and stilled the madness of the people. Remember how he associated with the Fathers of our land; traced the principles of our Government with his pen; and signed that great Charter of our Freedom, the Federal Constitution; and, as the First President of the United States, reduced to practice the transcendent theory of Government, which his wisdom had conceived: and when he retired to private life, to prepare to mount to a world more congenial with his spirit, remember how like the prophet Elijah he dropt his mantle upon us in his last legacy to the people. Would you learn the true interest of America? Study attentively this precious relic; and as you study, bless, gratefully bless, the sainted lips which pronounced it.

WOULD you learn to devote your whole lives to the service of your country? See WASHINGTON, when new dangers threatened our country, again issue from the peaceful scenes of domestic life, from the bosom of his family, and inspired by a love for you, again arm his aged limbs for battle, and close his well spent life in your service.

BUT there are many in this assembly, who may despair of imitating these illustrious deeds; but to the meanest of you, in the humblest walks of private life, I repeat, copy WASHINGTON; for he was not only the glory, the wonder of public, but the brightest ornament of private life.

IF it be not your ambition, my humble friends, to be elevated in the armies or the councils of your country, yet would you fill the minor offices of society? I point you to the great WASHINGTON, once the leader of our armies; once and again the First Magistrate of our Union; with all his blushing honours thick upon him, filling the place of a common juryman at a State Court in Virginia, and humbly thanking his fellows for raising him to the importance of their foreman.

WOULD you excel as farmers? See WASHINGTON, the husbandman, following his own plough, and tracing the furrow in his native fields.

WOULD you become estimable in married life? Would you be loved and respected as affectionate husbands? Where shall I shew you a brighter example of conjugal excellence? Would you know what a husband WASHINGTON was; go to the mournful halls of Mount Vernon; seek there the sorrowing widowed matron, who, with our nation this day, deplores her mighty loss.—Oh! she will tell you that though the fame of her hero, his wisdom in council, his might in battle, have delighted her ears; yet it was the milder virtues of the husband which touched her heart.

MINGLE your tears with hers, my fair countrywomen. They are the tears of virtue; and they adorn the fairest cheek. Man may admire her fortitude, but it is the female heart alone which can participate in her griefs. When she lost a husband, you lost a friend. It was his arm which protected you, and the helpless innocence of your babes in the rage of battle; he respected your sex in the person of this amiable woman; and will you not sympathize with her in her affliction and sorrow? Some of you perhaps have been separated from excellent men by the stroke of death. Oh! at those solitary moments, when busy, meddling memory, in barbarous succession, musters up the fond endearments of your tender heart; at those cheerless moments when you recollect pressing the clay cold hand of a dying husband, wiping the clammy sweat from his forehead, while his fixed eyeballs gave the last look of affection upon you, and closed forever; when you remember that heart rending hour, when you thought all happiness flown from you forever, and you felt yourself alone, and the world was a blank before you; then, while your agonized bosoms throb with anguish at your own loss; think on the pangs of her who mourns a WASHINGTON.

BUT, to return to the delightful theme of his virtues, would you, my friends, practice charity?

> "He had an eye suffus'd with pity's softest drops,
> And a hand open as day to melting charity."

He was the kindest neighbour, the humanest master, the firmest friend the world ever saw. In a word, he loved his country and reverenced his God. His belief in the Christian verity was not ostentatiously displayed from his lips; but he conformed to the outward duties of Religion; he reverenced the holy ministers of the Gospel, and I trust his deeds are recorded in the Lamb's Book of Life.

SUCH was the man whom we lament; and such was the man whom the world applauds. The world is filled with the fame of our departed hero; and the sighs we this day raise, and the lamentation we utter, will be reechoed across the broad Atlantic. The citizens of France will weep over the cor[p]se of their great perceptor in the school of Liberty; and British generosity, in spite of British pride, will deplore the death of the man who, with strong arm rent asunder their empire. —While on the distant shores of Africa, if they are saddened with the report of his death, the sooty native shall bless the memory of the man who, with his last breath, emancipated hundreds of their countrymen from the shackles of slavery. But though the world may do justice to this transcendent merit, it is we alone who can truly feel his loss. Perhaps the ungenerous policy of European Courts may profit themselves by our loss, and sudden invasion may succeed his decease. If, my fellow citizens, we of this generation should be again exposed to the ravages of foreign invasion; if we should again see our towns sacked, and our wives and children again driven from their peaceful habitations by a ferocious, foreign soldiery; then shall we truly bemoan the death of WASHINGTON; for then, citizens of America, and then only, will you know the worth of the man you have lost.

BUT let us not spend our breath in unavailing sorrow: let it be ours to profit by his great example.

LET the aged among us, whose gray hairs give certain presage that they shall soon follow him, console themselves with the sure and certain hope that they shall see him in the world of spirits.—

LET those, who are engaged in the active scenes of busy life, when they would serve their generation, remember WASHINGTON: and though they may justly despair of imitating his great exemplar, let them reflect that the man who can achieve one solitary deed, or practice one virtue of WASHINGTON, will deserve well of his country. Let our youth be taught to look to his conduct as their polar star, in their passage through the boisterous ocean of human life. And even, my little friends, who came with your parents to weep over the grave of your political father; though you are too young to value his worth, or know your loss; yet, if you would become the comfort of your parents, and the pride of your country, reflect, and let it excite your emulation, that this unrivalled hero, this delight of every heart, this matchless WASHINGTON was once an infant in the cradle. Those lips, which spake a language which would have adorned the Roman Forum in Rome's proudest days, once lisped his native tongue with infantine accent. Once like you he was a pupil of the schools, and his expanding virtues were marked only by his preceptors, and perhaps only appreciated by parental affection. Who, at that early day, could have foretold the revolution of our country? What prophetic spirit, "rapt into future times," could have pointed to the blooming boy, and said, in that child you see the saviour of his country? Five millions of happy people shall bless him while he lives; a nation shall lament him when he dies.

And who but the Omniscient can declare that I do not, among the smallest of you, see some future statesman who shall give energy to our public councils; some warrior who shall free our country from invasion; or some little WASHINGTON, who, like his great predecessor, shall unite all talents and all hearts?

THE hopes of our country, fellow citizens, are in the rising generation. In a few more hasty revolving years, the sages, the warriors, the statesmen, who conducted our American revolution, will be numbered with the mighty dead. WASHINGTON is not; and Adams stands on the summit of the age of man, plumes his wings, and prepares to mount to glory. Where are Greene, Warren, Mercer, and Montgomery? Where is the good Chittenden,[11] who founded our state? Alas! the places which once knew them shall know them no more. Where are the brave Starks and Warner,[12] under whose banners many of you, who now hear me, fought the battles of your country in yonder field of victory, and gave the first check to British superiority in arms?

WHERE are Fay and Walbridge;[13] those youthful heroes, who, when the desolating Hessians hung over you like a black cloud sur-

[11] Thomas Chittenden (1730–1797), one of the founders of Vermont and its first and third governor.

[12] John Stark (1728–1822). As a Colonel he and his regiment did good service during the Revolution at Bunker Hill and during the Canadian and New Jersey campaigns. As a Brigadier General of militia he commanded a force of men with whom, on Aug. 16, 1777, near Bennington, Vt., he defeated two detachments of General John Burgoyne's army.

Seth Warner (1743–1784). A friend of Ethan Allen, Warner was with him and Benedict Arnold at the capture of Ft. Ticonderoga in May, 1775. He was elected commandant of the Green Mountain Boys in July of that year. During the battle of Bennington the timely arrival of Warner and his regiment in the latter part of the contest turned the tide in favor of the Colonials.

[13] Why Tyler singled out the heroism of Fay and Walbridge is not known. Four young men from Bennington were killed during the battle: John Fay, Henry Walbridge, Samuel Warner and Nathan Clark. John Fay was one of the five sons sent into the fray by the Vermont patriot Stephen Fay, landlord of the Catamount Tavern in Bennington.

charged with destruction, though new in arms, girded themselves for war, and, in defense of your property, your wives, and your little ones, this pleasant town, and this temple; went forth to the fight, fought like veterans, and sealed their country's liberty with their blood. Their precious memory is embalmed in our hearts; but we shall see their faces no more. Their hope in the hour of dissolution was fixed on God and the rising generation. The consolation of WASHINGTON in his dying hour was, that he saw the defenders of Liberty growing up around him—and that the Independence he had established would be maintained by our posterity to the latest generation.

Let us not disappoint his dying hopes. On this day, fellow citizens, on this wide extended continent, men of adverse, political sentiment have drowned their animosity in the tears shed for our common loss. On this day, good men, unhappily differing about the interests of their country, perhaps, equally dear to them all, have forgotten their dislike; and, like the children of one great family, are come to weep over their father's grave.

THUS united in affliction, let us be united in love; and at this moment, while we recline over his bier, let us resolve never more to separate; but to inhabit the goodly heritage, which God has given us, like a band of brothers; and let it add to the glory of our lamented WASHINGTON, that he, who in his life, obtained for us Freedom and Independence, by his death bound us together in one bundle of fraternal love; "So," shall it be said of him as it was of the Israelitish man of might, "the dead which he slew at his death, were more than those which he slew in his life."[14]

FINALLY, brethern, farewel—retire to your habitations; and if, perchance, your homes salute you with a father's honoured name; go, call your sons; tell them of WASHINGTON; instruct them what a debt they owe their ancestors, and make them swear to pay it, by transmitting down entire, those sacred rights which WASHINGTON obtained.

FINIS.

[14] This was spoken by Sampson in *Judges*, 16:30.

Miscellaneous Essays

THIS SECTION will gather together all of Tyler's prose which does not fit into any of the other major divisions of this volume. These essays, covering a wide span of time and a wider span of subject, are isolated pieces contributed to various newspapers between 1794 and 1817.

Most of these works are short, satiric essays. They include his earliest prose pieces—the four "Saunterer" columns in 1794—and some of his final published efforts as a contributor to *The American Yeoman* in 1817. Only those essays that can be attributed to Tyler with certainty are included here. He undoubtedly composed many others but because of his habit of switching pseudonyms at will, using several different initials to diguise his contributions, or not even bothering to sign his pieces, it will never be possible to collect all of Tyler's prose, especially those empherical anecdotes and jeux de mots in which he delighted.

The pieces in this section will be presented in chronological order although it must be remembered that other large blocks of his prose output, such as the "Spondee" and "Author's Evenings" essays, and contributions to the *Polyanthos* and *New-England Galaxy* have been grouped together elsewhere in this volume.[1]

In the following commentary an attempt will also be made to mention some of the various other literary works which Tyler contemplated but which were lost or never completed. Clues of what these works were come from various correspondence, entries in diaries, hints in newspapers and fragments among his manuscript papers. In the hopes that these works may come to light at some future date all the available information will be presented here.

The verse and prose from "The Shop of Messrs. Colon and Spondee," which started in July, 1794, were not the first fruits of the friendship between Tyler and Dennie. In March of that year, on the urging of Isaiah Thomas, Dennie had contributed the first number of a column entitled "Saunterer" to *The Newhampshire and Vermont Journal*. Who deserves credit for the column's inception and format is not known, but it is obvious that the young Dennie did not feel sufficiently confident to carry out the entire series himself. He enlisted Tyler and their mutual friend, John C. Chamberlain, to contribute a major share of the "Saunterer" columns.[2]

[1] For a full chronological listing of Tyler's prose see the Chronological Index, p. 484.

[2] Chamberlain (1772–1834), a Harvard graduate, was a fellow law student with Dennie at Charlestown. He served in Congress from 1809 to 1810. He was the "Hermit" in *The Farmer's Weekly Museum* and is best remembered as author of *A Narrative of the Captivity of Mrs. Johnson* (Walpole, 1796).

Tyler composed four "Saunterer" essays during the spring and summer of 1794, but by September of that year the growing reputation of "Colon and Spondee" in *The Eagle* forced Tyler, and finally Dennie, to drop the "Saunterer" and concentrate on their contributions to the Hanover paper.[3]

For the remainder of 1794 and through 1802 Tyler's prose efforts appeared nearly exclusively under the "Colon and Spondee" masthead in *The Eagle, The Federal Orrery, The Newhampshire and Vermont Journal* and its successor, *The Farmer's Weekly Museum,* and *The Port Folio.* The only piece which was published outside the pages of these newspapers was one comical essay, "To the Lovers of Cider," which Thomas included in his *Massachusetts Spy* in Worcester in May, 1797. The column is signed "U. Underhill," the pseudonym Tyler was to make famous a few months later when *The Algerine Captive* was published by Carlisle at Walpole. Although Thomas had severed his ties with Walpole in March, 1796, he had remained on good terms with Tyler and Dennie and had reprinted several "Colon and Spondee" pieces in both the *Massachusetts Spy* and *Massachusetts Magazine.*[4]

Though the great bulk of Tyler's contribution to *The Newhampshire and Vermont Journal* and *The Farmer's Weekly Museum* were "Spondee" essays, he also gave Dennie a considerable number of anecdotes, epigrams and other short pieces to be used by the editor as "fillers." Most of these are of little literary value. The best ones, together with a couple of non "Spondee" columns by Tyler, were included in *The Spirit of the Farmer's Museum,* and the ones which were attributed to Tyler in the copy of the book which Dennie annotated are included here.[5]

In 1797 Tyler contemplated a project which must have been of some magnitude since it was to involve the assistance of the Reverend Timothy Dwight, President of Yale College. In 1797 Dwight embarked upon his famous journey through northern New England. In September, while passing through Vermont, he stopped at Guilford for a visit with Tyler. The latter kindly offered to serve as Dwight's guide up the Connecticut River through Brattleboro to Bellows Falls where Dwight voiced interest in seeing the famous waterfall there.

Following his return to New Haven, Dwight wrote to Tyler, thanked him for his hospitality in Guilford and discussed a "literary scheme that they

[3] For further details on the "Saunterer" column see below, p. 291.

[4] For example, see the *Massachusetts Spy* for Feb. 18 and March 25, 1795; May 17 and May 24, 1797; and April 10, 1799. See also *The Massachusetts Magazine,* VIII, No. 8 (Aug., 1796), 447–8.

[5] For comment upon Dennie's annotated copy of *The Spirit of the Farmer's Museum* see above, footnote 27, p. 201.

had agreed upon."[6] What this was, it is impossible to say since the correspondence between the two men has not survived outside of one fragment and no further mention of the project can be found.

It might have been the "historical labors" which Tyler had undertaken in April, 1797, or else the new play and opera which Dennie mentioned Tyler was to write that year.[7] On the other hand, Tyler might have been looking forward to and enlisting Dwight's support for his projected legal reports and law dictionary. The compilation of Vermont's law reports had been under consideration for some time. The only volume of that state's law reports issued up to that time had been assembled by the late Chief Justice, Nathaniel Chipman, but they were completed only through 1793.

During 1801 Tyler compiled the reports of "cases adjudged in the Supreme Court of Judicature and Court of Chancery of the State of Vermont, during the year 1801" to which was to be added "certain sundry cases adjudged in the same courts during the year 1797." Proposals were issued on October 5 for publishing this as Volume II of Chipman's Reports. The number of subscribers obtained, however, was not sufficient to make the book economically feasible and the project was postponed for several years.[8]

In 1803 a new weekly paper in his hometown attracted Tyler's full attention. *The Reporter* was established by William Fessenden on February 21. He served as both editor and publisher until October, 1809, when his

[6] The account of Dwight's visit with Tyler is contained in the former's *Travels in New-England and New York* (New Haven, 1821), II, 91, 101–8, 291–3.

The sole correspondence between the two men which survives is the fragment of a letter from Dwight to Tyler, dated from New Haven, June 9, 1798. It is quoted in "TPT Memoir," p. 127, where mention is also made of the "literary scheme" the two men discussed. A long anecdote involving Dwight, Tyler and Dennie which grew out of Dwight's visit is also recounted in "TPT Memoir," pp. 125–7.

The falls which Dwight visited had been famous even before the arrival of the white man. The site was held in awe by the Indians. John Trumbull had gone there in 1791 to sketch the cataract and "the first cantilever bridge in this country" which stretched from the Vermont to New Hampshire sides of the river. (The Trumbull drawing is at the Fordham University Library.)

[7] Mention of these proposed works is made by Dennie in a letter to Tyler, dated from Walpole, April 14, 1797. Quoted in "TPT Memoir," pp. 113–4 and *The Letters of Joseph Dennie*, pp. 155–6.

[8] "TPT Memoir," pp. 155–6. Background on the Vermont Supreme Court bench at this period, as well as a letter from Governor Issac Tichenor to Tyler, dated from Bennington, Dec. 17, 1801, is contained in pp. 152–5. Further details on the Court at this period are well presented by Russell S. Taft, "The Supreme Court in Vermont," *The Green Bag. An Entertaining Magazine for Lawyers*, V (1894); 553–64, VI (1895), 16–35, 72–91, 122–41, 176–92.

more famous brother, Thomas Green Fessenden, took over the editorship. The Fessendens were a noted Brattleboro family and extremely close to Judge and Mrs. Tyler. In Tyler's final years, when he was beset by physical and financial hardship, the Fessendens and Holbrooks, to whom the former were related by marriage, were unselfish in their aid of the Tyler family.[9]

This kindness was probably in gratitude for the considerable contributions Tyler had made in elevating the literary tone of *The Reporter* during the early months of its existence. Although Tyler was to contribute to *The Reporter* for less than a year, he retained an active interest in the journalistic efforts of the Fessenden family. Thomas Green Fessenden continued as editor of *The Reporter* until December, 1816, when he left to edit the *Vermont Intelligencer and Bellows Falls Advertiser*. In 1822 Tyler sent Fessenden a number of poems, the last to be published in the author's lifetime.[10]

Late in 1803 an amusing incident occurred which exhibited how Tyler's wit could mislead even the most scholarly and discerning. Noah Webster had published *A Brief History of Epidemic and Pestilential Diseases* in 1799. It immediately achieved a wide circulation and was highly regarded as an authoritative work. In his account of the famine which hit sections of the eastern seaboard in the spring of 1789, Webster recounted, with high seriousness, how "in Vermont, people were reduced to the necessity of feeding on tad-poles boiled with peastraw. . . . None of the human race were actually starved to death, but a few died of a flux in consequence of a bad diet."[11]

Webster's naiveté was brought to light in 1803 when William Coleman, then editor of the *New York Evening Post*, wrote the following to his friend Tyler:

It happens in the course of my motley labors, that I have run a tilt against the thrice renowned Noah Webster, Esq., and it is in your power to furnish me with a weapon. I have an indistinct recollection that you, one evening in Newfane [*Vermont*], amused us with an experiment you made on Webster's credulity, by informing him, that the people of Vermont had been so reduced by famine in '89, as to be under the necessity of subsisting on boiled tadpoles and peastraw. What was my surprise to find this gravely inserted in the first vol. of his history of pestilence. I have already had a hit at him with it; but I shall have occasion to make more of it, and I wish to be prepared to contradict

[9] The entries concerning both the Fessendens and Holbrooks are numerous in both Tyler's "Day Book" and Mrs. Tyler's "Diary." The former is a daily record between June 8, 1817–Dec. 1, 1821 (with a gap between May 16, 1820–March 14, 1821). The "Diary" extends from Dec. 2, 1821 until after Tyler's death in 1826.
[10] See *Tyler Verse*, pp. 181–9.
[11] Noah Webster, *A Brief History of Epidemic and Pestilential Diseases* (Hartford, 1799), I, 286.

him on the fact, that this story had made its appearance in the *gazettes of the day*. Was it ever heard of but in your letter?[12]

Since none of the other histories of the period made mention of this example of Yankee dietary ingenuity, it does appear that Tyler had given Webster an "exclusive" news source and that Webster included it in his history without question.

One of the reasons Tyler did not find time to continue his contributions to *The Reporter* in 1803 was his growing involvement in the affairs of the young University of Vermont at Burlington. With pride he informed his wife in January, 1802, that he had decided to accept the university's offer to become a trustee and member of the Board of Corporation. He also hinted that he hoped to play an increasingly important role in the leadership of the university and for this reason contemplated moving the entire Tyler family to Burlington.[13]

Tyler had apparently become quite intimate with the university's first president, Reverend Daniel C. Sanders, since the invitation to become a trustee had come from Sanders himself. The President also wrote to Tyler asking him to be present at the commencement exercises on August 17, 1804 and added the following:

We fear your distant residence may prevent your frequent attendance on the board of trust, but your good counsels may be communicated by letter. Do you think of anything for the benefit of this infant institution? Can its government receive a better form? Are we not too much confined to the scholastic rules of the 15th Century? Can any innovations be usefully made in the college? You would prove highly pleasing by being often communicative of your opinions; of your sentiments on the best mode of

---

[12] The letter from Coleman to Tyler, dated from New York, Oct. 26, 1803, is quoted in "TPT Memoir," p. 180. Coleman (1766–1829) was known as the most effective Federalist journalist of his era. He had become acquainted with Tyler during their service in supressing Shays' Rebellion and had remained close friends after Coleman set up his law practice in Greenfield, Mass. After moving to New York Coleman was befriended by Alexander Hamilton and rose to the editorship of the Federalist *Evening Post* in 1800.

[13] Tyler postponed and finally canceled the move to Burlington because of the war clouds on the northern frontier. See "TPT Memoir," p. 283. Tyler did, however, send his son, Royall Jr., to the university.

The university had been chartered by an act of the first general assembly held after the state joined the union. For a history of the school's early years see Julian I. Lindsay, *Tradition Looks Forward. The University of Vermont: A History* (Burlington, 1954).

Tyler told his wife of his election to the Board of Corporation in a letter dated from Middlebury, Jan. 20, 1802. It is quoted in "TPT Memoir," p. 160.

collegiate education; on the books to be adopted; on the exercises to be enjoined; on the whole system to be pursued.[14]

Tyler took an active role in the activities of the university. The minutes of the Board of Corporation show that he managed to attend a fair number of meetings despite his residence in Guilford and his duties as jurist. It appears that he and the Reverend Sanders talked further about the form the university's curriculum should take. The result of these conversations was that Tyler and William C. Bradley were asked in 1811 to be a committee of two to draw up a new set of regulations for the government and direction of the faculty and students.

As can be expected, with Tyler's Harvard background, the rules which were submitted follow closely those in force at Harvard when Tyler was a student at Cambridge. The regulations touch upon every subject mentioned by Reverend Sanders in the letter to Tyler mentioned above. The manuscript draft of the laws still exists, with the letter of transmittal to the trustees from Tyler and Bradley attached. Although in the hand of a copyist, the several notations in Tyler's hand show how deeply he was involved in this project.[15]

In recognition of this and other contributions to the university, it awarded Tyler a Master of Arts degree in 1811, and immediately appointed him Professor of Jurisprudence. He held the position until 1814 when his failing health forced him to relinquish it. He had remained as a member of the University Corporation until 1813.

[14] "TPT Memoir," p. 179.

[15] The minutes of the Corporation, which preserve Tyler's record of attendance at the meetings of the trustees, are in the office of the University Treasurer. Notations of the conversations with Sanders and the letters which passed between them are in "TPT Memoir," pp. 179–80, 226–30, 279–81 and 183–84.

The Ms., "The Laws of the University of Vermont [1811]," is in the University Archives. This copy is the one retained apparently by Tyler when the regulations were approved by the trustees. In the margins next to the various sections of the laws is written several times in Tyler's hand the word "passed."

William Bradley (1782–1867) was the son of Stephen R. Bradley, U.S. Senator from Vermont. William, a noted attorney, served in the 13th, 18th and 19th Congresses and was an agent of the U.S. Government under the Treaty of Ghent to fix the Maine-Canadian boundry line, 1815–20.

Senator Jonathan Robinson congratulated Tyler on his service with the university in a letter dated from Washington, D.C., Jan. 21, 1811. Robinson also mentioned the university awarding Tyler an honorary degree. (In the collection of the New Hampshire Historical Society.)

Outside of the work he accomplished in drawing up the university's laws, the only concrete fruit of his association with the institution was that it gave him time to work on the compilation of Vermont law reports he had started in 1801. It also made him think of starting on his long-standing dream of putting together an American law dictionary. Unfortunately, although it appears some of the book was completed and even printed, it was never issued.[16]

By November, 1808, however, Tyler was far enough along on the law reports to approach Issac Riley, the New York printer, about possible publication. After detailed correspondence of some months, the first volume of *Reports of Cases Argued and Determined in the Supreme Court of Judicature of the State of Vermont* appeared in December, 1809, and the second volume was off the presses at the end of 1810.[17]

Since April, 1803, when he had submitted his last column to *The Reporter*, Tyler's muse had been quiet. However, it was too restless to remain stilled for long, and as he had come to Fessenden's aid in 1803, so Tyler took an active interest in the efforts of Simeon Ide to issue a new weekly newspaper entitled *The American Yeoman* in Brattleboro in 1816. In a town where the great majority of citizens were aligned with the Federalist party, Ide knew he would have a difficult time making a success of a paper which pointedly was to support the Republican viewpoint. Ide admitted as much in correspondence with prospective supporters. Tyler offered Ide his full

[16] On May 10, 1810, Tyler wrote to Isaac Riley that he had been "sometime engaged in collecting materials for an American Law Dictionary. This work will be entirely original . . ." ("TPT Memoir," p. 277.) Pliny H. White, in his article, "Early Poets of Vermont," *Proceedings of the Vermont Historical Society, 1917–1918* (1920), 119, said that the Law Dictionary was to be "after the style of Jacob's Dictionary." White also noted approximately four quarto pages were printed, but did not say where he had seen these printed pages. All trace of them has since been lost.

[17] The correspondence between Tyler and Riley about the *Law Reports* is in "TPT Memoir," pp. 144–78. See also *Royall Tyler*, pp. 39–42. A further discussion of Tyler's legal career is contained below, pp. 354–66.

On July 22, 1809, Tyler wrote to Riley that he had "on hand sufficient matter to make at least four more volumes, with one or two in Chancery." (Quoted in "TPT Memoir," p. 262.) These additional volumes were never completed. A letter from Tyler to Cornelius Van Ness, dated from Brattleboro, June 15, 1811, mentions the *Law Reports* (in the "RT Collection," Ms. No. 810365). A letter from Isaac Tichenor, the former governor, to Tyler, dated from Bennington, Nov. 29, 1810, mentions Volume I and other legal writings contemplated by Tyler. Although not stated specifically, these might refer to the additional four volumes and the Law Dictionary. (The letter is in the Wilbur Collection, University of Vermont.)

support but counseled him against attempting to establish the new publication.[18]

Despite these warnings Ide went ahead and in the spring of 1816 issued proposals for the paper. The immediate reaction was not overwhelming and subscribers were slow in coming forward. By the beginning of 1817, however, Ide had secured 150 subscribers from Brattleboro and its immediate vicinity and sufficient financial backing to allow him to proceed. The first issue of *The American Yeoman,* printed in Ide's small shop over G. F. Atherton's store at the corner of Main and West streets, appeared on February 4, 1817. True to his word, Tyler supported the paper as much as his busy legal schedule and mounting financial problems allowed.[19]

Tyler befriended the young publisher because of his engaging personality, ambition in the face of hardship and their similar political views. Ide was entertained several times by the Tylers during his stay in Brattleboro and Tyler was to materially assist him in the management of the paper. In fact, Tyler may have been the actual, if not publicly admitted editor of the *Yeoman.* This possibility is given credence by the following chain of events. On February 18, Darius Clark, editor of the Bennington *Vermont Gazette,* praised the first two issues of the *Yeoman.* He said that Tyler had lent his considerable reputation to the paper and was acting as its editor.[20]

On February 25, Ide felt he had to make the following statement:

Though we might with good reason be proud of having our press conducted by a gentleman of the Hon. Mr. TYLER'S talents, in justice to him, it is our duty to assure Mr. CLARK, that the Yeoman has no *professed editor.* . . . Mr. C. will do us a favor by contradicting the statement we have alluded to; as the gentleman to whom he has imputed the conduct of the Yeoman might otherwise be burdened with a responsibility which does not belong to him.[21]

---

[18] See Louis W. Flanders, *Simeon Ide, Yeoman, Freeman, Pioneer Printer* (Rutland, 1931), pp. 41–43. Besides relating Ide's stay in Brattleboro, this work covers in excellent detail Ide's career both before and after he established *The American Yeoman.* The volume also includes a genealogy of the Ide family by Edith Flanders Dunbar and a bibliography of Ide's imprints by R. W. G. Vail.

Ide's worries over starting the *Yeoman* were outlined in a letter from Ide to Charles Phelps, dated from New Ipswich, N.H., April 11, 1816. The Ms. letter is at the American Antiquarian Society, Worcester, Mass.

[19] A copy of the broadside proposal, dated April, 1816, is at the American Antiquarian Society. The number of subscribers and the location of the print shop are mentioned in Flanders, *Simeon Ide,* pp. 42–44.

[20] *Vermont Gazette,* VIII, No. 25 (Feb. 18, 1817), 3.

[21] *The American Yeoman,* I, No. 4 (Feb. 25, 1817), 3.

In the face of this rejoinder, Clark, in the next issue of the *Gazette,* seemingly apologized, but with a definite touch of sarcasm, repeated "the Yeoman has no *professed editor*."[22] He was probably saying, therefore, that although Ide would not publicly admit to Tyler being editor, he was, in fact, although undeclared.

It is hard to believe that a publisher of Clark's reputation would have made the statement originally if it were untrue, and secondly, it appears unlikely Ide would have felt called upon to issue such a strong denial unless the report had some validity. It would have been disastrous for Tyler if it became known he had become engaged in a commercial venture, especially one with ties to Republican politics, since his appointive position as Register of Probate normally excluded involvement in partisan politics.

The numerous records of meetings with Ide and the notes of contributions to the *Yeoman* in Tyler's "Day Book" also belie Ide's disclaimer. The "Day Book" entry for December 28, 1817, gives an excellent example of Tyler's close involvement in the paper's management. On that day, while Ide was visiting at his home, Tyler wrote the column "Small Talk," an article on slavery, the Notice to Correspondents and the headnote to a series of letters by Reverend Ignatius Thompson. In other words, Tyler composed nearly everything in the next issue of the paper which was not foreign or domestic news cribbed from other publications![23]

The piece on slaves is especially noteworthy. It exists in manuscript and is replete with instructions to Ide's typesetters. The copy is filled with notations such as "vide loose sheet," "[*add*] discription of Preceptress, " and even more explicit instructions such as: "*Joseph*—when you have inserted the sketch of the moonstruck—no—moon light lovers—than tack on the finale—and contrive to annex this memorandum to the manuscript . . ."[24]

There could be no better example of Tyler's close relationship with Ide and the *Yeoman.* No one would have given such instructions to the typesetter unless he had worked with him for some time, knew him and trusted him. It illustrates how closely Tyler was involved in the paper's production and that he had been so for some time before this date.

---

[22] *Vermont Gazette,* VIII, No. 27 (March 4, 1817), 3.

[23] For further details of these contributions see below, pp. 320–21. The record of the other visits between Ide and Tyler and the latter's contributions to the *Yeoman* are in the "Day Book," entries for July 11, Aug. 7, 9, 11 and 19, Sept. 19 and Nov. 18, 1817; Jan. 27 and Feb. 16, 1818.

[24] Tyler's holograph Ms. of this composition is on a single sheet bound in at the rear of a fair copy of "The Chestnut Tree" ("RT Collection," Ms. No. 25).

By the end of 1817 Ide had increased the number of subscribers from the initial 150 to about 400, but he was still not happy with Brattleboro's coolness to the *Yeoman's* political philosophy. In January, 1818, Jesse Cochran, publisher of the *Vermont Republican* in Windsor offered to sell Ide his entire plant and the paper itself. Ide accepted the proposition. The last issue of the *Yeoman* came out on January 27, 1818. Ide moved shortly thereafter to Windsor and merged the *Yeoman* with the *Vermont Republican*.

Ide's departure meant the end of another project on which Tyler had been working. In an attempt to earn a little royalty income for his family, Tyler had started to compose in 1817 a book entitled, *The Touchstone; or a Humble, Modest Inquiry into the Nature of Religious Intolerance*. Taking the pseudonym, "A Berean," Tyler proposed to outline some of the current attitudes toward religion and to comment upon them. As Ide later described the book, "It was . . . a very caustic and by no means 'dry' commentary on the *beauties* of 'Calvinism,' 'Hopkintonianism,' &c. &c."[25]

Tyler worked on the manuscript through the summer and fall of 1817 and as soon as copy was ready sent it on to Ide to be set in type. In a letter written years later to Tyler's son, Ide said that at least four or five forms (containing 18 pages each) were completed before he moved to Windsor in February, 1818. The publisher stated he definitely did not complete the entire book, but apparently someone did bind the finished sheets since at one time a copy of more than 36 pages, complete with title page, did exist.[26] It has since been lost and no other trace of *The Touchstone* remains.

*   *   *   *

[25] The letter to Thomas Pickman Tyler, undated, is in the "RT Collection," Ms. No. 62. The full title page of the work was: *The Touchstone; or a Humble Modest Inquiry into the Nature of Religious Intolerance. Whether it ever existed? Whether those who practice it are conscious of it? Whether it is found in these regions? And the way to detect it in ourselves.* By a member of the Berean Society. [Motto] Brattleborough, Vt. Published by Simeon Ide, 1817.

Entries relating to his composition of the book are in Tyler's "Day Book," Aug. 3 and 11, 1817.

[26] For additional details see *Tyler Verse,* pp. xxxi-ii. Ide copyrighted the book on April 26, 1817. He and Tyler drew up an agreement on Jan. 26, 1818, regarding the amount of copy the author was to furnish and who was to bear the financial burden if the book was not printed. (The contract, in Tyler's hand, is in the collection of the New York Historical Society.)

Marcus D. Gilman was apparently the one to discover the bound, partly completed copy of *The Touchstone* at the University of Vermont about 1879, but because of the pseudonym on the title page ("By a member of the Berean Society") did not associate Tyler as the author. Gilman made the first recorded citation of the volume in his *The*

THE "SAUNTERER" COLUMN

THE FIRST "Saunterer" essay appeared in *The Newhampshire and Vermont Journal* in March, 1794. The initial numbers were contributed by Dennie.

The fifth column, published on April 18, was the first one by Tyler and carried at the bottom his initial "T." Dennie and Chamberlain wrote additional pieces intermittently during the summer of that year.[27]

Tyler's final three contributions, also signed "T.", were numbers nine, ten and eleven which appeared on August 1, August 8 and September 5 respectively. After a few more numbers the column was discontinued as Tyler and Dennie found themselves increasingly occupied with "The Shop of Messrs. Colon and Spondee" which they had opened in Hanover.

*   *   *   *   *

For the Farmer's Weekly Museum.
The SAUNTERER. No. V.

"Such, and *so various,* are the tastes of men."
Dr. Akenside.[28]

Mankind, in their progress through life, may be aptly likened to a party of travellers, whose journey is directed to the same place, but who differ in their mode of travelling. The object of their journey is happiness, and the various expedients employed to smooth the way, display the variety of human character. Every man's humour is indicated by his gait and mode of travelling. One party are seen driving in furious haste with whip and spur, leaping ditches and fences, and overturning every thing in their way, these are men of ardent and impetuous tempers; desperate adventurers, who can endure no delay,

Bibliography of Vermont (Burlington, 1897), p. 279. Since the unique University of Vermont copy has been misplaced for several decades modern day scholars have relied on Gilman's initial citation. See Marcus A. McCorison, *Vermont Imprints, 1778–1820* (Worcester, 1963), p. 408, citation No. 1956, and Flanders, *Simeon Ide,* p. 146.

[27] A discussion of the "Saunterer" column, including the attribution of those signed "T." to Tyler, is contained in Ellis, p. 85.

[28] The quotation is from Akenside's *The Pleasure of Imagination* (London: R. Dodsley, 1744), III, 1. 567.

and place no medium between being first in the road, or breaking their necks in the attempt. As these hast[y] pilgrims are generally unhorsed and tumbled into a ditch, or wear out with fatigue, both themselves and their beasts, there are others, who with moderate, but steady movements, pass calmly on, discreetly choose the smooth path, and making *regular* stages, arrive, without fatigue, at their journey's end. One of this class is he, who, in the language of scripture, "taketh heed in his ways."

As the SAUNTERER has assured the public, that he is neither a factious partizan, nor a man of professional engagement, it must surprize that motly crowd, in which he "keeps the noiseless tenor of his way," how a being can exist, who neither digs in the mines of wealth, nor climbs preferment's ladder. On dull minds the glare of gold darts so intensely, that they, by consequence are dazzled. Spirits more refined are attracted by honors and political preeminence. The third band, consist of those whose "eyes in a fine frenzy roll"; men of keen sensibility to pleasure and an ardency of passion, so extravagant, as to render them deficient in the quality of dullness, necessary to collect cash, or of prudence to attain popular favor. These unhappy wretches, careless of the respect that follows riches, and deriding the sacred vox populi, pass unregarded along, poor and stationless, unplaced and unpensioned. The wise ones of the two former classes, as they view the decayed libertine, cry, "Ah a," wagging their heads, and remark sagaciously "that they always feared he would run himself out." Now, as the SAUNTERER has not characterized the club, to which he belongs, it may be thought that, disclaiming a connexion with opulence and ambition, he is necessitated to enroll himself a member of that sect of philosophers, called stoics—Men, without the passions of humanity, and citizens, regardless of the social compact. Between the horns of this dilemma he is not, however, suspended. A man may yet be conceived, who is neither plodding in quest of wealth, nor sevile to an elector, neither dissipated with passion nor frozen into apathy.

From that endless variety of objects, held up to pursuit in civilized society, this essential advantage flows, that to genius of every species, opportunity is given, to exert itself in its proper sphere. In the savage state, among roving tribes of Tartars and Indians, that wretched individual, who can neither war not hunt, is a despised exile from the community. Among polished nations, and more particularly in our own, a resource is found for those, who labor under almost any deficiency. None can attain eminence in all, but each in some, of the vocations of life. He, to whom nature has denied vivacious wit, may allowably recompense the defect, by assuming the character of a man of deep judgement, and claim a judicial department. He, who has been sent into this world, without innate ideas, and is incapable of furnishing himself with others, from a deficiency of the intellectual apparatus, may add one to that numerous band of worthy citizens, who daily discharge the functions of representatives, selectmen, and other *high* offices, without the troublesome charge of sense, or learning. He, whose infirm and baby mind is too feeble to struggle with speculation, and is acquainted, not so much with the contents of a book, as a band box, let him repair to the nearest tea table, and doubt not but that he will secure, not only reception, but applause. Lastly, even the SAUNTERER, who neither opens a pill box, nor pores over a writ nor a sermon, who is too much of an Englishman, to dangle after women, and too much of a Frenchmen to keep a warehouse—Even this solitary soldier, who belongs to none of the *regiments* of life, finds a *peculiar* employment: Now choosing as a centinel, to ascend the watch tower and *survey,* and now, as a cavalier, to throw a gauntlet, and break a lance with the champions of vice and folly.

T.

*   *   *   *   *

For the Farmer's Weekly Museum.
The SAUNTERER. No. IX.

> The rabble gather round the man of news,
> And listen with their mouths;
> Some tell, some hear, some judge of news,
>   some make it,
> And he that lies most loud is most believ'd.
>   Dryden.

An essayist, in the present state of political affairs, has but a small chance to be much regarded. Stories of battles and defeats of French and English victories or losses, will at any time draw the attention of most readers from the moral or humorous Essay.—This avidity for European politics is more ridiculous than the inquisitive curiosity of the searchers after village scandal, though more harmless. The capture of a French or German town, by the one party or the other, of the situation of which, or the effects of its capture, we must be as ignorant as if it where in the moon, will be eagerly inquired after.—Selftaught statemen, leaving the plough and hoe, the counter or the cobbler's stall, will assume to arbitrate the differences of nations, though possessed of no other means of information than the vague rumors circulating in an obscure village, or an equivocal paragraph in a weekly paper.—This credulity of the populace and eagerness to hear and believe something is the stronghold of demagogues, who thereby take advantage to turn the current of opinion as their own views require. The rabble never deliberate, and that party which *lies most loud* is sure of success.—The French fight for civil liberty: This is loudly proclaimed and gains them many patrons. Great Britain fights to defend her constitution from destruction by French anarchy. This is also taken as a truth, and gains to their side all those whose prejudices or principles attach them to that constitution. Each party is candidly supposed to fight for the orthodoxy of a political creed. But although this controversy is thus generally looked upon as a war of principles, of metaphysical politicians, for speculative opinions, it is much more probable that the leaders on both sides use them as badges of party distinction, to keep up a tumult in which they find benefit—it were singular indeed, if speculative differences in opinions concerning government should succeed diversity of religious sentiments as the ground of war and persecution. If it be the case we must, from analogy conclude that the present is an age of ignorance and darkness in the science of government, as the ages of religious wars and persecution were times of equal ignorance in religion.—As the world grows enlightened, religious toleration takes place; and political toleration must ensue from similar progress in knowledge. It was long supposed that uniformity was necessary in religion, for the support of it.—This is now found not to be the case.—Why may it not be equally unnecessary that there should be a political uniformity?—Let every one be content to fulfil the duties of a good citizen of that government where he resides, when a majority concur in the maintenance of it, nor seek to make converts to his political creed by exciting civil broils, but rest satisfied with the peaceful means of persuasion. What must essentially contribute to render every considerate man aversed to political parties is, that all who engage therein, whatever their pretensions may be, are uniformly and apparently actuated by private and selfish policy.—HUME seems to be of opinion, that no one ever suffered as a martyr, for the cause of protestantism, who would not in similar circumstances with his popish persecutors, inflict upon them the same punishments. When episcopal persecution drove our ancestors to America, in their settlements they exercised towards those over whom their power extended the same prerogative of persecution, by which they had suffered.—Perhaps the present times may exhibit to posterity a more irrational scene, Americans declaring, and fighting for, the equal Rights of Man, while allowing the existence among themselves, of the most rigorous slavery. In general those who make the most noise and outcry concerning liberty and patriotism, are the most intolerant towards all who differ from them, and seem to conceive of freedom as appropriate to themselves.   T.

* * * * *

For the Farmer's Weekly Museum.
The SAUNTERER. No. X.

An honest man is the noblest work of God.
Pope.

Thus saith the Poet. But he certainly meant something more by the word honesty, than is included in the term, as it is commonly used. He who escapes the penalty of the statute, who regards morality, so far as character and reputation only are concerned; or is merely not guilty of a fraud within reach of proof, may be, according to the vulgar sense of Honesty, complimented as the noblest work of God.

If we reflect upon the application which the world frequently makes of this virtue, to men destitute of principle, of benevolence, of liberality, and of every social virtue, it would induce us to suppose that the poet had chosen for the noblest work the most contemptible part of God's works.—The miser, the prodigal, and even the sharper may be honest men.—I once heard of an honest gentleman, who may serve as a specimen of this sort of character.—By preying upon the necessities of those he dealt with, making advantage of the wants and distresses of his neighbours, he had screwed himself into a large estate; always ready to oblige the needy, by lending upon a pledge of double value; and always careful to make a proper use of the ignorance or inexperience of those he dealt with; cautious and cool himself, always vigilant to take hold of the unthinking and imprudent—Perfectly skilled in the art of deceiving by insinuation and hypocrisy, a much more successful method, as well as more detestable and injurious to society, than that of the professed knave.—Though possessed of great and useless wealth, so scrupulously attached to the precept of PAUL, to take care of his own, that no consideration of public good or private charity, could induce him to employ in those uses, the smallest part of it. This man, though without any qualities to be useful or agreeable, and with qualities to be despised and detested, was yet able from a smooth demeanour, careful and wary conduct in life, pretending to great strictness and fidelity in his dealings, and the external profession of those virtues, of which he was in reality destitute, to maintain and preserve in life, a reputable and respected character, and when any one who had suffered by his rapacity, or was witness to his meanness exclaimed, people were ready to say, it is true he is a rather hard man, and pretty sharp in his dealings, but we never knew any thing but that he was *honest*.—If any work of public utility is to be done, or any occasion which calls for exertion, instead of contributing with cheerfulness and liberality, the only point which he kept in view, would be how to turn the public necessities to his own advantage. It is a real and essential injury to a town that has such an honest man for a citizen. Like a noxious weed he creates a barren waste around him, and is continually dispossessing some poorer, though more useful inhabitant.

Of all sharpers, the honest sharp man is the most dangerous, and under an appearance of strict faith, and a high regard to the exactitude of his conduct, he will frequently commit acts of extortion and meanness, which even a professed knave would despise.

SHYLOCK was an honest man of his sort, and SHAKESPEARE, in the character of the Jew, has drawn the likeness of many modern christians. In scripture history we also find an example of this species of character. JACOB when he bought the birthright of his brother with the morsel, which extreme necessity only made valuable, and extorted from that necessity, to which it was his duty, even by the ordinary laws of humanity to administer relief, displayed his acquaintance with the science of making an honest bargain. JACOB was rather hard, to be sure, in the business, but he was an *honest* man.

The virtue of honesty may thus consist with characters, which we would be unwilling to esteem the noblest works of God; and if the poet had not a more enlarged sense of the word, in his own mind when he wrote, his ideas of excellence in the works of God, must have been very imperfect. The preceeding line will explain the poet's meaning. He introduces the honest man, after mentioning and passing over with contempt, the wit and the chief. Thus intending to assert the comparative futility of characters, founded on the usual objects of admiration, with one formed upon virtue; and the idea which existed in his mind, when he makes the honest man the noblest, was far from confining that quality to mere exemption from guilt. Merit consists in action, and the indolent and inactive can never attain the praise of virtue, which must be evidenced by something more than a happy escape from the commission of crimes.   T.

* * * * *

For the Farmer's Weekly Museum.
The SAUNTERER. No. XI.

From instances of popular tumults, seditions, factions, panics, and of all passions which are shared with a multitude, we may learn the influence of Society in exciting and supporting any emotion; while the most ungovernable disorders are raised we find by that means from the slightest and most frivolous occasions.— He must be more or less than man who kindles not in the common blaze.
HUME.

A propensity to the formation of clubs or societies for promoting particular purposes and principles, appear to be a distinguishing feature of the present times. Democratic, constitutional and a variety of other clubs are continually forming and exerting themselves to extend their own principles. Many reasons may be given for this tendency to association. Forming a number of men of similar views, into a body, by collecting and composing them into a club, enables them to act with a force and effect far greater than when scattered and dispersed throughout society. Hence those who would propagate any new doctrines or opinions, or would keep alive particular principles in societies, always collect and establish some society or club to serve as regular and disciplined forces for attack or defence. Thus many important effects have been produced by the instrumentality of clubs. Of this the Jacobins in France have afforded a striking example, and have shewn that a set of noisy fellows, formed into a political club and acting in concert, may usurp and retain the power of a state.— PITT and the British government appear to dread the efficacy of this mode of attack by clubbing, and though no greater crime can be alledged against those societies than are the necessary consequence of the existence of a political club, appear as solicitous to suppress a conventicle of dissenters. But though the extreme soreness of the British government when touched by any thing which looks revolutionary may induce them to start a harmless society of political reformers, yet the propriety of setting up clubs to censure and condemn, to make noisy harangues and factious addresses may be very well questioned. The great principle upon which civil establishments are founded is, the necessity of them to secure the peace and liberty of individuals living under them, and while this purpose is answered by the great association within the former, though in Russia or Turkey, in any country where the subjects are notwithstanding their civil government liable to oppression, and perhaps even from that very source whence they ought to receive protection, these internal associations may then serve for mutual defence and mitigate the severity of despotism. But leaving political clubs to indulge their humour, in meeting, haranguing, addressing and drinking patriotic toasts, as long as their restless spirit can find no more innocent employments, there is another class of clubs which deserve consideration. Those whose professed designs are, the promotion of discoveries and improvements in science or in arts.[29] The only misfortune attending these respectable bodies is, that they for some unaccountable reason are generally defective in answering the purpose of their institution. Though academies meet, organize themselves, receive contributions and publish their learned lumber, they are not commonly the authors of any great improvements, and societies the great engines for promoting political purposes rather retard than otherwise the progress of knowledge. Though Europe is full of those collections of literati, their exertions appear to produce no other effects than to add folios of transactions to the library of oblivion.

There appears to be some reason for the observation of the poet when we consider the fate of literary clubs;

---

[29] Tyler pokes fun at such learned societies in a poem, "An Irregular Supplicatory Address to the American Academies of Arts and Sciences," written in 1797. See *Tyler Verse*, pp. 55–9.

"For tho' most hands dispatch apace,
And make light work (the proverb says)
Yet many different intellects
Are found to have contrary effects."

Religion, as well as Politics or Science, has its clubs and associations, some of which have been very remarkable, and the most powerful and artful club that ever existed, the society of jesuits, was instituted on religious pretences. This society was to religion what at present Jacobins are to republicanism, and perhaps each were of equal advantage to their pretended objects of attention. Indeed religion is a fruitful source of clubs. Fanatic sectaries form as many different clubs as different creeds, and every individual church constitutes a distinct club.—But the most harmless and perhaps the best institutions of the club species, are those founded for social and benevolent purposes, and the most ancient as well respectable society in the world is or assumes to be founded on those principles. Unions of political or religious sectaries are liable to pernicious tendencies, but associations to improve and promote social and humane purposes may stimulate men to useful actions. To the honor of America there are more of this latter species than of any of the former,—Although societies may be beneficial when united for humane purposes and innocent and harmless when merely to countenance each other in mirth and good humour yet as similar institutions may be turned to injurious purposes and as there is a contractedness in confining ones views within the bounds of any one club, it may perhaps be safely concluded that he is the wisest and best citizen who adheres to no other political society but the great one, composed of all his fellow citizens, to no religious society, but that in which all may unite, and extends his views of benevolence beyond the limits of any particular set of men.[30]

T.

*   *   *   *   *

[30] A satire by Tyler of the Democratic-Republican clubs of this period is contained in "The Sun and the Bats. A Fable," a poem written in 1797. It is reprinted in *Tyler Verse*, pp. 67–71.

To the LOVERS of CIDER.[31]

What would you give to destroy the whole race of caterpillars? Give —I would give more than I'll say—but it is impossible. I have tried experiments until I am tired. Yes, you have tried flaming tow and lamp oil; you have shot their nests to pieces, with your musket, and pulled them down with your long forked pole; and all this you have done, on rainy days, when the caterpillars were mostly within their nests—and you have found, to your mortification, that they would often repair their nests the next day, or if you decreased the number for the present season, they were, after all your pains, as numerous the next.

NOW MIND ME.

You have often observed, that, at a certain time in the summer, the caterpillars appear to quit their nests entirely, and even the trees, and wander over the fields and on the fences. This generally happens, the latter end of June, or the beginning of July. Be that as it may, when this happens, do you take the old dried nest, break it open, and within it you will find a little pod, somewhat like the silkworm's cone; destroy that pod, for it contains the parent of the next year's race of caterpillars; which, like the queen bee, produces the whole family. This must be done, soon after the caterpillar quits the nest—for out of this pod comes a miller fly, who forms round and upon the small branches of the apple, or wild cherrytree, the latter seems to prefer a number of little cells, in which she deposits her eggs, and then covers them with a gluy substance, which effectually preserves them, until the next spring—*hinc illius ortus*. Hence springs the caterpillar family.

Now let the farmers, in a town, or vicinity, agree to search for the proper time, and effectually to destroy these pods, and my word for it, their neighborhood shall be a land of Goshen the next year.

U. UNDERHILL.

[31] This essay was printed in the *Massachusetts Spy*, XXV, No. 1258 (May 24, 1797), 4. As background Tyler might have read a paper delivered before the American Academy of Arts and Sciences by Mr. A. Crocket of Somerset, England, entitled, "A Practical Essay on Raising Appletrees and Making Cyder." A review of this and other papers contained in the Academy's Transactions, II, Part 1, was contained in *The Massachusetts Magazine*, VI, No. 3 (March, 1794), p. 173ff.

SPEECH OF DAVID WOOD[32]
While standing in the Pillory at Charlestown, N.H.
May 27th, 1797, for forging a deed.

SYMPATHIZING FRIENDS,

You come here this day to see a sad sight; a poor old man publicly disgraced for attempting to make a penny out of fifty acres of Vermont rocks; and yet I see some here in gay coats, mounted on naggish horses, who have made thousands out of lands, to which you had no more title, than I to David Dray's rocks. But you are great rogues, and wear silver spurs, and white beaver hats, and flourish your loaded whips, forget what you once were, drink your Madeira, and talk of your millions of acres, and sit at your ease; while poor I, who have speculated a little in a fifty acre lot, which would not maintain a woodchuck, must stand here; for I am a little rogue, and have no pretentions to be a great speculator.

Let me ask you, what is the difference, as to sin, between a man, who forges a deed and sells land under it, and a man who sells lands, who which he knows he has no title? You all know the great 'Squire——, he bought lands in Boston at the time all their great men got caught in the Georgia land trap. The 'Squire came home by the way of Hartford, at the very moment when the Hartford foxes were wailing for the loss of their tails, in the same spring trap. The 'Squire found he had bought the Devil, and was determined to sell him again on the best terms he could. He put spurs to his old mare, rode before the news, and sold to the widow Lowly and her two sons, who had just come of age, about fifty thousand acres of land, which lay the Lord knows where, and to which he knew he had no title, and took all their father, the old deacon's farm in mortgage, and threatens to turn the poor widow upon the town, and her two boys upon the world; but this is the way of the world. The 'Squire is a great speculator, he is of

---

[32] This column first appeared in *The Farmer's Weekly Museum*, V, No. 221 (June 26, 1797), 4. It was reprinted in *The Spirit of the Farmer's Museum*, pp. 204–6, where it was attributed to Tyler by Dennie's annotation.

the quorum, can sit on the sessions, and fine poor girls for natural missteps; but I am a little rogue, who speculated in only fifty acres of rocks, and must stand here in the pillory.

Then there is the state of Georgia. They sold millions of acres, to which they had no more title, than I to David Dray's land. Their great men pocketed the money; and their Honourable Assembly publicly burnt all the records of their conveyance, and are now selling the lands again. But Georgia is a great Honourable State. They can keep Negro slaves, race horses, gouge out eyes, send members to fight duels at Congress, and cry out for France and the guillotine, and be honoured in the land; while poor I, who never murdered any one, who never fought a duel or gouged an eye; *and had too much honour to burn my forged deed, when I had once been wicked enough to make it,* must stand here in the pillory, for I am a little rogue. Take warning by my sad fate; and if you must speculate in lands, let in be in millions of acres; and if you must be rogues, take warning by my unhappy fate and become great rogues.—For as it is said in a pair of verses I read when I was a boy,

> Little villains must submit to fate,
> That great ones may enjoy the world in state.

And again,

> A little knavery is a dangerous thing,
> Great cheats will flourish, while the small ones swing.

* * * * *

The following anecdotes and jeux de mots *are selected from that department of the Museum which was appropriated for that purpose. The Editor has been careful to cull those only of genuine humor, and Attic acidity, and has been assiduous to reject those which appeared stale and barren of wit.*[33]

ANEXDOTES and *JEUX DE MOTS.*

Riches may be entailed, and nobility may become hereditary. Wit and wisdom can never be made their looms. There are few names more respectable among the patriarchs of Massachusetts, than Governor Dudley and Judge Sewall,[34] yet the former had a daughter, who could scarce keep out of the fire and water, and the latter a son of equal abilities. The prudence of the old gentlemen intermarried these wiseacres. In due time after the marriage, Judge Sewall, then sitting at the council board in Boston, received a letter informing him that his daughter in law was delivered of a fine son, he communicated the billet to the Governor, who after perusing it, observed, with an arch severity, "Brother Sewall, I am thinking how we shall contrive to prevent this grandson of ours from being as great a fool as his father." "I believe," retorted Judge Sewall, "I believe brother Dudley, we must not let him suck his mother."

———

The battle of Monmouth, is fresh in the memory of every one, Gen. LEE, who commanded the advance of the American army. from some cause, not yet developed, had beaten a retreat, and met the

[33] Literally hundreds of anecdotes and epigrams appeared in the Walpole newspaper during Tyler's association with it and although he probably contributed more than his share very few can be attributed definitely to him. The few that are included here are placed in Tyler's canon on the strength of Dennie's annotations in his copy of *The Spirit of the Farmer's Museum.* The complete citation of where these various anecdotes first appeared will be found in the Appendix, pp. 468–73.

[34] Joseph Dudley (1647–1720), son of Thomas Dudley, second governor of the Massachusetts Bay Colony. In 1684, when the charter was declared vacant Dudley was made temporary governor of Massachusetts. He held the office until 1686 and after a stay in England returned as governor in 1702, serving until 1715.

Samuel Sewall (1652–1730). He took part in the judging of the witches during the Salem witchcraft trials and of all the judges who participated he was the only one to publicly confess his error. In 1718 he became chief justice, retiring in 1728.

intrepid WASHINGTON, marching to his support, with the whole
line of the army. Gen. Washington, with surprize, immediately accosted him with, "What is the reason of this highly extraordinary
retreat?" "Sir," replied Lee, "your troops will not fight British
Grenadiers." Washington immediately retorted, "Sir, *you* never
tried it."[35]

The bill for preventing the exportation of arms has passed by 78
yeas against a contemptible minority. The noisy and braggart Lyon
was the only northern member, who voted on the same side with
M'Clanagan.[36] The latter of these Hibernians might address his *honied*
votary in the phrase of Luke in the Poor Soldier:[37]

> "You know I'm your priest and your conscience is mine."
> While Lyon in the "Irish howl," might reply,
> "I went to confess me to father O'Flanagan,
> Told him my case, made an end, then began again."

In a Sermon, printed for a Ward at the Duck and Rainbow, Little
Britain, in the year 1676, by the Rev. Humphrey Harris, the Preacher

[35] General Charles Lee's actions at the battle of Monmouth on June 28, 1778, led to
his being relieved of his command by Washington. He was tried by a court martial and
convicted of disobedience of orders, misbehavior before the enemy and disrespect to the
Commander-in-Chief. Years later Lafayette charged that Lee, the second ranking
American general on the field, deliberately tried to lose the battle to the British. For an
unbiased and full account of the affair, with a report of Lee's trial, see Samuel S. Smith,
The Battle of Monmouth (Monmouth Beach, N.J., 1964). The trial itself is reported in
*Proceedings of a General Court-Martial . . . by the Order of . . . Gen. Washington . . . for the
Trial of Major-General Lee* (New York, 1864).
   A description of Lee's person and an account of his service in Charlestown and
Cambridge is contained in the Ms. memoir of Mrs. Tyler's mother, Elizabeth Hunt
Palmer, pp. 8–9. See also *GTB*, p. 44.
[36] Another one of Tyler's caustic comments on Matthew Lyon. "M'Clanagan" is a
phonetic spelling of Blair McClenachan (*d.* 1812), Representative from Pennsylvania
in the 5th Congress. He was one of the founders of the First Troop of Philadelphia
Cavalry in the Revolution. McClenachan also subscribed a large sum of money to help
the American forces and aided the Continental Congress with money and credit.
[37] John O'Keeffe's drama, *The Poor Soldier,* was played at the Federal Street Theater
in Boston during its first season on May 28, June 2 and July 4, 1794, and later on Nov.
28, 1796, and June 22, 1797.

thus inveighs, in the characteristic punnery of Charles the Second's reign, against fashion; by which it appears that the *short waists* were the mode upwards of a hundred years ago. "I shall speak my mind quaintly against the damsels of my charge—ye are crazy; ye know how to *patch*, but not to *dispatch*. Ye are extravagant, ye are all wasting and yet ye have no *waist*; ye are voluptuous; for, if ye are not *all bellied* ye are all *belli'd*."

———

Perhaps the folly and fondness of self delusion, which is so conspicuous in the larger moiety of mankind, are no where so glaring, as in the encouragement and patronage afforded by them to itinerant and imposing quackery. One would think that the maladies, incident to the fragile machines which we occupy, were sufficiently numerous, without tendering a premium to those whose profession it is to increase them. Whether it be from the prevalence of ignorance, whether from the novelty of any particular nostrum, or the desparing wishes of invalids, who are anxious to try every medicine, however, inefficacious, we shall observe that the man who professes to cure "all the ills that flesh is heir to" is generally well received. The inventor of a drastic pill battens on the folly of his fellow creatures, while the regularly bred physician, who is not sufficiently disingenuous to conceal from a patient the limit of his power, is obliged to comfort with

"The lean and fallow abstinence."

Dr. G. W. Adelersterren, from Lancaster, formerly surgeon in the hospitals of the Emperor of Germany, advertises, in the Fredericksburg paper, a variety of German medicines, unrivalled for their healing excellences. Among others, for only the small sum of seven shillings and six pence, he offers to the Fair, "an infallible remedy for female diseases." As he has neither prefaced, nor succeeded the title of his panacea by any explanatory observation, we must suppose that its operation is of a most general nature, and wherever the disorder lurks, its penetrating powers will eradicate the latent cause. Sheridan's satire upon the spaw of Kilkenny might well prefix the advertisement of his wonderful empyric.[38]

"If lady's cheek be green as leek,
    When she comes from her dwelling,
The kindling rose within it glows,
    When she's at Ballyspellin.

The sooty brown, who comes from town,
    Grows here as fair as Helen;
Then back she goes to kill the beaux,
    By dint of Ballyspellin.

Death throws no darts through all these parts,
    No sections here are knelling;
Come judge and try, you'll never die.
    But LIVE at Ballyspellin.

A songster, whose subject is the late battle of Aboukir, thus humourously causes Admiral Villeneuve to speak of the disaster of the fleet to the Directory;[39]

But des English have got such a damn'd vay of fighting,
To close quarters dey come, which we take no delight in;
Deir courage, begar, ve very soon felta,
And had you been dere, more dam powder you'd smalt a.

And concludes his song with the following very expressive compliment to the adversary admiral.

So now, mes sages sirs, we must give up de notion,
And let England peaceably govern de ocean;

[38] Tyler is probably referring here to Sheridan's caustic comments in *The School for Scandal,* II, ii, and III, iii.

[39] Admiral Pierre Charles Jean Baptiste Silvestre Villeneuve (1763–1806). Although he suffered a reverse from the English fleet while in command of the French rear-guard at the battle of Aboukir (1796), Villeneuve is unfortunately best remembered as the commander-in-chief of the French fleet which was overwhelmed by Nelson at Trafalgar.

As old Neptune won't grant us de rule of de sea,
He may give his damn'd pitchfork to Nelson for me.

A Parisian wit, in a sprightly *jeu de mots,* observes that every thing is gay and lively in the metropolis. We laugh, says he, we dance, we sing, always *sans souci,* and often *sans six sous.* We would carry the play a little farther, and observe that in so doing they frequently act like children, *sous six ans.*

A German Princess is said to have lately fallen in love with a *fiddler* at Munich. She seems, says a London wit, to have been of the Duke's mind in Shakespeare's comedy.

> "If music be the food of love, play on."[40]

She might with equal propriety sing the song of the wild Hoyden in Mother Goose's melody.

> I won't be my father's Jack,
> I won't be my father's Jill,
> I will be the fiddler's wife,
> And have music when I will.
> T'other little tune, t'other little tune;
> Prythee, love, play me t'other little tune.

The proprietor of a *travelling* Museum, in this town, lately announced in his printed exhibition bill, among his wax work figures, "*The* OLD PRODIGAL, *receiving his lost son.*" And Mr. Bowen, keeper of the stationary Museum in Boston,[41] in his exhibition sheet,

---

[40] *Twelfth Night,* I. i, 1.

[41] Daniel Bowen was the first person to exhibit wax works in Boston, initially at the American Coffee House on State Street. In 1795 it assumed the name of "Columbian Museum" and was established in an elegant hall at the head of the mall on the corner of Broomfield's Lane. After several changes of location the collection was finally sold to the New England Museum in 1825.

For another mention of the wax works emporium in the poem, "Epilogue to the Theatrical Season," see *Tyler Verse,* p. 136.

among his musical clocks advertises "King Herod, beheading John the Baptist, and his daughter holding the charger to receive the head." We refer the learned proprietor of the travelling museum, to the XV chapter of St. Luke; and as Mr. B, with other Literati, may not think it presuming to recommend *rare treatises,* which may throw light upon his valuable collections; we would recommend Mr. Bowen to procure access to the old South Library, in Boston, where he will probably find an old book dedicated to King James. In the second part, first division, written by St. Matthew, Chap. 14, he may find that King Herod did not personally behead John the Baptist, and that the damsel, who received the head in a charger, was not the daughter of Herod. JOSEPHUS, as Mr. Bowen *well knows,* seems to countenance this opinion, but we speak with great diffidence as the erudite Mr. Bowen has probably in his library books of greater authenticity than those we have mentioned.

———

The Editor of the Gazette of the United States,[42] in the following caustic and witty manner, notices the "Primary Assemblies" of our towns. "In the index to the second volume of the laws of New York, *Greenleaf's Edition,* occurs this odd reference, SWINE, see *town meetings.*"

———

In a Boston paper of the 5th inst. we observe that Thomas Williams, a black man, has advertised the elopement of his Wife Delia. To sooth his sorrows in solitude, we recommend to the desponding African, to sing

> Ah! Delia, see the fatal hour,
> Farewell, my soul's delight;
> Oh! How can wretched Damon live,
> Thus banish'd from thy sight.

* * * * *

[42] John W. Fenno, a protege of Alexander Hamilton, made the *Gazette of the United States* a champion of Federalist political viewpoints.

THE "OLD SIMON" COLUMN

THE FIRST ISSUE of William Fessenden's *The Reporter*, a weekly newspaper in Brattleboro, appeared on February 21, 1803. In the opening months Tyler proved to be of considerable assistance to Fessenden by providing some needed original material of a literary cast.

On March 28 Tyler made his first appearance in *The Reporter* a notable one. He contributed two poems, "Hymn to the Supreme Being" and "A Riddle for the Ladies."[43] Equally important, Tyler assumed for the first time the new pseudonym "Old Simon" and used the disguise to submit the first of a series of four columns entitled "The Lucubrations of Old Simon" to the newspaper.[44]

Tyler, who at this time was 46 years old, explained in the first "Old Simon" piece that the column was to contain folksy, moralistic observations on various topical subjects from a mature man who had retired to his "fireside and easy chair."[45] The full expectations which the author had for the future development of the column were not realized in the brief span of only four essays.

"The Lucubrations of Old Simon" ran in four consecutive issues of *The Reporter* between March 28 and April 18, inclusive. After the appearance of the fourth column on the latter date "Old Simon" disappeared from the pages of the newspaper. Tyler never again used the pseudonym and why he decided to sever his ties with *The Reporter* is unknown.

*   *   *   *   *

[43] Tyler also composed the headnote epigram for the paper's obituary column which was employed by Fessenden from March 28 to June 27, inclusive. For the texts of the poems see *Tyler Verse*, pp. 118–24.

[44] The holograph manuscript of the "Hymn to the Supreme Being" proves that Tyler was using his old initial "S." in *The Reporter*. Since all the "Old Simon" pieces are also signed "S." this collaborates the attribution of the pseudonym to Tyler. Further details are found in *Tyler Verse*, p. 123.

[45] The use of the homespun character called Old Simon as a *raconteur* of country anecdotes and moralistic tales was not unique with Tyler. For example, Old Simon appeared in Asa Houghton's *The Ladies and Gentlemen's Diary and Almanack . . . for the year . . . 1822* (Bellows Falls, Vt., Bill Blake & Co. [1821]), pp. 42–3.

FOR THE REPORTER.

MR. EDITOR,

I am an Old Man, who have read, travelled and reflected, have been busily engaged in the bustle of life, but am now decently retired to my fire side and easy chair. In the sports of my grandchildren and in reading I find my amusement, and my consolation *in preparing for a better world. Such extracts from the books I read or such reflections as are the companions of my fire side, I shall occasionally send you for insertion, under the head of*

THE LUCUBRATIONS OF
OLD SIMON.

There is much sound sense in the following extract from *Volney's Lectures on History,* and the compliment paid to our country is pleasing.[46]

"Accustomed as we are to the uniform influence of the press, we are not sufficiently sensible of all the moral and political advantages it produces. To estimate the effects of its privation, it is necessary to have lived in a country where the art of printing does not exist. There we soon feel what confusion in accounts, absurdity in reports, uncertainty in opinions, obstacles to information and general ignorance, the want of books and newspapers creates. History owes benedictions to him who first published articles of intelligence in Venice, for the little piece of money called a *gazetta*; the name of which journals of news still bear. Gazettes, indeed, are historical monuments of infinite importance: they are instructive and valuable even in their deviations from strict impartiality; since they thereby exhibit the prevailing spirit of the times in which they are published; and their contradictions always afford materials for the elucidation of facts. Thus, when we are informed that the first thing the Anglo Americans do in forming their new establishments is to cut a road and to commence a newspaper, it appears to me, that, in this double operation, they attain the

[46] Constantin Francois Chasseboeuf, Comte de Volney (1757–1820). His *Lecons d'Histoire,* first published in 1799, was soon translated into English and widely used in Great Britain and America.

object and exhibit the analysis, of every good social system: for *society is nothing more than the easy and free communication of persons and thoughts*; and all the art of government consists in preventing those violent shocks which tend to its destruction. As a contrast to this people, civilized as it were in the cradle, let us take a view of the nations of Asia, which have passed from infancy to decay, and, through every stage of their progress, have still been ignorant and barbarous. Doubtless they have been confined to this condition, because they neither knew the art of printing, nor were capable of constructing roads or canals."

In the *Port Folio* of March 12th Mr. Oldschool has made himself and readers merry by "a specimen of the *Ægis* Editor's style:"[47] but we are sorry to notice that he precludes his wit with a paragraph *"which we incline most to the opinion,"* no, *"we do not incline to the opinion,"* favors somewhat of the irritability of an angry man. Those Editors are certainly both men of classical taste; both are engaged in amusing and instructing the public and then they play with the foils of wit for our entertainment, I am pleased with their dexterity, and as either prevail, am ready to exclaim with Osric in Hamlet,
"A hit a very palpable hit:"
But we should grieve to see either of them assume the dagger of the revengeful or the cudgel of the vulgar. The family of Literature is very small in the United States, and like other families is too much divided by political sentiment; but when her children sport in the public's eye, "let them a brother's wager frankly play," and not like the sightless Sampson bring destruction upon themselves while they are making sport for the Philistines. I ardently desire to see a compacted union among men of science and devoutly wish that Literature would adopt the language of inspiration, and say unto her followers, "by this shall men know that ye are my disciples because ye love one another."   S

* * * * *

[47] "Dr. Oliver Oldschool" was one of Dennie's favorite pseudonyms while editor of *The Port Folio.* The *National Aegis,* established at Worcester, Mass., in 1801, was edited by Francis Blake under the pseudonym of "Hector Ironside."

THE LUCUBRATIONS OF
OLD SIMON.

I am no horseman and have oftener visited the library than the stud, but should like to inquire of some of the *knowing ones* of the turf, whether the following description of The HORSE, extracted from Shakespeare's Venus and Adonis, does not comprise all the points now esteemed excellent in that noble animal, excepting, perhaps in some of the minor beauties, where fashion, who delights to play her pranks with horses tails' as well as ladies' heads, and sometimes docks the former and sometimes frizzles the latter, may have marred that line of grace which filled the poet's eye.

> "Look when a painter would surpass the life,
> In limning out a well proportion'd steed,
> His art, with nature's workmanship at strife,
> As if the dead the living should succeed:
> So did his horse excel a common one
> In shape, and carriage, color, pace, and bone.
>
> Round hooft, short jointed, fetlocks shag and long,
> Broad breast, full eyes, small head, and nostril wide,
> High crest, short ears, straight legs and passing strong,
> Thin mane, thick tail, broad buttock, tender hide:
> Look what a horse should have he did not lack,
> Save a proud rider on so proud a back."

Last evening as I sat musing by my fire side upon the evils attendant on human life, and the petulance with which man bears them; the remembrance of my cousin Simon came fresh to my mind. I can well recollect how cheerfully he would sit in his easy chair, coeval in age with himself, and with an old man's garrulity and a large fund of that useful philosophy which is the handmaid of religion and daughter of experience, recommended that patience in adversity which his whole life had exemplified. I had thoughts of affording your readers the benefit of some of his practical lectures, but when I wrote them in plain prose, they had so much the appearance of sermons of an excellent preacher I have frequently read, that although I knew they would be relished highly by readers of reflection and matured taste, yet I apprehended that their sober appearance might frighten the youthful and unreflecting. In aid of virtue all innocent means may be used. Perhaps those who might turn with disgust from a sermon may read and relish wisdom in

A SONG.
OLD SIMON.
(Tune—in a Mouldering Cave.)

In his crazy arm chair, on the downhill of life,
    Old Simon, sat calm and resign'd;
He had outliv'd his friends, he had buried his wife,
    Old Simon was lame, deaf and blind.

But the Being of Love! who still tempers the blast,
    With devotion had sweet'ned his mind;
Her gay smiles, o'er his wrinkles, contentment had cast,
    And cheer'd him tho' lame, deaf and blind.

His misfortunes, his woes, could you hear him relate;
    Insisting, they all were design'd
To reclaim him from ill, *or some bliss* to create,
    You'd long to be lame, deaf and blind.

When I learn, says Old Simon, that topics of State,
    Inflame each political chief;
That they back-bite, snarl, slander, in noisy debate;
    Old Simon's content to be deaf.

When Fashion, that tempter, than the serpent more sly,
    To folly, Eve's daughters inclin'd;
When with scarce a fig-leaf, they obtrude on the eye;
    Old Simon's content to be blind.

When battles' fell trumpets so frequently sound
    And blood marks our annals with shame,
When *abroad,* war and murder, are raging around;
    At *home,* I'm content to be lame.

Thus, this worthy old man, by contentment and pray'r,
  To the ills of his life was resign'd;
And in death, he exclaim'd, as he sunk in his chair,
  What bliss, to the lame, deaf and blind.

With chaplets of joy in regions above,
  His temples the angels entwin'd,
Old Simon *there* blesses the Being of Love,
  Who *here* made him lame, deaf and blind.

MORAL REFLECTION.

Sweet are the uses of adversity, says some poet; man's calamity is God's opportunity, says the pious Flavel; and true it is, in adversity the heart is made ductile by sorrow, and we are ready to receive those religious impressions which in prosperity we disregard; or if we noticed them, it was only like the Governor of Judea, to defer the consideration of them to a future season. But adversity shews us the evil we should have avoided and impels us to consider seriously of reforming our conduct. Thus misfortunes are often blessings in disguise; he who has been prospered may say I have known pleasure; but he who has been in adversity may say I have learnt wisdom. The prosperous man, feels amidst his riches and pleasures, the unsatisfying nature of worldly enjoyment; and he has little more to expect; but the unfortunate man, is ever cheered by hope, has much to desire and much to expect in this life; and if the uses of adversity have been sweet to him, he is probably better prepared for a full fruition of durable riches, and unfading, uncloying pleasures in the world to come.

* * * * *

FOR THE REPORTER.

THE LUCUBRATIONS OF OLD SIMON.

I read the sermons of many elegant and eloquent preachers, but though I am pleased with Seed, instructed by Fordyce, amused with Sterne and rapt with Bourdaloue and Saucio,[48] yet there is something in the eloquence, if eloquence it can be called, of the good old Puritan Paul Baxter,[49] which never fails to interest my affections; while others gratify the scholar, he speaks home to the man and the christian. In his "Exhortation to Seriousness," in his Saints Everlasting Rest, page 129, he puts the following questions, which may vie with the most precious morals of pulpit rhetoric.

Quest. 1. If you could grow rich by religion, or get lands and lordships thereby; or if you could be recovered from sickness by it, or could live forever in prosperity on earth; what kind of lives would you then lead, and what pains would you take in the service of your God? and is not the Rest of Saints a more excellent happiness than all this?

Quest. 2. If the law of the land did punish every breach of the Sabbath, or every omission of family duties, or secret duties, or every cold and heartless prayer, with death. If it were felony or treason to be negligent in worship, and loose in your lives; what manner of persons would you then be? And what lives would you lead? And is not eternal death more terrible than temporal?

[48] Jeremiah Seed (1700–1747). Dr. Johnson was among those who praised his preaching.

James Fordyce (1720–1796), Presbyterian divine and poet. Garrick went to hear him preach and Boswell wrote of his friendship with Johnson.

Laurence Sterne (1713–1768). Although best remembered as a novelist and humorist, his first appearance in print (1747) was a sermon and many of them were published in his lifetime. Cardinal Newman, among others, admired his eloquence.

Louis Bourdaloue (1632–1704). This famous Jesuit became so renowned for his oratory that Louis XIV requested he preach before the King and his court.

[49] Tyler has given the Rev. Richard Baxter the wrong Christian name. He cited it correctly in "The Bay Boy," Chapter IX, footnote 18, p. 114.

Quest. 3. If it were God's ordinary course to punish every sin with some present judgement, so that every time a man swears, or is drunk, or speaks a lie, or backbiteth his neighbor, he should be struck dead, or blind, or lame in the place. If God did punish every cold prayer, or neglect of duty with some remarkable plague; what manner of persons would you be? if you should suddenly fall down dead like Ananias and Sapphira, with the sin in your hands; or the plague of God should seize upon you as upon the Israelites, while their sweet morsels were yet in their mouths. If but a mark should be set in the forehead of every one that neglected a duty or committed a sin, what kind of lives would you then lead? and is not eternal wrath more terrible than this?

Quest. 4. If you had seen the general dissolution of the world, and all the pomp and glory of it consumed to ashes: if you saw all on fire about you, sumptuous buildings, cities, kingdoms, land, water, earth, heaven, all flaming about your ears: if you had seen all that men labored for, and sold their lives for, gone: the place of your former abode gone: the history ended, and all come down, what would such a sight as this persuade you to do? why, such a sight thou shalt certainly see, I put my question to thee in the words of the Apostle, 2 Pet. iii. *Seeing all these things shall be dissolved, what manner of persons ought you to be in all holy conversation and godliness, looking for, and hasting unto the coming of the day of God, wherein the heavens being on fire shall be dissolved, and the elements shall melt with fervent heat?* As if we should say, we cannot possibly conceive or express what manner of persons we should be in all holiness and godliness, when we do but think of the sudden and certain, and terrible dissolution of things below.

Quest. 5. What if you had seen the proof of the judgement of the great day? if you had seen the wicked stand trembling on the left hand of the Judge, and Christ himself accusing them of their rebellions and neglects and remembering them of all their former slightings of his grace, and at last condemning them to perpetual perdition? if you had seen the godly standing on the right hand, and Jesus Christ acknowledging their faithful obedience and adjudging them to the possession of the joy of their Lord?—What manner of persons would you have been after such a sight as this? why, this sight you shall one day see, as sure as thou livest. And why then should not the fore-knowledge of such a day awake thee to thy duty?

Quest. 6. What if you had once seen hell open, and all the damned there in their ceaseless torments, and had heard them crying out of their slothfulness in the day of their visitation, and wishing that they had but another life to live, and that God would but try them once again? one crying out of his neglect of duty, and another of his loitering and trifling, when he should have been laboring for his life? what manner of persons would you have been after such a sight as this? what if you had seen heaven opened, as Stephen did, and all the Saints there triumphing in glory, and enjoying the end of their labors and sufferings? what a life would you live after such a sight as this? why, you will see this with your eyes before it be long.

Quest. 7. What if you had been in hell but one year, or one day, or hour, and there felt those torments that now you do but hear? and God should turn you into the world again, and try you with another life-time, and say, I will see whether thou wilt yet be any better: what manner of persons would you be? if you were to live a thousand years, would you not live as strictly as the precisest Saints, and spend all those years in prayer and duty, so you might but escape the torment which you suffered? how seriously then would you speak of hell! and pray against it! and hear, read, watch and obey! how earnestly would you admonish the careless to take heed, and look about them to prevent their ruin! and will not you take God's word for the truth of this, except you feel it? is it not your wisdom to spend this life in laboring for heaven, while yet we have it, rather than to lie in torment, wishing for more time in vain.

* * * * *

FOR THE REPORTER.

THE LUCUBRATIONS OF
OLD SIMON.

I generally close my evening lucubrations by reading some book upon a religious subject. Last evening I chanced to delight myself with Dr. Newton's dissertation on the Prophecies which have been remarkably fulfilled in the world at this time.[50] The following passage extracted from his first volume p. 314, pleased me, and may probably gratify many of your readers.   S.

Amos ix. 11, 12. Acts xv. 16, 17. "I will return, and will build again the tabernacle of David, which is fallen down; and I will build again the ruins thereof, and I will set it up; That the residue of men might seek after the Lord, all the Gentiles upon whom my name is called, saith the Lord, who doeth all these things."

This concern of Daniel, and affection for his religion and country, show him in a very amiable light, and give an additional lustre and glory to his character. But not only in this instance, but in every other, he manifests the same kind of public spirit, and appears no less eminently a patriot than a prophet. Though he was torn early from his country, and enjoyed all the advantages that he could enjoy in foreign service, yet nothing could make him forget his native home: and in the next chapter we see him pouring out his soul in prayer, and supplicating most earnestly and devoutly for the pardon and restoration of his captive nation. It is a gross mistake therefore, to think, that religion will ever extinguish or abate our love for our country. The scriptures will rather incite and inflame it, exhibit several illustrious examples of it, and recommend and enforce this, as well as all other moral and social virtues; and especially when the interests of true religion, and of our country are so blended and interwoven, that they cannot well be separated the one from the other. This is a double

[50] Newton's *Observations Upon the Prophecies of Daniel and the Apocalypse* appeared in 1733.

incentive to the love of our country; and with the same zeal that every pious Jew might say formerly, every honest American may say now, with the good Psalmist, Psal. cxxii, 6, &c.

"Oh pray for the peace of Jerusalem; they shall prosper that love thee. Peace be within thy walls, and plenteousness within thy palaces. For my brethren and companions sake will I wish thee prosperity; yea, because of the house of the Lord our God, I will seek to do the good."

Hannah Adams in her *View of Religion*,[51] quoting Dusresnoy's Chronology of Tables, mentions the EICETÆ, a denomination in the year 680, who affirmed that in order to make prayer acceptable to God, it should be performed *dancing*. Were not these Eicetæ the fathers of the Shaking Quakers?

* * * * *

THE AMERICAN YEOMAN

THE *YEOMAN* is the repository of some of Tyler's last published prose. During the year Ide published the newspaper in Brattleboro Tyler was a frequent and fairly regular contributor. As noted above he may also have been editor of the weekly.[52]

It is fortunate that a great number of Tyler's contributions to the *Yeoman* can be identified by the notations for 1817 in his "Day Book." Not only do these entries pinpoint some of his literary efforts, but also identify the legal public notices and advertisements he was required to place as Register of Probate.

Tyler's most regular appearance in the newspaper was as author of a column of levity entitled, "Small Talk." Appearing under the masthead of local Brattleboro news, it served as a pleasant divertissement from the weighty recountings of politics and wars.[53] All the "Small Talk" and Tyler's other contributions to the *Yeoman* will be presented here.

---

[51] Hannah Adams (1755–1831). This work was first published at Boston in 1784 under the title, *An Alphabetical Compedium of the Various Sects which have Appeared in the World from the Beginning of the Christian Era to the Present Day*. It is better known as *A View of Religions*, the title given to the second and third editions of 1791 and 1801.

[52] See above, pp. 288–89.

On Tuesday, January 27, 1818, Ide advertised that everyone should settle their accounts with him since he would leave Brattleboro "on the ensuing Thursday."[54] With his departure for Windsor Ide deprived Tyler of a local outlet for his literary productions. In fact, 1817–1818 marked the decline of Tyler's literary career. The contributions to the *Yeoman,* outside of the "Postumi" pieces in the *Polyanthos* in 1818 and a few poems published in 1822, were the last efforts of his pen to appear in print.

*   *   *   *   *

SMALL TALK.

These are thy glorious works,—Mil.

We hear that King Ferdinand, of Spain, a prince pre-eminent for his devotion to the Catholic faith, as delivered by the Monks, and prescribed by the Inquisition. While his subjects in the Peninsula are divided into powerful factions, and one half of them are employed to coerce the other moiety into abject servitude—and while his colonial subjects in South America are practicing their first lessons in the great American School-Book for nations, and will probably be soon able to spell those words so odious to Kings, *Republicanism* and *Independence.*

We learn that at this eventful period, this illustrious Legitimate is constantly employed, *in embroidering with his own princely fingers, a fringed petticoat for the image of the Virgin Mary at Loretto.*—It is added by the last advices from Madrid, that his Royal and Serene Highness— Don Alonzo Francis Gasper—Glaudio Genzalo Herrero—Joseph Juan Lopez Lazero Miguel Melichor Philip Paulo Xavier Ximenes de Compostolla Duke de Medina Cela—President of the Council of both the Indias, has the enviable and transcendant honor to approach the august presence of his Master, and to—thread his needle. Hide your diminished heads, ye presidents and secretaries of a Republican govern-

---

[53] Tyler's authorship of this column is confirmed by his "Day Book" entry for Dec. 28, 1817: "Mr. Ide here in Even'g—Wrote some small talk . . ."

[54] *The American Yeoman,* I, No. 52 (Jan. 27, 1818), 3.

ment, and blush before the splendid achievements of KINGS! Let us one and all petition Congress to avoid a war with his potent Potentate —for, should he turn the puissant point of his redoubtable needle from punctuating the petticoat of the Virgin of Loretto to the modest drapery of the lovely virgins of our land—who could stand—?

MORE SMALL TALK.
Short reckonings make long friends.
Poor Richard.

That there is actually existing an account courant between public Men and those who appoint them, which is kept in the Mental Ledger of every man, cannot be doubted. Perhaps it would not be amiss to see how it would look upon paper. We have sometimes fancied a member of Congress presenting something like the following to his constituents:—

The Hon. —— ——, Acc't. Cour. with his Constitutents.[55]

Washington, March 5, 1817.

Dr.

To	ware and tare of Conscience, in abusing others to get myself elected, ——	$244,60
"	two Carboys of rectified spirit of Fiction —— 3 Frails of assorted Fibs—seven dozen of *imitation* Facts, and a large hank of equivocations, as per Invoice by ship Ocean, ——	50,00
"	sundry *public* speeches delivered in my *counting-house,* upon the scandalous waste of public money, ——	344,60
"	do. against Bonaparte, ——	480,25
"	do. do. Town and Country Meetings, ——	20,00
"	paring 3 bu. of apples, and cracking 5 do. walnuts for the good nation in my seat in Congress, ——	180,00

[55] John Noyes of Brattleboro was one of Vermont's Congressional delegation to the 14th Congress. A staunch Federalist, he may be the subject of this column.

”	do. almonds, filberts, and ground-nuts, ——	90,00
”	attending 9 President's Levees, ——	45,00
”	eating myself into a surfeit at 14 Presidential dinners, ——	3,50
”	drinking do. ——	.30
”	do. British ambassadors, ——	.50
”	133 Nays—delivered in the house *ex tempore,* at 25 cts. per nay, ——	33,25
”	one Yea —$1,500 per ann. ——	3000,00
”	being kept awake 3 nights, setting out the question, ——	6000,00
”	exposing myself to *heat* and cold, by bolting two unpopular question, —— $12,00	
	Box of pills and solution, .75 ——	12,75
”	loss of popularity in voting the Salary Bill, ——	100,00
”	loss of credit in voting its repeal, ——	1000,00
”	sundries—barbers, shoe-blacks—charity, and hacks,	.60
		5611,35

SUPRA—CR.

By	salary 2 years, ——	$3000,00,0
”	travel—a brace of sessions, ——	650,00,0
”	privilege of franking 240 letters to wife in Home Department, ——	60,00,0
”	ditto to daughter Lydia, on contravailing duties and non-intercourse, ——	3,30,0
”	do. do. son Sam on Finances, ——	3,30,0
”	do. 1 do. to half a gross constituents, to be read in Society, ——	25,00,0
”	the honor gained by a seat in Congress, ——	4,5
”	sundry comfortable dozes when the member from Maine was up, 6 cts. pr. doze, ——[56]	48,0

[56] This probably refers to a long, unexciting speech given by Representative Cyrus King of Saco on Feb. 19, 1817, during House debate on a resolution to repeal the internal duties. He had earlier delivered an equally dull speech on the Internal Improvement bill on Feb. 6. See: *The Debates and Proceedings in the Congress of the United States*

    "   a pleasant dream—that I regained the confidence of
my constituents, ——   50,00,0

    "   the pleasure of viewing the Spanish ambassador, 5
Osagee Indian Chiefs, 2 Squaws, and a papoose
at Washington, ——   2,25,0

    "   the honor of being unanimously elected a member
of the committee of the whole house, ——   50,00,0

    "   transports, while bolting, ——   5,00,0

    "   three newspapers furnished by Congress, ——   18,00,0

    "   influence gained, ——   4,5

    "   stationary, treacle, &c., ——   52,82,0

Ballance carried to next Election—see account of
Public Sales—Journal No. 1818.

       Errors *ac*-cepted. $3895,49,0

*   *   *   *   *

SMALL TALK.

The Great Snow of 1717.—The Boston News Letter, quoted in the
account of this Snow, (see second page of this paper) mentions the
depth as six feet on the 25th of February; but though it notices successive falls of Snow until the 4th of March, it does not state the *greatest*
depth. The writer of this article well recollects, that when a boy his
grandfather often spoke of this great snow, and once told him, that it
was on a level with the eves of a certain chaise-house—which must
have been at least nine and a half, or ten feet high. The inhabitants of
Boston dug arched passages under the snow to open a communication
with their wells and their neighbors. The poor were so distressed for
fire, as in some cases to burn part of their household furniture. The
overseers of the poor sent persons on snow-rackets through the town,

... *Fourteenth Congress—Second Session* ... (Washington, 1854), pp. 876–78, 933, 991,
997–1003, 1014.

    In the third census of 1810 Massachusetts was assigned 20 representatives in Congress,
seven of whom had to be from the District of Maine.

to administer to the wants of the sick and needy—who entered their dwellings through the chamber windows.

It would really be a gratification of curiosity, if we could commune a few minutes with the shade of some long departed Sachem, who planted his wigwam on the base of the Green Mountains and used to trap Wapperknockers on the banks of the *Wantastic,* just to ask him how deep the snow was in his hunting-ground, about 1200 moons ago—That is all——[57]

If some of our members of Congress have not proved themselves to be elegant Orators—Candor must allow that they have shown themselves to be virtuous men; for, like the primitive Christians, their whole conversation on the floor of the house has been—*Yea, yea; or Nay, nay.*

It has been said, (says the Trenton True American) that if *the stripes* on our flag were as numerous as our states, they could not be *as plainly seen.* This however, is of little consequence, if we can but make them *severely felt.*

*   *   *   *   *

SMALL TALK.

Major Zebulon CASH, of this state, relates a very merry incident which happened on a late visit to his brother in the City of New-York.

A fellow-passenger in the steam-boat happened to be familiarly acquainted with his brother, politely gave him directions to his lodgings at the great hotel; and, after shewing him the street, and describing the house as a large handsome building, told him to enter it without knocking, and any of the boarders would *shew* him his brother.—The first house which appeared to answer the description, chanced to be a bank—he entered and accosted the cashier with—*Is*

---

[57] When this colmn was written in Feb., 1817, *Yeoman* subscribers would have retained frigid memories of the "Cold Year" of 1816, when snow actually fell in all 12 months.

Cash within? Will you be so obliging as to shew me Cash? The cashier
stuck his pen behind his ear, dropped his ream of soft, silky dollars,
and stared like the pig in the proverb—Indeed it must be confessed,
that in the whole commercial world no place was so improper to
obtrude such a question, as in—A BANK—At first he took it for an
insult, and imagined the honest Major to be some envious stock-holder
of the United States' Bank; or envoy from the National Treasurer, or
speculator from New-England, come to spy the nakedness of his
vault—and every genteel particle of his blood boiled into efferves-
cence, as he piteously pondered the Craven provisions of that un-
gentleman-like law—the act of New-York against duelling. But soon
discovering that Maj. Cash was not the wicked one come to spirit
away the departed soul of his defunct paper, but merely a simple
Vermontee, with this all-attractive surname, he very pleasantly
replied: "Sir, your namesake used to occupy these apartments—but
being of a very delicate habit, during the last war he was thrown into
hysterics, by some runnegate runners from Boston, and in his fright
hid himself in the snug little parlour below the ground floor, where
he has lain perdue ever since—obstinately denying himself to all
visitors, excepting to a few particular friends, who were going a long
voyage to the East-Indies, and wished to shake hands with him before
they sailed. But if you will please to call again on the 20th of February,
you will find your namesake at his old lodgings, happy to be seen by
all who come well recommended."[58]

* * * * *

[58] The debate in the House of Representatives on Jan. 7 and 10 over the difficulties
facing the Bank of the United States at this time can be found in *The Debates and
Proceedings in the Congress of the United States . . . Fourteenth Congress—Second Session,*
pp. 431–36, 454–59.

Immediately following this column is the request that Darius Clark of the *Bennington
Gazette* retract his allegation that Tyler was editor of the *Yeoman*. See above, pp. 288.

SMALL TALK.

When untaught genius spreads her sounding wings
    The unletter'd sons of science must retire;
For in her lofty flight she proudly flings
    This plodding scholar 'midst his kindred mire.
                     SANCONIATHAN.

Figures of Rhetoric.—Messrs. Glib and Sappy, two self-educated lawyers, lately argued a cause before a Justice of the Peace.—Mr. Sappy, in the midst of his harrangue, burst into a most boisterous laugh. On being reprimanded by the Magistrate, he observed, that "all the time his brother Glib had been speaking, he had noticed a fly which had repeatedly attempted to walk up his forehead, but the surface was so *slippery,* that the insect, like the learned advocate's reasoning, continually lost ground."—When Counsellor Glib proceeded to reply, he was also seized with a fit of the risables, still more obstrepulous—for he likewise had noticed a fly attempting to walk up his brother Sappy's pericranium, but the surface was so *soft,* that the insect slumped in.

Among the singularities of the late severe cold, we hear that Mr. — Howe discovered on the ice of the Connecticut River, opposite Vernon, a wild Duck—upon his dog's approaching it, the bird fluttered its wings, but seemed unable to rise.—After a violent struggle it flew; and on Mr. H. examining the spot, he found nearly all the breast feathers of the duck adhering to the ice.

*   *   *   *   *

SMALL TALK.

In a jovial company, a respectable old gentleman, equally remarkable in this vicinity, for his ready wit and temperance, was invited to drink grog—but he declared; observing, that he had been taught a valuable lesson by his old mare—and that was, Not to drink when he was not thirsty, and when *he was,* never to drink too much.

A gentleman travelling in a barren part of a neighboring state, was so struck with the sterility of the soil, and the meagre aspect of both man and beast, that, on observing one of the inhabitants issuing from the door of a miserable log hut, followed by a score of ragged children he could not help addressing him—"My good friend, what evil fortune has destined you to inhabit this region of sterility and want? from my heart I pity you." The inhabitant of F——a[59] replied with a smile—"Spare your pity, my dear sir; I am much *richer* than you imagine, for *I do not own but five acres of this land.*"

* * * * *

SMALL TALK.
WRIFFORD OUT DONE!

A young dashy Boston Shopkeeper, on a visit to his family in this vicinity, was boasting of his hand-writing—"I write (said he) two hands; one an elegant merchantile running hand, and another in the best mode of the celebrated Wrifford." "Well Tom (said his father), I see nothing extraordinary in all this—I, who never have had a Boston education, do something in the writing way still more wonderful. I also write two kinds of hand-writing. First I write a hand *which nobody can read but myself*; and secondly—mark me Tom—I write a hand *which neither I myself nor anybody else can read.*

* * * * *

SMALL TALK.
THE SQUINT EYED CONSCIENCE.

An Attorney, remarkably squint eyed, was settling an account with his client, who requested him to read the charges. Upon the lawyer's reading an item of $25.03, the client noticed it as very extravagant, observing that he had frequently done the same business for little more

[59] Obviously Franconia, in the White Mountains. Tyler apparently first used this anecdote in conversation with friends as far back as 1806, according to "TPT Memoir," p. 187.

than $3.00. The wiley attorney, finding that his client noticed the imposition, replied, "I beg your pardon, sir, it should have been $3.25, the mistake was entirely owing to the obliquity of my eye."— "Say rather," muttered the client, "to the SQUINT OF YOUR CONSCIENCE."

BONAPARTE Bunged up!

It is reported by arrivals from the West Indies, that Bonaparte has made his escape from St. Helena, in a water-cask, on board an American frigate.—(Much doubted in this region.)

* * * * *

SMALL TALK.

We are so greatly pleased with the following from a New-Bedford paper,[60] that we engage to publish any *notice* of the kind from our Thirsty friends, on either side of the Connecticut, free of expense.

Particular Notice—I, Jesse Reynolds, of New-Bedford, having very severely suffered, and being reduced to poverty, and frequently to deep distress, by intemperance, and knowing that my thirst for spiritous liquors often denied me of the exercise of my judgement: Do, by these presents, earnestly request all retailers of liquors not to give me credit for either cider or spirits of any kind; hoping, if they will withhold it from me, I shall be able to guard against its use, and thereby become a reputable citizen; and by my industry yet be able to maintain my family in comfort and ease.

JESSE REYNOLDS.

New-Bedford, March 5, 1817.

* * * * *

[60] This notice appeared initially in the *New-Bedford Mercury*, X, No. 33 (March 7, 1817), 3.

SMALL TALK.
ANECDOTE OF DR. FRANKLIN.

Dr. Franklin had occasion, in company with an Englishman to mention Lord Cholmondely, which he pronounced as spelled. The Englishman burst into a boisterous laugh, and informed the Doctor that it should be pronounced *Shumley*.—Without seeming to notice the Englishman's impoliteness, the Doctor calmly inquired if there were not families in London who spelled their name C,u,n,n,i,n,g, h,a,m? "Yes," replied the Englishman, "several." "Pray, sir, how do you pronounce their name?" "Why Cunningham, to be sure, *as it is spelled.*" "Well, observed the Doctor, it is very fortunate for me, that you did not pronounce it so in my presence, when I was a little ignorant soap-boiler's apprentice: for I should probably have then been silly enough to have laughed in your face; as we in Boston always pronounced it *Kinninkum*.

Scarcity of Cash.—Great complaint has been recently made of the scarcity of money in Brattleboro'. Where can it be gone? cry the farmer, the merchant and the mechanick. It must be *hid* somewhere, exclaim the lawyer and the sheriff. And so it seems it has been. It is now discovered, that this slippery being, *Cash,* has betaken itself to our *Town Treasury,* (the last place, it must be confessed, where a person would have thought of looking for it) as our late worthy Town Treasurer assures us he never saw the face of it in the Town Till, all the years he was in office.

"We bid the stranger welcome."

* * * * *

SMALL TALK.

MARINE JOURNAL.
BRATTLEBORO' SHIP INTELLIGENCE

Last Saturday evening, came to anchor in the lower harbour, the

Superscratch, Capt. OLIVER HASTINGS, fr. Hartford, (being the first Spring arrival at this port from a foreign voyage.)—Cargo 40 Tirces Salt—Rum—10 bbls. Beef—10 do. Shad—Box Looking-glasses, Chalk, &c. to Goodhue & Co.—Rosin, Rum and Junk Bottles to Clark & Hunt. Her letterbag was not opened when this went to press—and we are concerned to find that Capt. H. has brought no London papers. It is said one of the passengers brought Lloyd's List, but loaned it to a friend at Coombs Geese, at which port she touched on her passage.[61]

Extract from her log-book.—N. L. 44 27, E. L. 43 00, Miller's Falls,[62] bearing S.E., saw the hull of a vessel, no name on her stern—lugger-built, her dead lights calked—loaded with Cod Fish, Loaf Sugar, &c., supposed to be the Neptune. Took an observation at Parker's Bar, foot of Swift water.

* * * * *

SMALL TALK.

A CHARADE,
FOR THE READERS OF THE BOSTON
INTELLIGENCER.
My first is a Quiz—my second a Bore—and my whole a Hoax.

———

FAITH vs. GOOD WORKS.

The pious Jeremy Seed very gravely gives us the following anec-dote, as illustrative of the estimation some professors entertain of the

[61] Tyler was indulging here in a little whimsy. The Connecticut River was navigable up to Brattleboro, but not for large ocean-going vessels. Any substantial cargo had to be transferred at Hartford or Springfield to smaller river boats or flatboats for the trip up-river. The craft mentioned by Tyler may have been the usual flatboat, but he treated it facetiously as if it were a much larger ocean-going ship, possibly with the intention of advancing the many current plans to improve the river's navigation.

Tyler may also have been giving a free boost to two of the newspaper's best adver-tisers. Both mercantile concerns mentioned—Goodhue & Co. and Clark & Hunt—frequently placed notices in the *Yeoman.*

[62] This cataract was located on the Miller's River close to where it joined the Con-necticut east of Greenfield, Mass.

superiority of Faith over Good Works.—A worthy farmer crossing his neighbour's field, which lay contiguous to his own, improvidently thrust his cane into a dry cow-dab, and tossed it over the fence into his own enclosure. No sooner had he done it, than his conscience smote him with the reflection, that though his prize was of little value, yet this was actually defrauding his neighbour—he immediately resolved to make restitution, and, under the impulse of conscience, again pierced the savoury prize, and had actually raised his staff to throw it back into his neighbour's meadow—when suddenly recollecting his creed, he forbore to restore it, for this would be relying on a good work, which to him appeared horrible hetrodoxy.

* * * * *

SMALL TALK.
FROM A BLACK LETTER JEST BOOK.

Now it chaunced that the gude shippe HECTOR caste anchour in the Thames river, and the captaine thereof being much given to witte, and iollitie, inuited that cunninge poete, Mr. Beniamin Iohnson to drinke with him in his said shippe, whereupon this poete did with all speede repaire thither, and did sette down with the aforesaid captaine, and they two did quaffe wine together in gude fellowshippe, for a grate space of time, till finallie the captaine raising himself from his seate, and holding mightilie by the side of the cabbin, saide, "Now frende Iohnson addresse my gude shippe with an essaie of verse"; whereupon Iohnson replyed "Most willinglie—what is the name of your gude shippe?" "Hector" reioyned the captaine: then Iohnson, raisinge with the gobblette of wine in his sinister, and supporting himselfe as he mought with his dexter, lowdly did proclaime as followeth,

> "Oh! thou grate Hector, sonne of Priamm,
> Behold thy master's drunke as I amm."

Whereupon, in an extasie of joye they bothe emptyed their gobblettes and as it were spontaneouslie prostrated themselves beneath the table."[63]

[63] In the column adjoining this "Small Talk" article is an advertisement asking

* * * * *

AMERICAN YEOMAN.
Brattleborough, Tuesday, August 12, 1817.[64]

"*Cobbett eclipsed.*"—The political essay of Mr. WOOLER, an English printer, which we present to our readers in this paper, is replete with the true "fire of the flint." He is, perhaps, rather too indignant at the conduct of the run-away patriot, Cobbett, whose cowardice, we presume, is constitutional, and who still wishes well to the great and good cause of reform. But Wooler would "eclipse" Cobbett, at a "time that tries men's souls," were they fellow-labourers in the same political field. Cobbett exceeds all writers in the *quantity* of his productions, and the *quality* is, upon the whole, pretty good; but we cannot regard him as a prodigy of original genius. His powers are those of argument and amplification, rather than those of invention and illumination. The style of his political writings, in which he imitates Dean SWIFT, and of course expresses plain and bold ideas in plain and bold language, is calculated to produce the greatest possible degree of political effect. He has done wonders in preparing the minds of the English people for a state of revolution, but he has not courage enough to become an actor in the revolution itself. It would seem that a great political change, *of some sort,* must soon take place in Great Britain, and at such a crisis Cobbett must yield to such "master spirits" as Burdett and Wooler.[65] Could we hope that Wooler would be

readers to be on the lookout for a thief who had made off with some promissory notes and escaped from his guardian, Simeon Eaton of Brattleboro. This case had been taken by Tyler, as the following July 11 entry in the "Day Book" proves: "Drew advertiz't for Mr. Eaton. Inserted in Yeoman & Hand bills struck off."

[64] This article of Aug. 12 and the later one of Aug. 19, both on the subject of William Corbett, can be attributed to Tyler by the following citation of Aug. 11 in the "Day Book"; "Wrote piece about Cobbet for Yeoman."

Cobbett (1762–1835), an English reformer and journalist, was in political exile in the United States from 1792–1800 and 1817–1819. Under the pseudonym of "Peter Porcupine" he became famous and infamous as a party journalist for the Federalists. He was publisher and editor of *Porcupine's Gazette.*

[65] Sir Francis Burdett (1770–1844), a fighter against the continued encroachment of popular rights by the English Government. A champion for the freedom of speech, he

suffered to continue his labours, we should anticipate the most important consequences from them. He is a man of genius and industry. His
powers are calculated to infuse into the publick mind that noble contempt of danger and death, and that ardent and unconquerable passion
for glory, without which nothing can be accomplished in a struggle
for Freedom. His words are "words of sunshine," and his images are
replete with "rainbow hues." He has talents for a storm. Give him
"ample room, and verge enough," and he would display, with powerful effect, the "meteor flag" of Genius and Courage, amidst the
"thunder," and "lightning," and "blood" of Revolution and War.

God forbid that we should indulge in a wish to see the horrors of
the French Revolution acted over again in Great Britain. But the
British people are reduced to such a deplorable state of slavery and
misery, that it would be unworthy an American republican not to
pray that the British government, in the order of Divine Province,
may be speedily compelled to restore the people over whom they
now tyrannize, the liberties "to which the laws of nature and of
nature's God entitle them."

* * * * *

TO MY CREDITORS.

The humble petition of George
Loveland, respectfully
sheweth —[66]

That he is now above sixty years of age, and has a wife and children

capped his career by working for the passage of the Reform Bill by Parliament.
Thomas J. Wooler (1786?–1853), journalist and politician, who also worked for
British parliamentary reform.

[66] This petition is more than the mere advertisement of a case taken by Tyler at this
time. It is as much a piece of prose as a legal notice. It is included here for that reason and
is attributed to Tyler because of this notation in his "Day Book" on Aug. 7: "Wrote
Loveland out petition to his creditors for Yeoman."

In this same issue of the *Yeoman* (Aug. 12) there are two legal notices attested by
Tyler as Register of Probate. They are for the estates of John Peeler of Vernon and
Jonathan Witt of Wilmington. Both were repeated in the *Yeoman* on Aug. 19 and 26.

dependant on him, under Providence, for their daily bread—That when a youth he engaged in the revolutionary army, and fought during the whole war, until our Independence was established.—That he has lived to see the day when all the blessings which our old patriots used to tell us in our day of trouble would succeed our labours in the field, have been bestowed abundantly upon their posterity. But while thousands who were then unborn, are now rejoicing and flourishing, and eating and drinking, faring sumptuously, and enjoying the fruits of the old soldier's labours, your petitioner is poor, depressed—and his wife and family in want of almost the common necessaries of life—and what little they do receive is from day to day procured by his labours—That your petitioner has been committed to gaol on a small demand—That unable to pay it, he took the poor man's oath—That while in confinement he found that the State made no provision for the support of poor debtors, and he should actually have starved had it not been for the humanity of the gaoler, and a worthy family in the neighbourhood—That by the charity of some Christian friends in Brattleborough, he was released from prison, and had just returned to his family, when this day he is arrested, and is now going with the officer to close confinement, leaving his family to suffer while he takes once more the poor man's oath.

Now your petitioner humbly prays his creditors, if not for his sake, for their own; that they would not oppress him and his family, without the least profit to themselves—The old soldier, Honoured Creditors, who fought for the blessings you now enjoy, is not envious of your prosperity—he can rejoice to see you rich, if he is poor—but Washington, Green, Sullivan, and all his old commanders are departed, and but few of the old revolutionary soldiers remain—and we hope soon to go where there are no gaols, or single writs. Pray do not give us cause to curse the government we fought to establish; but rather, though we are poor, allow us to walk abroad in the fresh air, and rejoice in your prosperity.—And as in duty bound shall ever pray.

GEORGE LOVELAND.

Brattleborough, Aug. 7.

* * * * *

AMERICAN YEOMAN.
Brattleborough, Tuesday, August 19, 1817.

William Cobbett.—Soon after this political fugitive sought safety in the United States, and announced the publication of a periodical paper, we considered it to be our bounden duty to guard our republican friends against committing themselves by a decided approbation and patronage of a writer who came among us in a questionable character, and whose versatile pen had so often put his applauders and patrons to open shame. Our admonitions were re-printed by but few of our more independent brethren of the type, while the great body of editors on both sides of the question, if they did not applaud, at least preserved a respectful silence as to Mr. Cobbett and the fungi of his transported press.

We considered his retreat from Great Britain as a recreant abandonment of his friends in the hour of danger.

And we augured that he would terminate his visit by abusing those who might applaud and patronize him.

The correctness of our former position is amply confirmed by Mr. Wooler's "Farewel to Mr. Cobbett," which occupied four or five columns of our last number.

As to our second position, we have before us in its support his Political Register of July 31, 1817, entitled "The Last Hundred Days of British Liberty." Perhaps the glittering annals of flattery do not afford a more egregious example of adulation, than has heretofore been bestowed by Cobbett upon Sir Francis Burdett—in Cobbett's phrase, the Great, the Profound, the Learned, the Eloquent, the Patriotick Sir Francis Burdett—And yet this whole number of his Register, containing 16 large octavo pages, is devoted to abuse and belittle this same paragon of political perfection, Sir Francis Burdett—and we are promised another number to the same consistant effect.

We cannot, therefore, consider ourselves to have been uncandid or unfounded in our opinion of Mr. Wm. Cobbett; and we can render by analogy a pithy reason for our preconceived opinion:—Our children sometimes take a cub fox and rear it up in the family. It will play a thousand pretty tricks, and by its activity and gambols amuse and delight the simple young folks mightily. But discerning people know that this cub will one day make havock in the poultryyard, and become so mischievous, that he will make those curse the hour that they entertained him. How do these discerning ones know this? Why they know, and we know—"*It is the nature of the beast.*"

* * * * *

SMALL TALK.

Singular Scarecrow!—A farmer near Herkimer (N.Y.) last spring manufactured a sort of likeness about the size of one of the would be kings of New-England, to which he affixed this label in large letters, —"HARTFORD CONVENTION."[67] The consequence was that neither Crow nor Black Worm destroyed a single blade of corn in that field, nor for any considerable distance around.

In another field, "it is said," he exposed a board, decorated with white roses, on which it was written in flaming capitals, "WASHINGTON BENEVOLENT SOCIETY."[68] It had the same effect —all the crows and worms; and even Woodchucks quitted the premises. Some of the learned in the nature of crows imagine that these unerring birds were apprehensive, that they might be taken to be members of the society, and concluded it proper to imitate the Benevolents, by skulking into obscurity about these times.—Hence we learn that the Hartford Convention and Washington Benevolent

[67] New England Federalists felt that the national government was sacrificing commercial interests by imposing an embargo during the War of 1812. In turn, the government feared that the New England mercantile class would attempt to secede from the union. The Federalists met in secret session at Hartford during December, 1814–January, 1815, to discuss a course of action but the victory at New Orleans precluded further action.

[68] The first society was founded in Alexandria, Va., in 1800 but the movement did not grow until 1808, reaching a peak of more than 200 by 1815. It was an attempt by younger Federalists to band together in a fraternal and political society so as to survive in the face of Jeffersonian republicanism.

Societies are good for something, not withstanding the unmerited abuse cast on them by the Democrats.

*   *   *   *   *

SMALL TALK.

Look out girls—A market for dairy-women. An opulent planter on the banks of West River, near Annapolis, Maryland, requested a traveller from this vicinity to send him a good dairy-woman—gravely observing, that he would give a Thousand Dollars for a girl who could make good cheese. The traveller replied, that we did not sell that *kind of stock* in New-England.—The old man concluded, by his advice, to send his son to get him a New-England wife, and the young man is directed to choose his wife by tasting her cheese.—So, *look out girls.*[69]

*   *   *   *   *

SMALL TALK.

Rhodomontade.—A traveller, on his return from the State of Ohio, where he had been to purchase a farm, in that "land of milk and honey," gave this account of the State of Promise: "Sir—As I was driving my team, I observed a hat in the path; I reached with my whip-stick to take it up from the mud.——'What are you doing with my hat?' cried a voice under it. I soon discovered under the chapeau a brother emigrant, up to his ears in the mire. 'Pray let me help you out,' said I.—'Thank you,' said the bemired traveller, 'I have a good long-legged horse under me, who has carried me through worse

---

[69] This piece appeared in the *Yeoman* of Sept. 2. No more "Small Talk" was published until Oct. 14. A number of legal notices, however, were printed in the interval. On Sept. 19 Tyler wrote in the "Day Book," "Drafted Petition for Divorce—Persis Haywood vs. David Haywood, sent to Yeoman." This advertisement, signed by Tyler as Mrs. Haywood's attorney, appeared in the paper on Sept. 23 and was reprinted on Sept. 30, Oct. 7 and Oct. 14. Notices attested by Tyler for the estates of Park Holland of Newfane, Joseph Goodale of Marlboro and James Boyden of Guilford appeared on Oct. 7, 14 and 21.

sloughs than this: I am only stopping to breathe my nag; as this is the firmest footing I have found in fifty miles.'

"Driving my team a little further, I saw my old neighbour Restless, from merry-meeting Bay, up to his waistband in a puddle of water. 'What are you after there, neighbour?' 'Only resting myself a bit.' 'Resting yourself? what a foolish fellow you are to stop to rest in a puddle of water.' 'Not so foolish as you think, neighbour Grumble. This hole, d'you see, holds water—and so I *guess* it has got a bottom: and by jingo this is the only spot in the Ohio roads where I have found any bottom for seventy miles on end—' "

It is computed (but we will not vouch its accuracy, though the computation was made by an industrious maiden lady, who marked the numbers with her knitting pin on the lid of her snuff box, and is positive she is correct to a single pole) that since the 1st of June last there have passed through this village, to take the turnpike over the Green Mountains, on their way to the west and south western parts of the Union,

> 132 Men,
> 194 Women, (not including old maids)
> 234 Boys and girls,
> and   64 Sucking babies,

transported by 36 ox-teams, 42 horse do. principally from Massachusetts proper, New-Hampshire and this state: besides 17 one-horse wagons, 1 handcart, and a wheel-barrow from the District of Maine.

> 26 Returned *on foot.*

Kentucky, Louisiana, Mississippi, and Ohio, tho' to be sure they very much resemble it in some particulars, cannot be said to be that

> ——————— "undiscovered country,
> From whose bourne no traveller returns,"

For we daily see,

> "Faint and wearily, the way-worn traveller,"

retracing his "weary way" from the land of golden hopes and agues, to his native regions of competency and health.

"Paris, Aug. 11.—Prince Talleyrand was lately riding to his calash in Pau, when his horse ran away and threw him into a hollow 11 feet deep; but neither he nor any of the persons in his company were seriously hurt."

Now we can see nothing extraordinary in all this. Prince Talleyrand has in his day fallen into many deeper holes than this, and, when all supposed he was killed, came out unhurt. To be sure, we cannot observe the same of many of his old companions.

* * * * *

SMALL TALK.

We were much amused with the exhibition of the honest prejudices of a Connecticut ambulating merchant, who was returning home through this village, from a long indigo voyage. It so happened, that one of our neighbours was reading the candid account of the late election in that renovated state, from the American Mercury of Tuesday last, when the following dialogue ensued:

Itinerant Merchant.—If I may be so bold, what paper is that you are reading?

Vermonter—The American Mercury, printed at Hartford, Connecticut, by Elisha Babcock & Son.

It. Mer.—Our Minister says it is edited by the father of lies, and so says our deacon, and so says the squire—but do let us hear what new lies old Bab. has conjured up, to deceive the poor ignorant Democrats.

Verm.—The paper says, that Connecticut has become the most Democratick state in the union.

It. Mer.—Whew!!!

Verm.—There is 72 Democratick majority in the House of Representatives.

It. Mar.—That's a whapper with a vengeance!

Verm.—The House of Representatives have elected a Republican speaker, and two Democratick Clerks.

It. Mer.—I guess now——you are poking fun at me. Come, say so, and I'll treat.

Verm.—Hear more: the old Steady-Habit Councillors are put out of the nomination.

It. Mer.—They dare not do that. None of your tricks upon travellers. The Democrats, I know, are pretty bold of late—but they dare not *stand up* and vote against the wisest, the best, and most pious men in the state—Any more of Bab's lies?

Verm.—The Democratick House of Representatives was opened with prayer, by the Rev. Mr. Mervin.

It. Merchant.—Aye, now I've caught you—now I know it is all a Democratick Jacobin fudge.——Democrats pray!—ha? ha? Democrats have any religion?——That's a good one. I guess you don't know Democrats. Our minister says that they burn every bible that comes in their way—and that they would burn the meeting-houses and the ministers in them, if it were not that we stuck so close to Steady-Habits—and so says our deacon, and so says our squire.

———

Ludicrous Antithesis.—There is a very pleasant antithesis in the Connecticut Herald, published by Messrs. Flagg & Gray, New-Haven. After detailing, in a lurid and handsome style, the debates in the House of Representatives, these Editors make the following "Note.— We are not permitted to give the proceedings of the Council. They sit in *secret,* because their business is of a *publick* nature."

* * * * *

SMALL TALK.

For a number of weeks past we have seen in the papers notices of a new celebrated actress in London, who has recently made her appearance in this country. The following paragraphs have been in type some time, and were omitted to make room for more *important* matters.

MISS CARRABOO.[70]

A gentleman who left Philadelphia on Tuesday morning, called on the editors yesterday, and communicated the following particulars respecting Miss Mary Baker, alias Miss Carraboo.

He informs us that he is recently from Whiteredge, in Devonshire, where Miss Carraboo was brought up, and says he knows her connections. He states that Miss Baker is a most beautiful woman, now about twenty years of age, rather tall, but elegantly formed, her hair, eyes and eyebrows are very black; she writes the Carraboo language with great facility, having made several private exhibitions of her capability in this respect in Philadelphia. Our informant adds, that a number of gentlemen in Philadelphia have taken a warm interest in her behalf, having satisfied themselves of the rarity of her character and views. Under the charge and direction of those gentlemen this beautiful and fascinating young lady will, in a few days, exhibit herself at the Philadelphia Washington Hall, in the same dress which she wore in England when *hoxing* the people of Bristol. As soon as the curiosity of the Philadelphians is satisfied, Miss Carraboo intends to visit this city. In the mean time, we expect a further and more minute sketch of this singular stranger.——*N.Y. Gaz.*[71]

MISS CARRABOO.

The English papers have represented Miss Carraboo as being a great

[70] The Englishwoman, Mary Baker, alias "Carraboo," created a considerable stir during her United States tour of 1817, although she had already been exposed as a fraud in her homeland. Among the books which outlined the deception are: *Full Particulars of the Life, Character, and Adventures of Carraboo, alias Mary Baker* (Bristol: Harry Bonner [1817?]); Walter Bates, *Companion for Caraboo* [*sic*]. *A Narrative of the Conduct and Adventures of Henry Frederic Moon . . . And a Postscript, Containing Some Account of Caraboo, the Late Female Imposter* . . . (London: Allman & Co., 1817); and *Caraboo. A Narrative of a Singular Imposition, Practiced . . . by a Young Woman of the Name of Mary Willcocks, alias Baker, alias Bakerstenddht, alias Caraboo, Princess of Javasu. . . .* (Bristol: J. M. Gutch. London: Balwin, Cradock & Joy, 1817).

[71] This report appeared in the *New York Gazette & General Advertiser*, XXVIII, No. 11161 (Sept. 13, 1817), 2. Printed immediately below it was a notice from Mary Baker, admitting to the pseudonym "Carraboo." Other stories on Carraboo appeared in the same newspaper on Sept. 20 and 30, and Oct. 7 and 20, all on p. 2.

diver and an expert swimmer. If the following can be relied upon, they have not violated the truth.

N.Y. Eve. Post.

From the Patterson, (N. J.) Express, Sept. 24.[72]

Miss Carraboo, lately arrived from England, visited on the 20th of Sept. 1817, with a few confidential friends, the Passaick Falls, she precipitated herself, in their presence, from the highest rock, down into the basin, performed some wonderful exploits in the swimming way, and then to the great astonishment of the spectators, swam up the falls to the summit of the rock, where she was received with repeated cheers by her companions.

In witness whereof she with her friends have signed this with their names in the Carraboo language.

To the Editors of the Norfolk and Portsmouth Herald.[73]

Gentlemen—Having seen it mentioned in a late New-York paper, that the famous Miss Carraboo, whose arrival at Philadelphia you noticed in your paper some time past, was about to pay a visit to New-York, I beg leave through the medium of your paper, to undeceive the publick upon that highly important subject; Miss Carraboo, allow me to say, has lately arrived in this borough, and rented the brick house, No. 1, near the head of Talbot-street, where she has established herself with a numerous retinue, and may be seen at all hours of the day. It is a subject of much regret with the respectable inhabitants of that neighbourhood, that for decency's sake the police of the borough have not, ere this, waited on her ladyship and conducted her and her maids of honour to more suitable lodgings. This

[72] This item was carried in the *New York Evening Post*, No. 4771 (Sept. 25, 1817), 2. A biography of Carraboo had been printed in No. 4766 (Sept. 19, 1817), 2.

[73] Printed in the *New-York Evening Post*, No. 4776 (Oct. 1, 1817), 2. Another notice of Carraboo had appeared in No. 4772 (Sept. 26, 1817), 2.

much for the present, messrs editors: perhaps you may hear more of it by and bye.

I am,

NO JOKER.

A publisher in England posted at his door, the following notice, to draw the attention of the publick:—Here is to be had the full, true, and particular account of Miss Caraboo, the wonderful lady who dropt from the clouds, and speaks the language of the moon.

The curiosity excited by the appearance of Miss Carraboo in Philadelphia seems to have excited the displeasure of certain of our brethren of the type, who appear to consider it rather degrading to the Philadelphians to be imposed upon by a last English hoax—but it seems they have not rightly considered the subject. The citizens of Philadelphia did not go to see this out-cast as the London folks did, supposing her to be a Japanese Princess—but merely to see what awkward imitations of Royalty can impose upon the credulity of Englishmen.

———

By keeping up the hacknied cry of "dull times for news," which from every quarter assails our ears, we are almost induced to believe, that our readers think we are culpable for the unparalled scarcity of this *valuable* commodity—as though we had at command, not only the boisterous elements of nature, which produce hurricanes, tornadoes, and the like—but also the more unwieldy, incongruous, and wicked passions of man, from whence proceed the desolating scourge of wars; which together, in the estimation of some news-mongers, produce all the *pleasing varieties* that can profitably occupy the columns of a newspaper.—Now, if there are any among our patrons who have thus egregiously misapprehended the nature of their contract with the printer, be it known to them, that, so far from having the absolute control of these gigantick engines of destruction, he is the most dependent and impotent creature living.

*   *   *   *   *

COMMUNICATION.[74]

The period has at length arrived, when a Republican Government is generally acknowledged to possess both strength and permanency. Altho' few people have been dissatisfied with the constitution since its adoption, yet there have been some ambitious men, and other perhaps from principle, who have occasionally suggested their doubts of its utility; and even gone so far as to predict the time of its final dissolution. An eminent writer (Mr. Ames)[75] has compared it with a white birch root, which can retain its soundness only a certain number of years—while others have considered it well adapted to the sunshine of peace, but incapable of withstanding the more gloomy season of war.

Whatever may have been the source of these ominous conjectures, the whole train of events, from the days of Fisher Ames, down to the present, incontestibly prove them to have been groundless. The fiery ordeal through which we have recently been obliged to pass, and which many feared would prove injurious to the constitution, has given it additional strength and vigour.

The prudent and effective measures which it enabled the administration to pursue, in prosecuting and bringing the war to an honourable conclusion, have greatly increased the reputation of our constitution abroad, and augmented the citizen's confidence at home. In proof of this, we need only refer to the result of the elections, which, in every

[74] This column of Nov. 4 entitled "Communication" and a similarly headed one on Nov. 11 are placed in Tyler's canon because they are both signed with the initial "S", the most popular disguise of his literary career.

An editorial note immediately following this column stated that the *Yeoman* office had received the first two numbers of Joseph T. Buckingham's new Boston publication, *New England Galaxy & Masonick Magazine.* In his "Day Book" (p. 57) on March 6, 1818, Tyler noted, "Mail arrived from Boston—brought letter ... from Buckingham proposing that I should write for Masonick Magazine—".

The contributions Tyler sent to the *New-England Galaxy* are reprinted below, pp. 427–37.

[75] Fisher Ames (1758–1808), publicist, statesman and orator. A Federalist, he defeated Samuel Adams to be elected to the 1st Congress. Ames was re-elected to the 2nd, 3rd and 4th Congresses but declined to stand for another term in 1796. A brilliant man, he was noted for his eloquence and his speech on the Jay Treaty in April, 1796, has been called one of the greatest ever heard in Congress.

department, since the machinations of foreign enemies, and domestick malcontents were baffled, have uniformly terminated in favour of government—and the increasing interest with which every thing "relating to America is heard and observed in Europe."——The reasons, therefore, for the durability of our national government are too obvious to admit the idea of affixing to it any determinate limits.

S.

* * * * *

SMALL TALK.

A singing-master in the vicinity, whilst teaching his pupils, was visited by a brother of the tuneful art. The visitor observing that this chorister pitched the tunes *vocally,* said, "Sir, you do not use a pipe?" ——"No sir, I *chew,*" with admirable gravity replied Semi-breve.

"IN HOC EST HOAX CUM QUIZ."

Mr. Yeoman—A great deal of noise has been made in this country by the outlandish name of Miss CARRABOO. This is a name which one might suppose would make fun—and it has made fun enough. CARRABOO has not doubt been spoken more than 20,000,000 times in the U.S. since it was reported that the Bristol hoaxer was coming to this country. Indeed, CARRABOO, is now become the fashionable word for little babies to begin to talk with, and the old expression "*ah goo!*" is no more thought of by them. When it was said she had arrived in Philadelphia, the newspapers rang from Maine to Georgia with the information. Some styled her "the innocent and interesting, the accomplished Miss Mary Baker." Some said, "Miss Baker"—and one in Baltimore, with a horrible grin, vociferated, "*Poll* Baker"—and among them all, there was a most prodigious *Carrabooing, Baker-booing,* and all sorts of *booing.*—Now, Mr. Yeoman, this great stir is *boo et preterea nihit*; for no such person has ever been in this country, or in England: no *hoax* has been played, unless upon the punning Philadelphians, by the pretended appearance of the *lunatick lady* at the concert, and upon the editors of the newspapers and others,

who have told the story. It is time now to undeceive the *bam-boo-zled* publick, in this matter, and begin some new joke.   Yours, &c.
                                    LARRABOOREE.[76]

*   *   *   *   *

COMMUNICATION.

Perhaps there is no nation, in which political economy is so much an object of individual consideration, and none in which it is so much under the influence of publick opinion, as in the United States. In G. Britain, where the people neither make laws, nor, in reality, choose those who legislate, the national expenditure and necessary taxes are almost wholly under the control of a nobility and king. The revenue and debts of government are subjects about which the great mass of the community are generally uninformed, and over which they have very little influence. They know when their taxes become oppressive —but they likewise know, that any exertions on their part to remove them are regarded only "as the idle wind"—Their humble petitions may be thrown with impunity under the table; and their mobs receive correction from the gibbet and the halter. From circumstances like these the nation is involved in debt, and the poor in want. Of 16,000,000 of inhabitants, not less than one sixteenth part are said to be actual paupers, dependant upon publick charity for subsistence.— Hence, likewise, the extravagant pay of the military, and the enormous salaries of civil officers.

From such evils the United States is exempted. The citizen is neither deprived of natural rights, nor burdened with unnecessary and excessive taxes. The national expenditure, which, in time of peace, principally consists of office-salaries, is much less than in any nation, equal in wealth and population. This mode of administration derives its cheapness, not more from the patriotism of publick officers, who in some instances are at liberty to assess their own wages, than from a spirit of economy in the people. The magistrate being the servant of

[76] In this same issue of the paper, Nov. 4, there is a notice attested by Tyler as Register of Probate for the estate of John Underwood of Guilford. It was reprinted on Nov. 25.

his constituents, is obliged to serve them for what it is really worth. Hence no salary is extravagant, while some, perhaps, particularly in the judiciary departments, are less than the duties of the office justly merit.[77]

S.

* * * * *

SMALL TALK.
From the Columbian Centinel.

NOTICE.

A young gentleman, of good family and estate, aged about 25 years, who has a fine house, well furnished, wishes to obtain a partner for life, who possesses the following qualifications:—A humble heart, subdued and influenced by grace, which prosperity will neither too much elate nor adversity deject; a uniform, mild and amiable temper, which the trifling incidents of life will not easily irritate; a well cultivated mind, with an improved taste for reading, graceful and pleasing manners, rather modest than assuming; habits of prudence and industry; a decided partiality for domestick enjoyments, a good healthy constitution; respectable parentage, and a fortune of from ten to twenty Thousand Dollars. If there is a young lady within three hundred miles of this place, between eighteen and twenty two years of age, who really possesses these qualifications, and is willing to unite herself with a man whose happiness would consist in endeavours to render her happy; and whose united fortunes under the blessings of providence, would render them independent and even affluent through life. She may open the way to become acquainted with one who would endeavour to be such, by addressing a line prior to the first day of January next, with the postage paid, to J. Z. D. to the care of the Editor of the Columbian Centinel, in Boston, stating place of residence, and such other particulars as may be considered necessary.

November 19.

---

[77] Tyler had a personal interest in this subject. While he was Chief Justice of Vermont his salary had been only $1,000 annually.

Within three hundred miles of Boston.

The Editor of the Columbian Centinel, is respectfully requested, to inform Mr. J. Z. D. that there are in Vermont, above fifty Young Ladies, who will suit his description to a single dimple: with each a fortune, from fifty to one hundred thousand dollars, at her own disposal; as per margin—But the Gentleman "in the fine house well furnished" must condescend, to come and sigh among our mountains, for unfortunately there is not one of these accomplished *heiresses* who possesses so humble a heart, as to attempt a *Courting Voyage,* even through the channel of a Courtly Newspaper. Like Milton's Eve

"They would be woo'd; and not unsought be won."

P.S. Postage saved—

Inventory of the *Personal Estate* of each of the Young Ladies abovesaid—

In possession—

Two Ruby Lips	appraised at	$ 10,000
A pair of Diamond eyes—Brilliants of the first water, *weight 60 carats,*		15,000
A profusion of Golden tresses,		5,000
A mouth full of *Ora-entel* and dental pearls, $500 each,		12,000
Two Carnation cheeks and sundry deep ingrained blushes,		5,000
An ivory skin and Alabaster neck,		7,000
One charming tongue tip'd with the silver accents of kindness and modesty,		20,000
		$ 74,000

In expectency—

On the decrease of maiden life she will become a Crown of Gold to her husband at a fair price in the market valued at	30,000
	$104,000[78]

[78] In the Dec. 16 issue of the *Yeoman* Tyler recorded estate notices for the heirs of Jonathan Gates of Whitingham and Philip Maxwell, both of Guilford. The latter one was also reprinted in Dec. 23.

* * * * *

SMALL TALK.

An oppulent farmer in a neighboring town, who had long been accustomed to the cheering comforts of a good blazing fire, burning in a capacious old-fashioned fireplace, was urged by his sons to cover up the fireplace, and replace it with a Cooking Stove—. "I love," said the old man, "when I come in from work, to pull off my boots and set down before a comfortable fire:—the very sight of the blaze refreshes me. I don't love to part with the sight of this old friend." *Son.* "Father, wood grows scarce and these stoves, the merchants say, will save half the wood."—*Father.* "Well, son, tell the merchants to let you have *two* Cooking Stoves, then, and that will save the *whole of it.*"[79]

* * * * *

FOR THE YEOMAN.[80]

MR. EDITOR,

You will oblige a number of your subscribers in this place, by re-publishing the following letters from the Rev. Ignatius Thompson, late minister of the Gospel of Christ in Pomfret, in this state. Though some time has passed since they were first published, yet we believe "the warning voice" may be well-timed in even these days.—The disgraceful scenes of riot nearly approaching bloodshed, and the state of confusion into which the once flourishing College of Dartmouth, at Hanover has been brought, are but the fruits of the overbearing and

[79] An advertisement for such a type of "patent fire place" was inserted in the *Yeoman* on Dec. 30, 1817, and Jan. 13, 1818. This particular example, which the ad said could be examined "at the bookstore in Brattleborough and also at the tavern in Walpole, N.H." had been invented by a William Salisbury of Derby, Vt.

[80] On Dec. 28 in the "Day Book" Tyler wrote: "Mr. Ide here in Even'g—Wrote some small talk—Slaves—Notice to Correspondents, head of Rev'd Ig. Thompson letters—"

The "head" of the Thompson column is included here. The letters, between Thompson and an unidentified correspondent [*Tyler?*], are dated in 1813 and deal with the political involvement of some clergymen in the affairs of the University of Vermont.

uncharitable spirit of Despotism which good Mr. Thompson mentions in his letters.

Halifax, December 23, 1817.

* * * * *

AMERICAN YEOMAN.
Brattleboro, Tuesday, January 13, 1817.[81]

In our last we reluctantly compiled with the request of certain of our subscribers in Halifax, in publishing the letters of Mr. Thompson. —Whatever may have been agitated by our Rev. Clergy at the dates given by Mr. Thompson,—we could not for a moment give credence to imputations against any denominations of professors of the present day, so criminally henious, as he has laid to the charge of the Congregationalists. We do not believe there are any so much the enemies of the peace of society, and so much at war with the precepts of the religion they are commissioned to propagate, as to seriously engage in such schemes; and unless we had the most positive proof of it, it would be an unpardonable dereliction of duty to pass by, without comment, any thing which might indicate a different opinion.— Neither do we think that the great mass of the federalists, at any period, were justly chargeable with the intentions attributed to them in these letters. In the heat of party strife, they no doubt did many things which later experience has proved were impolitick: and this may be said with regard to the republicans, or any description of partizans, who have suffered their passions to get the better of their reason. But now we have done with those petty contentions; candour and liberality have moved the veil of prejudice: we no longer war about names. It is our duty, as well as our interest, to drop all animadversions, upon any subject, which tend to revive those disagreeable animosities; and, if there is any contention among us, to strive for

[81] Apparently the Thompson letters stirred up more reader reaction than Tyler and Ide anticipated. Although this column cannot be definitely attributed to Tyler, it is included here as a very probable fruit of his pen, attempting to explain the *Yeoman's* position in publishing the letters in the previous issue.

such objects as can be obtained without the sacrifice of order and decorum—such objects as will promote the general prosperity of our beloved country—in a word—to contend for that most satisfactory object, the heartfelt

—————————— "luxury of *doing good*."

Even were it true, that one, two, nay, half a dozen ministers of the Gospel have so far strayed from the paths of primitive virtue and simplicity, as to hanker after the "flesh-pots of Egypt"—as long for the arrival of the time, when those of their persuasion (no matter whether they be baptists, quakers, methodists, episcopalians, &c.) shall become a privileged order, or be endowed with exemptions and benefices not equally extended to every sect—admitting this to be the case—can they entertain the most distant hope of ever seeing their wishes consummated? No; verily we believe they cannot. The people of America know too well the condition of those countries where such things are in fashion, to suffer their introduction among us. They too well remember the stories of their venerable ancestors, to give ear to the craving voice of such anti-Christian pretenders. They have no idea of relinquishing so soon the sweet endearments of social life, and seeking, in "the watery waste," another unexplored Columbia, on which the hand of fanaticks has not laid its iron grasp. No—we aver, the time is far distant, when they will forget the import of the word, AMERICAN—when that appellation shall no longer entitle its possessor to such "modes of faith" and worship, as comport most clearly with his acceptations of the Word of God.

Perhaps our correspondent can furnish further proof of the existence of such designs as Mr. Thompson has attributed to a portion of our Rev. Clergy. If this be really the case, (which we think is far otherwise,) it would be uncharitable and unjust to condemn the whole for the faults of a few. It is an acknowledged maxim, that every persuasion has its bad, as well as good members.—But until such proof is exhibited, we shall adhere to the belief, that *all* upright ministers—all, of *every denomination,* who profess and practice the doctrines of the "meek and lowly" Redeemer, will ever condemn a connexion of church and state, as an unhallowed profanation of their character and calling.

We sincerely regret having had occasion for these remarks—and hope they will do away any erroneous impressions which the unseasonable introduction of Mr. Thompson's letters into our last may have left upon the minds of any of our readers. We would not intentionally lift a finger to wound the feelings of any sincere Christian:—above all things would we avoid giving rise to, or, in any case, participating in *religious controversies*; especially at a time, when, from a want of other employment of our will-natured propensities, such controversies would defeat the benign purposes for which our holy religion was given us:—subvert the order and harmony among families and neighbours it so forcibly inculcates,—and eventually being unmerited reproach upon the best institution man ever enjoyed.

* * * * *

Addenda[82]

Aboriginals
Negroes—
  Ladies coming from Clerical Lecture—vide loose sheet.
  Address complimentary to our English ancestors, "Land of [. . .] of Arts and [*ancestors?*]." Loose sheet.
  Half witted Tom—who draws watter and runs errands for all the poor widows in the village—and who cannot distinguish a cent from an Eagle—old manuscript—
  Village school—education perfected without the aid of the rod—Apostrophe to the Patroness unborn—Discription of the Preceptress. See my brain—
  Happiness of the village to be correctly attributed to the early

[82] This piece exists only in a holograph manuscript by Tyler appended to a fair copy manuscript of "The Chestnut Tree." It is included in this volume as a possible memorandum on the article on slaves Tyler said he was writing for Ide on Dec. 28 (see above, footnote 80). The actual column was never printed before Ide's departure from Brattleboro a few weeks later.

settlement of printing and the diffusion of Knowledge of the books edited and brought here.

Joseph—When you have inserted the sketch of the Moonstruck—no—moon light lovers—then tack on the Finale—and contrive to annex this memorandum to the Manuscript—that if we should feel disposed hereafter to finish the works we may know where to apply for the fragments & [. . .]thing.—

The great lesson taught by Solomon that there is nothing new under the Sun. Fashions may change but the human heart, its passions, virtues & follies is the same in all ages—near the C[. . .]—

The Law Cases

DESPITE TYLER'S considerable output as a versifier, novelist and essayist, it must not be forgotten that literature was only an avocation and that the law was his chosen career. That he served long and well in his profession was recognized in his own day but outside of a few anecdotes about his eloquence and wit before the bar and the learning he brought to the bench, little concrete is known of his talents as an attorney and judge.[1]

It is known that he was successful in every regard except one. His generosity and kindness to the unfortunate prevented his practice from ever providing him and his own large family with an overly comfortable way of life. To Tyler this was apparently something relatively unimportant. If he could help the downtrodden he was willing to forego for himself the monetary rewards of his practice.

Tyler's youthful career as an attorney started in Boston when, after his graduation from Harvard and several years of reading law, he was admitted to the Suffolk County Inferior Court of Common Pleas on August 19, 1780.[2] Following a short period of practice in Quincy and Braintree, Massachusetts, Tyler went to Falmouth, District of Maine, but his stay there was brief.[3]

In January, 1791, he made his decision to build a future in the new State of Vermont. It appears his talents and personality found favor with the local populace since his docket for the June, 1793, term of court at Windsor showed 63 cases, of which 22 were new ones that term. During the succeeding November term he pleaded 48 cases, 22 of which were again new.[4]

---

[1] Examples of these anecdotes and selected details of Tyler's legal career are contained in: Frederick Tupper, "Royall Tyler, Man of Law and Man of Letters," *Proceedings of the Vermont Historical Society*, IV (1928), 65–101; Thomas Pickman Tyler, "Royall Tyler," *Argus and Patriot*, Montpelier, Vt. (Nov. 5, 1879), 1 (reprinted in *Vermont Bar Association Proceedings, 1878–1881*, 44–62); Henry Burnham, *Brattleboro, Windham County, Vermont. An Early History* (Brattleboro, 1880), p. 101; Tanselle, *Royall Tyler*, pp. 34–46; Taft, "Royall Tyler," *The Green Bag*, XX (1908), 1–5; and "TPT Memoir," pp. 19–20, 83–84, 123, 152–70, 175–78, 180–87, 195–203, 234–36, 279–84.

[2] Tyler was recommended for admission to the bar by Atty. Benjamin Hichborne on July 18, 1780, but the favorable vote of that day was not officially recorded until Aug. 19. See Ms. Ch. F 11.97 in the Chamberlain Collection, Boston Public Library, and Inferior Court Records, Vol. 1780, Suffolk County Court House, Boston.

[3] An amusing anecdote of Tyler's short sojourn in Falmouth is recounted in William Willis, *The History of Portland* (Portland, 1833), II, 215, and "TPT Memoir," pp. 19–20.

[4] These figures can be arrived at by an examination of the notations of cases taken and pleaded in five different manuscript ledgers (dealing mainly, but not exclusively, with

His rising reputation caused Tyler to be named State's Attorney for Windham County in 1794. He served in that position until October 12, 1801, when he was elected assistant or side judge of the Vermont Supreme Court. In 1807, when the Republicans swept the state election, Chief Justice Jonathan Robinson was elected to the United States Senate and Tyler was sworn in as Vermont's ninth Chief Justice. He served until 1813, in all being elected to the bench twelve times, six as assistant judge and six as Chief Justice.[5]

legal matters) among the Tyler papers in the "RT Collection." Two of these ledgers relate to this period while three cover the years between 1815–1818 (see below, footnote 13). The total is also quoted in "MPT Memoir," p. 114. In 1797 the total of cases in the Vermont courts had increased to 69, together with an unspecified number in New Hampshire jurisdictions. See "TPT Memoir," pp. 83–84, 123.

There is an early holograph decision by Tyler in the case of Reuben Attwater vs. Samuel Damon, Windham County Court, November 1796 term, in the Elliot Papers, p. 35, Boston Public Library.

In the "Vermont State Papers," Office of the Secretary of State, Montpelier (hereafter cited as VSP), are the following manuscript documents relating to Tyler's law practice: Vol. 20, p. 151, Tyler as attorney for James Greenleaf, petition for new trial in Page vs. Greenleaf, Aug. 27, 1798; Vol. 20, p. 356, Tyler's petition for Windsor Turnpike, Oct. 16, 1799; Vol. 44, p. 173, Tyler's petition for new trial in Baxter vs. Tyler, Sept, 25, 1804; Vol. 80, p. 169, Tyler as remonstrator against White River Turnpike, Oct. 16, 1816; Vol. 53, p. 44, Tyler named in petition of Issac French for remission of fine, Oct. 14, 1817; Vol. 53, p. 47, Tyler as attorney for John P. Hill, petition for pardon, Oct. 14, 1817.

[5] Few documents survive from Tyler's days as State's Attorney. The following manuscript material is in the VSP: Vol. 11, p. 154, Tyler's account as State's Attorney for services and expenses in August 1796 term of Supreme Court; Vol. 19, p. 353, petition of Tyler as State's Attorney for appointment of agent to dispose of lands, Oct. 11, 1796; Vol. 11, p. 162, Tyler as State's Attorney named in report of Auditor Elisha Clark, Oct. 26, 1796; Vol. 78, p. 1, statement by Tyler as State's Attorney of actions in favor of State in August 1801 term of Windham County Court, Nov. 2, 1801.

The official document appointing Tyler Chief Justice from Oct. 17, 1809–Oct. 17, 1810, is in the "RT Collection," Ms. No. 810170. It is signed by Gov. Jonas Galusha and embossed with the State Seal. The Vermont Legislature's resolution on the appointment of Tyler as Chief Justice, dated Oct. 15, 1810, for the 1810–1811 term, is found in VSP, Vol. 68, p. 20.

Tyler held the post of Chief Justice the longest of any judge under the old judicial system. For a convenient listing of the state's Supreme Court chief and assistant justices and their years of service, together with a history of the court, see Taft, "The Supreme Court in Vermont." The chart is in VI, 192.

There is also a good section on the court, with details on the atmosphere of the times and a discussion of the major personalities, in "TPT Memoir," p. 132ff. For the friendship which developed between the newly elected Senator Robinson and the newly elected Chief Justice Tyler see pp. 176–77. This ripened into an intimate correspondence of several years duration. Some of these letters are reprinted on p. 195ff. There is a

As Vermont's dominant legal figure, Tyler earned a statewide reputation as a man with a far-reaching intellect and sound legal mind, able to judge fairly on any number of matters of a public interest. Because of this reputation, he was requested by both the Governor and Legislature to head several state commissions, panels or boards.

In October, 1808, Tyler was appointed to chair a commission established to inspect the branches of the Vermont State Bank.[6] Two years later he was a member of another board named to examine and audit the accounts of the commissioner charged with building the State Prison.[7] In 1813 he was involved as chairman of the commission appointed by the State Legislature, charged with investigating and auditing certain accounts of the Middlebury Branch, Vermont State Bank. This case, concerning irregularities in the management of the branch bank, involved several prominent citizens. The matter, which dragged on for some months, required great diplomacy and tact on Tyler's part. The panel, with broad powers to pass final judgement, made a searching examination of the case and returned to the Legislature its findings in favor of the State and against the three individuals charged.[8]

From 1811 to 1814 Tyler was professor of jurisprudence at the University of Vermont at Burlington. He was not in residence at the university and taught courses only when his travels about the state placed him in the proximity of Burlington. He was, however, the first to teach law at the new

---

letter in "TPT Memoir," p. 217, from Robinson to Tyler, dated from Washington, D.C., Feb. 12, 1808, in which the Senator passed on the good reports he had received of Tyler's work on the bench.

None of Tyler's law library exists in the "RT Collection." There is, however, in the general collection of the Vermont Historical Society one of his books autographed on the title page. It is a copy of *The Crown Circuit Companion . . . by W. Stubbs and G. Talmash . . . The Sixth Edition . . .* (Dublin, 1791).

[6] Manuscript documents relating to this commission are in the VSP, Vol. 67, p. 1, and Vol. 74, p. 4. The former, dated Oct. 22, 1808, is the panel's final report on the branches at Burlington, Middlebury, Woodstock and Westminster. It is signed by Tyler and the other judges of the Supreme Court which made up the commission. The latter, dated Oct. 27, 1808, is the judges' request for extra salary for the special sittings of the court constituted as a commission.

[7] See VSP, Vol. 67, p. 20, for the report of the commission, signed by Tyler as chairman, Nov. 2, 1810; and Vol. 68, p. 20, for the original legislative resolution appointing Tyler and the other members of the board, Oct. 25, 1810.

[8] This commission was made up of the three judges of the Supreme Court with Tyler, as Chief Justice, being named chairman. The final report of their investigation, signed by all three and dated Oct. 27, 1813, is in the VSP, Vol. 67, p. 30. There are further resolutions and reports by Tyler and the other two judges in Vol. 68, p. 45 (Oct. 28), and Vol. 74, p. 44 (Nov. 9).

institution. At the time of his appointment to the post he was presented with an honorary Masters of Arts degree by the university.

The last public office he was to hold was Register of Probate for Windham County. He obtained the position in December, 1815, through the kind intercession of Judge Gilbert Denison of Brattleboro, one of the many friends who attempted to help Tyler when his failing health forced a severe curtailment of his law practice. Tyler's deteriorating eyesight forced him finally to relinquish the position in December, 1822.[9]

One of the highlights of Tyler's career was the publication of *Reports of Cases Argued and Determined in the Supreme Court of Judicature of the State of Vermont*. The two volumes which were finally published were issued by the New York printer, Isaac Riley, in 1809 and 1810. They cover the years 1800 to 1803 and contain the cases decided by the Supreme Court in Vermont during that period.[10]

Tyler had no assistance in compiling the two volumes, outside of the notes sent to him by his fellow justices.[11] The two books were completely his own work. He gathered together the resumé of the facts in each case, presented the pleadings of the attorneys and concluded with the opinion or opinions handed down by the bench.

In Tyler's day there were no court reporters in the Vermont judicial system and the reporting of cases was a haphazard affair, dependent mostly on the willingness or ability of the various judges to take notations of the cases which came before the court. Tyler was, apparently, diligent in this regard since the reports of the cases for 1800–1803 which he assembled for publication in 1809–1810 seem to be quite complete and well edited.

At times, however, the irregularity of available notes resulted in an un-

---

[9] "MPT Diary" for that date records the unfortunate event. The entries for the days and months preceding recount Tyler's declining health and inability to attend to his duties. On June 10, 1822, Mrs. Tyler lamented that her sick husband had to travel to the Newfane County Court with one cent in his pocket.

[10] See above, pp. 287.

[11] A Ms. letter from Isaac Tichenor to Tyler, dated from Bennington, Vt., Nov. 29, 1810, mentions the help Tichenor was giving Tyler with the first volume of the reports (in the Wilbur Collection, Guy W. Bailey Library, University of Vermont). The two volumes were well received. For example, see the following letters: Tyler to Orsamus C. Merrill (Sen. Robinson's son-in-law and postmaster at Bennington), dated from Brattleboro, March 22, 1809 ("TPT Memoir," pp. 255–56); Tyler to Robinson, dated from Brattleboro, March, 1809 (*Ibid.*, pp. 256–57); Robinson to Tyler, dated from Washington, *c.* March, 1809 (*Ibid.*); William A. Palmer (later Senator and Governor) to Tyler, dated from Danville, Vt., July 21, 1810 (*Ibid.*, p. 278); and R. C. Mallery to Tyler, dated from Castleton, Vt., Aug. 3, 1810 (*Ibid.*).

evenness in the quality of the reporting.[12] In footnotes Tyler admitted that the reports of certain cases were imperfect, in others he attempted to cover these inadequacies by saying that because of the length of the pleading or the duplication of certain testimony he was abridging the report of a particular case.

By and large, however, the transcription of the judges' decisions is better than the resumés of the facts of the cases. Probably because he had time to revise them thoroughly, Tyler's decisions are always cogent and most readable. Considering the verbage of his profession and the state of law in that era, his opinions can be easily understood by modern readers. He is logical in his exposition of the facts and the law and his facility with the English language helped him put forth his thoughts in a clear fashion.

Tyler's surviving correspondence, his ledgers and "Day Book" preserve some of the sketchy details of his legal career. Unfortunately, the actual opinions he wrote and delivered, due to the above mentioned poor system of law reporting, have, for the most part, been lost.[13] This section will present all those opinions, charges to the jury or other comments from the bench by Tyler which are now available. These number nine with a fragmentary note of one other.[14]

[12] The problems encountered in gathering these notes are well illustrated in a letter from Sen. Robinson to Tyler, dated from Bennington, April 25–26, 1809 (in the Wilbur Collection). Robinson said, "I have rolled and packed all my minutes agreeable to your Request . . ." In a postscript, however, he added, "I know of no way to get them to you . . . as there is a half bushell of them."

[13] The only records are a few scattered single sheets in manuscript, the "Day Book" which presents some citations of Tyler's legal affairs between 1817–1821, and the above mentioned manuscript ledgers, all in the "RT Collection."

See specifically Ms. 21 entitled: "Royall Tyler's/ Docket —/ County Court —/ December Term —/ 1818 —"; Ms. 22 entitled: "Royall Tyler Esqr/ Docket/ Windham County Court/ Decr Term 1815"; Ms. 23, undated and untitled docket, two-thirds of the way through there is the notation, "New Entries June 1818 —"; and Ms. 35, an account book in Tyler's hand for March 1818–Dec. 1818 and Jan. 1819–Jan. 1820.

Ms. 21 is especially complete. The contents include records of cases taken and their disposition for the December 1817 and June 1818 terms of court, together with the docket of the Supreme Court for the January 1818 term. The booklet also includes partial reports of two cases: (1) Asa Burns vs. Isaac Webb, Chittenden County Court January 1801 term; and (2) Asa Porter vs. John Russell and Leonard Hodges, undated.

[14] Eight of the cases which will be included below are available in Tyler's own Law Reports. In chronological order they are: Pease vs. Goddard, 1 Tyl. 373 (1802); Adams vs. Brownson, 1 Tyl. 452 (1802); Windover and Hopkins vs. Robbins, 2 Tyl. 1 (1802); Robbins vs. Windover and Hopkins, 2 Tyl. 11 (1802); Selectmen of Windsor vs. Jacob, 2 Tyl. 192 (1802); Rich vs. Trimble, 2 Tyl. 349 (1803); State vs. White, 2 Tyl. 352 (1803); and Bowne et al vs. Graham, 2 Tyl. 411 (1803).

The ninth is Tyler's charge to the jury in the trial of Cyrus Dean, while the frag-

As will be outlined below, the "Blacksnake" affair was historically the most important case in which Tyler became involved. From a legal point-of-view Tyler's opinion in the case of Selectmen *v.* Jacob was his most significant. This landmark case dealt with the question of whether the bill of sale for a slave entered into in another state was valid in Vermont since in its Constitution of 1791 Vermont had been the first state in the union of specifically make slavery illegal.

In 1783 Stephen Jacob, together with a female slave, Dinah, came to Vermont and settled in Windsor. After several years she was hired away from Jacob by others who desired her services. Jacob, knowing that under the laws of Vermont Dinah was not bound to him by slavery, did not contest her departure and did not seek legal redress to recover her.[15]

Many years later, infirm and blind, Dinah became a ward of the town of Windsor when her second owners no longer desired to support her. The selectmen of that community, holding Jacob's title of ownership still valid, sued him for the monies expended by the town for her upkeep.

During the August, 1803, term of the Supreme Court, Tyler ruled that although the laws of the United States and other states might read otherwise, the Vermont Constitution was specific; that slavery in any form was an institution not adapted to the needs of Vermonters. No inhabitant of this state could hold a bill of sale transferring a person as a slave, even though valid in another state, since the moment he became a resident of Vermont the bill of sale became void.

During the February, 1805, term of the Supreme Court in Bennington County, Tyler participated in a case which, at that time, caused widespread local excitement because of the scandalous circumstances surrounding it.

A quack doctor, John Johnson, had been arraigned on the charge of

---

mentary notation deals with the trial of John Johnson for the murder of Hannah Everts. Both are found in "TPT Memoir."

Tanselle, in *Royall Tyler*, p. 239, footnote 101, also lists Tyler as making a statement in Harris *vs.* Huntington *et al*, 1 Tyl. 129 (1802). Tyler did deliver the opinion of the court since Chief Justice Robinson was counsel for the plaintiff. However, it was a *curia* decision, that is, written by the court as a whole, not by a particular judge. Since there is no way of definitely attributing it to Tyler it is not included in this volume. [Tyler also read another *curia* decision in Brackett *vs.* State, 1 Tyl. 152 (1802)]. Tanselle cites Tyler's charge to the jury in Robbins *vs.* Windover and Hopkins but neglects to note his opinion in Windover and Hopkins *vs.* Robbins.

[15] Jacob, an assistant judge on the Supreme Court, did not sit on the bench, being a party in this case. For a biography of Jacob see "The Supreme Court in Vermont," pp. 74–75. The close relationship between Tyler and Jacob is illustrated by the correspondence between the two ("TPT Memoir," p. 176ff.).

murdering an insane young girl, Hannah Everts. The girl had been confined in an out-house under the contemporary methods of dealing with the mentally ill. The charlatan, a stranger in the community, had ingratiated himself with the Everts family and despite what others considered "intemperate" habits, had convinced them he could work a cure of the girl.

Dissolving an ounce of opium into a quart of rum he secreted himself with the girl in the out-house and after three quarters of an hour finally forced her to drink the potion. Hannah died before nightfall. Johnson was immediately charged with her murder although the excited townspeople believed the poor girl had also been criminally assaulted.

The Supreme Court convicted Johnson of manslaughter and sentenced him to a public whipping and fine. Due to the widespread interest in the case Tyler decided to publish a report of the trial. Although there exist newspaper advertisements for the projected pamphlet and Tyler's son states it was published, there are no extant copies. The only remaining fragment is a transcription of Judge Tyler's "Editor's Address" for the pamphlet which Thomas Pickman Tyler included in the manuscript memoir of his father.[16]

It is included below as the sole remnant of Tyler's involvement in the Johnson-Everts case.

Unfortunately, outside of the "Blacksnake" affair, none of Tyler's opinions or statements exist for the years when he was Chief Justice (1807–1813).[17] Following the publication of his own Vermont Law Reports

---

[16] The above circumstances of the case are taken from "TPT Memoir," pp. 184–85. It appears that in making a synopsis of the facts Thomas Pickman Tyler had in front of him the pamphlet and/or his father's retained manuscript text of it.

On Sept. 21, 1805, there appeared in the *Rutland Herald* a proposal, dated Aug. 31, 1805, to publish "A Report of the Solemn Trial of John Johnson for an indictment for the murder of Miss Hannah Everts, before the Supreme Court of the State of Vermont, at their session holden in Manchester, Bennington County, Feb. term, A.D. 1805." (See Marcus A. McCorison, *Vermont Imprints, 1778–1820* (Worcester, 1963), p. 172, citation 794. In his comprehensive survey McCorison was unable to locate a copy of the pamphlet.)

In the VSP, Vol. 44, p. 95, there is a statement and certificate attesting to the compensation due to Messrs. Lot Hall and Abel Spencer, the court appointed attorneys for Johnson. In their statement Hall and Spencer say that the trial had been "long and tidious." The compensation agreed upon for defending Johnson was $40.00. The certificate, dated Sept. 24, 1805, is signed by Chief Justice Robinson and Side Judges Tyler and Theophelus Herrington.

[17] The following manuscript material, relating to Tyler's service as Chief Justice is in the VSP: Vol. 72, p. 5, report in case of State Treasurer *vs.* Nathan Deane, Jr., *et al*, August 1808 term of Supreme Court at Woodstock, Windsor County (this detailed

covering the years 1800–1803 there were no further published Vermont Supreme Court decisions until 1826.

The "Blacksnake" case, or the trial of Cyrus Dean, as it was also known, marked the highpoint of Tyler's years as Chief Justice. The hardship caused to New England farmers and mercantile interests by the Embargo Act of 1807 led to bitter feelings, especially in northern Vermont where all legal

seven-page clerk's copy report does not, unfortunately, state which of the three judges rendered the opinion of the court); Vol. 72, p. 61, Tyler named in deposition re State Treasurer *vs.* Deane *et al*, Oct. 7, 1808; Vol. 67, p. 2, certificate of judges of Supreme Court re guard for prisoners in gaol at Danville, Oct. 28, 1808; Vol. 78, p. 4, certificate of Chief Justice Tyler, qualifying Robert Temple as notary public, Feb. 2, 1809; Vol. 72, p. 31, copy of indictment and judgement in State *vs.* Jonathan Dorr, Jr., February 1800 term of Supreme Court at Manchester, Bennington County (Dorr was indicted for performing an abortion on an unmarried girl, Esther Gaby, and for "severely beating her . . . endangering her life." He was found guilty only of the second charge. Again, the report of the case does not state which judge handed down the decision of the court.); Vol. 66, p. 10, Tyler's certificate for holding session of court and completion of gaol and gaol house, Jefferson County, Oct. 15, 1811; Vol. 75, p. 1, Tyler's bonding of clerk of Supreme Court, Jan. 8, 1812; Vol. 75, p. 1, *Ibid.*, Oct. 3, 1812; Vol. 78, p. 7, Tyler's certificate, appended to copy of docket of cases before Supreme Court, September 1813 term, Orange County (important for listing the variety of cases, both civil and criminal, in which Tyler and the court were involved); Vol. 50, p. 93, report of George Worthington, surveyor of public buildings, of books belonging to state obtained from Tyler, retired as Chief Justice, Oct. 31, 1815.

Other manuscript papers of these Supreme Court years are scattered in various libraries and historical societies: (1) writ of error, John Law and Benjamin Boardman indebted to James Sawyer; and Orange Smith and Roger Enos indebted to Boardman Oct. 26–27, 1802 (at the Historical Society of Pennsylvania); (2) notice of indebtedness of Lyman King to Zalvez G. Fitch, Jan. 12, 1805 (at the Vermont Historical Society, accession no. 23917); (3) recognizance, Richard Skinner in writ of error to Frederick Dibble, Feb. 24, 1806 (in the collection of the editor); (4) writ of error, Loyal Cace to Seth Starr, Oct. 15, 1807 (at the Vermont Historical Society, accession no. 23917); (5) writ of error, Asa Fuller and Chauncy Langdon indebted to James Griswold, Feb. 11, 1808 (at the William L. Clements Library, University of Michigan); (6) recognizance, Anson J. Sperry indebted to Thomas Daves, Feb. 15, 1808 (at the Vermont Historical Society, accession no. 23917); (7) writ of error, Samuel Purdy indebted to Humphrey Richardson; and Elisha Houghton indebted to Richardson, Feb. 22, 1808 (at the Clifton W. Barrett Library, University of Virginia); (8) indenture between the University of Vermont and Solomon Goodell, witnessed by Tyler as member of the university corporation, July 13, 1808 (at the Boston Public Library); (9) writ of error, Thomas Huntington indebted to Isaac, Stephen and Nathan Warren; and Moses Strong indebted to Peter Ludlow, Feb. 1–2, 1809 (at the William L. Clement Library); (10) writ of error, Solomon Morton indebted to Issac, Stephen and Nathan Warren; and Robert Wilbur indebted to Benjamin Carver, Feb. 3–4, 1809 (at the Historical Society of Pennsylvania (11) certification of marriage, Thomas Harns and Abigail Chapin, May 18, 1809 (in the collection of the editor); (12) summons, Aaron Willard, Jr., to J. R. Gibson, July 5, commerce with Canada came to an end. The "Blacksnake" affair was the immediate result of efforts to enforce the embargo.[18]

For many years previous Vermont and northern New Yorkers had traded locally-made potash to the Canadians in exchange for the much needed salt employed to preserve their pork and beef. The embargo did not deter many individualistic Vermonters from smuggling these and other commodities across the Vermont-Canadian border, either overland or by means of vessels plying Lake Champlain.

A small force of militia had been stationed at Windmill Point near the Canadian line to patrol the lake and enforce the embargo. At the beginning of August, 1808, a boat called the "Blacksnake," owned by a known smuggler, was reported returning from a trip to Canada loaded with contraband. A Lt. Daniel Farrington and a crew of 13 militiamen were detailed to take the revenue cutter, the "Fly," intercept the "Blacksnake" and apprehend her and her crew. After searching the lake and its inlets for a couple of days, Farrington learned that the "Blacksnake" had been secreted along the bank of the Winooski (Onion) River close to where it entered the lake a few miles north of Burlington, Vermont.

Farrington took the "Fly" up the river mouth, discovered the camouflaged "Blacksnake" and detailed a number of his men to pull it out of its hiding place in the bushes so that they could row it back to the open lake. The crew of the "Blacksnake," standing on the bank, vowed death to Farrington and his men if they attempted to take possession of the smuggler.

Nonetheless, the Lieutenant's men refloated the vessel, and accompanied by the "Fly," commenced to row it down the river. The crew of the "Blacksnake" followed, walking along the bank and uttering dire warnings

1809 (at the Baker Library, Dartmouth College); (13) writ of error, James Cummeins [sic], Lemuel Bostwich, John Fetch, William McKnight and Elisha Smith indebted to Benjamin Paine, Oct. 25, 1810 (in the Elliot Papers, p. 139, Boston Public Library); (14) notation of Tyler to Jonathan Jones, clerk of the Supreme Court, re divorce and alimony, Rebeccah Perry vs. Daniel Perry; with postscript re transfer of persons to the State Prison, Feb. 16, 1812 (at the Clifton W. Barrett Library).

[18] The following resumé of the incident is taken primarily from A. M. Hemenway, ed., Vermont Historical Gazeteer (Burlington, 1871), 342–47; Walter H. Crockett, Vermont: The Green Mountain State (New York, 1921), III, 3–15; Ralph Nading Hill, The Winooski. Heartway of Vermont (New York, 1949), pp. 127–32; and "TPT Memoir," a 14-page insert between pp. 243–44.

The embargo had been passed by Congress on Dec. 22, 1807. Dr. Jebez Penniman had been appointed U.S. Collector of Customs at Colchester, Vt. For a discussion of the embargo in Vermont see: H. N. Muller, "Smuggling into Canada: How the Champlain Valley Defied Jefferson's Embargo," Vermont History, XXXVIII, No. 1 (Winter, 1969), 5–21.

of disaster. At a spot called Joy's Landing the smugglers opened fire from the shore, one of the shots killing Farrington's helmsman. Landing the militiamen, Farrington advanced upon the smugglers who posted themselves behind fences, trees and bushes. Some of the smugglers fled but a number of them, including Cyrus Dean, stood firm and fired at the approaching soldiers.

Farrington was wounded and two of his men were killed. The smugglers were immediately arrested and placed in the prison at Burlington. The case fanned extreme public excitement with sides being taken depending on individual political allegiance. The Republicans, the party in power in the state and supporters of the embargo statutes, called for the immediate trial and execution of the alleged murderers. The Federalists, on the other hand, felt that the smugglers were merely poor, oppressed, common citizens driven to acts of desperation to protect their property and make a livelihood.

In any case, everyone agreed the Supreme Court should act on the matter as soon as possible before the emotional atmosphere led to further difficulties. Tyler immediately suspended the Court, then on its circuit in the eastern part of the state, and convened it in a special session at Burlington on August 23, 1808.[19]

The State's Attorney for Chittenden County, William C. Harrington, gave evidence to the Grand Jury charging Dean and six others with murder. On August 26 the Grand Jury presented to the Supreme Court an indictment charging the seven with the crime. Separate trials were requested by the defendants. Dean's trial elicited the most interest and is the only one which was publically reported at length.[20]

---

[19] Sitting on the bench with Tyler were Assistant Judges Jonas Galusha and Theophelus Herrington (also spelled "Herrinton"). Biographical sketches of these two are in: "The Supreme Court in Vermont," pp. 75–77. Comments on them by Tyler and evaluations by Thomas Pickman Tyler are in "TPT Memoir," pp. 180–81, 195–202.

[20] *The Trial of Cyrus B. Dean, for the Murder of Jonathan Ormsby and Asa March, Before the Supreme Court of Judicature of the State of Vermont . . . Revised and Corrected from the Minutes of the Judges* (Burlington, 1809).

The trial of Samuel Mott started on Aug. 29 and closed on Sept. 1 with a verdict of guilty of murder. On Sept. 2 Dean was put before the bar for trial but challenges made it impossible to fill the jury and the court called for additional jurors. Dean's trial commenced on Sept. 3 and was closed on Sept. 5 with a verdict of guilty of murder. David Sheffield was found guilty of murder on Sept. 9. New trials were granted to Mott and Sheffield after their attorneys argued a motion in arrest of judgement. Dean was sentenced to be hung on Oct. 28. A respite of two weeks was granted by the Governor but on Nov. 11 he was hung before 10,000 spectators.

The case was a difficult one for Tyler. The embargo had caused a near universal split throughout the land in all levels of society. The public controversy raised by the arrest of the smugglers extended outside the borders of Vermont. The Chief Justice was especially aware of the case's relationship to the national political picture.[21]

Tyler also realized that improperly handled the emotional issues could obliterate the trial's legal aspects and could throw the court into disrepute if emotion took the upper hand. The responsibility for the climate in which the trial was conducted and the tone which it took rested upon Tyler, the Chief Justice, rather than with the two assistant judges, Theophelus Herrington and Jonas Galusha. For that reason Tyler felt called upon, on the first day of the special session, to make a fairly long plea to the Grand Jury, urging it to view the case in a proper context and in a proper frame of mind. This charge to the Grand Jury survives and is included in this volume. Unfortunately, although Tyler seems to have taken part in the trial itself his statements have not been preserved.[22]

Tyler's faith in the court and the citizens of Chittenden County serving on the Jury was justified. The trial was conducted in an atmosphere of calm, Dean was found guilty and hung on November 11. The decision and the execution of the sentence was carried out without incident and the local situation returned to normal.

No additional trials took place during the special term. At the next regular term of the court in Jan. 1809, Truman Mudgett was tried. The trial ended in a hung jury and he was retried at the Jan. 1810 term. The State entered a plea of *nolle prosequi* and Mudgett was discharged. At the Jan. 1809 term Mott, Sheffield and Francis Ledgard were convicted of manslaughter and sentenced to the State Prison.

[21] Tyler's views on the embargo and other contemporary domestic and foreign political matters can be ascertained from surviving correspondence. See Jonathan Robinson to Tyler, dated from Washington, D.C., Jan. 8, 1810 (at the Historical Society of Pennsylvania); Robinson to Tyler, dated from Washington, Jan. 21, 1811 (at the New Hampshire Historical Society); and Robinson to Tyler, dated from Washington, Dec. 1, 1811 (at the Butler Library, Columbia University). See also a long series of letters between Tyler and Robinson, Sen. Stephen Bradley and Rep. Thomas Witherell in "TPT Memoir," pp. 218–259.

[22] See below, p. 407, State *vs.* Dean, footnote 1. A document in VSP, Vol. 68, p. 10, attests to the controversy caused by Dean's trial. On Oct. 14, 1808, the State House of Representatives passed a resolution asking the Supreme Court to explain its charge to the jury, especially that portion which differentiated between the crime of murder and the crime of manslaughter. (Dean had pleaded guilty of manslaughter only.) A reply, signed by Tyler and undoubtedly drafted by him since it was his charge which was being questioned, defends the court's charge to the jury, cites the Vermont law on which he based his charge and concludes that the jury returned a verdict consistent with that law and the evidence presented.

The charge to the Grand Jury in the "Blacksnake" case is the last available document relating to Tyler's years as Chief Justice.

* * * * *

ADDISON COUNTY, JANUARY TERM,
A. D. 1802.

JONATHAN ROBINSON, Chief Judge.

ROYALL TYLER,
STEPHEN JACOB, } *Assistant Judges.*

RICHARD PEARSE, Appellee,
against
MOSES GODDARD, Appellant.

And now the said *Richard Pearse,* appellee, complaint makes,[1] that by the consideration of the County Court holden at *Middlebury,* within and for the County of *Addison* aforesaid, on the first *Monday of March,* A.D. 1801, he recovered judgement against the abovementioned *Moses Goddard,* for the sum of 353 dols 33 cts. damages, and the sum of 11 dols. 45 cts. costs of suit; from which judgement the said *Moses* appealed to this present term of the Supreme Court; and on the first day of the term entered his appeal in said Court; but on the sixth day of the same term, being thrice solemnly called to prosecute his said appeal to effect, did not appear, but thereof made default, which default is regularly entered on the docket of the said Supreme Court.

Now the complainant having here ready in Court to be produced,

---

[1] [As is the case in similar reports, the citations and supportive material in Tyler's *Law Reports* were presented as marginal notations. For the sake of textual uniformity they will be placed here at the bottom of the page in footnote form.]

When the appellant is defaulted, the appellee cannot file a complaint as in case of the non-entry of the appellant, and thus recover 12 per cent, as increase of damages, but must take his debt and usual cost in the action appealed.

attested copies of said judgement and other necessary evidence, prays the Court to affirm said original judgement with additional costs, and allow the complainant appellee interest on the damages so by him recovered as increase of damages occasioned by the appellant's delay in neglecting to enter and prosecute said appeal to effect at the rate of twelve per centum per annum, as is provided by the fourth section of the act entitled, an act constituting the Supreme Court of Judicature and County Courts, defining their powers, and regulating judicial proceedings.[2]

By his attorney,

S. Miller.

The question made is, shall this complaint be sustained?

JACOB, Judge. This complaint is novel; but I consider the judgment of the Court below ought to be affirmed, and the damages increased by the twelve per cent. interest.

The object of the Legislature was to prevent unnecessary delay in the collection of debts. They have therefore enacted, that if an appellant shall neglect to enter and prosecute his appeal to effect he shall, upon complaint made by the appellee, and affirmation of the original judgment, remunerate the appellee by increase of damages occasioned by his delay, at the rate of twelve per centum per annum.

It appears to me, that this salutary statute check upon the delays of debtors would be entirely evaded by permitting the appellant to make a mere formal entry of his appeal, and then instantly suffer a default.

TYLER, Judge. The words of the statute, "shall neglect to enter *and* prosecute his appeal to effect," are in the *conjunctive*. The appellant must neglect both, or he is not liable on complaint to the payment of the twelve per cent. interest; otherwise, if in the *disjunctive*, "neglect to enter *or* prosecute," if he then had failed in either, I should have been for sustaining the complaint.

Chief Judge. I am in opinion with Judge TYLER. Further it appears to me, that if we sustain this complaint, we shall encounter a

---

[2] *Vermont* Stat. vol. 1, p. 55.

difficulty in disposing of the proceedings already had upon the appeal. Here is a default entered, and, to make the record complete, costs must be taxed and damages ascertained. And although the general practice has been, when a party suffering a default intends to be heard in the assessment of damages, that the default is suffered under a rule that the defendant shall be heard in damages, yet as the statute provides, that "when judgment shall be rendered by default, or on deumurrer, in any Court in this State, the Judges of such Court shall have full power, by themselves, by the Jury in Court, the report of the clerk, or the report on oath of one or more judicious person or persons, to be appointed as an inquest by the Court to ascertain the sum due."[3] I do not conceive we could bar the appellant from yet being heard in damages on the default. In which case there would be a complete judgment on the appeal, and another judgment on the affirmation under the complaint if it should be sustained, and full costs in both; and perhaps the result of the inquiry after damages upon the default might lessen the judgment in the Court below to a sum merely nominal.

I will observe further, that a default entered on the docket is not by our practice conclusive against a party until after the rising of the Court. The statute provides,[4] that after default recorded and judgment entered thereon, if before the third day inclusive of the first day of the sitting of the Court, the defendant shall come into Court and move for a trial, he shall be admitted to it upon paying to the adverse party his legal costs. The Court have considered this statute provision to apply only to cases where there has been no appearance by the defendant in Court: therefore, in those cases which the statute did not reach, it has been the practice of the Court on motion, under considerations of equity, to take off a default at any day of the term, under a rule securing to the adverse party ample compensation for all the inconveniences he may sustain by it.

[3] *Vermont* Stat. vol. 1, p. 75.
[4] *Vermont* Stat. vol. 1, p. 75. A default entered on the docket is not conclusive until the rising of the Court.

The complainant had leave to discontinue, and judgment entered upon the default.

Samuel Miller, for appellee.
Josias Smith, for appellant.

* * * * *

RUTLAND COUNTY, JULY ADJOURNED
TERM, A.D. 1802

JONATHAN ROBINSON, Chief Judge.
ROYALL TYLER,
STEPHEN JACOB, } *Assistant Judges.*

JEREMIAH ADAMS *against* JOHN BROWNSON.

CASE on promissory note.[1]

Attach *John Brownson,* surviving partner of the late firm of *Hyde & Brownson,* to answer, &c. to *Jeremiah Adams,* &c. for that whereas *Lemuel Hyde,* since deceased, and the said *John Brownson,* merchants, trading in company at *Whitehall,* in the County of *Washington* and State of *New-York,* to wit, at *Rutland,* &c. on the 1st day of *August,* 1799, did make, execute and deliver to the plaintiff their certain memorandum or note in writing commonly called a promissory note, of that date, subscribed with the proper hand of the said *Lemuel Hyde,* for himself and the said *John Brownson,* under the firm of *Hyde & Brownson,* in and by which promissory note, for value received of the plaintiff, they promised to pay him 500 dollars in six months from the date of said note, with legal interest of the State of *New-York.* By reason of all which the said *John Brownson,* as surviving partner of said firm, became obligated to pay, &c. and assumed, &c.

[1] In an action brought against a surviving partner upon a promissory note, alleged to have been signed by the deceased partner in his life-time, in the name of the firm, proofs of his confession that he signed it, admitted to be given in evidence.

Plea, *non assumpsit.*

Defence, that no partnership ever existed between the defendent and *Lemuel Hyde.*

The plaintiff offered in evidence the note declared upon, and offered to prove the signature of *Hyde* by his confession.

The counsel for the defendant insisted, that as there is a subscribing witness to the note, he should be produced. They observed, that it was not the most substantial part of their defence that the note was not signed by *Hyde*; but they wished to examine the subscribing witness, and expected to have shewn by him, that though the note might have been signed by *Hyde* in the name of the supposed firm of *Hyde & Brownson,* yet that the plaintiff did not credit or rely entirely on the existence of the partnership at the time of the contract, but charged the goods, which were the consideration of the note, thirty per cent. above their real value in the market; and it was well understood between the plaintiff and *Hyde,* at the time of making the note, that the extra advance was made in the price of the goods, on account, as the plaintiff expressed it, of its being uncertain whether he could prove the partnership; that relying upon the plaintiff's producing the witness, the defendant had failed to summon him. They therefore objected to the confession of *Hyde* being heard in evidence.

JACOB, Judge. I am for admitting the confession of *Hyde* to prove the execution of the note. This is a distinct matter from the question of copartnership. To put the plaintiff upon producing the subscribing witness, will operate a surprise upon him.

TYLER, Judge. I have long considered that some general rule ought to be adopted to prevent the defendant in action upon promissory note from surprising the plaintiff by insisting on trial upon the testimony of the subscribing witness, in cases where it is obvious the execution of the note is not designed as a substantial defence, but merely to operate delay. Perhaps this evil can better be corrected in Courts which have the original jurisdiction of causes of this nature; and it would be desirable that the several County Courts would adopt as a general rule, "that in all actions upon promissory note, the execution of the note should be considered as confined, unless the defendant, by the second day of the term of entry, should give notice to the plaintiff, by a minute on the docket, signed by his counsel, or attested by the Clerk of the Court, that he meant to contest its execution."

As no such rule exists, in the present case I consider that the defendant has a right to examine the subscribing witness, and might safely rely on the plaintiff's producing him.

It is not stated that the defendant personally signed this note, or had any individual knowledge of the contract. If he has assumed to pay it, it is by operation of law, and dependent on the existence of the partnership between him and *Lemuel Hyde,* since deceased. The principle of law which renders the partners in a firm of merchants accountable for the contracts of each other, is directed to prevent imposition, that he who is bankrupt shall not obtain credit by a connection merely ostensible with him who is opulent, and that he who is opulent shall not take the avails of a contract made by a seeming partner, who is unable to respond for them. Therefore, in all cases of this nature, the Court have allowed a very liberal latitude. In the proof of partnership a plaintiff prosecuting defendants as partners in trade has not been confined to shew articles of copartnership, the annunciation of the firm in the public newspapers, an open store, sign-board, or books of the company. But he may shew a variety of joint contracts made by them in such manner as would induce a general and rational belief that they were connected in trade. This has been done to prevent imposition upon those who might deal with them.

If in the course of this trial it should remain doubtful whether the defendant was in partnership with the deceased at the time of the contract, and the testimony should rather preponderate in favour of a partnership, it would be a matter of importance with me to discover in what light the plaintiff viewed the connection between *Brownson* and *Hyde* at the time of the making the note in question. Did he part with his property upon the credit of the firm, or did he contract with *Hyde,* understanding that the partnership was a matter of uncertainty, and that its existence was denied by the defendant? Is the plaintiff one whom the law will and ought to protect from imposition, or has he voluntarily and with his eyes open, entered into the contract with *Hyde,* and made an advance upon his property as a premium for his risk in proving the partnership.

I am not therefore for dispensing with the attendance of the subscribing witness; and it is my opinion that evidence of the confession of *Hyde* to the execution of this note, cannot be admitted. But as I would not prejudice the plaintiff, I shall be inclined to grant him a continuance.

Chief Judge.   If the action had been originally commenced in this Court, I should not be for admitting the confession of the maker of the note to be heard in evidence, but I consider that the defendant, who put the plaintiff upon proof of the partnership, has, by the trial at the lower Court, had access to the note declared upon, discovered who was the subscribing witness, and had sufficient time to inquire whether his appearance on the stand would benefit him. If he considered his testimony material in his defence, he should have summoned him to appear.

I am therefore admitting the evidence of the confession of *Hyde* to the making of the note.

Evidence admitted.

Cephas Smith, Junior, and *John Cook,* for plaintiff.
Smith & Prentice and *Chauncey Langdon,* for defendant.

*   *   *   *   *

RUTLAND COUNTY, JULY ADJOURNED
TERM, A.D. 1802.

JONATHAN ROBINSON, Chief Judge.
ROYALL TYLER, }
STEPHEN JACOB, } *Assistant Judges.*

STEPHEN WINDOVER and JOSEPH HOPKINS, Appellees,
against
JOHN ROBBINS, Appellant.

THE plaintiffs,[1] as merchants trading in company, declare in trespass on the case, that at the city of *New-York,* on the 27th of *November,*
1795, one *James Robinson* was indebted to them in the sum of 144*l.*
2*s.* 11*d.* New-York currency, balance due from said *Robinson,* on account of goods, &c. sold to him. That *Robinson* was then, and ever
since hath been, a bankrupt, which was unknown to the plaintiffs, and
well known by the defendant. That the defendant conspiring with
Robinson to defraud the plaintiffs, and to procure the plaintiffs to sell
to *Robinson* on credit, goods, wares, and merchandise, to the amount
of 610*l.* 11*s.* 10*d.* New-York currency, did advance *Robinson,* as of his
own proper moneys, the sum of 310*l.* of the same currency, with
intent that *Robinson* should be able to pay the plaintiffs the sum due
to them, and to purchase of them goods to the amount of 610*l.* 11*s.*
10*d.* as aforesaid, the residue of said 320*l.* going in part and prompt
payment towards said goods. That the said *James Robinson,* conspiring
as aforesaid, on the 20th of *November,* 1795, did in the said city of
New-York, apply to the plaintiffs to vend him goods to the amount of
610*l.* 11*s.* 10*d.* and did then and there promise and offer to advance the
plaintiffs, in hand, 320*l.* as aforesaid, to pay the above balance of 144*l.*
2*s.* 11*d.* and towards the amount of the goods so to be sold, on condition that the plaintiffs would give credit and a day of payment for the

[1] An action will lie for the advancing money to a bankrupt, with intent and to enable
him to obtain on a credit, merchandise which goes into possession of the lender,
although the plaintiff never had any view or even knowledge of the defendent.

remainder, or balance to be due for said goods, &c. amounting to the sum of 434*l*. 4*s*. 9*d*. of the same currency, equal in value to the sum of 1,086 dols. 84 cts. of the current moneys of the *United States*. Whereupon the plaintiffs, deceived by the conspiracy and fraud of the said *Robbins* and *Robinson,* did sell and deliver to the said *James Robinson,* goods, wares, and merchandise, to the said amount of 610*l*. 11*s*. 10*d*. and the plaintiffs then and there received of said *James Robinson* the said sum of 320*l*. in full discharge and payment of said balance due them upon said former account, amounting to the said sum of 144*l*. 2*s*. 11*d*. and in part payment of said sum of 610*l*. 11*s*. 10*d*. and did then and there credit the said *James Robinson* for the balance then due, amounting to the sum of 434*l*. 4*s*. 9*d*. as aforesaid, to be paid to them when he the said *James Robinson* should be thereto requested. And the plaintiffs in fact say, that the said *James Robinson,* conspiring as aforesaid, and in pursuance of the fraudulent combination with the defendant as aforesaid, having so received said goods, &c. of the plaintiffs, then and there forthwith delivered the same to the defendant for his the defendant's sole use and benefit, and that the defendant then and there forthwith received the same, and hath converted them to his own proper use. And the plaintiffs in fact further say, that the said *James Robinson* has never since been able to pay to them the aforesaid sum of 434*l*. 11*s*. 10*d*. *New-York* currency, nor any part thereof, although often thereunto requested and demanded. Wherefore the plaintiffs say, that by the fraudulent and deceitful conduct of the defendant, combining and conspiring with the said *James Robinson,* they have been injured, *ad damnum,* 2,000 dollars.

General issue joined, and put to the Jury.

In support of the declaration, the plaintiffs' counsel offered to show in evidence *the confessions of James Robinson to prove the conspiracy.*

The defendant's counsel objected, That *James Robinson* was not a party to the suit; and if he were, his confessions ought not to prejudice the defendant. That if it should be understood to have been the decision of the Court, that *Robinson's* acts or words were admitted in evidence to charge the defendant, it would follow that a plaintiff might hereafter maintain an action for the most aggravated fraud against the most honest man, merely by coupling him in his declaration with a villain, and showing the confessions of the latter to charge the former.

Sed per Curiam.[2] This is an action of deceit in nature of a conspiracy brought against *John Robbins,* and *James Robinson* is alleged to have been his agent in the fraud. The uniform practice of the Court in similar cases has been, to call upon the plaintiff to show a privity between the defendant and the person coupled with him in the fraud. The Court will decide whether this be sufficiently proved or not. Until it is proved, the confessions or acts of the alleged agent in the fraud cannot be admitted. At present, therefore, the confessions of *Robinson* cannot be shown to the Jury. Let the plaintiffs proceed to prove the *privity,* and when shown to the satisfaction of the Court, the most liberal latitude will be allowed in the proof of the conduct and confessions of *Robinson* as a *particeps.*

On the trial by the Jury, it appeared in evidence,

That on the 27th day of *November,* 1795, *James Robinson,* then a bankrupt, was indebted to the plaintiffs 144*l.* 2*s.* 11*d.* *New-York* currency.

That in *October* preceding, the defendant, then an inhabitant of *Rutland,* observed to Messrs. *Willoughby* & *Miller,* that he could procure goods at ten shillings on the pound, if *he dared to risk somebody.* When requested to explain, he said, after some hesitation, perhaps it is by letting a man have money to establish a credit at the different banks.

That in *November,* 1795, the defendant and *James Robinson,* long known to the former as a bankrupt, went to the city of *New-York* in company. The defendant there told a witness that he had concluded

[2] In an action of deceit, in nature of a conspiracy, the acts or speeches of an alleged particeps in the fraud cannot be admitted in evidence to the Jury until a privity between him and the defendant is first shown, to the satisfaction of the Court. But when proved, the most liberal latitude will be allowed in showing the conduct and confession of the particeps.

to let *Robinson* have 1,500 dollars, and that he was to have 100*l.* as a premium, and double the amount in goods as his security.

On the 27th of *November,* 1795, *Robinson,* by advancing to the plaintiffs 320*l. New-York* currency, extinguished the debt of 144*l.* 11*s.* 2*d.* then, due, and the balance was passed to his credit on amount of goods and merchandise sold and delivered to him at that time, the invoice of which footed at 610*l.* 11*s.* 10*d.* and after deducting the credit, balanced in favour of the plaintiffs, 434*l.* 4*s.* 9*d.*

The goods were packed, and the bales marked *J. R.* Before they were removed, a bill of sale from *Robinson* to the defendant was endorsed upon the invoice. When the bales were shipped, they were delivered to the defendant, who with chalk, to the initials of *J. R.* added *obbins.* They were conveyed by the defendant to *Clarendon, Rutland* County, and exposed for sale in a store occupied by *Robinson* ostensibly as his property; but the defendant officiated as his clerk.

A dispute soon happened between *Robinson* and the defendant on account of the former paying sundry debts from these goods. In their altercation the defendant stated the contract between them, vis. "that he and his horses were to be at the service of *Robinson* from *October,* 1795, to the *May* following; that he was to receive 100*l.* lawful money, and to have goods pledged for his security; that he had advanced 1,500 dollars; and they had further agreed that the goods purchased by *Robinson* in *New-York* from the plaintiffs and others, amounting in value, at the *New-York* prices, to upwards of 6,000 dollars, should be pledged with him; conditioned, that if *Robinson,* by the 20th of *May,* 1796, paid the 100*l.* and repaid the 1,500 dollars, with all expenses and incidental charges, he was to surrender his lien on the goods; otherwise they were to become his absolute property." *Robinson* did not deny the contract, but complained that it was a hard bargain. An accommodation then took place. The defendant gave *Robinson* 500 dollars, who relinquished all claim on the goods. The defendant took them into possession, and converted them to his own use. *Robinson* the next day absconded the State.

The only points in defence were,

That as the plaintiffs, during the whole transaction, never had any view or even knowledge of the existence of the defendant, it could not be intended that they parted with their property through any reliance upon him.

That the defendant's loaning money to *James Robinson,* to buttress his declining credit, so far from being a fraudulent, was a lawful and meritorious act; that this was frequently done by the fairest merchants, and often operated a substantial benefit to creditors by saving a failing trader from bankruptcy. In support of this the defendant's counsel cited 2 *Burr. Rep.* p. 933. *Foxcraft et al. Assignees of Satterthwaite, bankrupt,* v. *Devonshire et al.* wherein Lord *Mansfield,* in delivering the opinion of the Court of King's Bench, observed: "A notion, 'that lending money to traders, knowing them to be in dubious, tottering or distressed circumstances, upon mortgages or *liens,* is fraudulent, and consequently the contract void in case a bankruptcy ensues,' would throw all mercantile dealing into inextricable confusion. Men lend their money to traders upon mortgages or consignment of goods, because they suspect their circumstances, and will not run the risk of their general credit."

TYLER, Assistant Judge, in charge to the Jury, laid it down as settled, that where *A.* and *B.* combine to defraud *C.* of property, and it is carried into effect, though *A.* should keep concealed from *C.* during the whole transaction, and *B.* should be the active partner in the conspiracy, yet the fraudulent combination being proved to have existed between them, *A.* shall be charged in damages; for it may appear that the *summa ars* of the covin was to secret *A.* from the knowledge of *C.* An adverse doctrine would lead to the conclusion, that the grossest fraud might be practised and fully proved in our courts of justice, and the law be found inadeqate to relieve. But the arm of the law is not shortened, that it cannot save, and courts and jurors will with eagle eyes trace fraud through all its secret and crooked paths, and render both the agent who appears, and the prime mover who plots in darkness, amenable.

The case cited from *Burrow*, addressed to the Court, but read in presence of the Jury, he declared to be not in point.

The defendants in that case had honoured certain bills and drafts made upon them by *Satterthwaite*. Afterwards, effects of this bankrupt came into their possession by his assignment, which they sold and converted into money; and the question was, whether this money should become the trust property of his assignees, or go to remunerate the defendants for the bills and drafts they had accepted and paid. It appears, that these bills and drafts were accepted and paid by the defendants before the commission of bankruptcy, which was in *August*, 1752.

The defendants were to receive merely the amount of what they had advanced with the customary commissions. Some secret acts of bankruptcy committed by *Satterthwaite*, about *Christmas*, 1751, were attempted to be proved by the plaintiffs, which "overreached the consignment of the goods, the sale of them, the receipt of the moneys for which they were sold, and likewise the time when the defendants advanced the moneys to the use and order of the bankrupt"; and the fraud attempted to be charged upon the defendants was this, "that they were privy to *Satterthwaite's* insolvency, at the time when they advanced the money to discharge his bills." But all this was done away by counter proof; it appearing, that if any of these secret acts of bankruptcy existed, they were done away by his again appearing publicly as usual, and continuing so to do, until *August*, 1752, when he stopped payment, and the commission was taken out.

If such secret acts of bankruptcy in *Satterthwaite* had been proved, and within the knowledge of the defendants, it is probable the decision would have been adverse, and the transaction amounted to a fraud in law, at least; or if the consignment of the goods, the sale of them, the receipt of the moneys for which they were sold, and likewise the time when the defendants advanced the moneys to the use and order of the bankrupt, had all been subsequent to the taking out of the commission of bankruptcy, the question must have turned upon the validity of payment, under the act of 19 *Geo*. II. c. 32. without noticing several other points mooted by the learned counsel. The question decided in that cause was simply, whether payment of bills to support the credit of a declining trader, without notice of bankruptcy, be fraudulent.

We should not consider it so here, for the law should always aid rather than discountenance the social virtues.

But does the case, or the reason of the decision, apply? Here is a premeditated *fraud in fact,* of the grossest nature, alleged.

It is in proof that the defendant *Robbins,* a few weeks before the plaintiffs vended their merchandise to *Robinson,* declared his intention of defrauding *somebody.* He said he could obtain goods at half their value. He detailed his iniquitous scheme, which was by loaning money to some one who might thereby obtain a credit. He did not indeed say he intended to loan to a bankrupt, but he described him as an unresponsible man; for he added, "if he could venture to trust somebody."

He had been long and familiarly acquainted with *Robinson,* and knew he was bankrupt. He accompanied him to *New-York.* He advanced him 1,500 dollars, part of which money it is not contended was paid by *Robinson* to the plaintiffs, and was the inducement for them to give him a credit to a large amount. Before the goods purchased by *Robinson* were removed from the plaintiff's store, this defendant took a bill of sale of the whole invoice. When the property is shipped, the defendant takes it into his possession, and marks his name upon the packages. Under his care the goods were transported to *Clarendon.* They were, it is true, exposed to sale in the store occupied by *Robinson*; but the defendant officiated as clerk, and evidenced his interest in and control over the property, by restraining his ostensible principal from applying any part of them to the payment of his debts. A dispute happened, and terminated in a final accommodation, by which *Robinson,* in consideration of 500 dollars, relinquished his claim to the whole merchandise in the store, which included not only the goods purchased of the plaintiffs, but other goods to the amount of more than 6,000 dollars, obtained by *Robinson* in the same mode and time from others. The defendant took possession of the whole, and *Robinson* immediately absconded.

Does the case read from the *English* authority apply? By advancing money to *James Robinson,* was the defendant engaged in the laudable business of loaning his money to support the credit of a declining trader without notice of any act of bankruptcy?

Verdict for the plaintiffs, 1,556 dols. 58 cts.

Darius Chipman and *John Cook,* for plaintiffs.
Cephas Smith, Chauncey Langdon, and *Smith & Prentice,* for defendant.

* * * * *

JOHN ROBBINS
against
STEPHEN WINDOVER and JOSEPH HOPKINS

MOTION for new trial.[1]
The defendant in the preceding cause moved for a new trial; stating,

First. That some of the Jurors of the Jury who tried the cause, after the cause was submitted to them, witnessed or related to others of the panel certain matters and things in relation to the issue not witnessed or related on the trial of the cause in Court.

Secondly. That since the trial of the cause he had discovered *new,* as he is advised, material evidence.

---

[1] When an action of fraud is brought against *A.*, and *B.* is coupled with him in the declaration as a particeps, it is not material to the general issue to show in defense that the plaintiff had no knowledge of the defendant, and was not *immediately* defrauded by him, and therefore the exhibition of such evidence by affidavit, though newly discovered, is no ground for a new trial.

On motion for a new trial in a *civil cause,* the affidavit of one of the panel who tried it cannot be read to show what passed in the jury room during the deliberations of the jury while agreeing to their verdict.

In support of the first point,

Chauncey Langdon, for defendant, offered to read the affidavit of one of the Jurors.

To the reading of this affidavit an objection was taken.

Langdon cited 1 *Wils. Rep.* p. 329. *Rex* v. *Simmons,* a Jew; and 1 *Burr. Rep.* p. 383. *Cogan* v. *Ebden and another.*

Darius Chipman, for plaintiffs, read, *as advisory, Leib* v. *Bolton,* from *Dallas's Pennsylvania Reports.*[2]

After hearing argument, the Court said they would take time to advise on this exception, and directed the defendant's counsel to proceed in support of his second cause for a new trial.

The counsel read the affidavit of *Paul Rogers,* upon which he principally relied, which testified, that some time after the institution of the suit of *Windover and Hopkins* v. *John Robbins,* and while the same was pending in the County Court, he was in the store of the plaintiffs in *New-York,* and heard them in conversation upon the subject of the suit, and either *Windover* or *Hopkins* said "they did expect to recover in the suit, although they did not deliver the goods upon the credit of *Robbins,* or upon any thing that *Robbins* had said or done within their knowledge; for they had delivered the goods to *Robinson* upon his credit only; but from information since the delivery of the goods, they hoped to be able to prove, that *Robbins* had some how or other been concerned with *Robinson* in partnership.

Upon the sixth day of the term,

TYLER, Assistant Judge, the Chief Judge being absent, delivered the opinion of the Court.

The defendant rests his motion on two grounds: The first is, that certain Jurors of the panel who tried the cause, witnessed or related certain matters and things in relation to the issue, to others of the

---

[2] This case may be found 2d edit vol. 1, p. 82.

panel after the cause was submitted to them, not witnessed on the trial of the cause in Court.

It may be observed here, that it is not alleged that these matters and things had any effect in determining the verdict; and the Court will not in any case set aside a verdict by intendment, where it appears that substantial justice has been done. But the previous question, whether the affidavit of one of the Jurors shall be admitted to show what passed during the investigation of the cause in the jury room, renders any further observation upon what would have been the effect of such testimony, if admitted, unnecessary.

Upon the point in question, the Court are decidedly of opinion, that the affidavit cannot be admitted to be read.

The common law requires, that the twelve Jurors shall unite in a verdict. Whoever considers the variety and intricacy of causes they have to determine, the difficulty of bringing twelve persons of different habits and modes of thinking, and of unequal abilities, fortuitously elected, to concur in opinion, will perceive the wisdom of the Legislature in directing that their deliberations should be secret; for it was to be expected, that in bringing about a union of sentiment in the panel, the subject under consideration would be presented in various lights; that futile objections would be met with inconclusive arguments, theory opposed to practice, and legal science to common sense; that the reputations of witnesses would be scanned, the character of parties too often adverted to, and the whole investigation illustrated by relations of what each Juror had heard or known in cases supposed similar; that the warmth of debate would excite an obstinacy of opinion, and a reluctant and tardy assent to the verdict, perhaps drawn from some one which, on after reflection, might leave in the Juror's mind a doubt of its rectitude.

It would be of dangerous tendency to admit Jurors by affidavit to detail these deliberations of the jury room, to testify to subjects not perfectly comprehended at the time, or but imperfectly recollected.

From a natural commiseration for the losing party, of a desire to apologize for the discharge of an ungrateful duty, after the Juror had been discharged from office, he would be too apt to intimate, that if some part of the testimony had been adverted to, or something not in evidence omitted, his opinion would have been otherwise, whilst others of the panel, with different impressions or different recollections, might testify favourably for the prevailing party. This would open a novel and alarming source of litigation, and it would be difficult to say when a suit was terminated.

The Court consider it to be far better to establish it as a general rule, that the affidavits of Jurors respecting the deliberations which led to their verdict, should in no civil cause be admitted; and they are confirmed in this opinion from the consideration of the provisions made by the Legislature to rectify improper verdicts.

If the verdict be contrary to law, the Court can grant a new trial.

If it is against evidence, the Court can send the Jury to a second and third consideration, stating the true points in the cause, detailing and applying the evidence, and affording them the light of their opinion which way the verdict ought to incline.

From the lower Courts an appeal lies. In this Court the cause may be reviewed where the verdict is not final; and when it is, the Court, in furtherance of justice, will be very liberal in granting new trials on application supported by *other testimony.*

We learn by the cases cited from the books, and from others within the recollection of the Court, that the *English* Judges consider the admission of such affidavits as not common, and of dangerous tendency.

The case of *Simmons,* the Jew, cited from *Wilson's Reports,* shows the caution with which the Judges of the Court of King's Bench, admitted the affidavits of petit jurymen. The ground of setting aside the verdict was not the exposition by affidavits of any *improper deliberations of the Jury,* not upon the affidavits of the Jury only, but because it was a criminal case, and that the verdict taken in Court was a mis-entry, as appeared by the affidavit of the foreman and all his fellows, supported by the declaration of Judge *Foster,* who presided on the trial at *Nisi Prius.*

In delivering his opinion, *Lee*, Chief Justice, said, "There is no doubt but a new trial may be granted in a *criminal* case, and the true reason for granting new trials is for obtaining of justice: but to grant them upon the affidavits of jurymen only, must be admitted to be of dangerous consequence. It appears from the *report* of my brother *Foster*, and the affidavit of *Dodson* the foreman, that this verdict was taken by *mistake*; for he swears that he declared in Court, "that they did not find the defendant guilty of any intent," and therefore this is not granting a new trial upon any AFTER-THOUGHT of the Jury, but upon what the foreman *Dodson* declared at the bar when they gave their verdict."

Wright, Justice, observed, "My brother *reports*, that he told them, if they did not believe the intent they must acquit him. The Jury now swear, "they did not hear him." Therefore I am of opinion that it is a verdict *mis-entered*, contrary to the declaration of the foreman, not contradicted by any of the rest at the time it was spoken at the bar; and that it is most plainly no *after-thought*; so that we may keep clear of the danger of granting new trials merely upon the *affidavits of jurymen*."

Denniston, Justice, added, "The Court will be very cautious how they grant new trials upon the affidavits of jurymen, because it would be of very dangerous tendency; but in this particular case, which *partly depends on my brother's report, and partly on the affidavits of all the jurymen,* I am very well satisfied, there ought to be a new trial, because it appears, both by the *report and affidavits,* that this verdict ought not to stand."

The case of *Cogan* v. *Ebden and another*, cited from *Burrow's Reports*, exhibits no decision.

It appeared, upon investigation, and recurrence to the reporting Judge's minutes, that there was a mistake, a mere slip in the verdict; and upon suggestion of Lord *Mansfield* to Mr. *Morton*, the plaintiff's counsel, he moved for a rule upon defendant to show cause why, upon reading the affidavits of eight of the jurymen, the verdict should not be amended and set right, according to the truth of the finding.

The rule was granted, *but it never came before the Court any more.*

But whatever may have been the opinions of the *English* jurists on this point, the Court consider that the mode of our trials affords so many opportunities for a losing party to have his cause reconsidered by Court and Jury, unknown in the mother country, that the reasons operative there, if any exist, for the admission of affidavits of jurymen, exhibiting the deliberations of the jury room, cannot apply here.

The case of *Leib* v. *Bolton,* cited from *Dallas's Reports,* decided in the Common Pleas, *Philadelphia* County, *Pennsylvania,* under the Presidency of the late venerable and learned Chief Justice *Shippen,* though read as advisory, has weight. It shows a coincidence of opinion in the Judges of a State eminently respectable for its jurisprudence, administering a municipal code of near affinity with our own.

The affidavit of the jurymen cannot therefore be read in evidence, and consequently the defendant cannot rest on the first ground of his motion.

Any reliance upon the affidavits of *Abel Spencer* and *Joseph Randall* being abandoned by the defendant's counsel, it remains only to be considered whether the subject matter of the affidavit of *Paul Rogers* be a sufficient ground for a new trial.

In order to obtain a new trial upon the exhibition of further testimony,

First. The evidence must have been discovered by the party subsequent to the trial.

Secondly. It must be material to the issue tried.

The time this evidence came to the defendant's knowledge has not been made to appear; but this is of small import, as the Court consider the evidence exhibited in the affidavit as totally irrelevant and immaterial to the matter lately in issue. It only goes to show, that the plaintiffs had no knowledge of *Robbins* during the transaction by which they were defrauded, and were not induced by his personal application to part with their property on credit to the bankrupt, and that they relied upon maintaining their action lately tried.

That the defendant was to keep concealed both as to acts and words from the plaintiffs' knowledge, appears to have been within the scheme and essence of the fraud.

On the trial, no reliance was had by the plaintiffs on any acts or speeches of the defendant, as applied immediately to them; but the fraud complained of, and the injury sustained, was *mediately* through *James Robinson*.

On the other hand, reliance was had by the defendant's counsel upon the circumstance, that as the plaintiffs, during the whole transaction, never had any view or even knowledge of the existence of the defendant, it could not be intended that they parted with their property through any reliance upon him. It was conceded by the plaintiffs that they had no such knowledge, and the defendant's counsel urged it in argument to the Jury.

As the Judge who charged the Jury expressed himself very fully upon this point, it was not apprehended that any further attempt would be made to attach this extraneous position to the cause. This repeated aberration in the counsel has manifestly arisen from confounding an action for fraud with an action upon a warranty. In the case of goods vended upon the express warranty of the ability of the purchaser by a third person, some privity of contract must be shown between the vendor and warrantor; but in cases of fraud it is not necessary to show any privity between the person defrauded and the principal in the fraud.

In this case *Robinson* was indebted to the plaintiffs, and was a bankrupt. He appeared at their store in a character every way the reverse. He was not only able to cancel their existing demand, but was able to deposit a considerable sum of money as prompt and part payment for a new invoice of goods. The plaintiffs, deceived by his apparent opulence, gave him credit for merchandise to a large amount, which he eloigned. They have now discovered the person who furnished this bankrupt with the means of deception, and they have traced their eloigned goods into his possession. It was manifestly part of the fraudulent design of the defendant to keep out of view of the plaintiffs. He might know or apprehend that his appearance might defeat the plan, entangle him as a *particeps* or warrantor, or at least draw the attention of the plaintiffs to some clew by which they might discover the place where the spoil was to be divided. Shall the defendant now say to the plaintiffs, "I have defrauded you. I have your property in my possession. You have exposed my fraud to the satisfaction of both Court and Jury; but as part of my plan was to keep from your view and knowledge, if the Court will afford me an opportunity to show, upon a new trial, that I have, by your own confession, succeeded in this part of my fraudulent scheme, I shall escape with impunity." Surely such showing would be inadmissible.

The subject matter of the affidavit of *Paul Rogers* cannot therefore be considered as material to the issue; and the defendant cannot take anything by his motion.

Motion dismissed, with costs.

Langdon, for defendant.
Darius Chipman, for plaintiffs.

* * * * *

WINDSOR COUNTY, AUGUST TERM,
A.D. 1802.

JONATHAN ROBINSON, Chief Judge.
ROYALL TYLER, }
STEPHEN JACOB, } *Assistant Judges.*

SELECTMEN of Windsor
against
STEPHEN JACOB, Esquire

THE plaintiffs, as selectmen and overseers of the poor of the town of Windsor, declared against the defendant in several counts of general *indebitatus assumpsit.*[1]

First.   For 100 dollars, money laid out and expended.

Secondly.   For work and labour done. Both stated to be on the 1st day of *January,* 1801.

The plaintiffs in their specification stated, That on the 26th of *July,* 1783, the defendant purchased of one *White, Dinah,* a negro slave, whom he then brought into the town of *Windsor;* that she continued to live with and serve him as a slave until some time in the year 1800, when she became infirm, sick, and blind, and in this condition was discarded by the defendant, and became a public charge, and that for the moneys expended by the corporation for medicine and attendance during her sickness, and for her support since, this action is brought.

General issue pleaded, and joinder.

In support of the declaration, the plaintiffs offered to read in evidence to the Jury the bill of sale from *White* to the defendant.

Marsh, counsel for defendant, objected. If this action can be supported, it must be on the principle of the implied contract a master is

---

[1] No inhabitant of this State can hold a slave, and though a bill of sale transferring a person as a slave may be valid by the *lex loci* of another State or dominion, yet when the master *becomes an inhabitant* of this State, his bill of sale ceases to operate here, and cannot be read to charge him with the maintenance of such person in sickness or the imbecility of old age.

under to maintain his slave. But we contend that no person can be held in slavery in this State; and the showing of a bill of sale can be no evidence that the unfortunate being supposed to be transferred by it as a human chattel, is a slave; for the contract in the bill of sale is void by our constitution, which, in the first article of the declaration of the rights of the inhabitants of the State of *Vermont,* declares, "That all men are born equally free and independent, and have certain natural, inherent, and inalienable rights, among which are the enjoying and defending life and liberty, acquiring, possessing, and protecting property, and pursuing and obtaining happiness and safety: Therefore no male person born in this country, or brought from over sea, ought to be holden by law to serve any person as a servant, *slave,* or apprentice, after he arrives to the age of twenty-one years, nor *female* in like manner after she arrives to the age of eighteen years, unless they are bound by their own consent after they arrive to such age, or bound by law for the payment of debts, damages, fines, costs, or the like."[2]

It will not be contended that the *African Dinah* is within the exceptions to this fundamental right.

Hubbard, for the plaintiffs, replied,

That though no person can hold a slave *de jure* by our constitution, yet there may exist among us a slave *de facto.* That if a master will hold an *African* in bondage as a slave, contrary to right, and for a succession of years, during which the slave *de facto* spends the vigour of her life in his service, and in which she may be presumed to have earned for the master sufficient to maintain her in the decrepitude of old age, there is a moral obligation upon the master to support her when incapable of labour; and the law of common justice, upon which all equitable actions are founded, will imply a promise in him to respond any necessary expenses incurred by others for her support.

That it would operate extremely hard upon corporations, who possessed no power to loose the shackles of slavery while the slave

---

[2] Constitution; *Vermont* Stat. vol. 1, p. 30.

continued in health, to be made a common infirmary for them when sick and useless.

That the position, "that slavery cannot exist in this State," must be taken *cum grano salis*; for in case a slave-holder should pass through our territory attended by his slave, the constituion of the *United States* protects the master's tenure in the slave, in case the slave should abscond. "No person held to service or labour in one State under the laws thereof, escaping into another, shall, in consequence of any law, or regulation therein, be discharged from such service or labour, but shall be delivered up on the claim of the party to whom such service of labour may be due;"[3] and by the act of the *United States* "respecting fugitives from justice, and persons escaping from the service of their masters,"[4] passed during the second session of the second Congress, the magistrates of this State are holden to aid in the arrest of fugitive slaves; and if they find, on examination, that the fugitive is a slave under the laws of the place from which he fled, they must certify the slavery; and the master or his agent may remove the fugitive *as such*, from this State, and annexing a penalty against all who may impede the slave-holder in seizing his property or rescuing the slave after he has been arrested. The bill of sale in ordinary cases must be admitted by the magistrates to substantiate the slave-holder's right. The principle upon which such bill is founded cannot be drawn into question, for that had been already settled by the article of the *United States* constitution cited. If, therefore, the bill of sale cannot be exhibited in evidence in this case, because it is void by our State constitution, it cannot be shown in any case; and this would avoid the constitution and laws of the *United States*; and, as if to meet the present case, the sixth article of the constitution of the *United States declares,* that this constitution, and the laws of the *United States* which shall be made in pursuance thereof, &c. shall be the supreme law of the land, and the Judges in every State shall be bound thereby, any thing in the *constitution* and laws of any State to the contrary notwithstanding.[5]

[3] Laws of the *U.S.* vol. I. 17. art. 4. s. 2.
[4] *Ib.* vol. 2, p. 166.
[5] Laws of the *U.S.* p. 18.

Marsh, contra. A distinction is attempted to be made between a slave holden *de jure* and a slave *de facto*; and it is urged, that in the latter case there exists a moral obligation in the master of such slave, who has received the benefit of her services, to bear the burthen of her infirmities. There is indeed a moral obligation upon all to be charitable, and to conduct conformably to the principles of natural justice, but we consider that such principles do not operate for, but against the plaintiffs. We beg liberty to state the facts, which, at the same time they do away an illiberal charge made against our client in the specification, will show, that no implied promise in the defendant can be raised in equity to respond moneys expended by the plaintiffs in support of the slave *de facto*.

Some time in the year 1783, the defendant brought the woman *Dinah* into this State. She continued in his family several years; and there can be but little doubt, from the excellent character and disposition of her master, she would have so continued until this time in sickness and in health; but several of the inhabitants of *Windsor,* represented in their corporate capacity by the present plaintiffs, discovering that she was an excellent servant, and wishing to profit themselves of her labours, inveigled her from her master's family and service by the syren songs of *liberty and equality,* which have too often turned wiser heads. She spent the vigour of her life with these people, and wasted her strength in their service; and now she is blind, paralytic, and incapable of labour, they aim by this suit to compel the defendant *solely* to maintain her; for as a member of the corporation, on the event of the failure of this suit, he must bear his proportion of the burthen.

When she was enticed from the defendant's service, he did not attempt by legal aid to reclaim her. As an inhabitant of the State, in obedience to the constitution, he considered that he could not hold her as a slave. Is it equitable then, that when the sovereign power had dissolved the tenure by which he held her services, and when he had been deprived of her labours by the enticement of others, that by the same power, and *virtually* at the suit of the same people who enticed her from his service, and who have profited by her labours when in vigour and health, he should now be compelled to maintain her in the decrepitancy of old age.

It is said, that it is extremely hard for a corporation, who possessed no power to remove the slave *de facto* from her master whilst in health, to be compelled to support her when sick or infirm.

The corporation of *Windsor* should have availed itself of the provision of the act in this as in all other like cases, by warning her to depart the town, which is the only mode pointed out in the statutes to avert from a town corporation the expense of maintaining a pauper.[6]

It is said, that by the operation of the constitution and laws of the *United States,* slavery may be said to exist in this State in a qualified sense. We are not disposed to investigate this position. It is certainly more curious than important in its application to the case in question. In this case the right of a claimant to a fugitive slave is not in issue. The simple point is, is the defendant obligated to refund moneys advanced by others for medicine and attendance, and in support of a woman who had formerly been in his service? We contend that it cannot be upon any other principle than that she is his slave; which cannot be admitted under our constitution of government.

TYLER, Assistant Judge.[7] The plaintiffs, as selectmen, and overseers of the poor of the town of *Windsor,* have declared in two general counts, and have displayed their cause of action in their specification, and rest it upon the implied liability the defendant is under to defray the expenses incurred by the sickness, and for the support of a blind aged person, who they allege is the defendant's slave, purchased by a

---

[6] *Vide.* An act in addition to an act, entitled, an act defining what shall be deemed and adjudged a legal settlement, and for the support of the poor, for designating the duties and powers of the overseers of the poor, and for the punishment of idle and disorderly persons, *Vermont* Stat. vol. I, p. 400. c. xxxix. No. 2. passed *November* 6, 1801. The act to which this is an addition was passed *March* 3, 1797. Same volume, p. 382. A former act, "providing for and ordering transient, idle, impotent, and poor persons," was passed *March* 9, 1787. *Vide Haswell's* edit. *Vermont* Stat. p. 126. repealed 10th *November,* 1797. *Vide Vermont* Stat. vol. 2, p. 416. c. cxi. No. 2.

[7] Jacob, Assistant Judge, being a party, did not sit in this cause.

regular bill of sale. In support of the declaration, this bill of sale is offered, and an exception is taken to its being read as evidence to the Jury. The question must turn upon the validity of operative force of this instrument *within this State.* If the bill of sale could by our constitution operate to bind the woman in slavery when brought by the defendant to inhabit within this State, then it ought to be admitted in evidence; and the law will raise a liability in the slave-holder to maintain her through all the vicissitudes of life; but if otherwise it is void.

Our State constitution is express, no inhabitant of the State can hold a slave; and though the bill of sale may be binding by the *lex loci* of another State or dominion, yet when the master becomes an inhabitant of this State, his bill of sale ceases to operate here.

With respect to what has been observed upon the constitution and laws of the Union, I will observe, that whoever views attentively the constitution of the *United States,* while he admires the wisdom which framed it, will perceive, that in order to unite the interests of a numerous people inhabiting a broad extent of territory, and possessing from education and habits, different modes of thinking upon important subjects, it was necessary to make numerous provisions in favour of local prejudices, and so to construct the constitution, and so to enact the laws made under it, that the rights or the supposed rights of all should be secured throughout the whole national domain. In compliance with the spirit of this constitution, upon our admission to the Federal Union, the statue laws of this State were revised, and a penal act,[8] which was supposed to militate against the third member of the 2d section of the 4th article of the constitution of the *United States,* was repealed; and if cases shall happen in which our local sentiments and feelings may be violated, yet I trust the good people of *Vermont* will on all such occasions submit with cheerfulness to the national constitution and laws, which, if we may in some particular wish more congenial to our modes of thinking, yet we must be sensible are

[8] The act to prevent the sale and transportation of negroes and mulattoes out of this State, passed October 30, 1786. *Haswell's* edition of the Statutes, p. 117.

productive of numerous and rich blessings to us as individuals, and to the State as an integral part of the Union.

The question under consideration is not affected by the constitution or laws of the *United States*. It depends solely upon the construction of our own State constitution, as operate upon the inhabitants of the State; which, as it does not admit of the idea of slavery in any of its inhabitants, the contract which considers a person inhabiting the State territory as such, must be void. I am therefore against admitting the bill of sale in evidence.

Chief Judge. I concur fully in opinion with the Assistant Judge. I shall always respect the constitution and laws of the Union; and though it may sometimes be a reluctant, yet I shall always render a prompt obedience to them, fully sensible, that while I reverence a constitution and laws which favour the opinions and prejudices of the citizens of other sections of the Union, the same constitution and laws contain also provisions which favour our peculiar opinions and prejudices, and which may possibly be equally irreconcilable with the sentiments of the inhabitants of other States, as the very idea of slavery is to us. But when the question of slavery involves solely the interests of the inhabitants of this State, I shall cheerfully carry into effect the enlightened principles of our State constitution.

The bill of sale cannot be read in evidence to the Jury.

Plaintiffs non suited.

Jonathan Hatch Hubbard and *Amasa Paine*, for plaintiffs.
Charles Marsh and *Jacob Smith*, for defendant.

*   *   *   *   *

ADDISON COUNTY, JANUARY TERM,
A.D. 1803.

JONATHAN ROBINSON, Chief Judge.
ROYALL TYLER, }
STEPHEN JACOB, } *Assistant Judges.*

NATHANIEL and LUCRETIA RICH, Appellants,
against
ALEXANDER TRIMBLE, Appellee.

DECLARATION in case upon a special promise made to the plaintiff *Lucretia* when sole.[1]

The plaintiffs declare, that the said *Lucretia,* when sole, had an illegitimate child born of her body, of which the defendant was the father, and by the law of nature and the land was obligated to aid and assist in its maintenance; in consideration whereof he promised the said *Lucretia* when sole, to wit, on the 5th of *March,* 1799, to pay her at the rate of one dollar per week, for each and every week that she should nurse, nurture, tend, support, maintain and take charge of said child during its infancy; that in consideration thereof she nursed, &c. and took charge of said child during its infancy, two hundred weeks, from, &c. to, &c. and then alleges an intermarriage between the plaintiff, and that the right of action hath accrued to both of them, &c.

There were also two general counts, one for 500 dollars, money had and received, and the other for the same sum for work and labour done.

The defendant pleaded in bar a release of the demand in writing for the consideration and receipt of 30 dollars, made on the 3d of September, 1800, by the plaintiff *Lucretia* when sole.

To this plea there was a traverse of the release, and issue to the country.

[1] The signature of a party to a release cannot be proved by comparison of handwritings if there be a *subscribing witness,* even though the witness resides *without* the State; for if the place of his residence be known, and he lives within a reasonable distance from the place of trial, his disposition should be taken.

The release was offered in evidence by the defendant's counsel, who offered to show its execution by a comparison of hand-writing.

Strong, for the plaintiffs, objected, that there was a subscribing witness, and relied on the case of *Stephen Pearl* v. *Ebenezer Allen, Chittenden* County, *January* term, A.D. 1800.[2]

Harrington, for defendant. We consider that case not in point. The objection there was, that the subscribing witness was *within process of the Court,* and that decision rested on this ground. But the subscribing witness to this release lives on the shores of Lake *George,* within the State of *New-York, beyond the process of the Court.*

TYLER, Assistant Judge. The State statutes provide for the taking the depositions of witnesses out of the State, to be used in the Judicial Courts within it, and the deposition of the subscribing witness might have been taken in this case.

The term *"process,"* as commonly applied, intends that proceeding by which a party is called into Court, but it has a more enlarged signification, and includes all the proceedings of the Court from the beginning to the end of a suit, and is defined in the books, *"processus; a procedendo ab initio usque ad finem."* And in this view all proceedings which may be had to bring testimony into Court, whether *viva voce* or in writing, may be considered to be within the process of the Court.

JACOB, Assistant Judge. I agree with my brother TYLER. There are two modes of obtaining testimony to be used in Court; one by bringing the witness into Court by process of *subpœna ad testificandum,* or in case of wilful neglect of appearance by *capias;* the other by taking the deposition of the witness, by the aid of government if the deponent lives within the State, and upon the party's own application if the witness resides in another State or dominion; but when the deposition is returned into Court, it is incorporated with the proceedings or process of the Court. I am therefore for not admitting the execution of the alleged release to be proved by comparison of hand-writing, as within the case of *Pearl* v. *Allen.*

[2] *Vide Vermont Rep.* vol. I, p. 4.

Chief Judge. Whether the case cited is in point, and the rejection of the comparison of hand-writing in this case can be included in that case or not, I am against the admission of comparisons of hand-writings, to show the execution of this release. I consider that our statute had made ample provision for the taking of depositions in civil causes. That when a question arises whether the presence or the deposition of a witness shall be supplied by a comparison of hand-writing, or other lesser evidence, in case the witness lives beyond the territorial lines of the State, the inquiry must be, whether the place of his residence is known with precision, and whether it is within such reasonable distance as that the party might procure his deposition? In this case I consider, that the place of residence of the subscribing witness being ascertained, and within reasonable distance, the defendant might readily have obtained his deposition, and therefore I agree with the assistant Judges, that a comparison of hand-writing to prove the plaintiff *Lucretia's* signature to the release, cannot be admitted.

Evidence not admitted.

Verdict for plaintiffs, 200 dollars.
Samuel Miller and *Moses Strong,* for plaintiffs.
W. C. Harrington and *Amos Marsh,* for defendant.

* * * * *

STATE against PETER WHITE.

INDICTMENT for larceny.[1]

The indictment charged the defendant, that at *Middlebury,* on the 25th of *December,* A.D. 1802, *vi et armis,* he stole, took, and carried away seven yards of muslin, a portmanteau, and sundry other chattels, principally tin ware, of the proper goods and chattels of *Thomas Clerk,* then and there being found, &c. *contra formam statuti.*

Trial by Jury.

It appeared in evidence, that *Thomas Clerk* was a tin manufacturer,

---

[1] A bailee of goods, who has the qualified possession of them, is guilty of larceny in privately eloigning and converting them.

and had hired the prisoner to work at his trade as a journeyman; that Clerk went a journey, and left his shop in the care of the defendant, under the superintendence of his brother *Samuel Clerk,* who on account of the prisoner's ill conduct in being frequently intoxicated in his brother's absence, dismissed him and shut up the shop. On *Thomas Clerk's* return the goods were discovered to be missing, the prisoner was pursued, overtaken in *Cornwall,* and the goods found in his custody.

The defense attempted to be made was, that the eloigning the goods was only a breach of trust in the prisoner; that he could be no trespasser in the eloigning, he having received the goods by consent of the owner, and if no trespass in taking, there could be no *theft,* as without a tortious taking there can be no larceny.

TYLER, Assistant Judge. After the repeated decisions of the Court upon this point, the present defense is certainly unexpected.

So long since as the year 1530, this doctrine has been abrogated in *England* by the statute of *Henry* VIII. c. 7. which in the preamble recites, "That divers persons had upon confidence and trust delivered unto their servants their caskets and other jewels, money, goods and chattels, safely to keep to the use of the said masters, &c. and that they had afterwards withdrawn themselves, and had gone away with the same or part thereof, to their own use, and *that it was doubtful whether this were felony or not at common law*": and then enacts, "that all and singular servants, (being of the age of eighteen, and not apprentices,) to whom any such caskets, &c. shall be delivered to keep, that if any such servant or servants withdraw him or them from their said masters or mistresses, and go away with the said caskets, &c. or any part thereof, with intent to steal same, and defraud his or their said masters or mistresses thereof, contrary to the trust and confidence in him or them put by his or their said masters or mistresses, or else being in the service of his said master or mistress, without their assent or command, he embezzle the same caskets, &c. or any part thereof, or otherwise convert the same to his own use, with like purpose, &c. if the caskets,

&c. shall be of the value of 40s. or above, then the same false, fraudulent and untrue act or demeanor from thenceforth shall be deemed and adjudged felony." And although, through the peculiar regard which the *English* Judges pay to the letter of the statutes, this was not extended to journeymen embezzling the goods of their masters, yet since the making of that statute it has ever been considered, that a journeyman or servant who takes his master's goods with an intent to steal them, is guilty of felony at common law.

A distinction in more modern times seems to be made between delivering the *property*, or the qualified *possession, being the care of goods*, to any one. If the *property be actually delivered*, there can indeed be no tortious taking; but if the mere qualified possession *or care* of the goods is only delivered, there may be a tortious taking, and it is committed the instant the bailee privily converts the goods to a purpose not comprehended in the implied or special contract on which the qualified possession or care of the goods was made.

It appears to me, that if this defense is pursued, the sole question to the Jury must be, whether the prisoner took the goods with a design to steal them, which, indeed, from the goods being found in his custody on his apprehension while on flight, can scarcely be questioned.

JACOB, Assistant Judge. It appears to me, that if the doctrine that the eloigning goods by a bailee is not larceny, but a breach of trust, were well founded, it could not apply in this case, for it is in evidence that the prisoner had been discharged from his master's service by the brother, who was his agent to superintend his business in his absence. Upon the prisoner's discharge, all right of possession had then ceased in the prisoner.

Chief Judge. If the prisoner's counsel insist, let this defence be urged to the Jury, and the Court will state the law as it is. In a criminal prosecution I had rather err through *indulgence* than *rigour*.

Miller, counsel for the prisoner, said, he should not press the defence any further, as he had learned from the State Attorney that he had witnesses in Court to prove the taking of some of the chattels mentioned in the indictment, which were not delivered by the owner to the charge of the prisoner.

Verdict guilty.

Daniel Chipman, for the State.
Samuel Miller, for the prisoner.

* * * * *

RUTLAND COUNTY, FEBRUARY TERM,
A.D. 1803.

JONATHAN ROBINSON, Chief Judge.
ROYALL TYLER,
STEPHEN JACOB, } *Assistant Judges.*

BOWNE et al., Appellants,
against
JOHN A. GRAHAM and NATHAN B. GRAHAM, Appellees.

TRESPASS *quare clausum fregit.*[1]

This was an action of trespass on the freehold. The plaintiffs, in their declaration stated, that on the 5th of *July,* A.D. 1801, the defendants *vi et armis* broke and entered their close, being the lot of land and the dwelling-house thereon, on which the said *Nathan B. Graham* now lives in *Rutland,* &c. and having so entered, with like force plucked and destroyed their apples, pears and peaches on their trees on said lot growing, and consumed and eat their garden stuffs growing on said lot, and broke ten panes of glass, and converted a certain brass knocker to their own use, *et alia enormia,* with a *continuando* to the 26th of *February,* A.D. 1802, being the day of the teste of the writ.

---

[1] In an action of trespass *quare clausum fregit* against two, the regular levy of an execution upon a judgement rendered against one of the defendants who had quitted possession before, and never intermeddled with the possession since the levy, cannot be given in evidence against the other, who was in adverse possession at the date of the levy, and has not surrendered his possession since.

The defendants pleaded severally not guilty, and issue to the Jury.

The counsel for the plaintiffs read in evidence a judgment rendered by the Circuit Court of the *United States,* holden at Windsor, within and for the District of *Vermont,* on the 5th day of *May,* A.D. 1801, in favour of their clients, against *John A. Graham,* for the sum of 2,704 dols. 49 cts. debt and costs, and the execution which issued on this judgment, with its levy on the 4th of *July,* 1801, on the premises, by *Thomas Leverett,* the marshal's deputy, who caused them to be appraised, and made record of his levy in *Rutland* town clerk's office the same day, and in the clerk's office from which the execution issued on the 18th of the same month.

It was conceded, that the plaintiffs made a demand of the possession of the premises of *Nathan B. Graham,* on the 6th day of *January,* A.D. 1802, who refused to deliver possession; and it appeared that *John A. Graham* had not been in possession since the year 1794. That *Nathan B. Graham* had held an adverse possession antecedent to the levy.

The question made is, whether the levy of the execution, and the consequent proceedings on the part of the plaintiffs, will show such a possession in them as will maintain an action *quare clausum fregit* against the defendants?

After argument, the Court delivered their opinion.

TYLER, Assistant Judge. The plaintiffs have brought their action *quare clausum fregit* against two defendants for trespass, done, as it is alleged in the declaration, on the 5th *July,* 1801, with a *continuando* to the 26th of *February,* 1802. The defendants have pleaded the general issue *severally.*

It appears that the plaintiffs recovered judgment against *John A. Graham,* one of the defendants, in *May,* 1801, and procured the land to be set off in part satisfaction of his execution on the 4th of *July,* 1801, by a regular levy. That the defendant *John A. Graham* has not been in possession since the levy, and no intermeddling with the close or tortious act is proved to have been done by him. That on the 6th of

January, 1802, the plaintiffs demanded possession of the land levied upon from *Nathan B. Graham,* who refused to surrender his possession, which he has held adverse to the other defendant, antecedent to the levy, and adverse to the plaintiff ever since. So that the question which should be made is, whether the regular levy of an execution upon a judgment rendered against one of the defendants, who had quitted possession before, and never intermeddled with the premises since the levy, can be given in evidence to maintain an action *quare clausum fregit* the other defendant, who has pleaded severally the general issue, and who was in adverse possession at the time of the levy, and has never surrendered his possession since?

It is an established principle, that before an entry and actual possession, one cannot maintain an action of trespass, though he hath *the freehold* in law. Therefore the books inform us, "that an heir before entry cannot have trespass against an abator, but a disseisee may have it against a disseisor *for the disseisin itself, because he was in possession,* but not for an injury against the disseisin." 2 *Roll. Abr.* 553.

This leads to the inquiry, what is the operation of the levy of our execution on lands; and this must be decided by a sound construction of our own statutes; for we can obtain little or no assistance from the writings of our *English* ancestors, as the *English* writ of *elegit* meddles only with the profits; but the levy of our writ of execution transfers the fee of the land, if held by the debtor.

How does it operate as against the debtor? Does it give the creditor possession as against him?

The third section of the act directing the levying and serving executions, in the latter clause enacts—"And all executions extended and levied upon any houses, lands, or tenements as aforesaid, with the return of the officer thereon, being recorded in the records of the lands of the town in which such houses, lands, or tenements, are situate, or in the office wherein deeds respecting the same are required by law to be recorded, and also returned into the office of the Clerk of the Court, or Justice of the Peace, from which such execution issued, and there recorded, shall, as *against* such debtor, his heirs or assigns, make a good title to the party for whom such estate was taken, his heirs and assigns for ever."[2]

But the mere levy of the execution and record made, create only a conditional interest in the estate levied upon in the creditor, and give no possession; for the 5th section provides, that the real estate, thus levied upon, may be redeemed by the debtor in six months from the date of the levy, by tendering or paying the full sums of debt, damages and costs mentioned in the writ of execution, and the officers' fees thereon, together with interest thereon at the rate of twelve per cent. per annum; and the 6th section declares what shall be the operation of the levy, as it respects both creditor and debtor, "that no person or persons to whom any houses, lands or tenements shall be appraised and set off as aforesaid, *shall enter and take possession of the same until six months* after the execution shall have been extended; and if such estate shall not be redeemed in manner as above provided within that time, the person or persons to whom such estate shall have been appraised as aforesaid, are hereby authorized and empowered to enter and take possession without giving any previous notice to the person or persons in possession, in as full and ample a manner as though seisin and possession of the same had been delivered by the officer who served such execution, or could have been given by the person in actual possession, any law, usage or custom to the contrary notwithstanding. But although, at the expiration of the six months, the creditor, on non-payment of the redemption money may enter and take possession without any previous notice; yet he must make an actual entry, and take an actual possession, which the statute has empowered him to do, and which, if not done, he cannot have possession by implication of law. The right of possession is one thing, and the statute has secured to the creditor as against the debtor and those who hold under him; but the actual possession must be taken by his own act; and if this be not done, he has not that possession which will enable him to maintain the present action. This actual entry must be without breach of the peace, or he himself is amenable to the law; and therefore the usual mode has

[2] *Vermont* Stat. vol. I, p. 323.

been for the creditor to bring an action of ejectment, and obtain a legal and peaceable entry by a writ of possession; and the statute seems to countenance a resort to the law in case a peaceable entry is refused by the debtor or his legal representatives, by giving an action to the creditor for the mesne profits, and a right to tender their amount by the debtor in case the creditor does not take possession in bar to an action for the mesne profits, which clearly implies, that the Legislature did not consider that the possession accompanied the levy, or accrued to the creditor upon the non-payment of the redemption money. The creditor, then, by the mere operation of the levy of an execution on lands, on the expiration of the statute term without redemption, does not obtain possession of the lands, and cannot maintain trespass grounded on such process.

But what is the operation of the levy of an execution on lands, as relative to strangers to the judgment? The statute seems to have decided this by confining its operation in a certain case to "the debtor or debtors, or their legal representatives remaining in possession."

A creditor may levy his execution at will upon any real property which he esteems to be the debtor's. The 9th section of the statute contemplates cases where execution may be extended on lands not the property of the debtor, and provides a remedy by allowing the creditor an *alias* execution on his judgment on process of *scire facias*. It would be absurd to suppose that such levy could decide the rights of others, strangers to the judgment, and not holding under the debtor.

It therefore appears to me, that the plaintiffs in this action not having been in possession by actual entry, or by operation of the levy of their execution, cannot maintain their declaration of trespass *quare clausum fregit* against either of the defendants, and more especially against *Nathan B. Graham,* who was an entire stranger to the creditor's judgment, and held a possession antecedent to the levy, and adverse to both the creditor and debtor. If the plaintiffs wish to try the validity of their title, accruing from the levy, as against either, they should resort to an action of ejectment.

JACOB, Assistant Judge. I agree with Judge TYLER. The object of the plaintiffs' attorney in bringing this action, was probably to try the title under it; and if this action had been brought solely against *John A. Graham,* the judgment debtor, he would have been estopped from showing title against the levy; but as it appears he has never been in possession since the levy, and has committed no tortious act, this action will not lie against him. If the plaintiffs wished to try the validity and operation of their levy against a stranger to their judgment, who holds by adverse possession, they should have resorted to an action of ejectment.

Chief Judge. It is much to be desired that the gentlemen of the bar would advise their clients, who claim title to land, to institute an action of ejectment against all in possession. A resort to other actions, by which the title may be collaterally tried, is certainly not beneficial, as the verdicts are not conclusive as to the title, even against the trespassers. If the title might be tried in the present action, which seems to have been the object of the attorney who drafted the declaration, a verdict for the plaintiff would only sound in damages; and a common writ of execution would issue, not a writ of possession, which can only follow the action of ejectment.

Plaintiffs nonsuited.

Cephas Smith, junior, for the plaintiffs.
Nathan B. Graham, pro se et al. def.

*   *   *   *   *

BENNINGTON COUNTY, FEBRUARY TERM,
A.D. 1805

A REPORT OF THE TRIAL
OF
JOHN JOHNSON
FOR THE MURDER OF
HANNAH EVERTS[1]

Editor's Address.

To the reader.

That the good people of Vermont, in common with their fellow citizens of the United States, are daily exposed in their property, health and lives, to the depredations of quacks and imposters is a truth which will not be denied. To put any effectual stop to the wickedness, folly and rashness of such swindling pretenders to medical skill, however desirable, is what has been in vain attempted in Europe; not even attempted in our sister states; and cannot be expected from any positive act of our Legislature; as the General Assembly would even find it hard to draw any line of distinction between him who is skillful, and those who are grossly ignorant; and they might be apprehensive that, while they endeavored to restrain quackery, they might restrain genius. We have it is true, some medical academies within the state, legally incorporated, which grant licenses to practice physic upon due examination of candidates; but this does not remedy the evil. Such licenses may and ought to give credence to those who are thus proved to possess knowledge in the healing art; but they do not restrain the unskilled from tampering with the health, limbs and lives of the community, and taking the bread from the mouths of those physicians who by a long course of study and practice have qualified themselves for real usefulness.

---

[1] The following preface, which was to be utilized in a printed report of the case, is found in "TPT Memoir," pp. 185–86.

To expose to our citizens the base arts, the inhuman folly and gross ignorance of such bold pretenders to medical science, is the object of publishing this trial; and, although it is apprehended, it may not check such hardened and desparate men from insinuating themselves into the families, picking the pockets, injuring the constitution, or destroying the lives of the simple, honest and industrious; yet it is ardently hoped that the perusal of the ensuing trial may operate as a solemn warning to parents and masters of families, how they commit those under their care to men of intemperate habits and profligate lives.

* * * * *

THE SUPREME COURT OF JUDICATURE OF THE STATE OF VERMONT

BURLINGTON, CHITTENDEN COUNTY, SPECIAL SESSION, AUGUST, 1808.

ROYALL TYLER, Chief Judge.
THEOPHELUS HERRINGTON, ⎱ *Assistant Judges.*
JONAS GALUSHA, ⎰

THE STATE OF VERMONT
against
CYRUS B. DEAN

The Grand Jury being impanelled, the Chief Justice gave the following charge.[1]

Gentlemen of the Grand Jury.

The awful and melancholy occasion of our present meeting must

---

[1] This charge to the Grand Jury was recopied in "TPT Memoir." It is included in a narrative of the "Blacksnake" affair, a separate gathering of 14 unnumbered pages, inserted between pp. 243-44, of the ms. memoir.

In a letter of Nov. 30, 1877, Thomas Pickman Tyler said that his brother, Rev.

be a subject of deep and lasting regret to every upright and feeling mind: it is so considered by this Court; we doubt not it is so viewed by you. We officially learn by the verdict of the Jury of inquest, that three of our peaceable, unoffending citizens have been willfully murdered: that our once peaceful and happy land has been polluted with human gore; and the voice of the blood of our brethren crieth from the ground.

Whether we contemplate this event as men, or as citizens, it excites only the most gloomy reflections: as men sympathizing with the surviving relations of the deceased, as citizens indignant at the daring violation of the good laws of our Country—yet, in the midst of this gloomy scene, we have one consolation—and blessed be a merciful *God,* it is a rich one—and that is, that our present meeting affords irrefragable evidence that we have still a government existing among us: a government of our own choice—a government founded in principles of rational liberty: a government which secures to every man retribution for individual wrong—and affords ample legal and constitutional redress for public grievances: a government which secures its citizens the full exercise and almost uncontrolled expression of private opinion: but a government which has provided wholesome laws to restrain and to punish acts of violence and of bloodshed; and which has energy sufficient in its Courts of Justice to bring the perpetrators of them, after conviction by impartial trial to condign punishment.

In times of general dismay when tragical scenes like these are acted; when the public mind is agitated; and some are ready to condemn the accused unheard; others perhaps to excuse, and if not to excuse, to palliate,[2] and when on every side the angry and intolerant passions

George P. Tyler, had deposited at the Vermont Historical Society their father's manuscript report of the trial. This manuscript, probably containing Tyler's notes of the case, would be invaluable but a present day search at the Society has failed to turn up the document. (The above mentioned letter is quoted in Marcus D. Gilman, ed., *The Bibliography of Vermont* [Burlington, 1897], pp. 283–84.)

[2] This phrase is also printed in Hemenway, *The Vermont Historical Gazetteer,* II, 346, in an account of the trial and Tyler's charge to the Grand Jury. The phraseology and punctuation is slightly different from that in "TPT Memoir" and it is possible that the

are excited, good men, however unhappily divided in private opinion, will find their minds irresistably united in one point:—they will instinctively turn their minds to the Supreme Court of Justice; for there they know popular clamors will have no effect: that Innocence will find a sanctuary and guilt only be condemned. Good men will at such times turn their eyes to the Court of Justice because they know that there Judges will preside chosen from the midst of their brethren —men, for whose faithful discharge of their official duties they have every obligation which the laws and the constitution can provide: Judges not only bound by oath, but who, not holding their commissions proudly independent of any control, must at the close of every year, submit their official conduct,—not to the clamorous decision of party zeal, or the volatile opinions of the giddy multitude, but to the calm and deliberate investigation of your representatives, the fathers of the people assembled in their Legislative capacity. Good men will look at their Court of Justice because they know that there they shall meet a Grand Jury, selected from the body of the County in the most fair and impartial mode, and embracing in its panel, whatever of wisdom, integrity and temperance we have among us; and because they know they shall meet a Jury of Trials, selected by lot and purged by challenge from every possibility of partiality or prejudice. Good men will look to the Court of Justice because they know that the accused, though prejudged by the popular voice, will have a candid and impartial trial: and because they especially know that even in these hours of peril, before such Judges and such Jurors, the good and wholesome laws of our country, made to restrain and to punish men of violence and blood, will be carried into effect with decision and firmness and not be suffered to be obscured by casuistry or perplexed into contempt by the subtlety of lettered ingenuity.

Therefore, when, in consequence of this melancholy event, we received the application from your respectable State's Attorney, we did not hesitate immediately to suspend the business of the Eastern

quotation used in Miss Hemenway's volume of 1871 was copied from the original manuscript notes of Tyler mentioned above.

Circuit, and to convene this special session of the Court, conceiving that mere decisions on civil contracts inferior in magnitude and importance to the enquiry into the murder of our Fellow Citizens, and the peace of this highly valued section of the State.

And now we have come among you, with your aid.—not to condemn unheard;—not to be instruments of popular indignation;—not to convict but to try;—not to condemn, but to coolly and impartially investigate—with such dispositions, so honorable to you as men and citizens, we doubt not the Grand Jury of the County of Chittenden is now convened before us.

It is made the duty of this Court, and your oath obligates you to present all such breeches of the law which come to your knowledge *according to your charge.* We do therefore as the Supreme Judiciary of the State charge you, in the first place to peruse, and to reperuse your *Oath,* and consider it not merely as a cold official formulary, necessary to be repeated for your induction into office, but as a solemn appeal to your *God* and your Country; to pause and reflect for what purpose and in whose presence you have lifted your hands to Heaven in this Court of Justice. In your Oath you will find a compleat directory to the conscientious discharge of your duty. You will find the scope of that excellent oath to be, that the moment you enter these walls, and are invested with the character of Grand Jurors, you are to consider yourselves as separated from your fellow citizens to do important duties, and are therefore to divest yourselves of all those prejudices and partialities which so readily attach to us in private life. Let not therefore your acquaintance or friendship for the deceased; the tears of the widow, the lamentations of the fatherless, or the distress of surviving relatives affect you. If possible, divest yourselves of that honest zeal, that holy indignation against the crime of murder, which good men, by some strange mental process, are apt to convert into a species of evidence against the accused. On the other hand, if you have associated with thoughtless and inconsiderate men who have spoken lightly of the crime of murder; who have palliated, if they have not had the boldness to justify the unlawful shedding of human blood; if in some hour of levity any of you have thought that the primary laws of society—those made for the preservation of human life ought, on this occasion to be relaxed, and be accommodated to certain supposed exigencies of the times; purify yourselves also from these prejudices.[3] In a word, if you are assailed by hatred or malice; by fear, favor, affection or hope of reward, repair to your oath. Remember it is not merely your guide now, but can be your only justification to your consciences hereafter.

[3] Miss Hemenway also used this section of the Grand Jury charge in her gazetteer, again with minor changes.

The "Trash" and "Postumi" Essays

ESSAYS IN
POLYANTHOS AND *THE NEW-ENGLAND*
GALAXY

IN DECEMBER, 1805, Joseph T. Buckingham established the *Polyanthos* in Boston. It was a monthly literary magazine, specializing in native verse, prose, theatrical reviews, criticism and biographies of notable figures. As a printer's apprentice at David Carlisle's press in Walpole, Buckingham had known both Tyler and Dennie, but in the intervening years the contacts with each other had not been closely maintained.

Early in 1806 some of Tyler's Boston friends sent him a copy of the new periodical. Without knowing who was the publisher, he praised its attempts at originality and indicated he would not mind contributing to the new venture. Tyler's laudatory comments filtered back to Boston and were heard by Buckingham. In March he wrote Tyler, identified himself as the publisher of the *Polyanthos,* said he was flattered to hear of Tyler's "generous offer of *literary assistance*" and would gladly accept everything Tyler could contribute.[1]

Tyler wrote back on April 3 and explained that he had not meant to suggest he could become a regular contributor. He continued:

For reasons, needless at present to explain, I cannot engage in the continued support of your, or any other periodical publication. I meant merely to intimate that I would occasionally furnish some original matter; . . . but as you have had your expectations raised, it would be wrong to disappoint them. Therefore I send you sufficient to fill your poetical department for one number. . . . I must, however, observe that the unvarying conditions upon which you are permitted to publish it, must be your solemn promise, that I am not known as the author, either by private communication to your friends or any public hints to patrons and subscribers[2]

Shortly thereafter Buckingham wrote to Tyler thanking him for the verses and approaching him about writing a series of essays and a biography of Dennie for future issues of the *Polyanthos.* On April 21 Tyler said, regard-

[1] The letter of March 22, 1806, from Buckingham to Tyler is quoted in "TPT Memoir," pp. 188–89.

[2] *Ibid.,* pp. 189–90. The verses mentioned by Tyler appeared in *Polyanthos,* April, 1806 (see *Tyler Verse,* pp. 131–41).

ing the life of Dennie, that "perhaps my intimacy with him would furnish me with all the necessary facts; and I flatter myself that he would as readily commit his character to my pen, as to most others; but without his express consent I should think it a violation of our long standing friendship."[3]

Concerning the possibiliy of writing a few essays, Tyler was no more encouraging. He wrote: "I have written a sheet of prose for you, divided into numbers under the head of—Trash; with a little exordium, explanatory of this quaint Title; but I omit sending it, as I have been so long out of the fashionable world, that I doubt if I can hit the fashionable taste."[4]

Apparently Buckingham was able to convince Tyler he was still "fashionable" for during the following months Tyler contributed several "Trash" essays to the *Polyanthos*. During the next year Tyler also contributed a number of important poems to the magazine.[5]

On May 20 Buckingham wrote to Tyler, "I am much pleased with your '*trash*' and hope you will long continue your favours, as I *mean to deserve them*. I also hope I shall be able at some future day to make you ample compensation for your generosity."[6]

Trash No. 1 appeared in the May, 1806, issue of the magazine. It contained the "little exordium" and had as its motto the Greek phrase, Φλυϛω χαι Φλυϛω, meaning "chatter and chatter." The motto was retained for the remainder of the Trash essays.

Trash No. 2 in June was taken up entirely with Tyler's poem, "The Town Eclogue" and his paraphrase of an ode by Horace. Since it contains no prose it is not included here.[7] Trash No. 3 was published in the April, 1807, issue and at that time Buckingham said in an editor's note that Trash No. 4 was "on file for publication."

The column which appeared the following month (May, 1807) was meant to be No. 4 but it was misnumbered No. 3. Because of the press of his legal duties, or for some other reason, Tyler lost interest in the column and no further prose by him was printed in the *Polyanthos*.

As will be seen below, however, Tyler did not forget Buckingham and when the Boston publisher established another magazine a few years later Tyler was again to become a contributor.

[3] *Ibid.*, p. 192.

[4] *Ibid.*, p. 192. The attribution of the "Trash" essays to Tyler is further reinforced by Buckingham's statement of his later years, "of the several writers from which I received aid, Judge Tyler of Vermont was the most liberal in his contribution. The series of numbers entitled 'Trash' . . . were supplied by him." (Buckingham, *Personal Memoirs and Recollections of Editorial Life* [Boston, 1852], I, 56.)

[5] *Tyler Verse*, pp. 131–44, 146–65.

[6] The letter is in the "RT Collection."

[7] *Tyler Verse*, pp. 148–49.

FOR THE POLYANTHOS

TRASH. . . . NO. 1.

Φλυςω χαι Φλυςω

Some years since, visiting an old college acquaintance, I observed in his library a book, labelled on the back in gold letters—"TRASH." The quaintness of the title induced me to inspect the volume. I discovered that it was made of a number of pamphlets, the ephemeral productions of past time. Here sermons and sonnets—almanacks and addresses—masonick songs and lyrick poems—essays on agriculture and collections of witty sayings, toasts, and conundrums—treatises on tar-water and news-carriers' odes—with the trial and last words of a noted malefactor, and a letter on the culture of hemp—cum catalogus eorum qui & te—alicujus Gradûs Laureâ donati sunt, were by the eccentrick humour of my friend compressed within the covers of a sizeable duodecimo. This is a very singular title,—said I. It is very significant,—he replied. But here are *two sermons,*—I observed rather gravely. One of them—he returned—is very dull, and the other I wrote myself. I still think my title very apposite: and I sincerely wish that every bookseller was obliged by law to impress on his volumes titles, which would as honestly exhibit their contents; we should then have less occasion for reviewers.

This anecdote, I trust, will serve as a plenary explanation of the *head* I have given to this department I propose to occupy in the Polyanthos. Those who are too wise, grave and learned to be *amused,* when they see my *title,* may pass my humble lucubrations—they can regale themselves on the *ripened* fruits of science; but there are many, who may wish to cheer the gloom of a stormy evening, or relieve the tedium of busy life, with what may relax without tainting the mind; and such may have a relish for TRASH.

During the contest between Charles the First of England and his parliament, when it was fashionable to give scripture names—when

Praise God Barebones and Fight the good fight of faith Milbourn were all the vogue,—a worthy pair were blest with a son, born on the day of the battle of Noseby, that decisive battle, which assured entire victory to the parliamentarians; and whilst this joyful event was celebrated with sermons and thanksgivings, this zealous couple, resolving not to be outdone by any, selected a whole text of scripture, commemorative of the national deliverance, as a name for this son— and the child was accordingly named—"*Who comforteth us in all our tribulation, that we may be able to comfort them which are in any trouble by the comfort wherewith we ourselves are comforted*" TICHBOURN.—And now, gentle reader, how do you suppose the family contrived to *abbreviate* this Alexandrine of a name for every day use?—Guess— Guess—Ay, I see it is in vain—I must tell you—They called the boy— Trib—

For the Classick Idler.
THE SACRIFICE.

O quale hoc hurly hurly fuit.
Drummond's Polemio-Middinia.[8]

Dum Thomas, in domo of a certain old gentleman vivens,
To his bed, comitante puella, retires in the winter:
She bearing in manu, a warming pan, illam comprimit,
Et certamina veneris the parties began to debellare:
In medio intrat, illud animal, call'd an old woman;
Et videt, horrendum! miro modo in pyxide stupum.
Interea flammae corripiunt totas bed cloathas;
And fir'd by the warming pan, fumum undique arises.

----

[8] William Drummond (1585–1649), poet, author of a history of Scotland and friend of Ben Jonson. In 1683 there was issued anonymously at Edinburgh a macaronic poem, "Polemo-Middinia inter Vitarvam et Nebernam." It was a farcical account of a quarrel between the tenants of two Scotish landowners. Reprinted at Oxford in 1691, it was attributed to Drummond at that time.

Sic clauditur scenum, by offering devout sacrifices;
Vulcano and Hecate et Veneri known by her sweet scents.

                                                    B.

————————

Leaving the great question, whether the stage is most conducive to vice or virtue, undecided, I never have yet heard it doubted, that it was an excellent school for enunciation. Indeed it seems natural to suppose that those, whose trade it is to repeat the literary works of others, should be emulous to express themselves according to the best rules of correct orthoepy. I must, to the honour of our Boston stage, declare, that I have had my pronunciation wonderfully corrected in various important particulars during my attendance to the theatre the past season;[9] and I feel the more grateful, as the instruction I have received, by which I have been enabled to correct and polish my Yankee utterance, could not have been derived from any other source: as I assure you I have sought for it in vain, in Sheridan, Walker, and others, who have *pretended* to instruct us in elocution. But all men are not *parfect*. Immediately after the season closed, I addressed the following *Varses* to my dear *Mistriss*; wherein I have attempted some of the graces of our theatrical style of pronunciation, by spelling the words as they were pronounced on the boards, as far as our sorry alphabet would enable me: for although our cris-cross row is abundantly ample to express the pronunciation of a Cicero, Ames, or Chatham, yet the poor letters often appear to make awkward and abortive efforts to delineate the elegant tones of our more polished players.   S.

Love Varses to the bucheous Daffodel.[10]

Alas! my *shweet* Daffodel's eyes
    Ave made a *greet ole* in my *art*:
With *rapchure* my *art* almost dies,
    When I see my *adjored* depart.

[9] Tyler never did journey to Boston at this time. He received all his details on the Boston theater from Buckingham's correspondence.

[10] In this poem Tyler is satirizing the diction of Gilbert Fox, an actor in the Boston

She's as *bucheous* as morning in May;
  No wonder to love I'm *injuc'd*:
She's the *shweetest* of *creachures* I say,
  That *nachure* has ever *projuc'd*.

Not *Harculus* boasts of more force;
  Not *Dougle-as*[11] shows more desire;
Not *Caato* more *virchus* resource;
  Nor *Uthellur* e'er rag'd with more fire—

Than I for *shweet* Daffodel feel,
  When *jest* by the woodlands we meet:
She's the *emblum* of all that's genteel;
  She's *parfect* in all that is *shweet*.

I made her a *promus* of love;
  To *ajore* her ever was my *juty*;
I was *onest* and true as a dove,
  For who could be false to such a *beauche*!

I never my *promus* will *breek*,
  Though the *whirld* should in *phalanx* oppose:
Her *virchue* will bind me to keep
  What her *radiunt* eyes did impose.

My *art haches* to think on her charms
  Lest *forchune* her aspect should *churn*:—
Was the *beauche* but once in my *harms*,
  She from me should never *rechurn*.

Company during 1805–06. There are several mentions of Fox's poor diction in *Polyanthos'* theatrical columns (February, 1806, 207–08, 211–12; March, 1806, 284. See also *Tyler Verse*, pp. 142–44).

[11] John Home's play, *Douglas,* was produced in Boston on Feb. 11, 1806. For a review of this production see *Polyanthos,* April, 1806, 21–5.

Shet out from her presence I mope;
The shepherds all call me *schupid*:
Would *forchune* then lend me a rope,
I'd soon bid *ajue* to *shweet* Cupid.

If I lose her, I'll mount on my *orse*,
To bid her *ajue* then inclin'd;
And to cheer my *art* under her loss,
I'll drink off a bottle of *wind*.

As is common with authors who make use of obscure words, we subjoin a glossary for the benefit of the *unlearned* reader.

GLOSSARY

Ave, have
Art, heart
Adjored, adored
Ajore, adore
Ajue, adieu
Bucheous, beauteous
Beauche, beauty
Breek, break
Creachures, creatures
Caato, Cato
Churn, turn
Dougle-as, Douglas
Emblum, emblem
Forchune, fortune
Greet, great
Harculus, Hercules
Harms, arms

Injuc'd, induced
Jest, just
Juty, duty
Nachure, nature
Ole, hole
Onest, honest
Orse, horse
Projuc'd, produced
Parfect, perfect
Promus, promise
Rapchure, rapture
Shweet, sweet
Shet, shut
Schupid, stupid
Uthellur, Othello
Virchue, virtue
Wind, wine

* * * * *

FOR THE POLYANTHOS

TRASH. . . . NO. 3.

Φλυϛω χαι Φλυϛω

To obtain a personal view of those personages who have conspicuously figured on the theatre of human action is, I believe, a desire common to all. Is the interesting personage living, how eagerly do we hasten to the church, the theatre, the mall, or the exchange, to catch even a faint glimpse of the Patriot, honoured by his country; the Orator, distinguished for the sublime and beautiful; the Author, admired for his wit and learning, for the Beauty and the Hero, alike famed for conquest! Have the objects of our sympathy or admiration been dead for years or ages, how grateful it is to view a statue, a portrait, a coin or seal, which afford some faint idea of their lineaments, or to gleam from the fields of literature, after the harvest of the historian.

To those who think with me, and who have read or been present at the representation of Rowe's tragedy of 'Jane Shore,'[12] some memoranda of that eminent martyr to meretricious pleasure may not be unacceptable,

JANE SHORE.

Shakespeare, in his first scene of Richard the third, has put the following sarcastick sketch of this celebrated beauty into the mouth of the tyrant:

> We say that Shore's wife hath a pretty foot,
> A cherry lip, a bonny eye, a passing pleasing tongue.[13]

---

[12] Nicholas Rowe's *Jane Shore,* was first played at Drury Lane, Feb. 2, 1713/14. The Boston Company presented it in that city on Nov. 11, 1795, and May 1, 1797. For notices of the play see the *Columbian Centinel,* XXVII (May 17, 1797), 3.

[13] *Richard III,* I, i, 93-4.

In the year 1593, Michael Drayton, an English bard, published a work entituled [sic] 'England Heroical Epistles'; these epistles are humble imitations of Ovid.[14] Drayton seldom rose above mediocrity as a poet, and these epistles are not among the most excellent of his labours. The learned Selden[15] has, fortunately for this writer's fame, enriched his work with annotations; and although Drayton is neglected as a poet, he is idolized and immortalized by the antiquarians.

One of these heroical epistles is styled,

EDWARD IV. TO JANE SHORE.[16]

According with the fashion of that day, the epistle is preluded with An Argument.

"Edward the fourth, bewitched with the report
Of Mistress Shore, resounded through his court,
Steals to the city, in strange disguise,
To view the beauty *whose transpiercing eyes
Had shot so many*—which did so content
The amorous King, that instantly he sent
These lines to her whose graces did allure him,
Whose answer back doth of her love assure him."

As the royal writer was a *lover,* it would be rash to look for a very correct description of the lady's beauty in the epistle itself, especially as it is made to appear to have been written whilst he was wooing this fair one to frailty and love; for, as our old friend Geoffrey Chaucer ryghte cunninglie plaineth,

[14] Michael Drayton (1563–1631), poet laureate of England. The book, *England's Heroical Epistles,* a series of letters in verse modeled after Ovid's *Heroides,* was published in 1597, not 1593 as Tyler states.

[15] John Selden (1584–1654), jurist, friend of Ben Jonson and Drayton. Best known for *Table Talk* (1689), he published *Notes on Drayton* in 1612.

[16] For the complete epistle of "Edward the Fourth to Mistres *Shore*" see William Hebel, ed., *The Works of Michael Drayton* (Oxford, 1932), II, 247–51. Tyler has correctly copied the original although he modernized the spelling in some instances and added some punctuation.

"Whenne lustee youthe to love incline,
They blinken ay with bleered eyne."[17]

But there is one compliment in the epistle so truly gallant, that I publish it for the benefit of our city beaux in Boston and New York, whose fine speeches, I am told by the young ladies, have become of late, "wearisome, stale, flat and unprofitable."

"If thou but please to walk into the pawn,
To buy thee cambrick, callico, or lawn;
If thou the whiteness of the same would prove,
From thy far whiter hand pluck off thy glove;
And those which buy as the beholders stand
Will take thy hand for lawn, lawn for thy hand."[18]

Now, with a little variation, would not this very courtly compliment apply to a lily hand examining laced muslin upon a William's-street or Cornhill counter?—The monarch concludes his tender epistle in the usual style of love letters ancient and modern, by assuring her that he was sickening, dying, and what is worse, *starving* to see her—

Till when these papers, by their lord's command,
By me shall kiss thy *sweet and dainty hand*.[19]

THE PORTRAIT.

A pair of Lovers from Selden's annotations upon Drayton's Heroical Epistles.

Jane Shore.

Two or three poems written by sundry men have magnified this woman's beauty; whom that ornament of England, and London's

---

[17] This quotation cannot be found in any concordance or modern edition of Chaucer. During Tyler's day there where many spurious works attributed to Chaucer and this passage may have been taken from one of these.
[18] "Edward the Fourth to Mistres *Shore*," ll. 95–100.
[19] *Ibid.,* ll. 169–70.

more particular glory, Sir Thomas More, very highly hath praised for her beauty, *she being alive in his time,* though poor and aged. Her stature was mean, (*middling*) her hair of a dark yellow, her face round and full, her eye grey, and delicate harmony being betwixt each part's proportion, and each proportion's colour; her body fat, white and smooth; her countenance cheerful and like her condition. That picture which I have seen of her, was such as she rose out of her bed in the morning, having nothing on but a rich mantle, cast under one arm, over her shoulder, and sitting in a chair, on which her naked arm did lie. What her father's name was, or where she was born, is not certainly known; but Shore, a young man of right goodly person, wealth and behaviour, abandoned her bed, after the king had made her his concubine. Richard the third, causing her to do open penance in Paul's Church-Yard, commanded that no man should relieve her; which the tyrant did not so much for his hatred to sin, but that making his brother's life odious, he might cover his horrible treasons the more cunningly.

I suspect from the eulogiums in the epistle, and the attitude of Mistress Shore in the picture, which was doubtlessly adapted to exhibit her beauty to the greatest possible advantage, that her hand, or, as the king more gallantly styles it, *"her sweet and dainty hand,"* was the most perfect of her personal charms.—What do *you* think, Ladies?

Edward IV.

Edward the Fourth was by nature very chivalrous and very amorous, applying his sweet admirable aspect to attain his wanton appetite the rather; which was so well known to Lewis, the French king, who, at their interview, invited him to Paris, that, as Comencus reports, being taken at his word, he notwithstanding brake off the matter, fearing the Parisian Dames, with their witty conversation, would detain him longer than should be for his benefit; by which means Edward was disappointed of his journey. And albeit princes whilst they live, have nothing in them but what is admirable, yet we need not mistrust the flattery of the court in those times; for certain it is that his shape was excellent, his hair drew near to a black, making his face's favour to appear more delectable, though the smallness of his eyes, full of shining moisture, as it took away some comeliness, so it argued much sharpness of understanding and cruelty mingled together. And indeed George Buchannan (that impetuous Scott)[20] chargeth him and other princes of those times, with affection of tyranny; as Richard the third manifestly did.

* * * * *

FOR THE POLYANTHOS

TRASH. . . . NO.. 3.

$\Phi\lambda\nu\varsigma\omega$ $\chi\alpha\iota$ $\Phi\lambda\nu\varsigma\omega$

There are more adults pleased with riddles than are willing to confess it; they are considered as an infantile amusement; and yet both sacred and profane history inform us, that in earlier ages they were held as the test of manly wit and wisdom. Sampson's riddle[21] has been thought worthy of preservation in that inspired volume, while that of Sphynx[22] adorns the pages of ancient profane history. It is long since I amused myself with riddles;[23] but when I have been in search of what would be called more rational amusement in the perusal of the elder English poets, repeatedly have I cast my eye upon the following, and sometimes in an idle moment have I attempted to solve it. It may be found in the Poetical Works of Sir Thomas Wyat, the Elder—who, with the accomplished Earl of Surry, were the most brilliant belle lettres ornaments of the court of Henry VIII.

[20] George Buchanan (1506–1582), historian and scholar, author of a history of England.

[21] Judges 14: 12–19.

[22] The riddle of the Sphynx was put forth many times in Greek literature, e.g., Apollodorus, *The Library*, III, v, 7–9; Sophocles, *Oedipus the King*, l. 391ff.; and Euripides, *The Phoenician Maidens*, l. 45ff.

[23] For the poem entitled, "A Riddle," see *Tyler Verse*, pp. 121–3.

A RIDDLE OF A GYFT BY A LADIE.[24]

A Lady gave me a gift she had not,
And I received her gift which I took not,
She gave it me willingly and yet she would not,
And I received it albeit I could not;
If she gave it me I force not,
And if she take it again she cares not;
Consider what this is and tell not,
For I am fast sworn I may not.—

CRITICISM

Dr. Johnson, in his life of Dryden, commenting upon his Ode for St. Cecilia's Day, observes "that it does not want its negligences; some of the lines are without correspondent rhymes; a defect which I never detected but after an acquaintance of *many years*." That is, while the Doctor for many years perused this divine poem with the simple design of gratifying himself with its rich and variegated beauties, he did not discover these negligences; but when he was engaged by the London Booksellers to write the Poet's biography, he commenced the critick, and discovered, for the first time, that "some of the lines are without correspondent rhymes."

Now this is the case with all of us when we sit down to criticise. We are forced to discover some defects in order to evidence that we have some penetration. But yet, great as the Doctor is, I, who am an enthusiastick admirer of the Ode, would no more thank him for his discovery, than I would the officious person who should approach me at dinner, and point out something disgusting in my favorite dish. At the literary feast, I wish to cater for myself, and an austere, captious critick is as disagreeable to me as the Physician in Don Quixotte was to Sancho Pancha, when he criticised away the best viands from the

---

[24] This verse by Wyatt is included in *Tottel's Miscellany* of 1557. It is Epigram No. 8 in *The Poems of Sir Thomas Wiat*, ed. A. K. Foxwell (London, 1913), p. 49.

table of that governour of the island of Barataria.[25] The inefficacy of criticism, as operating on publick taste, has often been displayed. The celebrated Bentley wrote a critique upon Addison's Cato, in which he condemned that popular work as a farrago of absurdities; and yet what critick is more reverenced than Bentley,[26] what tragedy more read than Cato?—Dr. Johnson, after insinuating an indifferent opinion of Pomfret's Poems,[27] observes, "that they please many, and that which pleases many must have merit." Here is the acknowledged triumph of publick taste over the fastidiosity of refined criticism.

S.

* * * * *

THE NEW-ENGLAND GALAXY

ALTHOUGH BUCKINGHAM showed good business sense and the *Polyanthos* was a quality publication, subscribers were slow to accept his rather novel concept of a literary magazine. Competition from *The Monthly Anthology* forced Buckingham to suspend publication between July, 1807, and February, 1812. Finally, in September, 1814, the *Polyanthos* ceased to exist.

On the prodding of his friends, however, Buckingham attempted again in late 1817 to establish a periodical in Boston. The fruit of his efforts was *The New-England Galaxy & Masonic Magazine*. The first issue appeared on October 10, 1817.

After an interval of ten years Buckingham again solicited literary contributions from Tyler. On March 6, 1818, Tyler noted in his "Day Book" that he had received a letter from the publisher "proposing that I should write for Masonick Magazine."[28] Tyler's answer on March 9 must have been in the affirmative, although he does not say so, for on July 6 he noted

---

[25] This subject apparently interested Tyler. See his play, "The Island of Barrataria," in original ms., "RT Collection." It has been printed in: Arthur W. Peach and George F. Newbrough, eds., *Four Plays by Royall Tyler* (Princeton, 1941).

[26] Richard Bentley (1662–1742), scholar, critic and controversial master of Trinity College, Cambridge. He was the brunt of several attacks by Pope, especially in the "Dunciad."

[27] John Pomfret (1667–1702). He is best remembered for his poem, "The Choice: a Poem written by a Person of Quality." (1700).

[28] Tyler's ms. "Day Book," 196 pp., is in the "RT Collection." It is a diary kept by

in his diary that he had "sent Postumi to Buckingham by this even'g mail."[29]

The column entitled "Postumi" appeared in *The New-England Galaxy* on July 10. It was intended to be the first installment of a project which had interested both Tyler and Buckingham as far back as 1806. Since Dennie's death in 1812, they and others had lamented that no biography of their late friend or a collected edition of his works had appeared.

In an editor's note Buckingham outlined the purpose of Tyler's contribution:

> We solicit the attention of the classical reader to an article on the preceeding page, entitled "POSTUMI," &c. It is hoped that the plan there proposed of collecting the scattered literary fragments of DENNIE, will receive the approbation of all who have taste to admire the writing, enthusiasm to reverence the genius, or feeling to regret that no monument is yet erected to perpetuate the memory, of one of the most accomplished scholars that have adorned the age.[30]

In the headnote to the column itself, although Tyler says that Dennie's friends had assembled a manuscript of his literary fragments of "more than fifty pages," it was probably the work mainly of Tyler himself. Unfortunately this effort to perpetuate Dennie's memory is now lost.

In the "Day Book" on July 8 Tyler wrote that he had completed another anecdote about Dennie.[31] It was sent immediately to Boston and appeared in the *Galaxy* on July 24 with the notation it was contributed "by J.T." (i.e., Judge Tyler). The column is a charming recounting of Dennie's unfortunate experience as a young lawyer.[32]

Despite the exhortations by Buckingham for other people to send in their reminiscences of Dennie, and Tyler's attempt to get the project underway with his two contributions, the plan was stillborn. Nothing more was heard in the pages of the *Galaxy* about the hopes to memorialize Dennie.

Tyler's other pieces in the magazine cannot be identified. On July 17

Tyler (and by his wife when he was absent from home) from June 8, 1817-Dec. 1, 1821. For the most part it is a daily record although there are a few gaps. The entry for March 6 is on p. 57.

Tyler had no qualms about contributing to the "Masonick Magazine." He was probably a Mason himself. This is borne out by the "Day Book" notation of June 25, 1820 (p. 164) where Mrs. Tyler mentions her husband went to hear a Masonic discourse in Guilford.

[29] *Ibid.*, p. 75.

[30] *The New-England Galaxy*, I, No. 39 (July 10, 1818), 3.

[31] "Day Book," p. 75.

[32] Buckingham commented on the anecdote in his *Specimens of Newspaper Literature*, II, 198.

Tyler noted he had sent another anecdote to the publisher, on July 20 he mailed some verse to Boston and on July 31 he "wrote to Buckingham enclosing Tear Droppes, anecdote & phenomenon to go by Major Atherton in stage."[33] None of these contributions can now be pinpointed in the *Galaxy* and they may not even have been published.

Nearly a year later Buckingham took a trip through north-central Massachusetts and southern Vermont. The account of his nine-day journey was published in the *Galaxy* in five installments in September and October, 1819. Buckingham included southern Vermont in his itinerary so as to visit Tyler in Brattleboro.[34]

One of the reasons for the visit was to again discuss the possibility of reviving the Dennie project. This is reinforced by a letter of March 20, 1820, from Buckingham to Tyler enclosing a note from Samuel L. Knapp about his proposed memorial volume of notable people. Buckingham suggested that Tyler himself was the best qualified person in the country to write the article on Dennie for the memorial edition.[35]

One tantalizing section of the letter talks about why Buckingham had not been able to publish some of Tyler's more recent verse and anecdotes in the *Galaxy*. Regretably, none of Tyler's contributions during this period are identifiable in the magazine. The only attributable Tyler pieces in the *Galaxy*, therefore, are the two anecdotes on Dennie in 1818.

* * * * *

FOR THE NEW-ENGLAND GALAXY.
POSTUMI,

Or Anecdotes and remains of the late JOSEPH DENNIE, Esq. Editor of the Port-Folio—Compiled by several of his intimate friends in aid of his Biographer.

It is *well*, though perhaps not *generally*, known, that soon after the decease of the late Joseph Dennie, editor of the "Farmer's Museum," and founder and editor of the "Port-Folio," several of his early friends resolved to collect such of his unpublished writings, letters, &c as they were able, and to preserve them in a manuscript for the use of his

[33] "Day Book," p. 78.

[34] The visit to Brattleboro by Buckingham is recounted in the *Galaxy*, III, No. 107 (Oct. 29, 1819), 3.

[35] The correspondence between Knapp and Buckingham and Tyler is in the Chamberlain Collection, Boston Public Library, Ms., No. Ch. A. 12. 48.

future biographer, and that this manuscript, of more than fifty pages, has been read with much interest in certain circles.

This compilation, however, tho' it may have been principally transcribed from the autographiæ of the deceased, does not afford indubitable evidence of its authenticity, and some of its contents are held by critical friends to be of sceptical origin. It would not be surprising that a compilation thus made should embrace some essays which, if genuine, the author surpressed as unworthy [of] his pen, or which may have been improperly, though honestly, imputed to him by injudicious friends. It has, therefore, been deemed advisable to publish extracts from this manuscript, with the expectation that some of the familiar friends of the lamented author may decide on their authenticity from their own knowledge, or from internal evidence; and it is also hoped that many of Mr. Dennie's friends, who have not contributed to this little preparatory compilation, may be induced from this publication, to furnish other reliquiæ.

As you, Mr. Editor, served your apprenticeship with the proprietor of the Farmer's Museum, and at a period when Mr. Dennie edited that celebrated Newspaper, it has been considered proper to publish these supposed or real remains of that elegant writer, in your Galaxy—and to request that you respectfully solicit further contributions of letters, essays, or well authenticated anecdotes and notices of our departed friend—with assurances that, if any such are deposited in your office, they shall not be published in your paper without express license, but shall be reserved to illustrate his life in a proposed biography, in which due acknowledgements will be made for all such contributions.

The reiterated complaint of Dr. Johnson, and almost all other English biographers, is, the want of attention in contemporaries in preserving the unpublished writings, with notices of the habits, familiar converse and vicissitudes of the private lives of men celebrated for their writings. Let not the future biographer of one of the first *professed* men of letters of the United States have reason to make the same complaint. In the phase of our common friend FLACCUS, we say to the surviving friends of Dennie, *Carpe Diem*.

EXTRACT FROM POSTUMI, &C.
THE LAY PREACHER.

Contributed by——.

"And Rebekah said to Isaac I am weary of my life because of the daughter
of Heth—if Jacob take a wife of the daughters of Heth such as these which
are of the daughters of the land, what good shall my life do me?"
Gen. chap. xxvii. 46.

What! shall the heir apparent of the illustrious house of Abraham,
the son of the opulent Isaac, "who had waxed great"—"very great,"
"and had possessions of flocks and possessions of herds, and great store
of servants" "and was envied by the Philistines"—shall he, the favourite of his mother—he who was well calculated to drive a bargin in
"the gate," for we read he was "a smooth man"—shall Jacob, who
had given such irrefragable proofs of a precocious capacity for mercantile business by speculating with a less accomplished brother for a
birth right and a blessing—shall he meanly obey the impulses of a
youthful heart, and marry for Love? Forbid it all the stately maxims
of family Pride!

In vain, Jacob, has some blooming, lovely virgin of Heth, caught
the youngling fancy,—in vain hast thou, like they father Isaac, "gone
forth in the field in the even tide to meditate" on her beauties, and to
conjure up delightful panoramas of conjugal bliss. In vain "is the
damsel fair and goodly to look upon," and as she leads her flock to
the well of Sichem, does thy pulse rebound to the fairy motion of
her feet, "beautiful with shoes." In vain is her "neck like a tower of
Ivory" and her eyes like the "fish pools of Heshbon." In vain does
thy frolic fancy sport with her "two young roes which are twins"—
In vain do the thousand graces of the Canaanitish belle mingle with
thy best affections, by that powerful affinity, that divine alchemy,
which, with unerring process, pairs the birds on the morn of Valentine
—In vain, Jacob, art thou sick of love—The potent hand of family
pride is preparing to strangle all the gay brood of thy young desires

in the nest. Thou must hie thee to Padanaram and seek thee a wife, for if thou marriest one of these daughters of Heth, thy mother "will be weary of her life."

But pause, we pray thee, thou ambitious mother. Consider that it is thy son's happiness is at stake, and not merely thy own—If thy darling son should make a preposterous love match, it is but a few years that in course of nature "thou canst be weary"; but if Jacob makes a match of interest it is thy son, who is doomed to be indeed weary through a patriarchial life. In a few years, Rebekah, all thy plottings, all thy anxieties for the aggrandizement of a favourite son; with thy family pride, and—happy for him!—thy husband's conjugal disquietudes will all rest quietly together in the cave of Macpelah—But it is fruitless to apostrophise maternal prejudice or family pride. Their ear is deaf to the calls of affection or the responses of reason. Jacob forsook his first love, and at his parents' command went to Padanaram to seek a wife. The matrimonial biography of the Patriarch as displayed in the context, is the best comment upon the maternal policy. He married into the family of the wealthy Leban, as his mother had directed him—he proved recreant to his love—and what was his reward?—ever a blear eyed Leah, and a beautiful barren Rachel, who constantly serenaded him with that dulcet note, so appalling to a married Patriarch's ear—"Give me Children or I die."—

Matrons of my country! ye proud Rebekahs of this land of equality, —Have ye never sent your Jacobs to seek their wives? and whilst tottering into your graves extended the palsied hand of age to sever the affections of a favourite son from some lovely daughter of Heth— you were once perhaps needy—Providence has blessed your industry —fortune favoured your speculations—you have become rich, and the mantle of Rebekah has descended upon you—Your son, your favourite son—the heir apparent of his father's wealth—the inheritor of his funded debt, his insurance stock, his houses in the city, and his wild lands in the Maine,—He could match with the daughter of the wealthy and the honourable. But alas! the unambitious youth is "sorely smitten" with the charms of some lovely lowly daughter of

Heth. Is the damsel beautiful, amiable, virtuous, innocent, modest, and alltogether lovely?—Yes, but her father is a mechanic and the family are poor, says PRIDE. Her father is a Democrat or aristocrat, says POLITICAL PREJUDICE. The family are Socinians or Universalists, says BIGOTRY; and even the damsel herself is unconverted. She does not attend our evening conferences, and is not willing to be made eternally miserable for the Glory of God.

* * * * *

FOR THE NEW-ENGLAND GALAXY.

POSTUMI,

Or Anecdotes and remains of the late JOSEPH DENNIE, Esq. Editor of the Port-Folio—Compiled by several of his intimate friends in aid of his Biographer.

Anecdote communicated by J. T——.

It was generally imagined that, to a mind imbued with a classic taste, and possessed of a fine fancy, there is something peculiarly forbidding in the study of law—The English biographers favour this idea, and notice frequent instances wherein the prudence or ambition of the parent had devoted a favourite son to this unalluring study, who, after lounging a few years at the Temple or Inns of Court, disgusted with the black lettered text of Rastell and Cemberbach,[36] and "smitten with the love of sacred song," had abandoned a science the study of which is so uncongenial with a refined taste for the belles-lettres.

Whatever may have been the case with others, it is certain Mr. Dennie was never disgusted with his professional studies. He read law with assiduous application for three years, under the direction of an eminent

---

[36] John Rastell (d. 1536), printer and lawyer. Trained as an attorney, he became noted as a printer of legal books and other works. Rastell was the brother-in-law of Sir Thomas Moore.

"Cemberbach" is unidentified.

432 The Prose of Royall Tyler

counsellor,[37] and had access to a well furnished library; his preceptor often spake of his attention to his books and his professional acquirements with high approbation, and I have heard him dilate upon *Tenant by Copie et per la verge, Escuage, Frankalmoigne* and *Attornment,* with a familiarity and precision which would have done honour to the "Parve Puer" of Lord Coke.[38]

To what cause then may we attribute his dereliction of a profession in which with common application he might have become eminent? The truth is Mr. Dennie was a gentleman of a refined taste and a fastidious sensibility, which attached him, not merely to the elegant in literature, but the elegant in manners, and which made him turn with equal disgust from a *bald writer* and a *vulgar speaker.* No man could with more propriety have adopted as the motto of his escutcheon the apostrophe of Horace—"*Odi profanum vulgus et arceo.*"

In his study he could read and admire the profound lucubrations of the English jurists; the theory was beautiful and interesting; but to carry his knowledge into practice—in the course of his professional business to encounter the gross familiarity of an ill-bred client, the vulgar sarcasm of an opposing advocate, and the unpolished prerogatives of the bench, his soul disdained—and it is highly probable that his extreme irritability of the mental nerve, would have caused him to abandon with equal promptitude any other profession or business which brought him into familiar contact with the coarser mass of common life. If he had studied Physic; the works of Harvey, Rush and Boerhaave[39] would have delighted him: but he never would have

---

[37] Dennie served his clerkship in the office of Benjamin West at Charlestown, N.H., starting in December, 1790.

[38] Sir Edward Coke (1552–1634), jurist and legal writer. As attorney general for the Crown he conducted the prosecution of Sir Walter Raleigh in 1603 and the gunpowder plotters in 1605. The author of a series of Law Reports.

[39] Gideon Harvey (1640?–1700?). He was physician to Charles II and also served as physician of the Tower under William and Mary. Harvey was the author of *The Family Physician* and other works, many of them critical of the College of Physicians.

Benjamin Rush (1745–1813), physician, patriot and humanitarian. A noted professor of chemistry and medicine, Rush was the author of the first American text on medicine and the first native work on personal hygiene. He was also a member of the Continental Congress and signer of the Declaration of Independence.

been qualified to deliver a clinical lecture. The privileged nausea of a sick chamber, the dictatorial prattle of the sagacious nurse or venerable aunt, would have been held by him as the Buan Upas of absurdity.

I well recollect that soon after he had terminated his noviciate, was admitted to the oath of an attorney and had opened an office, *I was present at his debut as an advocate at the bar.* No young lawyer ever entered on practice with more favourable auspices.—The senior members of the bar augured success, and he numbered all who were valuable among the juniors as particular friends. As it was generally known when he was to deliver "his maiden speech," by a kind of tacit agreement the gentlemen of the bar resolved to afford him the most favourable arena for the display of his eloquence. The opposing counsel had engaged to suspend all interference, although his statements deviated ever so far from fact.

Mr. Dennie had been engaged on behalf of the defendent to support a motion for an imparlance or continuance in an action brought by certain plaintiffs for the recovery of the contents of a promissory note. The execution of the note could not be contested, it was given for a valuable consideration, and was justly due. A very liberal indulgence had already been extended to the defendant by several previous imparlances, and nothing remained for the most adroit advocate to press upon the court but the untoward effects a judgement and consequence writ of execution would have upon the fortunes of his client.

The court opened, and, as if by previous concert, all other business was suspended, and our young advocate, after bowing gracefully assumed the attitude of an orator, and addressed the court.

I wish I could transcribe this address as the lawyers say, "in hæc verba," but I can give only a mere sketch. Twenty years have elapsed, and I remember it as I do an original picture of Claude Loraine—to do justice to the original I should possess the talents of the matchless artist.

He began with a luminous history of compulsory payments, he

Hermann Boerhaave (1668–1738), one of the most famous doctors of the eighteenth century. Under his rectorship the University of Leyden became the center of medical studies of world-wide import.

shewed clearly that as knowledge was diffused humanity prevailed
even from the savage era, when the debtor, his wife and children were
sold into slavery to satisfy the demands of the creditor and the corpse
of the insolvent was denied the rites of sepulture, through the iron age
of our English ancestors, when the debtor was incarcerated in "salva
et areta custodia," down to the present day, when by the amelioration
of the laws, the statutes of bankruptcy and gaol delivery had humanely
liberated the body of the unfortunate debtor from prison, upon the
surrender of his estate. He observed, that in the progress of knowledge,
the municipal courts had, by interposing the "law's delay" between
the vindictive avarice of the creditor, and the ruin of the debtor, always to the honour of the judiciary department, preceded the Legislative in the merciful march of humanity. That the time was not too far
distant when the Legislative would repeal those statutes which provided for imprisonment for debt, and punished a virtuous man as a
criminal merely because he was poor.

But aside of these general considerations, he begged leave to lay the
defendant's unhappy case before the court; he would "a round un-
varnished tale deliver." His client was a husbandman, a husband, and
the father of a large family, who depended *solely* on the labour of his
hands for bread—he had seen better days—but his patrimonial farm
had been sold for Continental money, and the whole lost by deprecia-
tion, whilst others had been getting gain—a deep scar in his side, occasioned by the thrust of a British bayonet at the battle of Bunker-Hill,
was all he had to remunerate him for his services as a soldier during the
revolutionary war. Here, the "poet's eye began to roll in a fine
phrenzy." We saw the hapless husbandman "plodding his weary way"
through the chill blast of a winter's storm, and seeking through the
drifting snow his log cottage, beneath the craggy side of an abrupt
precipice; "the taper's solitary ray" appears—vanishes—and again
lights up hope in his heart—the door opens—his children run "to lisp
their sire's return and climb his knees the envied kiss to share"—"the
busy housewife" prepares the frugal repast, the wicker chair is drawn
before the capacious hearth, "and the crackling faggot flies"; the

labours of the day are forgotten and all is serenity and domestic bliss
—the family bible is opened—the psalm is sung, and the father of the
family rises in the midst of his offspring and invokes a blessing upon
his country and his government, and fervently prays that its freedom
and independence may last as long as the sun and moon shall endure—
acknowledges his own trespasses and pours out his heart in gratitude,
that in the midst of judgement God had remembered mercy—that
though despoiled of wealth, the wife of his youth was continued unto
him. His children were blest with health, that they had a roof to cover
them from the wintery storm, and that under his Divine protection
they might sleep in peace with none to disturb them or make them
afraid. But scarcely does the incense of prayer ascend from that golden
censer, a good man's heart, when an appalling knock is heard; the
wooden latch is broken, the door is widely thrown open—Enter the
bailiff, "down whose hard unmeaning face ne'er stole the pitying
tear," with the writ of execution, issued in this cause; he arrests the
hapless father, and amidst the swoonings of the wife, and sobbings and
imbecile opposition of his children, he is dragged "through the pelting
of the pitiless storm" to a loathsome prison.

Was not this a case to be distinguished from the common herd of
parties, which cumbered the court's docket?—Was not some considerations to be had for a brave man who had bled for that Independence without which their honours would not now dignify the
bench as the magistrates of a free people?—was rigid justice untem-
pered with mercy to be alone found in the Judicial Courts of a people
renowned for their humanity? and shall "human laws, which should
be made only to check the arm of wickedness," be changed into instruments of oppression and cruelty?

The orator ceased—mute attention accompanied the delivery, and
at the close all were charmed and all silent; even the opposing counsel
sat hesitating betwixt his fees and his feelings, and forbore to reply.
This silence, which our young advocate seemed to notice with peculiar complacency, was broken from the bench. The Judge, an unlettered farmer, who, by the prevalence of party, had obtained the

summit of yeoman ambition, a seat on the bench of an Inferior Court, who knew only the technical jargon of the court, and to whom the language and pathos of Dennie were alike unintelligible, sat during the delivery of the address rolling a pair of "lack lustre eyes" with a vacant stare sometimes at the orator and then at the bar, as if seeking most curiously for meaning, and who was perhaps restrained only by the respectful attention of the latter from interrupting the speaker— The Judge broke silence.

Judge. I confess I am in rather a kind of quandary, I profess I am somewhat dubious, I cant say that I know for sartin *what the young gentleman would be at.*

Counsellor V.[40] My brother Dennie, may it please your honour, has been enforcing his motion for an Imparlance on the part of the defendant, in the cause of Patrick McGripinclaw *et alii* Plaintiffs, vs. Noadiah Chubber.

Judge. Oh! Aye! now I believe I understand—the young man wants the cause *to be hung up for the next term, duz he?*

Counsellor V. Yes, may it please the court.—

Judge. Well, well, if that's all he wants, why couldn't he say so in a few words, put to the purpose, without all this *larry cum lurry?*

Our advocate took his hat and gloves from the table, cast a look of ineffable contempt upon the Bæotian magistrate and stalked out of the court house.

Although Mr. Dennie affected to view his unlucky debut in its proper light, and would frequently tell the story of his discomfiture with great humour, yet his friends perceived he was deeply wounded —disgusted with the profession. To entice him to a second essay, some months afterwards, I observed to him, "That I was engaged as counsel in an action for seduction. An unfortunate girl, the daughter of a poor but respectable widow, had been ruined by the promises of a base but

---

[40] According to Ellis, pp. 31 and 96, this is Roger Vose, friend of both Tyler and Dennie. Vose (1763–1842), a classmate of Dennie's at Harvard, was a witty and able, but not brilliant lawyer. He was a frequent contributor to *The Farmer's Weekly Museum* under various pseudonyms. Vose also served in the U.S. Congress as a Representative, 1813–17.

wealthy man; that the facts would be well substantiated, and the whole effort of her counsel directed to the enhancement of damages: this depending principally upon the eloquence of her counsel, presented a fine opportunity for the display of his peculiar talents. That I would introduce him into the cause, and he might open it before a presiding Judge who possessed a taste for fine speaking and would justly appreciate the force and classical purity of his rhetoric."

His reply convinced me that he had taken *a final leave* of the "noisy bar."

D. "It may do for you, my friend, to pursue this sordid business —you can address the ignoble vulgar in their own Alsatia dialect. I remember the Bæotian Judge, and it is the last time I will ever attempt to batter down a mud wall with roses."

Manuscript title page of Tyler's projected anthology of his miscellaneous works, entitled "Utile Dulci." It remained uncompleted at the time of his death in 1826, and what the author intended to include in the volume is not known exactly. The anthology was planned as an effort to gain some royalties for his family since Tyler knew he did not have much longer to live. *In the Royall Tyler Collection of the Vermont Historical Society, gift of Helen Tyler Brown.*

Fragments of "Utile Dulci"

BESIDES "The Bay Boy," one other major effort of Tyler's last years remained unpublished upon his death in 1826. This was "Utile Dulci" which, according to the surviving manuscript title page, was intended to be a catch-all of the prose and verse which had accumulated in Tyler's desk drawers during a writing career that spanned close to four decades.

In his final years, when he was trying to assure his family of some continuing royalties after his death, Tyler thought of an anthology of his miscellaneous works. Like every other writer, he had piled up countless pieces of verse and prose of one sort or another that had never been completed or sent off to a publisher.

Knowing that his talents were declining and that his ambition was sporadic, Tyler felt that it would be easier to revise and update already completed works than to undertake another full-length book, especially since he was already burdened with finishing "The Bay Boy."

The first mention of a possible collection of Tyler's miscellaneous works is in a letter of October 4, 1824, to Tyler from his son, Edward. The latter agreed that a new edition of *The Algerine Captive* was needed, but he hoped that Tyler's other "select works" and "other fugitive pieces of merit" might also be issued. Edward felt there was enough material to fill two volumes.[1]

Work on the new volume progressed simultaneously with "The Bay Boy." Good headway was made and by early 1825 the manuscript was completed. On April 19 Mrs. Tyler wrote in her diary that "Mr. Williston set out for New York and carried with him the Manuscript of 'Utile Dulci,' a collection of Dramas, Fables—Tales, &c, &c—designed for the use of children and youth—directed to William's care to get published on the best terms he can."[2]

This was the first mention of the book's title. A month later Mrs. Tyler, in a letter to Edward, gave more details of the family's hopes for the manuscript:

---

[1] Ms. letter from Edward Tyler to Royall Tyler, dated from New Haven, Conn., Oct. 4, 1824. In the "RT Collection," Ms. No. 824554. The letter mentions specifically "The Sensitive Plant" (*Tyler Verse*, pp. 23–7), "The Chestnut Tree" (*Ibid.*, pp. 194–216) and "Elegy for Rev. Samuel Stillman" (*Ibid.*, pp. 155–8) as three poems which should be included in the collection.

[2] Mrs. Tyler's "Diary" entry for April 19, 1825. In the "RT Collection."

My opinion is that your Father's name alone would insure a sale of one Edition of that work. You forget that he is not unknown as an author. Many of his old friends know his merits as a Poet, altho' from many adverse circumstances justice has never been done to his productions. . . . I think if some judicious Bookseller would read Utile Dulci through Prefaces, etc., he would not fear to publish it. We contemplate unless we hear something more encouraging from N.Y. to direct Aunt Pickman to take it to John [*their son in Boston*], and have him try its fate in the Literary Emporium. I should like to hear the opinion of such men as Mr. Everett on its literary merits. I think the fables very beautiful and the Introduction to the poetry far superior to many things we see published of a serious cast.[3]

This letter, unfortunately, is the only surviving clue as to the contents of "Utile Dulci" outside of the broad guidelines mentioned by Mrs. Tyler in the diary entry quoted above and laid out more fully in the manuscript title page printed below. The prefaces and introduction to the poetry mentioned by Mrs. Tyler are now lost, although a short introduction to the Sacred Dramas survives.[4] Only three short fragments of two fables remain, as well as a number of poems Tyler wrote at the end of his life, probably specifically for inclusion in the anthology. There are also in the Tyler papers three pieces of incomplete biblical plays in verse and other scattered prose fragments.

What probably happened to "Utile Dulci" is that the manuscript became lost in New York or Boston or it was still in those cities when Tyler died less than a year and a half later and was never returned to his family.

The several poems and the dramatic fragments in blank verse are included in the separate volume on Tyler's poetry.[5] Thus the prose remaining to be included in this collecton are the title page, the fragments of the fables, the introduction of the Sacred Dramas and the sermon-essay entitled "Marriage" (Tyler also called it "Advise to Young Clergymen on Marriage"). Tyler might have intended to place in "Utile Dulci" the Sermon and Prayer he delivered on Christmas Day, 1793, as well as the Oration on George

---

[3] Ms. letter from Mary Palmer Tyler to Edward Tyler, dated from Brattleboro, Vt., May 15, 1825. In the "RT Collection." "Mr. Everett" was Edward Everett, the distinguished clergyman, statesman and orator who was also editor of the influential *North American Review*. A favorable comment by him on the worth of "Utile Dulci" would have greatly increased its chances of publication.

[4] The three sacred dramas and the earlier play, "The Island of Barrataria," are not included because of their availability in *Four Plays by Royall Tyler*. For a discussion of these and the author's lost or unpublished dramatic works see Marius B. Péladeau, "Royall Tyler's *Other* Plays," and Tanselle, "Royall Tyler, Judith Sargent Murray and *The Medium*," *New England Quarterly*, XLI, No. 1 (March, 1968), 115–7.

[5] *Tyler Verse*, pp. 216–29.

Washington, but they are included in this volume in their chronological sequence.[6]

Since the finished draft of "Utile Dulci" was sent off to New York it must be remembered that the surviving fragments were retained rough drafts and therefore most unpolished.

We are fortunate in having the title page of "Utile Dulci" so that at least Tyler's intentions as to the contents of the volume are known. The manuscript is a rough draft in Mrs. Tyler's hand, added to and revised, with two versions of a dedication to Mrs. John Holbrook on the reverse.

UTILE DULCI

Being
A Collection Compiled
From the More Juvenile and Unpublish'd
Works
Of the Author.

Embracing Dialogues, Sacred Dramas,
Fables in Prose and Verse, Tales,
&c.

Design'd to Allure the Youth
Of Both Sexes
To Profitable Studies.

By
Royall Tyler, A.M.—

Omne tulit punctum qui miscuit Utile Dulci.
Horace: Art Poet., Ver. 343.[7]

[6] See above, pp. 177–90, 272–80.

[7] This phrase, from Horace's *Ars Poetica,* may be translated as follows: "He will gain the vote of all who combines the useful with the pleasing." Thus, the anthology, "Utile Dulci," was to be a volume both useful and pleasing.

Dedication
[*Version 1*]

To Mrs. Sarah Holbrook, Consort
of John Holbrook, Esq.
of
Brattleboro, Vermont.

This Little Book
Is
Respectfully Dedicated
By
The Author.

———————

[*Version 2*]

To Mrs. Sarah Holbrook
Consort
of
John Holbrook, Esq.,
Brattleboro, Vermont.

In
Memorial of the Author's Profound
Respect
For Her Virtues
As One of the Most Excellent Wives and Best
Of Mothers.

This Little Work
Is Respectfully Dedicated
By
The Author.

INTRODUCTION TO THE SACRED DRAMAS

The three biblical plays Tyler completed during his last illness were nerver produced or printed and remained in manuscript until published by Princeton in 1941. There are fragments of a couple more similar sacred dramas which exist in manuscript. Tyler intended to preface these plays in "Utile Dulci" with a short introduction. It has never been printed and is included here for the first time.[8]

"Introduction to the Sacred Dramas"

The following Sacred Dramas are not published with the vain design of competing with a justly celebrated English writer. The unrivaled excellence of the parent Country in any art of science should not be permitted to confound us into inactivity, but should rather excite to emulation.

In the introduction of the webs of parnassian as well as mechanic looms we must necessarily begin those of a coarse fabric, as we began with coarse woolens before we rivaled the English broadcloths. The weavers of the stuffs of Helicon demand of Congress no protecting tariff—but will be amply gratified with the patriotic predilection which says we must purchase these wares, for the HOMESPUN.

*　*　*　*　*

MARRIAGE

As one who at one time considered entering the ministry, Tyler took a lifelong interest in the clergy and religious matters. Among his manuscripts at the time of his death was the following unpolished, lengthy "lecture" to young clergymen on the pitfalls of marriage. From its tone it appears to have been written fairly early in his career, yet it was never published during his lifetime.[9]

[8] The manuscript introduction is found on the reverse of the title page of "The Origin of the Feast of Purim," one of the sacred dramas. In the "RT Collection." See also below, footnote 26, p. 459.

[9] Ms. No. 70, "RT Collection." The fact that the manuscript is in Tyler's hand reinforces the belief it is an early work. Because of his poor eyesight most of the lengthy pieces of his last years are in Mrs. Tyler's handwriting.

"Marriage"

Let your courtship be brief. Marry as soon but by no means sooner than you obtain a settlement.

Your courtship should be brief, because the character of the suitor seldom sits easy upon young gentlemen of the cloth. Courtship is the season of pleasure; the rigid habit of our country seems to relax in their favour and the young couple expect and are allowed a thousand gay amusements, in which, however innocent, custom has forbidden you to participate.

The sister or the companion of the young lady may be invited to the dance or the sleighing ride which you cannot join or to the card table which you must not approach. The decent comeliness of your dress, carriage and conversation will be continually contrasted with the brilliancy of her acquaintances of other professions. You will hear parties for pleasure proposed to which you cannot assent; and you will hear, or fancy you hear, the last deep sighs of your mistress for those enjoyments, from which, by her union with you she is to be ever excluded. You will be often tempted to imprudence, to gratify the taste of the woman you love and to avoid the imputation of bigotry and parsimony: and the decorum of your character will ever damp your vivacity.

No lover should ever expose himself to any contrast in which he may suffer in any view in the eye of his mistress. Hasten then to the legal enjoyment of those substantial joys of connubial life in which you cannot suffer by comparison. The duties of the marriage state will soon wean the mind from its juvenile attachments and the delights of the matron will soon cause her to forget or despise the amusement and frolicks of the girl.

Marry as soon as you are settled.

Because all eyes are upon you in the pulpit, and many hearts will be set upon the best dress'd and perhaps the handsomest man in the assembly, and there should be but one great object of desire in a temple of worship. The Minister is ever a desirable match in the place; to be madam of the parish is "worth ambition." You will find it difficult to distribute your attentions to your fair parishioners with apparent impartiality. Your word being supposed peculiarly sacred, your very compliments will be construed literally, and you will perhaps make enemies of those you have most sedulously endeavoured to make your warmest friends.

Marry as soon as you are settled, because being debarred by custom from most of the gratifications of the world, your pleasures must in peculiar manner centre in domestick life. Because temptation awaits you on every side. Because mortification of the flesh by celibacy is no part of the Protestant Creed. Because the husband and the parent are respectable characters. Because the people yield a deference to precepts founded on experience and you will be habitually qualified to advise and console your flock under the perplexities, disappointments and vexations of this Vale of Sorrow.

Do not marry sooner than you obtain a settlement, because the disposition of your wife never can obtain one vote in your favour in a strange place, but may influence some people to vote against you. The Rev^d M^r A **** married an amiable, prudent girl before he settled in the Ministry, before he had a Call, but not until the people of a very opulent back-country parish were unanimously engaged in his favour. Soon after his marriage he carried his bride to the meeting arrayed in all the fashionable brilliancy of her wedding attire. The wedding times have been, from all antiquity, the season for dress. Those who are fond of types may probably see figured in the dress of the new married the garlands and ribbands with which the victims are adorned when led to be immolated upon the Altar of Connubial Love.

The Rev^d M^r A **** was never settled in that place and he has been candid enough to attribute his disappointment to the right cause: a substantial husbandman of that parish observed, "That it would be cheaper to settle a Minister with an up-country wife upon two hundred pounds per annum, than to give one thousand pounds to the husband of a woman with such a notion about dress. The entrance of such a grand dressing body into a parish with all her [. . .] would set the women agag and be the means of carrying out of the place three times the sallery in ribbands, gewgaws and top knots."

Do not marry before you settle.

Because the women, young and old, ever feel interested in an unmarried man, and never forget that the women have vast influence. Because the hopes of an alliance with you may influence some families in your favour and your actual alliance may make your life easy by disarming some powerful family in the opposition of its inveteracy.

"It will be in vain," said I to my friend M **** of the Great River, "that you have gained so large an interest in the church and congregation at X ****** if you do not secure the S **** family."

"True!" replied he, "but the women of that family are as remarkable for their prudence and beauty as the men are for their malice and inveteracy. I have courted the other families but I mean to marry in that."

He did so, and no clergyman is upon better terms with his people than the Rev^d M^r M ****.

Do not marry before your settlement.

Because in the choice of a parish you will have two persons instead of one to consult and please. In the institution of marriage we read that the twain became one flesh, but neither scripture, reason or experience justify us in expecting that the twain should be of one spirit. Old married pairs, from long and near intimacy, acquire an apparent similarity of manners and modes of thinking. Cattle long accustomed to the yoke cease to crowd too thick and to interfere, but a young wife will have an opinion of her own, possibly very different from yours; she will have her attachments to the manners, amusements and families of the place of her nativity or long residence.

You will perhaps say that when she married you she knew from your profession that you must carry her from her family and friends.

True, but wherever the place is, the place of her nativity and education will be the standard of its excellence, and possibly from a near acquaintance with the magnitude of your abilities, her love may induce her to suppose that you will readily obtain a settlement in some parish, equal, if not superior, to the place of her education in those very things for which she is most warmly attached to it.

But if she loves you, "Where thou goest she will go. Thy people will be as her people, etc."

Her affection for you may induce her to be silent and complying, but it cannot by some magical power at once change the inclinations of her past life. Love often actuates the conduct contrary to the inclination and therein exists its merit. But it never suddenly changes the taste, disconnects from old attachments to persons and things, and makes us regard vehemently what was ever disagreeable, because agreeable to the interest and palate of those we love.

Suppose your wife disliked olives as much as she loved you: would your regard for this classic vegetable at once render them as pleasing to her taste as a green apple to a school boy? As well may you expect that the marriage ceremony will at once transmute the attachment of the young lady of the seaport to balls, concerts, cards, tea and sleighing parties into a violent affection for the rustick joys of husking, quilting, and singing meetings; that it would as suddenly change her taste for the compositions of Abel or [. . .]¹⁰ and make her prefer Billings' lamentable lucubrations upon the rivers of Watertown to the Canzonets of [. . .]¹¹ or that the inhabitants of the river towns should prefer Indian Johnny Cakes to wheat bread.

I can give you a forcible instance where even a change from mediocrity to comparative affluence could not alter the inclination of the clergyman's wife. The Revᵈ Mʳ ****'s wife was adorned with all the

---

¹⁰ These brackets indicate a blank in the manuscript. Apparently Tyler did not get around to completing the comparison with the compositions of Karl Friedrich Abel (1725-1787), a celebrated player of the viol and composer of instrumental music.
¹¹ Again, Tyler was uncertain of the analogy he desired to make and left an empty space. The reference is to William Billings (1746-1800), a popular American singing master and composer.

useful ornaments of a country education: she could knit, spin, brew, bake and manage the dairy with peculiar dexterity. He married her in his vicinity and she was industrious and happy, but when the *Golden Trumpet* of religion with resistless clangor had summoned her husband from the pastoral care of that puny collection of homespun souls to a scene of greater evangelical usefulness, she brought his wife's person with him but she left her heart behind her, and tho' courted by the politest part of the most polite congregation in the politest town in New England to be polite, she still yearns for her early attachments.

He would give his best gown, nay relinquish the merry Mechanick's Company for a fortnight to make her a lady, could her love for him effect it. We might see her flaunting in a hoop petticoat immediately, but like the girl in the song:

> "Tho' she loves him passing well
> Still she turns her spinning wheel."

But suppose that your yoke mate, instead of being silent and complying, should pout, look glum, refuse to go and insist upon your declining an invitation to settle in a certain parish to which your supposed better judgement may incline you. You may not conceive of this, your education at the college and residence in a school may not have afforded you all that knowledge of the sex that we have who have disciplined for years in the School of Matrimony, who have taken our degrees and write LL. D.: "Legalis Luguriæ Doctor—in Conjugal Life."

We know that besides the persuasive rhetoric of a certain forensick and the metophysical subtlety of the Vapours and hystericks, wives are possessed of one cogent argument, if I am not mistaken, not to be met with among the Bocardos and Baraliptons of Watts' Logic[12] and that consist of three universal negatives.

But presume that your wife should from inclination, love or duty acquiesce in the place of your choice. You have her relations to consult. The mother and sisters cannot consent to her being so far sepa-

---

[12] See above, "The Bay Boy," Chapter IV, footnote 6, p. 66.

rated from them and the maiden aunt will be sure that she sees her dead and buried the moment she sets foot in that awful place. And lastly you will do well to consider the expense of a growing family, for the blessing of Noah seems to descend in full toll upon the families of Levi.

And you will also reflect upon the lesser expense of riding across the country to revisit your family and the opportunity that you thereby lose of ingratiating yourself with the people to whom you preach as a candidate.

Upon the choice of a wife.

Your mistical marriage with your flock will ever influence your carnal union. The character of the pastor will ever affect your conduct as a husband. If disagreements arise between married pairs, the usual opinion of the people is, that faults are on both sides. If they once conceive you to be a bad husband they will never allow you to be a good Minister. If you are unhappy at home you cannot, with men of secular employment, seek pleasure and ease abroad. You cannot move from, nor what is worse, even remove with your misfortunes. You cannot have the meagre consolation of the prudent of concealing your domestic disquietudes from the world.

The whole parish is interested in your family concerns and people have a claim to be familiarly acquainted with whatsoever they are interested in; and to speak of the subject familiarly. Every ungracious look will be noticed, every unkind expression will be recorded with a pen of steel and every false step in your marriage course you must consider as irretrievable. In the vexation of a moment of petulance you may say and do, with other married men, a thousand things which your reason would disapprove and your love for your wife cause you bitterly to repent.

So trust me, my reverend pupils. A sudden start of passion, a look misconceived, a word misapplied, a thoughtless action or expression, an opinion too hastily adopted and perhaps too pertinaciously adhered to, tho' the heart is pregnant with love, will often bind the brow of the married with care. Sensible married people prudently impute their folly to the imbecility of the human mind, and while they hasten to forgive, are anxious by an increase of affectionate attention to obliterate the memory of past unkindness. But in vain will you deplore your weakness; in vain will you proffer and receive mutual forgiveness. The tear which effaces your unkindness from your wife's bosom or cancels the remembrance of her folly from your own, will serve as the record of your conduct to your people. You may forgive and forget, they will never forget. One of the unkind charges exhibited against the late Rev^d M^r **** of ******, then at the age of sixty-seven, was a supposed domestic feud which happened at the age of thirty.

Be therefore peculiarly circumspect in the choice of a wife. Rest not the propriety of your conduct in married life, solely, upon your own prudence or the more sandy foundation of your wife's love. Your inflexible prudence may be diverted by your yearning after family peace and the affection of your wife may make her desire to *do*, but it cannot alone make her *know*, what is right.

Chuse, therefore, a woman so circumstanced by birth and education, by the gifts of nature and fortune, as will in the mere pursuance of her own gratifications pursue your inclinations and interest. Such a woman as will by her habitual carriage make you happy, and not merely happy at home, but respected abroad.

In the first place, *chuse a wife in the vicinity of your parish,* because a stranger is exposed to observation; her dress, her gait, her manners, her conversation, her pronunciation will be critically canvassed. If she is inferior she will be despised, if she excells, envied, and envy is the foster father of detraction.

A wife from the vicinity will find a thousand sources of enjoyment in the neighborhood of her nativity which would escape the notice or meet the contempt of a stranger. Her family will afford you a circle of visiting associates who are interested in your fame. It will give a stability to your character in your office and possibly support and protect you in the hour of adversity, for though you should not rely too much upon an arm of flesh, yet I have known a brawny secular arm raised in a clergyman's favour crush an aspersion which, if it had met with no other opposition than the purity of the minister's life and conversation, might have increased to such a scandal as to have endangered the peace of the parish.

A stranger of superior education can never mingle with your parishioners; if she visits them instead of introducing pleasure, she will impose restraint wherever she goes. Her appearances will be suspected and her very smiles of approbation will be construed into sneers of ineffable contempt. But to a wife from the vicinity, if of superior education, the people will readily yield a deference to which they have been habituated. Her mingling with the people will be esteemed a condescension, she will take a part in their enjoyments and conversation and preserve your influence among the gossips. And trust me, you lose sight of your true temporal interest when you neglect your influence among the matrons of your parish.

Chuse a woman who has been humbled but not lower'd by family misfortunes.

Happiness is not the portion of this world, and when people are once convinced of the folly of its pursuit, they often find content without looking for it. The young woman whose family has been exposed to great misfortunes, learns more of the world, obtains more of that useful knowledge which rectifies the affections and accommodates us to the vicissitudes of life in three months, than she would by the intense application of a whole life to Fordyce and Wilkie.[13] Misfortunes soften the heart, melicrate the affections, and by teaching us the vanity of expecting much, they learn us to be content with a little.

The woman whose family has been buffeted by misfortune will find pleasure in even the serene gratifications and still life of a country minister's family. The weather-beaten mariner hugs with rapture that

[13] James Fordyce (1720–1796), poet and presbyterian divine of great eloquence. William Wilkie (1721–1772), a prolific writer and imitator of Homer; called "the Scottish Homer."

scanty land, that bleak shore and desolated isle, which he would despise, if wafted to it under the auspices of an easy gale and clear sky.

Chuse a woman of strong good sense and great prudence.

Of good sense—because it is the indispensable qualification in the
bosom companion of a man of letters.

Of prudence—because a clergyman's wife keeps the key of her husband's reputation and peace of mind. Therefore, chuse a *woman of
constitutional slowness of speech,* one that seems literally to think twice
before she speaks once, for this is one of those rare excellencies which
we must look for from nature as we despair of procuring it by art.

*Let her have some taste for books, less passion for dress and the most genuine
relish for the duties of domestick life.*

Some taste for books is necessary to induce a love for your profession. A wife should always enthusiastically respect her husband's calling, and to enable her to share in and be improved by the conversation
of those with whom you more especially associate.

I say, *some taste in books,* for by all means avoid what is called the
woman of deep reading. A close application to books implies an inattention to the less respectable, not less important, and more amiable
duties of life. The man attached strongly to books is negligent of his
person, apparel, etc. The woman attached to books, etc., etc., etc.

I leave it to the Philosopher to discuss the cause, but it is certainly a
fact that the more a man reads the more liberal he becomes. The more
a woman reads, the more dogmatical. The man who owns a modern
library has sufficient domestic dogmatists on the shelves of his study,
and conjugal dogmatism is a solecism in connubial happiness.

A woman of deep reading may know, or what amounts to the same
thing, make the parish believe that she knows more than yourself.
Now propriety requires that the minister should be supposed to know
at least as much of books as any *woman* in the parish.

A refined taste for dress would be ill suited to the opinions of your people and worse adapted to your own finances. It would excite envy and continually create desires which you cannot gratify. The wish which we cannot gratify is a want. That which we can is a source of pleasure. Would you be happy? Suppress the former and increase by every possible means the latter. But although your wife should have but little passion for dress she cannot have too great a regard for personal neatness. She may dress too rich, too gay and too fine but she cannot dress too neatly.

Women love the admiration which our sex pay to their personal charms; it influences the whole sex. The handsome woman strives to be thought beautiful, the beautiful more so, whilst even the conscious homely strive to render their persons at least agreeable. It is innate with the sex. It is the active principle of their youthful life and when it ceases to impel as a principle it is continued at least through habit. The ancient lady composes the disordered pleats of her mob [*cap*] and smooths the rumples in her apron with the approach of the male visitor with the same promptness, if not with the same sensations, as she adjusted her tucker upon the same occasion in early life.

In your profound wisdom you may stigmatize this desire to be admired for mere external excellence with the opprobrium of folly. But believe me, if you root this enchanting weed of folly from the female heart you will tear up with it a thousand lovely flowers and fair fruits without which life itself would be a barren wild.

As you cannot support this desire to be admired for personal appearance in your wife by the grandeur or fashionable vanity of her dress, let her be remarkable and ever applauded for her neatness. Neatness, cleanliness, simplicity of person and apparel are jewels within the compass of a clergyman's purse and which shed a bewitching lustre over the person which diamonds of the first water cannot confer. Consider neatness then as indispensable in your wife. Set all your penetration to work to discover whether the lady you address is constitutionally and habitually so—*all your penetration,* for courtship is ever a state of deception.

The sexes deceive each other upon the most praiseworthy motives;

even the wish to appear agreeable to each other. In common life the man who deceives, condemns you, but the greater the lady's love for you the stronger will be her desire, and the more earnest her endeavour, to accommodate her sentiments, manners and person to your mode of thinking and to conceal those feelings which might displease or disgust you.

Judge not then of her neatness from her appearance at meeting a visitor, or at those stated times when she expects your presence. Visit her at unexpected and even unseasonable hours. Observe how long she makes you wait for her appearance. Listen for the bustle overhead and the repeated calls for the wash ball and comb, and inquiries after the strayed parts of her apparel. Notice whether her dress is adapted to the season of the day. Be cautious of a full dress; the finer the dress the easier the deception. It is the home, morning undress in which your wife is to appear to you the greater part of your life.

But should she appear as neat in her attire and person as your holy fancy represents the garb of a superior order of beings, suspend your judgement. Observe her working implements and the work itself. It is an indelible criterion that a woman is not neat if her work is generally soiled or her working implements mislaid, in bad order, or not clean. Observe the lesser ruffle upon the arm and the interior covering of her foot.

A lady, not remarkable for her beauty, sense or fortune, intoxicated a friend of mine merely by her neatness of person and apparel. She stood the test of the above mentioned criticisms. He lodged at her father's and was awakened the same night out of a delicious dream of the white-robed spotless innocent, by the cry of "Fire."

Full of the tenderest apprehensions for his mistress, he rushed out of his chamber in pursuit of her's. In the passageway he met a female figure whose face on one side was completely concealed by her disheveled tresses, whilst the other was umbrated by the nocturnal foliage of a torn nightcap, with a ribband of quality binding, which had been exalted from its service by day, bound slightly upon her head. A woolen stocking encircled her neck, a comfortable garment of the tyrian dye was thrown over her shoulders and the whole person presented the most squalid contour imaginable.

"And where is my angelic Nancy's chamber?" exclaimed the anxious lover.

"Here am I," said the figure.

It was his angelic Nancy herself. My friend consoled himself under this misfortune by reflecting that this accident, whilst it had saved him from a life of disquiet and disgust, armed him with the power of defending himself from a similar deception. Accordingly, by sometimes giving a boy a shilling to fire a bundle of straw in the road opposite the house at midnight, by the cry of "Thieves," and similar maneuvers, he contrived to make his female acquaintances pass in midnight review before him.

But I must in justice to the ladies add, for I have the highest respect for the ladies, that he had not alarmed above ten families before he brought four sisters into the passageway at one in the morn'ng all as neatly dressed as they appear'd in the evening preceding. He married the eldest.

It is true, I have heard it whisper'd, but I believe it to be mere malice, that the dear creatures had fortunately got a new novel to read that night and could not quit the Dear Caecilia until they knew she was happy with her divine Me[. . .].[14]

*   *   *   *   *

FRAGMENTS OF TWO MORAL TALES

The title page of "Utile Dulci" said it would contain "fables in prose . . . design'd to allure the youth of both sexes to profitable studies." The first mention of the moral fables is in 1797. In a letter to Tyler, Dennie said that Roger Vose, a fellow attorney and contributor to *The Farmer's Weekly Museum*, "has read your 'Moral Romances'; and, he assures me, it rendered a gloomy and snowy Fast day pleasant. He declares it more uniformly pure than Updike, and, in elegance, greatly its superior."[15]

[14] A tear in the paper obliterates the final word of the manuscript.
[15] Pedder, *The Letters of Joseph Dennie*, pp. 155–6.

Toward the end of 1799 Tyler made the acquaintance of Joseph Nancrede, at that time a well-known Boston publisher and bookseller.[16] The two apparently discussed the possibilities of bringing more of Tyler's work into press, following the success of *The Algerine Captive* and the "Colon and Spondee" essays and poems. The two specifically mulled over plans to publish a small book entitled, "Moral Tales for the Instruction of American Youth," and a larger work to be called "Cosmography."

The former was designed to fill the nearly complete lack of childrens' books of native origin, while the latter—a combination universal gazetteer and geography—would compete with similar works by Jedidiah Morse and others.

Tyler and Nancrede discussed the contents and terms of publication, but the "Cosmography" never seems to have progressed beyond the talking stage. The "Moral Tales," however, advanced to such a point that Tyler sent the finished manuscript off to the publisher, but unfortunately the book never came off Nancrede's presses. The pair exchanged several letters about the progress of the "Moral Tales," and since they give us several important details as to the book's contents, as well as revealing Tyler's epistolary talents, they are reprinted here at some length.

On February 11, 1800, Nancrede acknowledged receipt of the manuscript of the "Moral Tales." He was deeply touched by the oration delivered by Tyler at Bennington upon the death of George Washington and informed Tyler he would include it in the book as per the author's wishes. The publisher, however, complained that the manuscript was too short, would amount to no more than one hundred printed pages and would not return him his investment in its printing. For the copyright and in lieu of payment for the manuscript Nancrede offered Tyler 200 copies of the book.[17]

Four days later Tyler wrote back to the publisher. He firmly declined the 200 copies as full payment for his manuscript because he felt it would be both difficult and demeaning for the author to market his own work. Tyler then added:

[16] Paul Joseph Guérard de Nancrede (1761–1841), an immigrant from France, he fought in the American Revolution and became noted as an early publisher of French language books in the United States. He set himself up as a printer in Boston in 1796, returned to France in 1804 only to come back and settle in Philadelphia in 1812.

A discussion of the business relationship between Tyler and Nancrede is found in Tanselle, "Author and Publisher in 1800: Letters of Royall Tyler and Joseph Nancrede," *Harvard Library Bulletin,* XV, No. 2 (April, 1967), 129–39.

[17] "TPT Memoir," p. 132.

You certainly misconceived me if you concluded that I was always anxious to have the work published, or supposed my credit as a writer in the least degree interested in the success of the work. So far from this, it is with great degree of reluctance I have consented to its publication; sensible that merely writing upon such childish topics may induce an opinion that the author who can amuse children can never write anything worthy of men. No one can have a humbler opinion of the Moral Tales, but yet I can appreciate its being native and original; the first of its kind which has been written in America; and that some little credit I may have obtained as a fanciful writer, and some acquaintance in several states with literary people will go far to help off a small edition. . . . If the manuscript being too brief to make a bound volume were the principal objection, I can obviate that in three days . . . and if the copyright is worth merely your proffer, it cannot be mine to usher it to the public with my name at length. I have a profession, and my abilities in the exercise of it in this wooden world are esteemed above mediocrity. This profession affords me the comforts and conveniences of life . . . and I have learned that great secret of felicity to find enjoyment at home. From certain disgusts perhaps uncharitably admitted, I had renounced the ambition of authorship . . . [*and*] if writing for the public is attended with no more profit, I had rather fill legal process in my attorney's office, and endeavor to explain unintelligible law to Green Mountain jurors; and when the *cacoethes cribendi* assails me, I will write sonnets to rustic loves, and tales for children, and look to my reward in the exhilarating smiles of partial friends round my fireside.[18]

Tyler then concluded that if Nancrede wanted to go ahead and publish the "Moral Tales" at his own risk he could purchase the copyright for $200. and assign to Tyler all rights for future editions. The publisher apparently relented for on March 7 he wrote that he was going ahead with the printing of the book. After pointing out that the "Cosmography" would "yield a handsome income," he chided Tyler as follows:

I will not make any comment on your very "explicit and absolute answer" of an advance of 200 dollars for 100 small pages of a work for youth, which the author says cost him "eight days of amusement," but request you will furnish me with an instance of an author—the gigantic *Johnson, Pope, Swift, Voltaire, Rousseau* (I will not compare you to meaner writers) or any other, selling the amusements, or even the hard labors, of eight days for "200 dollars cash". . . .[19]

Nancrede added a postscript. It said that the "little fable for grown folks" had arrived by separate post and was being included in the "Moral Tales"

[18] *Ibid.,* pp. 133–5.

[19] *Ibid.,* p. 139. Although the "Cosmography" was never published Tyler did consider it seriously. In a Feb. 17 postscript to a letter of Jan. 30, 1800, from Mrs. Tyler to her mother, the former said that her husband "is offered three thousand dollars—to write a new Geography of the World and had thought of attempting it. Such is his extensive knowledge he would almost do it from his own head—he says all the difficulty is in writing it—it will require a vast deal of writing indeed we must all help." (Letter in Vermont Historical Society collection.)

then on the press. In his next letter of later that month Tyler politely but firmly put the printer in his place:

I have been highly entertained with your letter.... Without doubt your correspondence will ever command my esteem; for, although you may advance many things abhorrent to my interest, and perhaps some to my feelings; yet, I am assured your manner of writing will be amusing. I am only perplexed to discover how a person of your solid business talents should have so much wit. . . .

I must confess, however, that I am somewhat surprised that you should intimate that the value of a literary work should be estimated by the time taken to produce it. This I know to be an excellent rule when applied to wood-cutters and day-laborers; but if ever applied to a work of a genius, the surprise is that it should be made by a man of genius. It is not, however, new to me. An honest client, whose cause I have obtained, when he paid me my small fee, has sometimes observed: "Surely the squire makes money very easy; ten dollars for only half an hour's talking; and it seemed to come out so easy. I am sure it could not cost him much labor."[20]

The remainder of this lengthy but incomplete letter is devoted to further details of the "Moral Tales." Tyler said he had completed more text and was sending the new fables to Nancrede. They were: (1) "A little Green Mountain story, entitled 'Home,' with an introduction in the manner of Le Mercier's 'Night Cap'"; (2) "Dr. Franklin and His Mother; a Philosophical Experiment"; and (3) the "Story of the Tub-Woman." A part of this latter tale is all which survives.

Tyler again urged that the work go forward and that if more copy was still needed he would provide it immediately. He also outlined his plans for future volumes of the book in the same letter:

That a book which will amuse while it instructs children, will sell in this country I think may be fairly inferred from the number of imported books of this nature vended in this country; and even from the awkward attempts repeatedly made by our own compilers of localizing the European story by merely inserting the names of American places in lieu of those of France and England. . . . I have some hopes, therefore, that a book which is quite a home thing and which talks about folks, places and things which we all know, will be read; and if it is . . . I can see my account in it, to publish a second and third volume, and so on; forming a little library.

The second volume should contain Dialogues after the manner of Berquin; and infantile folly and virtue characterized, after the manner of [La] Bruyere and Theophrastus. For the third volume, I have somewhere among my manuscripts, an Accidence, or Grammer for young ladies.[21]

The letter concludes with Tyler's explanation of the comic grammer, but unfortunately his grandiose dreams for a series of little books for chil-

[20] Ibid., pp. 140–1.
[21] Ibid., p. 143. The comic grammar mentioned here may have been similar to the "Pap of Science" printed in 1799. See above, pp. 240–43.

dren never materialized. The "solid business talents" which Tyler praised did not prevent Nancrede from experiencing severe financial tribulations at this time and the publisher was not able to bring out even the first volume. Still more unfortunate, the manuscript was lost.[22]

Only three manuscript fragments of two tales survive. One of them is the introduction and comic letter of transmittal to the tale entitled "The Historiette of the Tub Woman" mentioned by Tyler in his letter to Nancrede, which would date its composition in 1799 or early 1800.[23]

The other two fragments are a prose and a dramatic rendering of the same fable, "The Tale of the Five Pumpkins." The latter dates from the end of 1824. At this time Thomas Pickman Tyler was attending Miss Rebecca Peck's school in Brattleboro and both parents showed a deep interest in their son's education. On December 14, 1824, Mrs. Tyler noted in her diary that "my husband began writing a Drama for Miss Peck's School—called Five Pumpkins."[24]

The following day she wrote that Tyler had completed the work and on December 16 she recopied it. Pickman probably took this copy of the skit with him to school. The versions of "The Tale of the Five Pumpkins" printed here are taken from the original manuscripts in Tyler's hand.[25]

Besides the various fables mentioned in the correspondence with Nancrede, Tyler left behind another tabulation of tentative tales intended for inclusion in "Utile Dulci." The incomplete listing is as follows:

"Fables, etc.

Sukey Blossom, or the folly of [*precipitation?*].
A Fable,
The Youth, etc.
The Thunder Storm.
The Tub Woman.
Parental Reverence Inculcated.
Home."[26]

[22] A puzzling aspect is a letter written by Tyler to a Mr. Scrolley in Boston: "There is a little book in the press, entitled 'Moral Tales for the Instruction of American Youth;' please to call upon Mr. Nancrede . . . and he will deliver you two copies." ("TPT Memoir," pp. 144-5.) How did Tyler know that complimentary copies were available if Nancrede had not informed him the book was off the presses?
[23] "RT Collection," Ms. No. 79.
[24] Mrs. Tyler's "Diary" entry for Dec. 12, 1824.
[25] "RT Collection," Ms. Nos. 30 and 48.
[26] This listing, in the "RT Collection," is on the reverse of the title page of "The Origin of the Feast of Purim" together with the "Introduction to the Sacred Dramas."

'The Historiette of the Tub Woman'

I design the following story expressly for you, young friend. I mean you, who while your gayer and more opulent schoolmates are at their sports or receiving from the music and the dancing master that higher polish of education which the penury of your parents cannot afford, are engaged every leisure hour with your book. I do not the less regard you because your clothes are tatter'd and your parentage is humble. I rather enter into your feelings. I know that you apprehend with despondency the time when you will be constrained to quit your school and your books and enter upon an apprenticeship to a laborious handicraft trade.

The letter you have read has excited your ambition to be eminent, but your ambition is depressed by poverty, and the ascent to greatness is so difficult and so distant that you despair of surmounting it. When you look abroad into the world you consider yourself a contemptable being among the thousands who people your state, a unit among the millions who compose our nation. You dare not even hope to become an ornament to the seat of judgement like the erudite and impartial Dana[27] or be the Saviour of your country like the illustrious Washington; to bless a nation while you live like the great Adams or be lamented when you die like the good Sumner.[28]

But be of good courage, my humble friend, the foundation of mighty states and empires have been laid in weakness and the founders of them may be trac'd to the humblest origin. You may read for your encouragement the *British Spectator,* a paper appropriated to this

[27] Francis Dana (1743–1811). A Son of Liberty, he went to England in 1774 in the interests of Anglo-American harmony. He returned in 1776 convinced reconciliation was impossible. In 1780 he was appointed U.S. Minister to Russia and represented American interests there from 1781–3. In 1785 he became associate justice of the Massachusetts Supreme Court, rising to become Chief Justice in 1791.

[28] Increase Sumner (1746–1799). Appointed associate justice of the Massachusetts Supreme Court in 1782, he was elected Federalist Governor of the Commonwealth in 1797. Sumner was re-elected in 1798 and 1799 and died shortly after being sworn in for his third term.

Tyler composed a rather conventional elegy on Sumner's death. It is reprinted in *Tyler Verse,* pp. 95–6.

subject. I cannot tell which number, as I have not the book at hand, in which amidst the most pertinent and consolatory observations an Eastern apologue is introduced.

When you are told that a single drop of that immense body of water which constitutes the Pacific Ocean once, like you, contemplated its own comparative insignificance. It felt that it was but an undistinguished particle of this watery world. It raised its feeble voice to deity from the bottom of the vasty deep. It complained that it was actuated by ambition to be distinguished [*but*] was curs'd with a sense of its own insignificance and the utter despair of being able to attain the object of its ambition.

The Indian Philosopher who invented the fable informs us that at the very moment when this wat'ry mite was accusing Heaven of unkindness an oyster opened its shells and swallowed this diminutive murmurer and by the fostering hand of Providence it indurated to a pearl of precious price; was taken by the pearl divers and in a short time became the most resplendent ornament in the turban of the Great Sophi of Persia.

Perhaps you will say this is a mere fable. Read then for your consolation:

The Historiette of the Tub Woman,
a true story.

[*A*] remembrance of me when I am dead and gone.

I received the precious relicts and have by observation perceiv'd so much truth in them that for the benefit of my youthful visitors, I got them copied in a fair hand and gave them an honorable place over my chimney piece, between the ballard of "The Cruel Stepmother" and "The Royal Game of Goose."

Understanding that you were about to publish a book for the amusement and instruction of our American youth, and hoping it may extend their usefullness, I enclose you the Golden Rules which you may publish as your own.

I am, with sincere regard,
Yours to serve,
Simpkin Greenhorn.

From this story you learn to do well* and to place a humble but sure confidence in that superintending Providence, which will assuredly place you in that situation of life most adapted to your abilities and your best interest; remembering that the same almighty power who took the shepherd boy, David, from his father's flocks and made him King of Israel can, of the most unpromising child, make a war [. . .]

*   *   *   *   *

"The Tale of Five Pumpkins"
[Version 1]

What, the sprightly Charlotte Airy looking pensive? You who always appear'd so cheerful and smiling that I thought your features could express nothing but good humour.

I am vex'd, Lucinda. I am really angry. I do not know that I was ever so sensibly affected in my life.

Is your trouble of such a nature as to be trusted to your friend? I never love to pry into secrets, but you know, my dear, the poet tells us, that our griefs when divided are hushed into peace.

It is no secret, Lucinda. I wish it was. Somebody has gone and spread a very malicious story about me and told all over the school that before breakfast this morning I ate five green pumpkins, each as big as a half bushel.

Ha, ha, ha. Excuse my laughing, my lovely friend, but the story seems in itself so ridiculous and so absurd when told about a delicate young lady that, I declare, was so foolish a tale repeated about me, it would not give me one moment's uneasiness.

It is the very folly of it that hurts me. I'm sure I never attempted to make anybody appear silly, and I think this must be done to make me ridiculous. Besides, I am fearful this report will come to the preceptor's

* The words "to do well" were crossed out on the original manuscript.

knowledge. He has prepared this commodious house as the place of our studies, and gave us liberty roving both these spacious gardens for our exercise and amusement. We have been restrained only from those things which would be of real hurt to us. He has forbidden us to trample down the beds, and especially to eat green trash. Now what would he think of me to hear such a story! I'll go and clear up my character to him immediately.

Pray, stop one minute, Charlotte, don't be too hasty. Indeed, you are much too vexed to act yourself. Come, suffer me to advise you. You know my friendship. You may possibly feel more keenly an indignity offered you than another, but cannot be more anxious to clear your character than your friend is to see it without blemish. Suppose you complain to the preceptor, he will only inquire into the truth of this ridiculous report, and its author will be exposed to his displeasure, which I am sure you would not wish to be the instrument of bringing upon any of our school.

I stand corrected, Lucinda. I am ashamed of my rashness. Under the semblance of vindicating my own character I was going to become a pitiful tale bearer. But what must I do then? I cannot bear to become the laughing stock of the school.

Do? Why, suppose you should go to the master or miss who reported this story, and expostulate with them and ask them why they could tell so foolish a tale. Who was it you heard reported this among others?

Why, Suky Glib told me that Miss Sally Chatter told it to her since school.

Well, very luckily here comes Miss Chatter. You had better ask her about it. Shall I introduce the subject? She will not deny it if she said so.

I'll thank you, Lucinda, if you mention it to her.

Miss Chatter, we were speaking about you. Our friend, Miss Airy, has had a very silly story told about her that she ate this morning five green pumpkins each as big as a half bushel and she is sorry to be informed that you are the author.

Indeed, I am not. I told some such story this morning in a laughing way to Miss Glib, but with no intention of hurting your feelings, my dear (to Miss Charlotte). Besides, I did not say five pumpkins, or as big as a half bushel. I only mentioned four as big as a peck.

Lucinda. Forgive me, my dear, but I think lessening the number does not lessen the unkindness of repeating or the sin of making such a story.

I told you I was not the author. Miss Prattle told the story to me. She was walking with me in the garden. I will send her to you.

So it seems, Miss Prattle, I am indebted to you for this fine story?

Not at all, I only told a story I heard, tho' it seems Miss Chatter has increased the story. As I heard it from Miss Prattapace, it was said you had eaten three green pumpkins as big as a half peck. But I tell you my author, my dear. I beg your pardon for anything I have said in this matter, and if you wish to see Miss Prattapace I will send her to you.

Why, Charlotte, one would think by the bustle about this story that you were really angry. I am come among the rest to clear myself. It seems Miss Prattle has told you that I said that you had eaten three green pumpkins as big as a half peck. Now you may thank her for one of them, my dear, for positively I never said more than two, and if I said anything about a peck it was that they both might be put into a half peck. And I'm sure I was never called a tale bearer and I can produce my informer. Miss Talkative told me, and she told the Missus coming to clear her. I'll hasten her.

Well, ladies, I believe I can produce you the author of this story. I confess I told Miss Prattapace the story but not with the least design of making you ridiculous or of exposing you to the master's displeasure, but merely in the way of chitchat. I am sure I can.

Well, but who told you?

Why before I tell you I must say in his defense that my informer did not speak of more than one great green pumpkin.

Well, but who was it?

Why, little Bob Erchin.

What, Bob Erchin? I do declare that boy makes more mischief than all the rest of the boys in the school.

He is mischievous boy, and the master ought to be informed of his tricks.

You will have him here immediately for Miss P. and Miss T. are gone to look in the back garden; and see they are bringing him along.

I'll tell all if you won't tell master.

Well, how came you to tell Miss Talkative that I ate a great green pumpkin? Come, do not deny it. Miss Talkative heard you say great pumpkin. This is positive.

Well, if you will let me speak I will tell you all I said. I told Miss T. that I saw Miss Charlotte Airy eat a great pear this morning as big as a pumpkin.

And so I did. It was one your brother gave you when he came here yesterday.

A general laugh.

Why, what a story was raised here from nothing. Everyone meant no harm and everyone added a little and meant no harm. And so from one misconceived speech the feelings of the most admirable girl among us have been injured.

If proved, you say well, if proved. Why I am positive he said great pumpkin. My story will not be like the other young ladies who are really somewhat to blame.

Well, for my part, I'll never believe a story until I have examined into it.

Nor I either.

Nor I.

Nor I.

Lucinda. But let is likewise remember not to add to a story when we tell it again for if everyone had not added a little, one pear could not in one morning have increased to five pumpkins.

*   *   *   *   *

"The Tale of Five Pumpkins"
[*Version 2*]

(Enter Miss Prattle and Miss Prattapace.)

Charlotte. And so it seems, Miss Prattle, I am indebted to your friendship for this pretty story.

Miss Prattle. Pray Miss Airy, how did Miss Chatter represent it to you?

Lucinda. Miss Chatter says that you told her that Charlotte had eaten four green pumpkins, each as big as a peck.

Miss Chatter. I am astonished, perfectly astonished. Four pumpkins as big as a peck! Well, this is just like Sally Chatter. She never yet repeated a story without adding to it. I am positive, ladies, I never mentioned but three pumpkins each as big as a half peck. It is amazing how some folk can add to stories. I certainly mentioned but three as big as a half peck, and to clear myself I have brought my author with me. Patty Prattapace reported it to me, and here she is to answer for herself.

Miss Prattapace. Miss Prattle, will you please to look me in the face. Will you undertake to say before these ladies that I ever told you of more than two pumpkins, and ever said one word about a half peck?

Miss Prattle. Why as to that, Miss Prattapace, there is no great difference between two or three, and I am not disposed to dispute with you about a single pumpkin. You certainly said something about a half peck.

Miss Prattapace. I never mentioned but two as I stand here, and if I said anything about a half peck, it was chey were so small that they might both be put into a half peck.

Lucinda. Perhaps, young ladies, this difference had better be adjusted amicably between yourselves. At present Miss Airy is determined to persist in searching this scandal to its source.

Charlotte. We will suppose, Miss Prattapace, that you said two pumpkins.

Miss Prattle. I am pretty certain she said three.

Miss Prattapace. I certainly mentioned but two.

Charlotte.   Well, two or three, am I to look upon you as the author?
Miss Prattapace.   I, the author? No, Miss Charlotte, I hope I never framed as ridiculous a story about any young lady, much more made it worse by adding to it. Miss Blab told the story to me. I will send her to you and she will prove that I am right as to the number. Please to remember, ladies, that I am positive Miss Blab said only two pumpkins.
(Exeunt Misses Chatter and Prattapace.)
Lucinda. I am anxious to find the author of this report.
Charlotte.   There must be blame. Some person must have invented it. [It] could not have grown out of nothing.
(Enter Miss Blab.)
[Miss Blab.] One would think, Miss Charlotte, by the bustle you are pleas'd to make about this story that you were really angry. I have come among the rest to clear myself.
Charlotte.   I should be happy to have you [recant] or even apologize for this report of the two pumpkins.
[Miss Blab.]   Two pumpkins! Did Miss Prattapace tell you two? She is vastly mistaken. I can produce you my informer, but I must do him justice to say that he never spoke of but one pumpkin.
Lucinda.   Well, who told you?
Miss Blab.   Little Bob Urchin.
Charlotte.   Who, Bob Urchin!
Lucinda.   He is a mischievous knave.[29]

*   *   *   *   *

---

[29] The last page of this manuscript fragment was employed originally as an envelope addressed to John Hampden Palmer, Mrs. Tyler's brother. The moral tale was written over the following: "Walpole March 10th 6./Mr. John Hambden [sic] Palmer/at Major Tyler's Guilford/Vermont."

Appendix

THIS APPENDIX will provide complete bibliographical data on all the Tyler material included in this volume. It will elaborate on the information contained in the text so as to allow scholars to locate the printed and manuscript prose works of Royall Tyler.

Unless otherwise noted all manuscripts are in the author's hand and are in the Royall Tyler Collection, gift of Helen Tyler Brown, at the Vermont Historical Society, Montpelier, Vt.

"THE BAY BOY"

Complete descriptions of the thirteen extant "Bay Boy" fragments are provided on pp. 37–39. Fragment 13 is contained in Thomas Pickman Tyler, "Memoirs of Honorable Royall Tyler, late Chief Justice of Vermont," pp. 112–13. The other twelve, either in Tyler's hand or that of his wife, exist in manuscript.

A SERMON AND PRAYER FOR CHRISTMAS DAY

Holograph manuscript No. 115.

THE "SPONDEE" ESSAYS

"To the Literati" [the Colon & Spondee advertisement] in The Eagle, II, No. 3 (July 28, 1794), 3. Reprinted in The Spirit of the Farmer's Museum, pp. 215–17.

"To Our Kind Customers" in The Eagle, II, No. 23 (Dec. 29, 1794), 4. Reprinted in The Newhampshire and Vermont Journal, V, No. 260 (March 27, 1798), 4; The Federal Galaxy, II, No. 124 (May 14, 1799), 4; and The Spirit of the Farmer's Museum, pp. 256–59.

"Amid the festivity . . ." in The Federal Orrery, I, No. 28 (Jan. 22, 1795), 111. Reprinted in The Eagle, II, No. 30 (Feb. 6, 1795), 4.

"Miscellany" in The Eagle, II, No. 27 (Jan. 26, 1795), 4, and simultaneously in The Federal Orrery, I, No. 29 (Jan. 26, 1795), 115. Reprinted in Thomas' Massachusetts Spy, XXIII, No. 1141 (Feb. 18, 1795), 4.

"Although to the man . . ." in The Federal Orrery, I, No. 40 (March 5, 1795), 158.

"Between You and I" in The Newhampshire and Vermont Journal, IV No. 161 (May 3, 1796), 1. Reprinted in The Eagle, III, No. 42 (May 9,

1796), 2; *The Federal Orrery,* IV, No. 7 (May 12, 1796), 1; and *The Spirit of the Farmer's Museum,* pp. 288–89.

"The Runner, *or* Indian Talk," in *The Newhampshire and Vermont Journal,* IV, No. 175 (Aug. 9, 1796), 1. Reprinted in *The Federal Orrery,* IV, No. 36 (Aug. 22, 1796), 1; and *The Spirit of the Farmer's Museum,* pp. 297–302.

"Fine Comb Points" in the *Farmer's Weekly Museum,* V, No. 210 (April 11, 1797), 4. Reprinted in *Thomas' Massachusetts Spy,* XXV, No. 1257 (May 17, 1797), 4; and *The Spirit of the Farmer's Museum,* pp. 277–81. (The *Farmer's Weekly Museum* was the direct successor of *The Newhampshire and Vermont Journal.*)

"Aristocracy" in the *Farmer's Weekly Museum,* V, No. 214 (May 9, 1797), 4. Reprinted in *Thomas' Massachusetts Spy,* XXV, No. 1258 (May 24, 1797) 4; and *The Spirit of the Farmer's Museum,* pp. 303–05.

"De Minimis *curat lex*" in the *Farmer's Weekly Museum,* V, No. 219 (June 12, 1797), 4. Retitled "Logic" it was reprinted in *The Port Folio,* I, No. 47 (Nov. 21, 1801), 371.

"To the *Public*" in the *Farmer's Weekly Museum,* V, No. 223 (July 10, 1797), 4. Reprinted in *The Spirit of the Farmer's Museum,* pp. 305–09.

"Oilnut, or Butternut" in the *Farmer's Weekly Museum,* V, No. 226 (July 31, 1797), 4. Reprinted in *The Spirit of the Farmer's Museum,* pp. 309–10.

"*To our constant* Customers *and the* Publick" in the *Farmer's Weekly Museum,* V, No. 234 (Aug. 25, 1797), 4. Reprinted in *The Spirit of the Farmer's Museum,* pp. 286–88.

"*In our last . . .*" in the *Farmer's Weekly Museum,* V, No. 235 (Oct. 2, 1797), 4. Reprinted in *The Spirit of the Farmer's Museum,* pp. 292–93.

"Paragraphs for the Chronicle" in the *Farmer's Weekly Museum,* VI, No. 263 (April 17, 1798), 4. Reprinted in *The Spirit of the Farmer's Museum,* pp. 293–96.

"Remnants" in the *Farmer's Weekly Museum,* VI, No. 268 (May 22, 1798), 4. Reprinted in *The Federal Galaxy,* II, No. 77 (June 17, 1798), 4; and *The Spirit of the Farmer's Museum,* pp. 252–53.

"The laudable rage . . ." in the *Farmer's Weekly Museum,* VI, No. 307 (Feb. 18, 1799), 4. Reprinted in *The Spirit of the Farmer's Museum,* pp. 271–74.

"Messrs. Colon & Spondee *to their kind Customers*" in the *Farmer's Weekly Museum,* VII, No. 313 (April 1, 1799), 4. Reprinted in the *Massachusetts Spy,* XXVIII, No. 1357 (April 10, 1799), 1; *The Spirit of the Farmer's Museum,* pp. 289–91; and *The Port Folio,* I, No. 43 (Oct. 24, 1801), 338–39.

"Although authors are . . ." in the *Farmer's Weekly Museum,* VII, No. 315

(April 15, 1799), 4. Reprinted in The Spirit of the Farmer's Museum, pp. 311–14.

"State of Literature in England and America" in the Farmer's Weekly Museum, VII, No. 321 (May 27, 1799), 4. Reprinted in The Spirit of the Farmer's Museum, pp. 302–03.

"Parables have . . ." in The Federal Galaxy, III, No. 141 (Sept. 9, 1799), 4.

"Attention, Haymakers" in The Spirit of the Farmer's Museum, pp. 266–69.

"An Author's Evenings" in The Port Folio, II, No. 2 (Jan. 21, 1802), 9–10.

"An Author's Evenings" in The Port Folio, II, No. 8 (Feb. 27, 1802), 57–58.

"An Author's Evenings" in The Port Folio, II, No. 19 (May 15, 1802), 148.

AN ORATION ON THE DEATH
OF GEORGE WASHINGTON

Fair copy manuscript No. 82. Printed in The Federal Galaxy, IV, No. 182 (June 28, 1800), 4; and as a separate imprint, AN/ORATION,/Pronounced at BENNINGTON, Vermont,/On the 22d February, 1800./IN COMMEMORATION OF THE DEATH OF/ General GEORGE WASHINGTON/[swelled rule]/By ROYALL TYLER, Esq./[swelled rule]/ WALPOLE, Newhampshire,/Printed For THOMAS & THOMAS,/ By DAVID CARLISLE./[short rule]/1800.

MISCELLANEOUS ESSAYS

"Saunterer, No. V" in The Newhampshire and Vermont Journal, II, No. 54 (April 18, 1794), 1.

"Saunterer, No. IX" in The Newhampshire and Vermont Journal, II, No. 69 (Aug. 1, 1794), 1.

"Saunterer, No. X" in The Newhampshire and Vermont Journal, II, No. 70 (Aug. 8. 1794), 1.

"Saunterer, No. XI" in The Newhampshire and Vermont Journal, II, No. 74 (Sept. 5, 1794), 1.

"To the Lovers of Cider" in Thomas' Massachusetts Spy, XXV, No. 1258 May 24, 1797), 4.

"Speech of David Wood" in the Farmer's Weekly Museum, V, No. 221 (June 26, 1797), 4. Reprinted in Thomas' Massachusetts Spy, XXV, No. 1265 (July 12, 1797), 4; and The Spirit of the Farmer's Museum, pp. 204–06.

"The following anecdotes . . ." [the headnote paragraph] in The Spirit of the Farmer's Museum, p, 150.

"Riches may be entailed . . ." [*also entitled,* "Original Newengland Anecdote"] in the *Farmer's Weekly Museum,* V, No. 210 (April 11, 1797), 4. Reprinted in *The Spirit of the Farmer's Museum,* p. 151, and in the *Greenfield Gazette,* VI, No. 13 (April 20, 1797), 4.

"The battle of Monmouth . . ." in *Farmer's Weekly Museum,* V, No. 258 (March 13, 1798), 4. Reprinted in *The Spirit of the Farmer's Museum,* p. 153.

"The bill for preventing . . ." in *The Spirit of the Farmer's Museum,* p. 53.

"In a Sermon . . ." in the *Farmer's Weekly Museum,* V, No. 259 (March 20, 1798), 3. Reprinted in *The Spirit of the Farmer's Museum,* pp. 55–56.

"Perhaps the folly . . ." in *The Spirit of the Farmer's Museum,* pp. 57–58.

"A songster . . ." in *The Spirit of the Farmer's Museum,* pp. 58–59.

"A Parisian wit . . ." in *The Spirit of the Farmer's Museum,* p. 59.

"A German Princess . . ." in *The Spirit of the Farmer's Museum,* p. 59.

"The proprietor . . ." in the *Farmer's Weekly Museum,* V, No. 259 (March 20, 1798), 3. Reprinted in *The Spirit of the Farmer's Museum,* pp. 59–60.

"The Editor of . . ." in *The Spirit of the Farmer's Museum,* p. 61.

"In a Boston paper . . ." in the *Farmer's Weekly Museum,* VII, No. 323 (June 10, 1799), 3. Reprinted in *The Spirit of the Farmer's Museum,* p. 65.

"The Lucubrations of Old Simon" in *The Reporter,* I, No. 6 (March 28, 1803), 2.

"The Lucubrations of Old Simon" in *The Reporter,* I, No. 7 (April 4, 1803), 4.

"The Lucubrations of Old Simon" in *The Reporter,* I, No. 8 (April 11, 1803), 2.

"The Lucubrations of Old Simon" in *The Reporter,* I, No. 9 (April 18, 1803), 4.

Small Talk ("We hear that . . .") in *The American Yeoman,* I, No. 2 (Feb. 11, 1817), 3.

Small Talk ("The Great Snow of 1717") in *The American Yeoman,* I, No. 3 (Feb. 18, 1817), 3.

Small Talk ("Major Zebulon Cash . . .") in *The American Yeoman,* I, No. 4 (Feb. 25, 1817), 3.

Small Talk ("*Figures of Rhetoric*") in *The American Yeoman,* I, No. 5 (March 4, 1817), 3.

Small Talk ("In a jovial company . . .") in *The American Yeoman,* I, No. 6 (March 11, 1817), 3.

Small Talk ("Wrifford Out Done!") in *The American Yeoman,* I, No. 7 (March 18, 1817), 3.

Small Talk ("The Squint Eyed Conscience.") in *The American Yeoman,* I, No. 8 (March 25, 1817), 3.

Small Talk ("We are so . . .") in *The American Yeoman*, I, No. 10 (April 8, 1817), 3.

Small Talk ("Anecdote of Dr. Franklin") in *The American Yeoman*, I, No. 15 (May 13, 1817), 3.

Small Talk (*"Marine Journal"*) in *The American Yeoman*, I, No. 16 (May 20, 1817), 3.

Small Talk ("A Charade") in *The American Yeoman*, I, No. 18 (June 3, 1817), 3.

Small Talk ("From a Black Letter Jest Book") in *The American Yeoman*, I, No. 24 (July 15, 1817), 3.

"Cobbett Eclipsed" in *The American Yeoman*, I, No. 28 (Aug. 12, 1817), 2.

"To My Creditors" in *The American Yeoman*, I, No. 28 (Aug. 12, 1817), 3.

"William Cobbett" in *The American Yeoman*, I, No. 29 (Aug. 19, 1817), 3.

Small Talk ("Singular Scarecrow") in *The American Yeoman*, I, No. 30 Aug. 26, 1817), 3.

Small Talk (*"Look our girls . . ."*) in *The American Yeoman*, I, No. 31 (Sept. 2, 1817), 3.

Small Talk (*"Rhodomontade"*) in *The American Yeoman*, I, No. 37 (Oct. 14, 1817), 3.

Small Talk ("We were much amused . . .") in *The American Yeoman*, I, No. 38 (Oct. 21, 1817), 3.

Small Talk ("For a number . . .") in *The American Yeoman*, I, No. 39 (Oct. 28, 1817), 3.

"Communication" in *The American Yeoman*, I, No. 40 (Nov. 4, 1817), 3.

Small Talk ("A singing-master . . .") in *The American Yeoman*, I, No. 40 (Nov. 4, 1817), 3.

"Communication" in *The American Yeoman*, I, No. 41 (Nov. 11, 1817), 3.

Small Talk ("A young gentleman . . .") in *The American Yeoman*, I, No. 43 (Nov. 25, 1817), 3.

Small Talk ("An oppulent farmer . . .") in *The American Yeoman*, I, No. 48 (Dec. 30, 1817), 3.

"Mr. Editor, you will oblige . . ." in *The American Yeoman*, I, No. 49 (Jan. 6, 1818), 1.

"In our last . . ." in *The American Yeoman*, I, No. 50 (Jan. 13, 1818), 2.

"Addenda/ Aboriginals/ Negroes—", manuscript single sheet tipped in at the end of fair copy manuscript of "The Chestnut Tree," No. 25.

THE LAW CASES

Pearse *vs.* Goddard in 1 Tyl 373. This and the following seven cases are to be found in Tyler's *Reports of Cases Argued and Determined in the Supreme Court of Judicature of Vermont* (New York: I. Riley, 1809–10), 2 vols.

Adams *vs.* Brownson in 1 Tyl 452.

Windover and Hopkins *vs.* Robbins in 2 Tyl 1.

Robbins *vs.* Windover and Hopkins in 2 Tyl 11.

Selectmen of Windsor *vs.* Jacob in 2 Tyl 192.

Rich *vs.* Trimble in 2 Tyl 349.

State *vs.* White in 2 Tyl 352.

Bowne *et al vs.* Graham and Graham in 2 Tyl 411.

State *vs.* Johnson in Thomas Pickman Tyler, "Memoirs of Honorable Royall Tyler," pp. 185–86.

State *vs.* Dean in Thomas Pickman Tyler, "Memoirs of Honorable Royall Tyler," 14 unnumbered pages tipped in between pp. 243–44.

THE "TRASH" AND "POSTUMI" ESSAYS

Trash No. 1 in the *Polyanthos*, II (May, 1806), 92–97.

Trash No. 3 in the *Polyanthos*, V (April, 1807), 14–19.

Trash No. 3 [*i.e., No. 4*] in the *Polyanthos*, V (May, 1807), 86–89.

Postumi ("It is *well* . . .") in *The New-England Galaxy*, I, No. 39 (July 10, 1818), 2.

Postumi ("It was generally . . .") in *The New-England Galaxy*, I, No. 41 (July 24, 1818), 2.

FRAGMENTS OF "UTILE DULCI"

Title Page and Dedication of "Utile Dulci" in an unnumbered manuscript. In Mrs. Tyler's hand.

Introduction to the Sacred Dramas at the end of an unnumbered fair copy manuscript of "The Origin of the Feast of Purim."

"Marriage" ("Advice to Young Clergymen Upon Marriage"), manuscript No. 70.

"The Historiette of the Tub Woman," manuscript No. 79.

"The Tale of Five Pumpkins" [*Version 1*], manuscript No. 30.

"The Tale of Five Pumpkins" [*Version 2*], manuscript No. 48.

Bibliography

Allen, Ira. *The Natural and Political History of the State of Vermont*. London: J. W. Myers, 1798.

Beckley, Hosea. *The History of Vermont*. Brattleboro, Vt.: G. H. Salisbury, 1846.

Billington, Ray A. *The Protestant Crusade, 1800–1860; a Study of the Origins of American Nativism*. New York: Macmillan Co., 1938.

Binkley, Wilfred E. *American Political Parties; their Natural History*. New York: A. A. Knopf, 1962. 4th ed.

Brigham, Clarence S. *History and Bibliography of American Newspapers, 1690–1820*. Worcester, Mass.: American Antiquarian Society, 1947.

———. *Journals and Journeymen: A Contribution to the History of Early American Newspapers*. Philadelphia: University of Pennsylvania Press, 1950.

Brown, Roger H. *The Republic in Peril*. New York: Columbia University Press, 1964.

Buck, Edward. *Massachusetts Ecclesiastical Law*. Boston: Gould & Lincoln, 1866.

Buckingham, Joseph T. *Personal Memoirs and Recollections of Editorial Life*. Boston: Ticknor, Reed and Fields, 1852.

———. *Specimens of Newspaper Literature: with Personal Memoirs, Anecdotes, and Reminiscences*. Boston: C. C. Little and S. Brown, 1850. 2 vols.

Burnham, Henry. *Brattleboro, Windham County, Vermont: An Early History*. Brattleboro, Vt.: E. Leonard, 1880.

Butterfield, Lyman H., ed. *The Earliest Diary of John Adams*. Cambridge: The Belknap Press, 1966.

Cabot, Mary R., ed. *The Annals of Brattleboro, 1681–1895*. Brattleboro, Vt.: E. Hildreth & Co., 1921–1922. 2 vols.

Cady, Edwin H., ed. *Literature of the Early Republic*. New York: Rinehart, 1950.

Cary, John H. *Joseph Warren: Physician, Politician, Patriot*. Urbana: University of Illinois Press, 1961.

Chapman, Bertrand W. *The Nativism of Royall Tyler*. University of Vermont, M.A. thesis, 1932.

Clapp, William W., Jr. *Joseph Dennie: Editor of "The Port Folio," and Author of "The Lay Preacher."* Cambridge: John Wilson & Son, 1880.

———. *A Record of the Boston Stage*. Boston: J. Munroe & Co., 1853.

Chorley, Edward C. *Men and Movements in the American Episcopal Church*. New York: Scribner's Sons, 1946.

Cooper, James Fenimore. *Early Critical Essays, 1820–1822*. Ed. James F. Beard, Jr. Gainesville, Fla.: Scholars' Facsimiles and Reprints, 1955.

Crockett, Walter H. *Vermont, the Green Mountain State*. New York: Century History Co., 1921–1923. 5 vols.

Cross, Arthur L. *The Anglican Episcopate and the American Colonies*. Hamden, Conn.: Archon Books, 1964.

Cushing, William. *Initials and Pseudonyms, a Dictionary of Literary Disguises*. New York: Thomas Y. Crowell & Co., 1886.

Davis, Richard B. "The Early American Lawyer and the Profession of Letters," *Harvard Literary Quarterly*, XII (Feb. 19, 1949), 191–206.

Deming, Leonard. *Catalogue of the Principal Officers of Vermont, as Connected with its Political History, from 1778–1851*. Middlebury, Vt.: Printed for the Author, 1851.

Dennie, Joseph. *The Lay Preacher*. Ed. H. Milton Ellis. New York: Scholars' Facsimiles and Reprints, 1943.

Drake, Samuel G. *History and Antiquities of Boston . . . from its Settlement in 1630, to the Year 1770. Also, an Introductory History of the Discovery and Settlement of New England*. Boston: I. Stevens, 1856.

Dunn, Richard S. *Puritans and Yankees; the Winthrop Dynasty of New England, 1630–1717*. Princeton: Princeton University Press, 1962.

Dwight, Timothy. *Travels; in New-England and New-York*. New Haven: 1821–1822. 4 vols.

Eames, Wilberforce. *Early New England Catechisms: A Bibliographical Account of Some Catechisms Published Before the Year 1800, for Use in New England*. Worcester: C. Hamilton, 1898.

Ellis, H. Milton. "Joseph Dennie and His Circle," *Bulletin of the University of Texas*, No. 40 (July 15, 1915).

Evans, Charles. *American Bibliography: A Chronological Dictionary of All Books, Pamphlets, and Periodical Publications Printed in the United States of America. . . .* Chicago: Blakely Press, Hollister Press, and Columbia Press; Worcester, Mass.: American Antiquarian Society, 1903–1959. 14 vols.

Flanders, Louis W. *Simeon Ide, Yeoman, Freeman, Pioneer Printer*. Rutland, Vt.: The Tuttle Co., 1931. Genealogy by Edith Flanders Dunbar; Bibliography by R. W. G. Vail.

Force, Peter, ed. *Tracts and Other Papers, Relating Principally to the Origin, Settlement, and Progress of the Colonies in North America from the Discovery of the Country to the Year 1776*. Washington, D.C.: Printed by the author, 1836–1846.

Forsythe, Robert S. " 'The Algerine Captive,' 1802," *Notes and Queries*, CLXXII (May 29, 1937), 389–90.

Gilman, M. D., comp. *The Bibliography of Vermont*. Burlington, Vt.: The Free Press Association, 1897.

Goen, C. C. *Revivalism and Separatism in New England, 1740–1800; Strict Congregationalists and Separate Baptists in the Great Awakening*. New Haven: Yale University Press, 1962.

Hall, Benjamin. *History of Eastern Vermont, from Its Earliest Settlement to the Close of the Eighteenth Century*. Albany: J. Munsell, 1865.

Hall, Hiland. *The History of Vermont*. Albany: J. Munsell, 1868.

Haroutunian, Joseph. *Piety Versus Moralism: the Passing of the New England Theology*. Hamden, Conn.: Archon Books, 1964. Rev. ed.

Haskins, George L. *Law and Authority in Early Massachusetts*. New York: Macmillian Co., 1960.

Heimert, Alan. *Religion and the American Mind from the Great Awakening to the Revolution*. Cambridge: Harvard University Press, 1966.

Hemenway, Abby M., ed. *Poets and Poetry of Vermont*. Rutland, Vt.: G. A. Tuttle & Co., 1858. Rev. ed., Boston: Brown, Taggard & Chase, 1860.

———. *The Vermont Historical Gazetter* . . . Burlington: Printed for the author, 1868–1891. 5 vols.

Hill, Ralph Narding. *Contrary Country, a Chronicle of Vermont*. New York: Rinehart, 1950. Rev. ed., Brattleboro, Vt.: Stephen Greene Press, 1961.

———. *The Winooski, Heartway of Vermont*. New York: Rinehart, 1949.

Hoskins, Nathan. *A History of the State of Vermont, from its Discovery and Settlement to the Close of the Year MDCCCXXX*. Vergennes, Vt.: J. Sheed, 1831.

Johnson, Merle. *American First Editions. Fourth Edition Revised and Enlarged by Jacob Blanck*. Cambridge: Research Classics, 1962.

Lathrop, G. P. "Early American Novelists," *Atlantic Monthly*, XXXVII (April 1876), 404–14.

Lehmann-Haupt, Hellmut. *The Book in America; a History of the Making, the Selling, and the Collecting of Books in the United States*. 2d ed., New York, R. R. Bowker, 1951.

Lindsay, Julian I. *Tradition Looks Forward. The University of Vermont: A History, 1791–1904*. Burlington, Vt.: University of Vermont, 1954.

Love, W. De Loss, Jr. *Fast and Thanksgiving Days of New England*. Boston: Houghton, Mifflin & Co., 1895.

Manross, William W. *The Episcopal Church in the United States, 1800–1840*. New York: Columbia University Press, 1938.

———. *A History of the American Episcopal Church*. 3d ed., New York: Morehouse-Gorham, 1959.

Marble, Annie. *From 'Prentice to Patron: The Life Story of Isaiah Thomas*.

New York: D. Appleton-Century Co., 1935.

———. *Heralds of American Literature: a Group of Patriot Writers of the Revolutionary and National Periods.* Chicago: University of Chicago Press, 1907.

McCorison, Marcus A. *Vermont Imprints, 1778–1820.* Worcester: American Antiquarian Society, 1963.

———. *Additions and Corrections to Vermont Imprints, 1778–1820.* Worcester: American Antiquarian Society, 1968.

McLoughlin, William G. "Essay Review. The American Revolution as a Religious Revival: 'The Millennium in One Country,'" *New England Quarterly*, XL (March, 1967), 99–110.

Miller, Perry. "The Marrow of Puritan Divinity," *Publications of the Colonial Society of Massachusetts*, XXXII (1937), 247–300.

———. *The New England Mind: From Colony to Province.* Cambridge: Harvard University Press, 1953.

———. *The New England Mind: The Seventeenth Century.* Cambridge: Harvard University Press, 1954.

———. " 'Preparation for Salvation,' in Seventeenth-Century New England," *Journal of the History of Ideas*, IV (June, 1943), 253–86.

Mode, Peter G. *Source Book and Bibliographical Guide for American Church History.* Menasha, Wisc.: George Banta Publishing Co., 1921.

Morgan, Edmund S. *The Puritan Dilemma; the Story of John Winthrop.* Boston: Little, Brown, 1958.

Morison, Samuel Eliot. *The Intellectual Life of Colonial New England.* New York: New York University Press, 1956.

Morton, Nathaniel. *New Englands Memoriall.* Cambridge: John Usher, 1669. Reprinted, New York: Scholars' Facsimiles and Reprints, 1937.

Newborough, George F. "Mary Tyler's Journal," *Vermont Quarterly*, XX (Jan., 1952), 19–31.

Northend, William D. *The Bay Colony; a Civil, Religious and Social History of the Massachusetts Colony and Its Settlements from the Landing at Cape Ann in 1624 to the Death of Governor Winthrop in 1650.* Boston: Estes and Lauriat, 1896.

Notestein, Wallace. *The English People on the Eve of Colonialization: 1603–1630.* New York: Harper & Brothers, 1954.

Osgood, Herbert L. *The American Colonies in the Eighteenth Century.* New York: Columbia University Press, 1924–1925. 4 vols.

———. *The American Colonies in the Seventeenth Century.* New York: The Macmillian Co., 1904–1907. 3 vols.

Peabody, Andrew R. "The Farmer's Weekly Museum," *Proceedings of the*

American Antiquarian Society, n.s., VI (Oct. 23, 1889), 106–29.

Pedder, Laura G., ed. *The Letters of Joseph Dennie, 1768–1812.* Orono, Me.: University of Maine Press, 1936.

Péladeau, Marius B. "Royall Tyler and Ethan Allen's Appendix to *Reason the Only Oracle of Man,*" *Vermont History*, XXXVI (Summer, 1968) 155–58.

———. "Royall Tyler's *Other* Plays," *New England Quarterly*, XL (March, 1967), 48–60.

———. *The Verse of Royall Tyler.* Charlottesville, Va.: The University of Virginia Press, 1968.

Perkins, Bradford. *The Cause of the War of 1812. National Honor or National Interest?* New York: Holt, Rinehart & Winston, 1962.

———. *Prologue to War; England and the United States, 1805–1812.* Berkeley, Cal.: University of California Press, 1961.

Prince, Thomas. *A Chronological History of New England in the Form of Annals* . . . Boston: Kneeland & Green for S. Gerrish, 1736. Reprinted. Boston: Cummings, Hilliard & Co., 1826.

Randall, Randolph C. "Authors of the *Port Folio* Revealed by the Hall Files," *American Literature*, XI (Jan., 1940), 379–416.

Richardson, Charles F. *American Literature, 1607–1885.* New York: G. P. Putnam's Sons, 1889. 2 vols.

Rutman, Darrett B. *Winthrop's Boston; Portrait of a Puritan Town, 1630–1649.* Chapel Hill, N.C.: University of North Carolina Press, 1965.

Sabin, Joseph, and Wilberforce Eames and R. W. G. Vail, eds. *Bibliotheca Americana: A Dictionary of Books Relating to America.* . . . New York: Sabin, and William Rudge Press; Portland, Me.: Southworth-Anthoensen Press, 1868–1936. 29 vols.

Shipton, Clifford K. *Isaiah Thomas, Printer, Patriot and Philanthropist, 1749–1831.* Rochester, N.Y.: Leo Hart, 1948.

Smith, Page. *John Adams.* Garden City, N.Y.: Doubleday & Co., 1962, 2 vols.

Spargo, John. "Early Vermont Printers and Printing," *Proceedings of the Vermont Historical Society*, n.s., X (Dec., 1942), 214–29.

Spencer, Benjamin. *The Quest for Nationality.* Syracuse, N.Y.: Syracuse University Press, 1957.

The Spirit of the Farmer's Museum, and Lay Preacher's Gazette. Walpole, N.H.: Printed for Thomas & Thomas by D. & T. Carlisle, 1801.

Sweet, William W. *Religion in Colonial America.* New York: C. Scribner's Sons, 1942.

Taft, Russell S. "Royall Tyler," *The Green Bag. An Entertaining Magazine for Lawyers*, XX (1908), 1–5.

———. "The Supreme Court in Vermont," *The Green Bag. An Entertaining Magazine for Lawyers*, V (1894), 553–63; VI (1895), 16–35, 72–91, 122–41, 176–92.

Tanselle, G. Thomas. "Attributions of Authorship in 'The Spirit of the Farmer's Museum' (1801)," *The Papers of the Bibliographical Society of America*, LIX, No. 2 (April-June, 1965), 170–76.

———. "Author and Publisher in 1800: Letters of Royall Tyler and Joseph Nancrede," *Harvard Library Bulletin*, XV, No. 2 (April, 1967), 129–39.

———. "Early American Fiction in England: The Case of *The Algerine Captive*," *Papers of the Bibliographical Society of America*, LIX, No. 4 (Oct.-Dec., 1965), 367–84.

———. *Royall Tyler*. Cambridge: Harvard University Press, 1967.

———. "Some Uncollected Authors XLII. Royall Tyler, 1757–1826," *The Book Collector*, XV, No. 3 (Autumn, 1966), 311–14.

Thacher, James. *American Medical Biography; or, Memoirs of Eminent Physicians Who Have Flourished in America*. Boston: Richardson & Lord, 1828. 2 vols.

Thatcher, B. B. *Indian Biography: an Historical Account of Those Individuals Who Have Been Distinguished Among the North American Natives* . . . New York: Harper, 1832. 2 vols.

[Tyler, Mary Palmer.] *Grandmother Tyler's Book. The Recollections of Mary Palmer Tyler (Mrs. Royall Tyler) 1775–1866*. Ed. Frederick Tupper and Helen Tyler Brown. New York: G. P. Putnam's Sons, 1925.

———. Ms., "Memoirs." In the possession of The Honorable William Royall Tyler, Washington, D.C.

———. Ms., "Diary." In the Royall Tyler Collection, gift of Helen Tyler Brown, Vermont Historical Society, Montpelier, Vermont.

Tyler, Moses C. *A History of American Literature During the Colonial Time*. New York: G. P. Putnam, 1878. 2 vols.

[Tyler, Royall.] *The Algerine Captive*, by Dr. Updike Underhill [*pseud.*] Walpole, N.H.: David Carlisle, 1797. Also: London: Printed for G. & J. Robinson by S. Hamilton, 1802; and Hartford, Conn.: Peter B. Gleason, 1816. Serialized in *The Lady's Magazine*. London: G. & J. Robinson, 1804. Vol. xxxv ff.

———. *Four Plays by Royall Tyler*. Ed. Arthur W. Peach and George F. Newborough. (America's Lost Plays, vol. XV.) Princeton: Princeton University Press, 1941.

———. *An Oration, Pronounced at Bennington, Vermont, on the 22d of February, 1800. In Commemoration of the Death of General George Washington*. Wal-

pole, N.H.: Printed for Thomas & Thomas by David Carlisle, 1800.
———. *Reports of Cases Argued and Determined in the Supreme Court of Judicature of Vermont* [1800–1803]. New York: I. Riley, 1809–1810. 2 vols.
[———.] "The Royall Tyler Collection, gift of Helen Tyler Brown," Vermont Historical Society collections, Montpelier, Vt.
[?———.] *The Trial of Cyrus B. Dean, for the Murder of Jonathan Ormsby and Asa Marsh, Before the Supreme Court of Judicature of the State of Vermont . . . Revised and Corrected from the Minutes of the Judges.* Burlington, Vt.: Samuel Mills, 1808.
———. *The Yankey in London.* New York: I. Riley, 1809.
Tyler, Thomas Pickman. "Memoirs of the Honorable Royall Tyler, Late Chief Justice of Vermont." In the collection of the Vermont Historical Society.
———. "Royall Tyler," *Vermont Bar Association Proceedings, 1878–1881,* pp. 44–62. Also in: *Argus and Patriot* (Montpelier, Vt.) n.s., XXIX (Nov. 5, 1879), 1.
Wegelin, Oscar. *Early American Fiction, 1774–1830.* Stamford, Conn.: The Compiler, 1902.
White, Pliny H. "Early Poets of Vermont," *Proceedings of the Vermont Historical Society, 1917–1918* (1920), 93–125.
Williams, Joseph J. *Voodoos and Obeahs. Phases of West India Witchcraft.* New York: Dial Press, 1932.
Wright, Lyle H. *American Fiction, 1774–1850: a Contribution Toward a Bibliography.* San Marino, Cal.: Henry E. Huntington Library Publications, 1948. Rev. ed.

Alphabetical Index

Chronological Index

Subject Index

Abel, Karl Friedrich, 447.
Abercrombie, Rev. James, 201.
Aboukir, Battle of, 307.
Adams, Abigail, 32.
Adams, Hannah, 320.
Adams, John Quincy, 229, 237, 250, 279, 460.
Adams, Samuel, 127.
Addison, Joseph, *Cato*, 36, 125, 143–48, 425.
Adelersterran, Dr. G. W., 306.
Adet, Pierre Auguste, 224.
Aiken, Dr. John, 262.
Akenside, Dr. Mark, 124, 291.
The American Yeoman, 281, 287–90, 320–21.
American Mercury, 340.
Ames, Fisher, 345, 416.
Annapolis, Md., 338.
Anvil, Mr. Ichabod, 50.
The Arabian Nights, 113.
Arminianism, 69, 70.
Asgil, Capt. Charles, 274.
Austin, Benjamin, 206, 237.

Bache, Benjamin Franklin, 237, 243.
Bacon, Francis (Baron Verulam), 125.
Bacon, Nathaniel, 53.
Baldwin, Abraham, 209.
Barry, Col. Henry, 167.
Baxter, Rev. Richard, 316; *The Dying Thoughts of*, 114.
Beddoes, Dr. Thomas, 262.
Belknap, Jeremy, 226.
Bellamy, Joseph, 34.
Bellington, Mrs. 54.
Bellows Falls, Vt., 282, 310.
Bennington, Vt., 270, 272, 456.
Bennington County, Vt., 360.
Bentley, Richard, 425.

Congregationalism, 34, 35, 36, 68, 69, 83, 168, 176, 351.
Congreve, Sir William, 37, 94.
Connecticut Herald, 341.
Connecticut River, 196, 222, 225, 269, 282, 327, 331.
Conti, Prince de, 223.
Cook, Atty. John, 372, 380.
Cooke, George F., 37, 147, 149.
Cooper, James Fenimore, 25.
Cooper, Rev. Samuel, 104.
Cooper, Thomas A., 37, 147.
Corbett, William, 237, 333–34, 336–37.
Culpeper, Nicholas, *Directory for Midwives*, 94.
Cutter of Coleman Street, 143.

Dana, Francis, 460.
Dartmouth College, 350.
Davis, John, 85.
Davy, Sir Humphrey, 50.
Dayton, Jonathan, 225.
Dean, Cyrus B., 362–64, 407.
"Dear Ally Croaker", 54, 58.
Declaration of Independence, 14, 269.
Defoe, Daniel, 93.
Della Crusca, 244, 247.
Denison, Judge Gilbert, 358.
Dennie, Joseph, 14, 18, 22, 23, 24, 46, 191–201, 281–82, 291, 312, 412–13, 426–37, 455.
Dennis, John, 146.
Diaway, Mrs., 31, 110–12, 118, 120–25, 155–56, 159–60, 162–63, 170, 172 173.
Diderot, Denis, 87.
Dilworth, Thomas, *A New Guide to the English Tongue*, 62, 65.
Don Quixote, 424.
Drayton, Michael, 420–23.
Drummond, William, 415.
Dryden, John, 142, 294, 424; *Alexander the Great*, 96.
Dudley, Gov. Joseph, 304.
Duncan, Admiral Adam, 238.
Dunham, Josiah, 191–92.
Dwight, Rev. Timothy, 282–83.